SINGLE-SHOT RIFLES

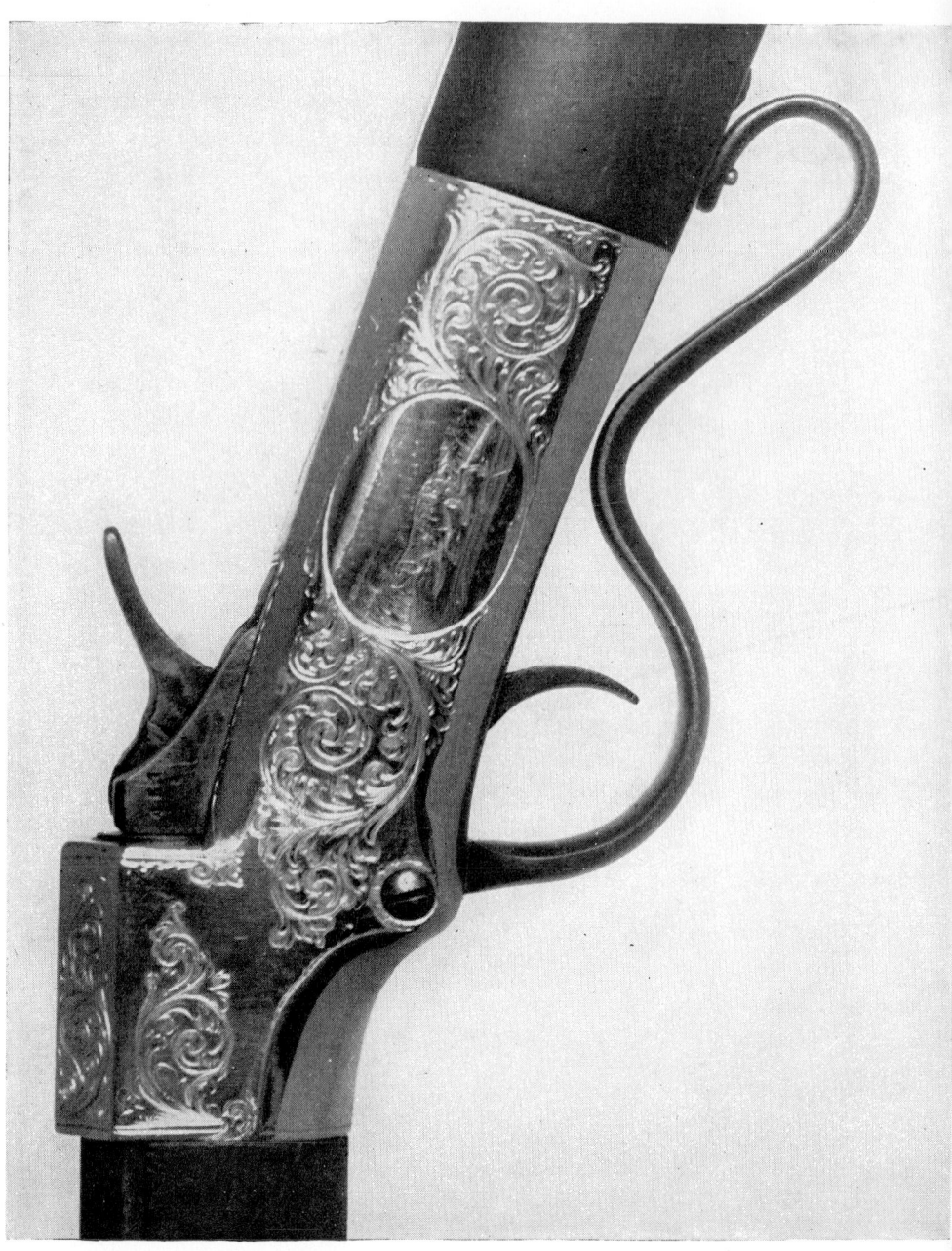

AN ENGRAVED, BRONZE FRAME BALLARD, CALIBER .38 RIM-FIRE, SERIAL NO. 1493, MARKED BALL & WILLIAMS; MERWIN BRAY, AGENTS, NEW YORK. BALLARDS PATENT NOVEMBER 5TH, 1861, BALL & WILLIAMS.

RIFLES

By

JAMES J. GRANT

NEW YORK

WILLIAM MORROW AND COMPANY

1947

COPYRIGHT, 1947,
By JAMES J. GRANT

All rights reserved
This book, or parts thereof, must not be reproduced
in any form without permission of the publisher.

FOURTH PRINTING, DECEMBER, 1964

PRINTED IN THE UNITED STATES OF AMERICA

TO JANE, MY WIFE, WHO
THROUGH A PATIENCE WITH AND
A TOLERANCE FOR AN ENGROSSING
HOBBY HAS MADE THIS
VOLUME POSSIBLE

Contents

	Introduction	ix
I.	The Ballard Single-shot Rifle	1
II.	Stevens Arms	50
III.	Remington Single-shot Rifles	114
IV.	The Sharps Rifle	165
V.	Winchester Single-shot Falling-block Rifles	201
VI.	F. Wesson Rifles	233
VII.	Wurfflein Rifles	241
VIII.	Peabody and Peabody-Martini Rifles	249
IX.	Whitney Rolling-block and Phoenix Rifles	268
X.	The Maynard Rifle	277
XI.	Bullard Single-shot, Hopkins & Allen, and Farrow Rifles	298
XII.	Foreign Single-shot Rifles	311
XIII.	Remodeling the Single-shot Rifle	338
	Appendix	371
	Index	379

Introduction

SINGLE-SHOT rifles were at one time very popular with all classes of shooters, both on the target ranges of this country and in the game fields. They have been made in higher and finer grades than any other firearm offered by American factories. As a group they are without doubt the most accurate of all rifles ever offered as a standard factory line. It is surprising to find so many men who appreciate this particular arm and yet who are unfamiliar with the models as they were made at the factories. The younger riflemen, in general, know nothing about them, and it is interesting to hear some of the comments made by those who see a fine specimen for the first time. Since so many of these fine old target guns have been converted into modern calibers, restocked, and otherwise rejuvenated, thus losing their identity as a separate and distinct type, it is no wonder that even among well-informed collectors the various distinguishing features are unrecognizable.

From time to time there have been interesting articles on the single-shot rifle in the *American Rifleman* magazine, but for the most part these have dealt with the various types mainly as foundations for modern varmint rifles. Surely the single-shot deserves more comprehensive treatment than this. Charles Winthrop Sawyer, in his book, *Our Rifles*, discusses and illustrates the single-shot to a certain extent, and W. O. Smith's book, *The Sharps Rifle*, clears many somewhat confused points on this one particular make. But as a whole the many once very popular models are suffering from a lack of understanding.

This volume will deal with the rifles as they have been made in standard models by various factories. I shall not attempt to discuss the Schuetzen [1] rifles made by custom gunsmiths such as H. M. Pope, Zischang, Schoyen, Peterson, and others. These are generally fine pieces as worked over by these old craftsmen, but there is so much

[1] The German word *Schützen*, meaning "marksman," has become a recognized term to express a high type of target rifle.

variety in their work that really every job is somewhat different. Although I own and shoot several fine specimens as altered by these men, I have never made an attempt to collect them as purposefully as I have the factory models. Many readers will undoubtedly disagree with me when I state my conviction that, as a type, the rifles as made originally at the factory were the finest of the lot. One would have a job on his hands were he to attempt to sell a dyed-in-the-wool Colt collector a percussion model that had been rebarreled by a custom gunsmith, and while this may be a rather obscure comparison, it is the way I feel about single-shot rifles. As another illustration, who would invest money in a Kentucky rifle that had been restocked or otherwise altered? The collector prefers them original or not at all, and the same holds true of the single-shot collector.

The actions of the Ballard, the Stevens, the Winchester, and other single-shot rifles of well-known make were in demand by the custom barrelmakers long before the present craze for high-velocity varment rifles. This accounts, no doubt, for the relative scarcity of the original specimens and possibly for the demand for them as collection pieces. If they were plentiful today there is no indication that they would be so sought after as collection pieces. The very fact that the supply of any commodity is limited seems to enhance its intrinsic value to a certain extent.

Single-shots have fascinated me from the first time I saw a really fine specimen. That was not so many years ago—in fact, it was comparatively few years ago. Even at that time they were considered an obsolete arm, and their popularity waned in favor of the military type. To me the single-shot typifies the leisurely life of the past century, before the advent of high-pressure living, when it was not considered necessary to live at a breakneck pace twenty-four hours a day. In those days it was not imperative to have a new automobile every year or the latest household gadgets in order to feel that you were really living. If a man had a good target rifle he had the means for a vast amount of pleasure and a certain amount of profit. This was his recreation, and who can deny that he wasn't happier for it? If he lived in a game country—and when these rifles were first made very few portions of the country were not game country—he had the satisfaction of getting his buck, or whatever his quarry might be, in a leisurely manner; stalking it the way a fine game animal deserves, and making the kill with one well-placed shot. What a contrast to present-day hunting procedure! Today the average hunter gets a few days off, jumps into his car, and tears off for the game country, where he mows his game down with a volley of shots from his autoloader or his slide-action rifle and must rush up and put his tag on the kill to prevent one of the other fifty-odd men who are hunting in the same square mile of territory from claiming it. Also what a contrast to the days when a knowledge of the habits of game and the capabilities of a man's own particular rifle were necessary to make a kill! A hunter had to know these things in those earlier days; he didn't trust to a magazine full of "flat-shooting" high-velocity cartridges to make up the deficiencies in his own knowledge.

But of course those days are gone forever. Today our game is to be found only in certain small localities, and the competition among sportsmen is keen. We are all, for the most part of our time, busily engaged in the prosaic pastime of making a living, which is as it should be, of course, in our present age, and we must take our enjoyment of hunting as it used to be from the relics of those early days. There will be no more days like those of old, nor will there be any more rifles like the original single-shot, so we treasure the more both the memories and the guns we have acquired.

Perhaps this book will help gun-minded men who have a genuine desire to know these rifles of another day; possibly it may even stimulate a renewed interest in them. But if it serves the purpose intended —to call attention to the real importance of single-shot rifles in the arms field and in the affections of real gun lovers—then it will add immeasurably to the vast amount of pleasure I have derived from collecting and studying this type of arm. Several of the old single-shot rifles had their origin as military rifles, but I have never cared for this particular version. Like most real gun lovers, I have no affection for nor patience with military arms. Their crudities have no place among the fine techniques of gunmakers anywhere.

Within these pages effort has been made to show all the standard models of single-shot rifles. Those of which I do not own a specimen and so could not provide actual or original photographs, I have reproduced from catalog illustrations.

J. J. G.

May, 1946

SINGLE-SHOT RIFLES

I

The Ballard Single-shot Rifle

It is fitting that the most famous and beloved of all the old single-shots should have the place of honor in a volume of this character. Therefore I nominate the Ballard rifle for this, the first chapter.

To me the Ballard is the most fascinating of all the single-shots made in America in the days when this was still a "nation of riflemen," and before the advent of the really successful repeating mechanisms. This was the action most favored and sought after by gunsmith and rifleman alike for a fine custom Schuetzen rifle. And it is no small testimonial to the undying popularity of the Ballard that even today, over fifty years after its official demise, the serious small-bore rifleman considers this arm the ideal foundation for a fine match .22 rifle.

Though not a particularly strong design, the Ballard was, nevertheless, well and finely fabricated, and the breechblock parts were glass hard, which accounts for their still being found in a condition even remotely suitable for shooting. The materials used in most models were the best that were available at the time, and when used with cartridges within their strength adaptations they are today perfectly adequate for the job. (The Ballard design is shown on page 49.)

I was in Charles C. Johnson's shop one day—in Thackery, Ohio—when a man who claimed to be a metallurgist argued with Mr. Johnson—who, incidentally, is a Ballard connoisseur—that the materials used in Ballard actions were good enough to hold the pressures obtained with small high-powered cartridges such as the R-2 Lovell, or .22/3000. I recall that Mr. Johnson had quite a time convincing this gentleman that it was not a question of the materials used in manufacturing the action but rather the design itself that mattered, and of course the Ballard design leaves a great deal to be desired as far as supporting a hot cartridge is concerned.

In view of the age of the Ballard patent and the cartridges the arm was originally designed to handle, it seems to me that the rifle has done remarkably well to survive as it has. Had there been an action available which combined all the excellent qualities of the Ballard and in addition offered more secure locking of the breech—in other words, a stronger design—there is no doubt that the Ballard would have been abandoned in its favor long ago. The only other good action designs available, however, were the Remington system and the Sharps system, in their various applications. Although these were inherently strong and simple designs, they did not incorporate the outstanding characteristic of the Ballard, which of course was the camming of the breechblock closely against the cartridge head.

There are many derogatory remarks heard concerning the Ballard. One of the most amusing is that the great expanse of metal in the action makes it a "very cold" rifle to handle in winter. However, the regard in which the rifle is held by its lovers is not lessened by any reason such as this. They know the Ballard is not strong enough for a Lovell cartridge, a .22 highpower, or other shell of this nature; they also know it is a somewhat rudimentary appearing action externally; they know, too, several other things that do not meet the casual eye. And despite these questionable points for argument they will still take a Ballard. Why? Well, it is a hard thing to explain. In fact, I cannot explain it. The best I can do is advise the unbeliever to get the Ballard fever, and if he gets it, I would venture to say it will be a lifelong malady and one for which he will not seek a cure.

The Ballard was in production over only a comparatively short period of time—1861 to about 1890—but during these years it was made by several manufacturers and in a great variety of styles. It is, therefore, small wonder that much confusion concerning the different models exists today.

The early pre-Marlin Ballard has been thoroughly and intelligently covered by Mr. L. D. Satterlee in his article "The Early Ballard" in the August, 1927, issue of the *American Rifleman*. It is my intention here to confine the story of the Ballard to a discussion of this arm as made by J. M. Marlin and the Marlin Firearms Company during the years 1875 to 1890. During this period the really fine and beautiful Ballards of outstanding performance on the various target ranges were in their heyday. These models are varied and complex, and an attempt to clarify them has long been desired and needed. There

THE BALLARD SINGLE-SHOT RIFLE 3

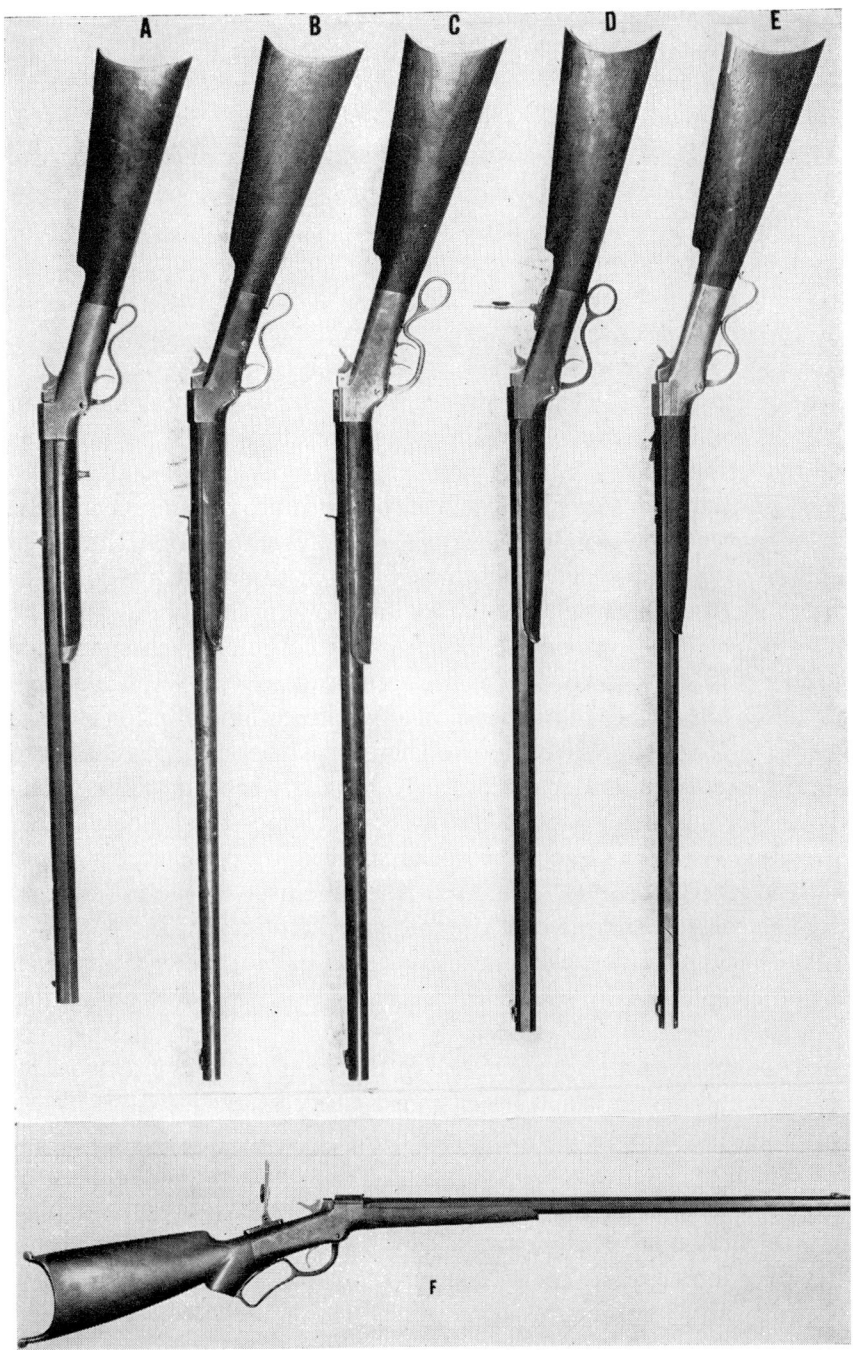

BALLARD RIFLES
(See page 36 for explanation)

has never been much attention paid to the calibers of these models and this in itself is a fascinating subject, one which I shall cover to the best of my ability.

The man who should write the Ballard story is Mr. M. G. Chandler of Detroit, Michigan, who has forgotten more about the Ballard than the rest of us will ever know. He collected Ballards in great and amazing variety at a time, years ago, when it was still possible to find many originals. His collection of years—or at least most of it—has been turned over to the Milwaukee Public Museum in Milwaukee, Wisconsin, and may be viewed there.

Of the early phase in the Ballard's history it is very hard to find a fine specimen of the higher grades intact and in original condition. So many of these rifles were, in years past, torn apart in order to get the action that it is small wonder the supply of originals is definitely limited. There will, of course, be no more of these available. I have never been able to ascertain definitely how high the serial numbers went. The highest known to me or to any of my collector friends is 39000. Does anyone know just how high they did go? The year the manufacture of the Ballard was completely discontinued is also rather hazy; some say 1888, some say 1890, 1891, 1892, and 1893. The latest date I have seen on a Marlin catalog offering Ballard models is 1888, though of course there must be later ones. Ballard catalogs are even harder to locate today than the fine rifles themselves. I have been able to get for myself only one—the January, 1882, issue—but I have had access to others dated 1879, 1886, 1887, and 1888. With these, plus the actual rifles themselves, we are able to visualize fairly accurately the rise and fall of the Ballard.

There was considerable variation offered in practically all the better grades of this rifle, so one finds almost no two that are identical in every respect. This is especially true of the engraved series, in which I feel almost secure in stating that you cannot find two that are identically engraved. The Marlin factory was evidently very accommodating and helpful in making the Ballard rifle to meet the customers' individual whims. The makers would do practically anything a customer wished, it seems; and apparently gun cranks then were as individual in their tastes as are those of today. Now, however, in order to satisfy idiosyncratic whims one must go to a custom gunsmith and pay him his own price—which is seldom inconsiderable—to bring into being one's pet ideas.

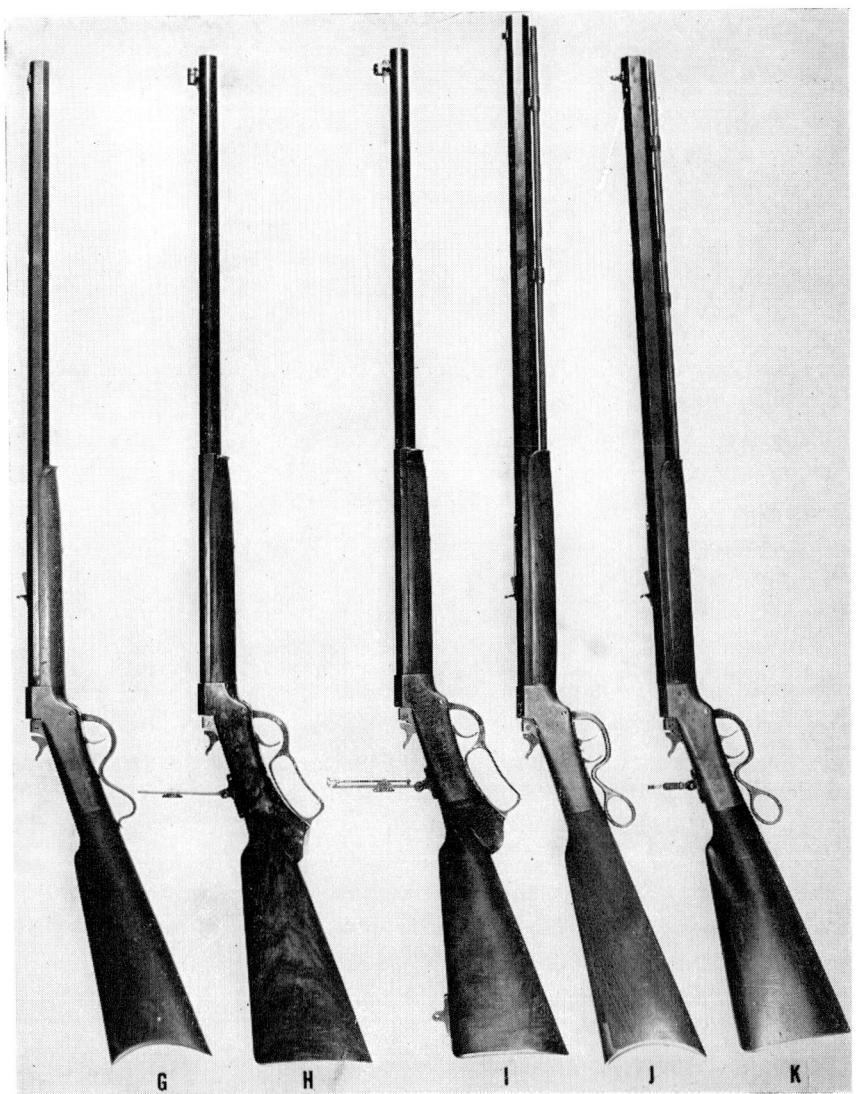

BALLARD RIFLES
(See page 37 for explanation)

Of course, Ballards—that is, the better grades—were not cheap; far from it. But in comparison with some other contemporary makes on the market they were very reasonable. The little No. 3 .22 rim-fire Ballard that sold in hardware stores almost everywhere in the early days at around $15 was certainly not expensive, and apparently it was very popular, judging by the number of these rifles to be found today. The plain cast-iron action of this No. 3 Ballard makes as fine shooting a .22 match rifle as any of the high-grade engraved series. One of these can be rebarreled without compunction, as the original barrels are always badly pitted or worn, thus saving a fine engraved original model for a deserving fate—that of being treasured for years to come by collectors. These little plain-lever, rim-fire Ballard actions lend themselves admirably to being rebarreled and restocked to your heart's content, and the lever can be altered to suit almost anyone's ideas. There will be more about this remodeling farther on in this book,[1] but in this chapter the original Ballard is revered and treated with the respect it deserves.

Following is a summary of the models as made by J. M. Marlin during the years 1875 to 1881. The J. M. Marlin Ballards incorporated Marlin patents covering the inside extractor and the reversible firing pin for center-fire or rim-fire cartridges. While there were a few sporting models made prior to 1875 by the Brown Manufacturing Company and others, as outlined by Satterlee, these utilized the under-barrel, sliding hand-operated extractor, and they are not to be confused with the Ballards made by J. M. Marlin after he had taken over their manufacture in 1875.

BALLARD HUNTER'S RIFLE. Introduced in 1875. This was the first model which appears to have been made for Schoverling and Daly by Marlin. It was a round-barrel model with the old-style hand extractor for the .44 Long rim-fire and center-fire cartridges, using the reversible firing pin. The following year, 1876, this model was announced as having the automatic extractor.

BALLARD HUNTER'S RIFLE No. 1. Introduced in 1876 and discontinued in 1880. This was the round-barrel, reversible firing pin model for the .44 Long rim-fire or center-fire cartridges. The barrel was offered in lengths of 26, 28, and 30 inches, in weights of from 8 to 9 pounds.

BALLARD SPORTING RIFLE No. 2. Introduced in 1876 and discontinued in 1880. This model was chambered for the .32 Long rim-fire or center-fire cartridges and was available in barrel lengths of 26, 28, and 30 inches. It had, of course, the automatic extractor as standard. It was also offered in .38 Long rim-fire or center-fire caliber, and for

[1] See Chapter XIII.

THE BALLARD SINGLE-SHOT RIFLE 7

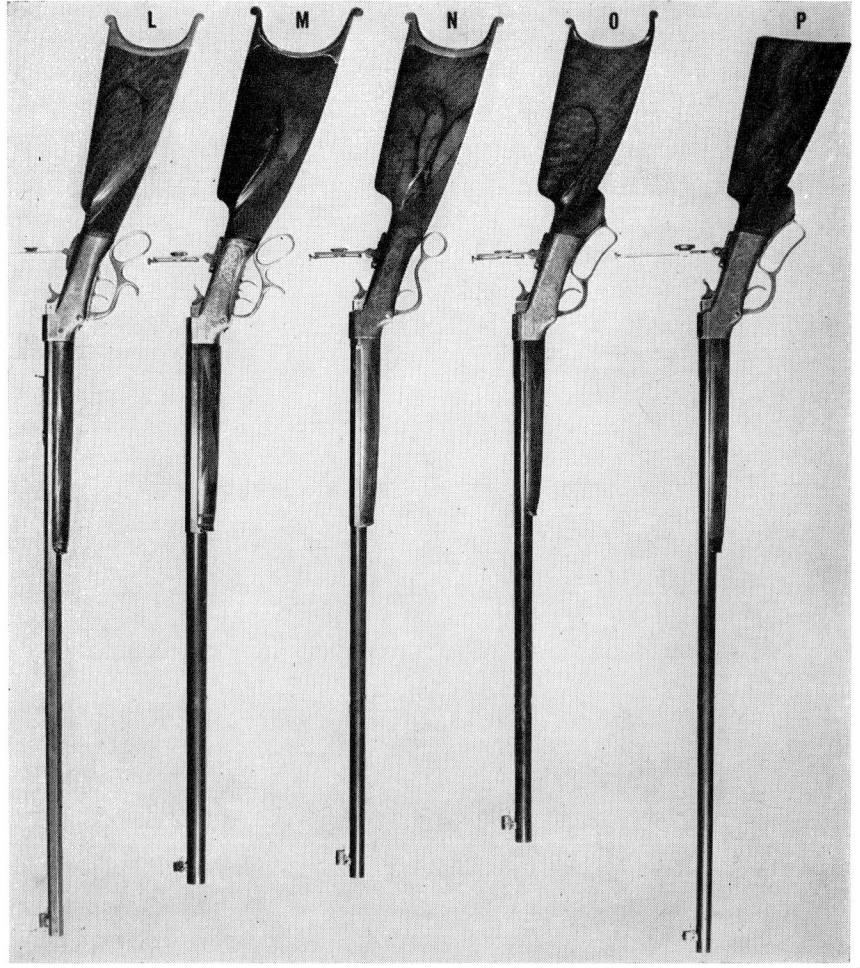

BALLARD RIFLES
(See page 38 for explanation)

a short period also in .44 Long Ballard or in .44 Extra Long Ballard center-fire caliber. This .44 Extra Long Ballard cartridge was superseded by the .44/40 Winchester center-fire, which was also abandoned in this model very shortly.

BALLARD GALLERY RIFLE No. 3. Introduced in 1876 and discontinued in 1880. This model was chambered for the .22 Short rim-fire cartridge and was in all other respects the same as the No. 2 rifle. It was also chambered for the .22 Long rim-fire but not for the .22

Long Rifle cartridge, as this had not as yet made its appearance. These No. 3 caliber .22 models had 24-, 26-, 28-, or 30-inch octagonal barrels and weighed from 7 to 9 pounds, which was comparatively heavy for a .22 rim-fire rifle.

BALLARD PERFECTION RIFLE NO. 4. Introduced in 1876 and discontinued in 1880. This rifle was first manufactured in large calibers —.40/70, and .44/77 Sharps necked, and .50/70 Government—with 26-, 28-, 30-, 32-, and 34-inch octagonal barrels. The frame was advertised as being of extra heavy Norway iron, casehardened, and weighing from 8½ to 12 pounds, depending on caliber and barrel length, of course.[2] The sights were of Rocky Mountain pattern. The .40/70 and .44/77 Sharps necked and the .50/70 Government calibers were discontinued in this model in 1880.

Calibers .38/50 Ballard Everlasting 1$^{15}/_{16}$″, .40/65 Ballard Everlasting 2⅜″, and .44/75 Ballard Everlasting 2¼″ proved to be very popular with riflemen, and they were continued for several years in this model.

BALLARD PACIFIC RIFLE NO. 5. Introduced in 1876. This was the early Pacific, with double-set triggers and a cleaning rod carried under the barrel in thimbles. The heavy octagonal barrel was standard. Some of the first Pacific actions may have been cast actions, but all I have examined appeared to be the drop-forged type. Calibers offered were .40/70 Sharps bottlenecked, .44/77 Sharps necked, and .50/70 Government center-fire. But these three calibers were discontinued in this model in 1880. Calibers continued on past 1880 were: .38/50 Everlasting 1$^{15}/_{16}$″, .40/65 Everlasting 2⅜″, .40/90 Everlasting 2$^{15}/_{16}$″, .44/75 Everlasting 2¼″, .45/70 Government 2$^1/_{10}$″, and the .44/100 Ballard Everlasting 2$^{13}/_{16}$″.

BALLARD SCHUETZEN OFFHAND RIFLE NO. 6. Introduced in 1876 and discontinued about 1880. This was the plain, non-engraved No. 6, with full-octagonal barrel, double-set triggers, and loop-and-spur lever. It had a handmade German pattern straight-grip stock with cheekpiece and special butt plate. The frame was pistol-grip type. (See L, page 7.) Barrels were 30 and 32 inches long and chambered for .40/65 Everlasting 2⅜″ case, and .44/75 Everlasting 2¼″ case. In 1879 the .38/50 in 1$^{15}/_{16}$″ case was added.

[2] This is the flat-sided receiver without the rabbet, or set-back, along the barrel housing.

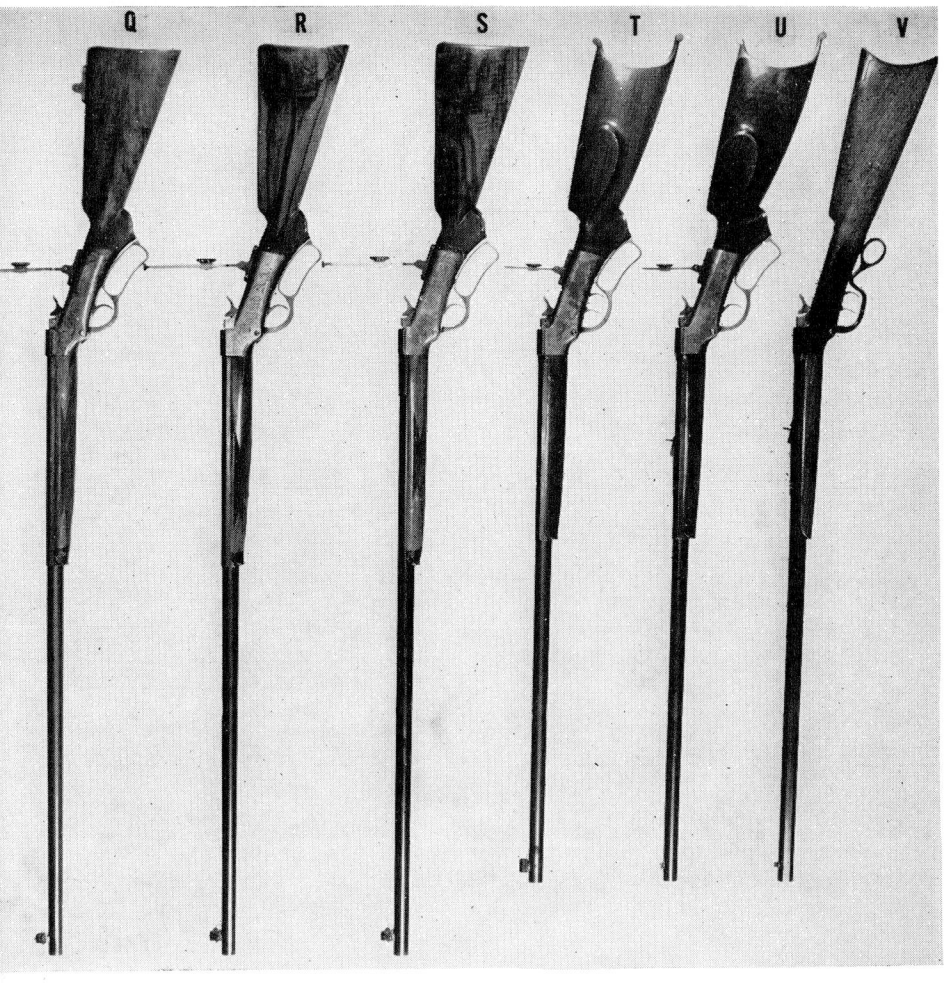

BALLARD RIFLES
(See page 39 for explanation)

BALLARD CREEDMOOR A-1 LONG RANGE RIFLE No. 7. Introduced in 1876 and discontinued sometime before 1886. Engraved on one side of the frame is "Ballard A-1"; on the other side is "Long Range." This was a special long-range target rifle with 34-inch full- or part-octagonal barrel in .44/100 Ballard Everlasting $2^{13}/_{16}''$ case. It was also chambered for the same load in $2\frac{5}{8}''$ case.[3] This model had a

---
[3] The .44/100 in $2\frac{5}{8}''$ case is the common .44/90 or .44/105 Sharps and Remington bottleneck case.

pistol-grip shotgun buttstock of selected walnut, a loop lever, a tall vernier rear sight, and a spirit-level, wind gauge, adjustable front sight. (See R, page 9.)

BALLARD LONG RANGE RIFLE NO. 7. This was essentially the same rifle as the Creedmoor A-1 No. 7, but of somewhat lower grade. It had a plain walnut stock of the same pattern as the A-1. Its sights were plain adjustable rear, and globe front. It was made in .44/100 Ballard Everlasting $2^{13}/_{16}''$ or $2\frac{5}{8}''$ case. Its frame did not have "Ballard A-1" and "Long Range" engraving. This model was discontinued in 1878.

BALLARD LONG RANGE RIFLE NO. 7-A-1. This third No. 7 Long Range rifle was still another version of the A-1. It had a straight-grip stock with shotgun butt plate, and was checkered at grip and forearm. It had a 34-inch full- or part-octagonal barrel, and the frame

BALLARD FINGER LEVERS

1. Lever without extractor recess milling, used on the pre-Marlin Ballards with hand operated extractor below forearm.
2. Same style as number 1, but with the extractor seat milled in. Used on Ballard No. 1 and No. 1½ rifles. Also seen on some No. 2 and No. 4 Ballard rifles in the early J. M. Marlin series.
3. Ring lever for single trigger. Used on several of the J. M. Marlin models including No. 2, No. 4 and No. 6½ offhand.
4. Scroll finger lever, common to the later J. M. Marlin and Marlin Firearms Ballards, seen on the No. 1½, No. 2, No. 3 and No. 4 Ballard rifles.
5. Four-finger loop-lever for single trigger. Used on J. M. Marlin and Marlin Firearms model Ballards of model Nos. 3F, 4½, 4½-A-1, 6½ Pistol Grip, No. 7 Long Range, No. 7-A-1 Long Range, and No. 9 Union Hill.
6. Ring lever for double-set triggers. This is the common Pacific lever, but is also found on several other models when ordered with set triggers, such as Ballard Far West Rifle No. 1¾, No. 2 Sporting Rifle, No. 3 Gallery Rifle, and No. 4 Perfection Ballard, also used on the No. 5½ Montana Ballard.
7. Four-finger loop-lever for double-set triggers. Used on the No. 6½ Pistol Grip, when ordered with double-set triggers. The standard lever for the Ballard No. 8 Union Hill rifle.
8. Schuetzen ball-and-spur lever for double-set triggers and straight-grip stock. Used principally on the No. 6 Schuetzen rifle.

Levers No. 2 to No. 8 comprise the complete styles of levers as offered by the J. M. Marlin and Marlin Firearms Company. There are no other styles as made originally at the factory for these rifles. Any of the styles shown here could be substituted for the regular lever of a specified model, providing, of course, the grip and triggers permitted. One sees today many levers which have been altered by gunsmiths in various ways, principally by the addition of spurs, finger rests, and wood fillers to the loop style lever. There are no further Marlin Ballard levers that are original, other than these seven.

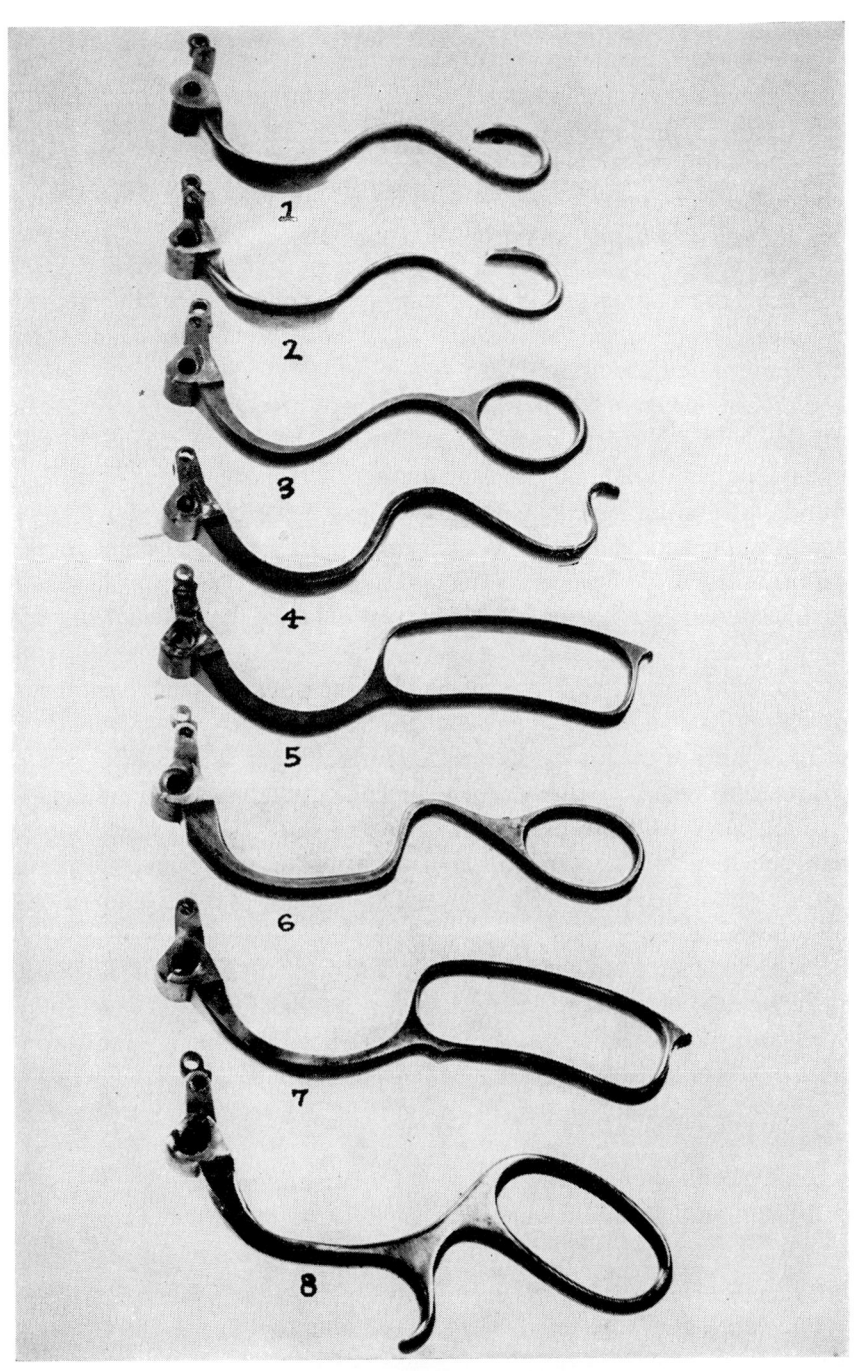

BALLARD FINGER LEVERS
(See facing page for explanation)

was engraved the same as the Ballard Creedmoor A-1 Long Range, with lettering in Text type or Old English. Sights were tall vernier rear, and wind gauge, spirit-level front. Caliber was the same as the two preceding models—.44/100 Ballard Everlasting $2^{13}/_{16}''$ case. This model was dropped probably about 1879.

There were a few models introduced a little later than the preceding ones. These were, for the most part, introduced in 1878, 1879, and 1880. They are as follows:

BALLARD HUNTER'S RIFLE NO. 1½. Introduced in 1879. This rifle had the heavy Norway iron frame. It was a round-barreled rifle, in barrel lengths of 28, 30, and 32 inches, weighing from 9 to 10½ pounds, and chambered in .45/70 Government caliber. This was a very popular model in the West, and was used extensively in the buffalo and other big-game fields. About 1880 it was also offered in .40/65 Everlasting $2\%''$ caliber, with a 30-inch barrel, weighing 9½ pounds. (See page 3, Figure B.)

BALLARD FAR WEST RIFLE NO. 1¾. Introduced in 1879 and discontinued in 1882. This was identical with the No. 1½ rifle except for the addition of double-set triggers. (See C, page 3.)

BALLARD SPORTING RIFLE NO. 2. Introduced in 1879 in .44/40 Winchester center-fire caliber. This was a somewhat lighter model than the regular No. 2 introduced in 1876. It had a 28-inch barrel and weighed approximately 8 pounds. It was discontinued in this caliber in 1882.

BALLARD TARGET RIFLE NO. 3½. Introduced in 1880. This rifle had a heavy octagonal barrel 30 inches long. Its caliber was .40/65 Everlasting $2\%''$. It had a shotgun butt type stock. Its sights were Marlin "Improved" peep rear, and globe front. Evidently it was not a popular model, for it was dropped after only two years of manufacture.

BALLARD SPORTING RIFLE NO. 4¼.[4] Introduced in 1878 and discontinued in 1880. This had the same straight-grip, plain lever as the No. 4 Perfection Rifle,[5] but its ramrod was below the barrel. It was made in .40/70 Sharps bottlenecked, .40/90 Sharps necked,

[4] Mr. Satterlee lists this No. 4¼ Sporting model and he had access to many early catalogs of Marlin's. I personally would accept his statement as true, in spite of certain museum experts' "guesses" confusing the number 4¼ with the No. 5, the Pacific Rifle. This model has eluded me so far.

[5] See G, page 5.

.38/50 Ballard Everlasting, .44/77 Sharps necked, .44/90 Sharps necked 2$\frac{7}{16}$" and 2$\frac{5}{8}$", .40/90 Ballard Everlasting, .44/75 Everlasting 2$\frac{1}{4}$", .44/100 Ballard Everlasting 2$\frac{13}{16}$", .45/70 Government, and .50/70 Government. This also was a short-lived model. It was identical with the No. 5, the Pacific Ballard, with the exception of having a single trigger and a single trigger lever.

BALLARD MID RANGE RIFLE NO. 4½. Introduced in 1878 and discontinued in 1882. This model had a pistol-grip frame and stock, shotgun butt plate, loop finger lever, nicely checkered grip and fore end, and 30-inch part-octagonal barrel. It was chambered for .40/65 Ballard Everlasting. Marlin's "Improved" tang rear sight and globe front sight were standard on this model. The rear sight was graduated to 700 yards. (See H, page 5.)

BALLARD MID RANGE A-1 RIFLE NO. 4½. Introduced in 1879 and discontinued in 1882. This was a very fine target model, same as the Mid Range No. 4½ except that it had a fine English walnut stock, and the frame was engraved on one side "Ballard A-1" and on the other, "Mid Range." Rear sight was Marlin Improved Vernier Mid Range, and there was a hooded wind gauge front sight. Like the other Mid Range model it had a 30-inch barrel, and it was chambered for .40/65 and also for .38/50 Ballard Everlasting 1$\frac{15}{16}$" case. This was a popular model among discriminating riflemen.

BALLARD RIGBY OFFHAND MID RANGE RIFLE NO. 6½. Introduced in 1880 and discontinued in 1882. This was a pistol-grip frame model, with a straight-grip stock, engraved frame, and Rigby barrels in 28- and 30-inch lengths, and was chambered for .38/50 Everlasting and .40/65 Everlasting. Wood used was fine English or Circassian walnut. This was a deluxe model made in limited quantities.

BALLARD LONG RANGE RIFLE NO. 7-A. Introduced in 1878. This rifle is one of the rather confusing models of about this period. It had an octagonal or part-octagonal 34-inch barrel and was chambered for caliber .44/100 Ballard Everlasting 2$\frac{13}{16}$" case. It had a vernier tang rear sight graduated up to 1300 yards, a pistol-grip frame and stock, shotgun butt, loop finger lever, checkered grip and fore end. A Morocco leather sight case came with this fine hand-finished model.

BALLARD LONG RANGE RIFLE NO. 7-A-1. This is the same as the No. 7-A except that it usually had a selected walnut pistol-grip stock, checkered finely. The frame was engraved "Ballard A-1" and

"Long Range," in Text type lettering. This model carried an extra base on the heel of the stock, for prone shooting, but most of the Creedmoor Ballard stocks were equipped with a plate inlet in the top of the stock so that the base of the vernier tang rear sight could be easily moved to that location if desired.

BALLARD LONG RANGE RIFLE NO. 7-A-1 EXTRA. Introduced in 1879. This was the highest grade Creedmoor Ballard and was largely a custom job. It usually had a deluxe Circassian walnut stock and special engraving, as well as a special Rigby 34-inch barrel. Its caliber was .44/100. A fine deluxe specimen of this model made to order may be seen on page 9, Fig. S.

BALLARD OFFHAND RIFLE NO. 6½. Introduced in 1880 and discontinued in 1881. A short-lived offhand rifle, with a plain frame, with no engraving, and a handmade, Swiss pattern, highly polished stock. It was chambered for the .40/65 Ballard Everlasting cartridge and had a half-octagonal barrel of 28- or 30-inch length. This model was designed for 200- and 300-yard offhand shooting on German ring targets. It had a single trigger of regulation pull.

BALLARD MONTANA RIFLE NO. 5½. Introduced in 1880 and discontinued in 1884. This model was brought out just before the reorganization of the Marlin Company. It was a Pacific rifle throughout, the only difference being that the Montana had a shotgun buttplate stock with checkered steel butt plate. It was made in .45 caliber, usually for the .45 Sharps 2⅞" cartridge. In 32-inch barrel length this model weighed 14 pounds.

In 1881 the Marlin Firearms Company was incorporated to manufacture the Marlin repeating rifle. At the time of this reorganization Mr. John M. Marlin was elected president of the new company and Daly of Schoverling and Daly became secretary. The Marlin Firearms Company continued the manufacture of Ballard rifles, and the following models were made and are marked with the new corporation name on the left side of the receiver. The J. M. Marlin name was, of course, dropped at this time.

BALLARD HUNTER'S RIFLE NO. 1½. Introduced in 1881 and discontinued in 1883. This was one of the models carried over into the newly organized company. It was the heavy frame, round barrel, 30- and 32-inch model chambered in .45/70 Government caliber. The sights were Rocky Mountain open rear, and blade front. This model weighed about 9½ pounds. It was also offered in .40/63 (Everlasting version of the .40/70 Ballard) 2⅜" case. This cartridge was one of the new ones introduced by the new company, and was designed for use with grooved bullets instead of the paper-patch type.

BALLARD SPORTING RIFLE No. 2. Introduced in 1881. This was one of the most popular models in the Ballard line. It was chambered for the .32 Long rim-fire or center-fire cartridge, and also for the .32 Extra Long center-fire Ballard cartridge. Barrel lengths were 24, 26, and 28 inches. It was also offered in .38 rim-fire and center-fire calibers, and later in .32/20 Winchester center-fire.

BALLARD GALLERY RIFLE No. 3. Introduced in 1883. This was the popular gallery model that was so widely used for indoor shooting. It was first offered in .22 Short and .22 Long rim-fire in 24-, 26-, and 28-inch barrel lengths, and in weights of 7½ to 8 pounds. Nickel plating on the frame was optional. A little later it was offered in .22 Extra Long rim-fire caliber.

In 1887 this model was chambered for the new Maynard .22 Extra Long center-fire cartridge, but the following year, 1888, this cartridge was largely superseded by the .22 Winchester center-fire, and the rifle was then chambered for this new cartridge.

BALLARD FINE GALLERY RIFLE No. 3F. Introduced in 1883. This was a deluxe version of the Ballard No. 3 gallery rifle. It had a pistol-grip frame (cast), short loop lever, full-octagonal 26-inch barrel, and was chambered for the .22 Long rim-fire cartridge. The stock was pistol-grip type, uncheckered, with small Swiss nickel-plated butt plate. The frame and levers were also available nickeled if so desired. The weight of this model was about 8½ pounds. It was a fine little model and is rather rare today.

Both the Gallery No. 3 and the Fine Gallery No. 3F were made with flat-top receiver housing, and also with the top flat of the barrel housing milled slightly concave to permit a lower sight line.

BALLARD PERFECTION RIFLE No. 4. Introduced in 1884. This is the straight-grip, plain lever, full-octagonal 28- or 30-inch barrel model, chambered for .40/63 Everlasting, .38/55 Everlasting, and .40/70 Ballard. In 1885, the .32/40 cartridge was added in Everlasting type to the calibers available for this model.

BALLARD PACIFIC RIFLE No. 5. Introduced in 1882. This model was the heavy, long-range hunting rifle with double-set triggers, and ramrod held under the barrel by two thimbles. The barrel was oc-

16 SINGLE-SHOT RIFLES

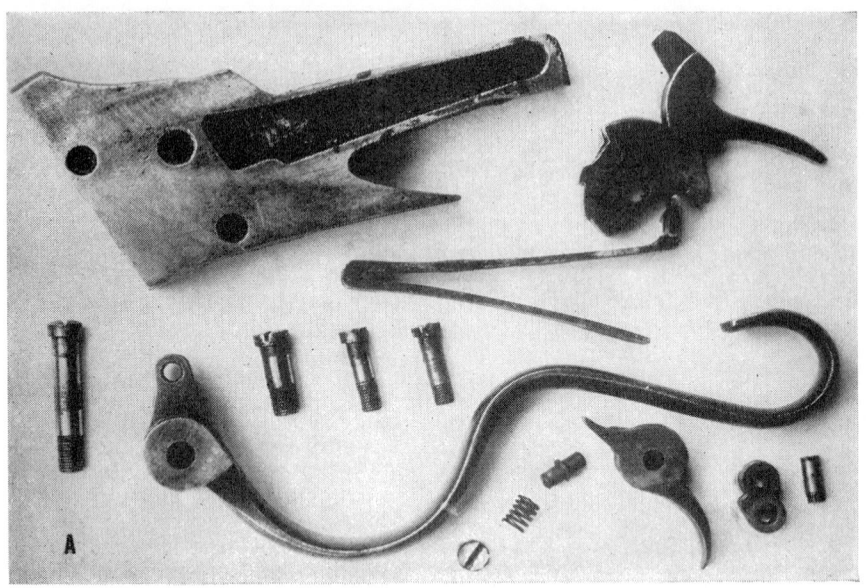

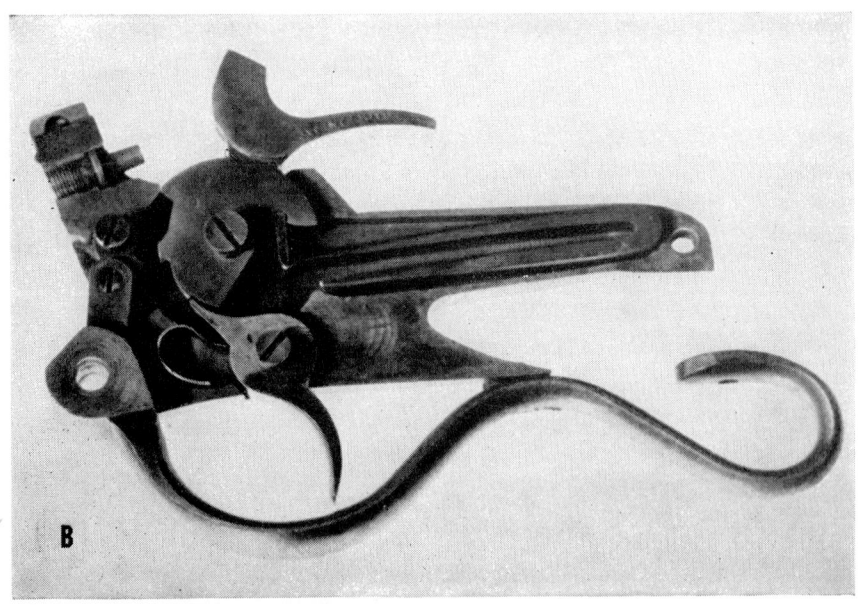

BALLARD BREECHBLOCKS AND SET TRIGGERS
(Explanation of these two pages appears on page 18)

THE BALLARD SINGLE-SHOT RIFLE

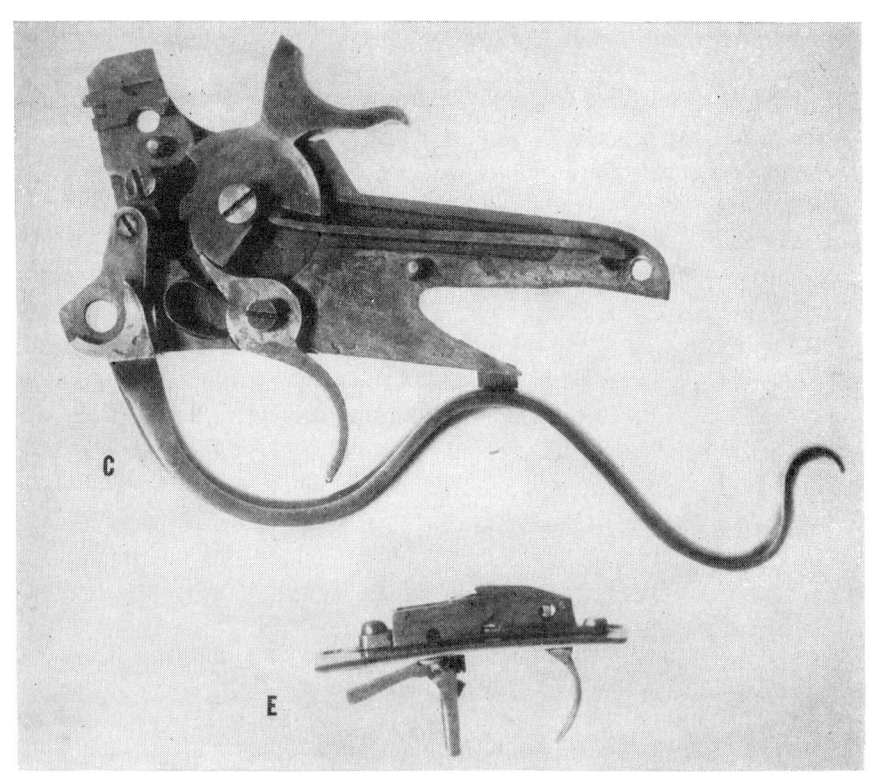

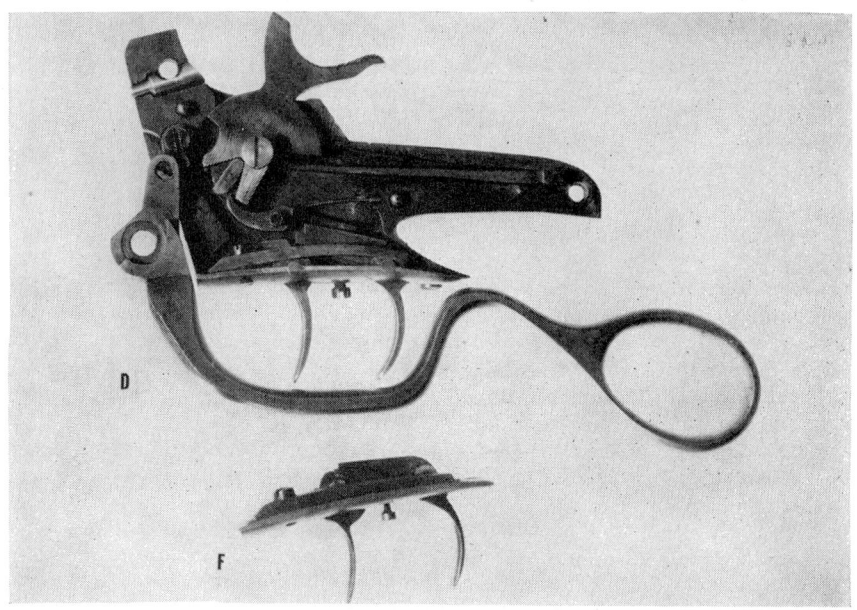

tagonal, and in 30- and 32-inch lengths. The frame was drop-forged, as was the case in all subsequent Ballard models up to the No. 10. This rifle was chambered for a variety of cartridges, among them the .38/55 Everlasting, .40/63 Everlasting, .40/85 Everlasting, .45/70 Government, and .45/100 Everlasting. Also a few were chambered for the .44/40 Winchester center-fire.

BALLARD MONTANA RIFLE NO. 5½. Introduced in 1883. This was essentially the same rifle as the Pacific, with the exception that the No. 5½ usually had a shotgun butt and checkered steel plate instead of the usual Pacific rifle plate. Some were chambered for the Sharps 2⅞-inch case, and came in barrel lengths of 30 and 32 inches.

BALLARD SCHUETZEN RIFLE NO. 6. Introduced in 1876. This was one of the popular engraved offhand target jobs, with part-octagonal barrel, double-set triggers, loop-and-spur lever, and straight-grip Schuetzen butt-plate stock with cheekpiece. The sights were Marlin vernier tang rear, and wind gauge. Barrel lengths were usually 32 inches, and calibers were .32/40 and .38/55 Ballard. This was a heavy arm, weighing from 13 to 15 pounds.

BALLARD PISTOL GRIP OFFHAND RIFLE NO. 6½. Introduced in 1883. This particular single-trigger, loop-lever, pistol-grip model was first offered in caliber .38/55 Ballard, and in 1885 in caliber .32/40 Ballard. It had the Rigby round barrel in 28- and 30-inch lengths. It introduced the new "offhand" nickeled butt plate, and it weighed just under 10 pounds.

BALLARD LONG RANGE RIFLE NO. 7-A-1. Introduced in 1883. This was the regular Creedmoor rifle with 34-inch Rigby barrel, chambered for caliber .45/100 in 2¹⁵⁄₁₆" case. It was a handsome pistol-

---

EXPLANATION OF ILLUSTRATIONS ON PAGES 16 AND 17

A   The Ballard one piece breechblock used in certain of the pre-Marlin Ballards.
B   Breechblock from a Brown Manufacturing Company Ballard, showing the rim-fire firing pin and also the nipple for use with percussion cap. This breechblock is from a .44 rim-fire hand extractor type rifle.
C   Breechblock from a No. 2 Ballard Sporting rifle, showing the reversible firing pin for rim- or center-fire cartridges.
D   An early Ballard double-set trigger breechblock, showing the heavy set triggers with trigger axles extending full width of trigger plate.
E   A set of gunsmith made set triggers for a Ballard. The front trigger is a straight piece of spring wire which is protected by a fixed shield at the rear of the trigger and a swinging shield to cover the front of trigger wire.
F   The more common Ballard set triggers of lighter construction and with small diameter, short axle pins.

grip shotgun butt model, with loop finger lever, and frame engraved "Ballard A-1" on one side and "Long Range" on the other. It had a vernier long-range rear sight and a spirit-level adjustable front sight. A Morocco leather sight box was supplied with this model. The weight was just under 10 pounds, to conform to the Creedmoor range rules.

BALLARD UNION HILL RIFLE No. 8. Introduced in 1884. This Union Hill model was produced in .32/40 and .38/55 Ballard calibers, and with 28- and 30-inch barrel lengths. The barrels were half-octagonal, and the rifles weighed 9½ to 9¾ pounds. The frame was pistol-grip type, and the stock was pistol-grip, cheekpiece type, with offhand butt plate and half-checkered grip. The lever was loop type for double-set triggers. The sights were adjustable tang rear, and globe front. This was one of the most popular models in the later Marlin line.

BALLARD UNION HILL RIFLE No. 9. Introduced in 1884. This was the same model as No. 8 except that it had a single trigger in order to conform with different club rules. Sights, barrel lengths, and calibers were the same as those of the No. 8.

BALLARD SCHUETZEN JUNIOR RIFLE No. 10. Introduced in 1885. This was the last Ballard model introduced. It was the same rifle as the No. 8 except that the barrel was 32 inches in length and extra heavy, making the rifle weigh from 13 to 15 pounds, depending on whether it was chambered for .32/40 or .38/55 caliber cartridges. The sights were the Marlin "Improved" vernier rear, and hooded wind gauge adjustable front. The wood in the stocks was usually of selected grade, as compared to that in the No. 8 and No. 9 stocks; but the pattern was the same in all three.

This concludes the list of Ballard models made by the J. M. Marlin Company and by the Marlin Fire Arms Company from about the year 1875 until the abandonment of the Ballard patent sometime around 1890 or 1891.

A more detailed description of the various basic models is to be found in the January, 1882, Marlin catalog, which reads as follows:

BALLARD RIFLES

. . . for the past four years [these rifles] have won more prizes in matches than any other make. . . .

Simplicity, durability, finish, and accuracy are their strong points. . . . Expert marksmen by using the Ballard have improved their shooting 3 to 5 points. . . .

They are approved and recommended by the best shots in the leading clubs in the United States, Great Britain, France, and Germany. . . .

The model of the Ballard Rifle is conceded to be the most elegant of any that is made. The breech mechanism is the most simple possible and will stand any strain that can be put upon it. The extractor is positive and, working on the same pin as the lever, cannot fail to act. The breechblock moves forward and upward, at the same time pushing the cartridge into the chamber, holding it firmly, greatly lessening the recoil, which is less in a Ballard than in any other rifle made; for close target shooting this is an item of more importance than is generally understood. . . .

When the lever is thrown down, the hammer is pushed to the half-cock notch, making the arm perfectly safe. . . .

The quality of the material and workmanship is unsurpassed. The browning, stock, and general finish is superior to any other rifle. No expense has been spared to secure accuracy of shooting, and the rifling is, we contend, the best ever produced.

PRICE LIST, JANUARY, 1882

These rifles are made only of the calibers, weights, and lengths herein enumerated for each particular style. A greater variety would involve an immense outlay, etc., in making such articles by machinery; special orders are usually filled without a profit, or at a positive loss. Hence the list will be strictly adhered to, and for orders of a caliber and weight not enumerated an extra charge will be made according to expense incurred. [*Alignment in the following list has been rearranged for the benefit of the reader, but the data and descriptive wording are identical with the original.*]

No. 1½ HUNTER'S RIFLE. Round barrel, extra heavy wrought frames, Rocky Mountain rear and knife-edge front sights. Using .45 Government cartridges and .40/63 Everlasting shells.

BARREL LENGTH	WEIGHT	PRICE
30-inch	9½ lbs.	$22.50
32-inch	10 lbs.	24.50

No. 2 SPORTING RIFLE. Octagon barrel, reversible firing pin. Using rim- and center-fire cartridges, .32 Long and .38 Long and .44 Colt and Winchester center-fire.

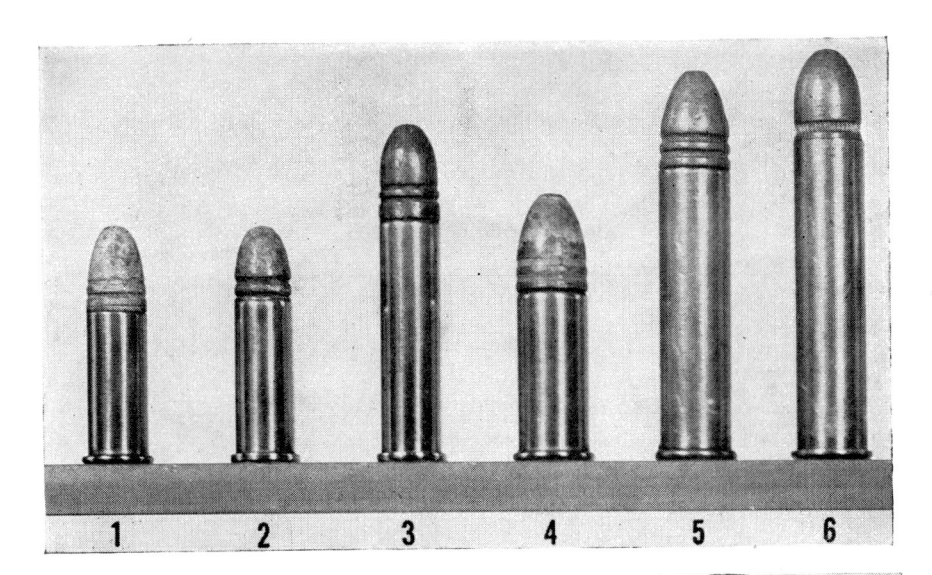

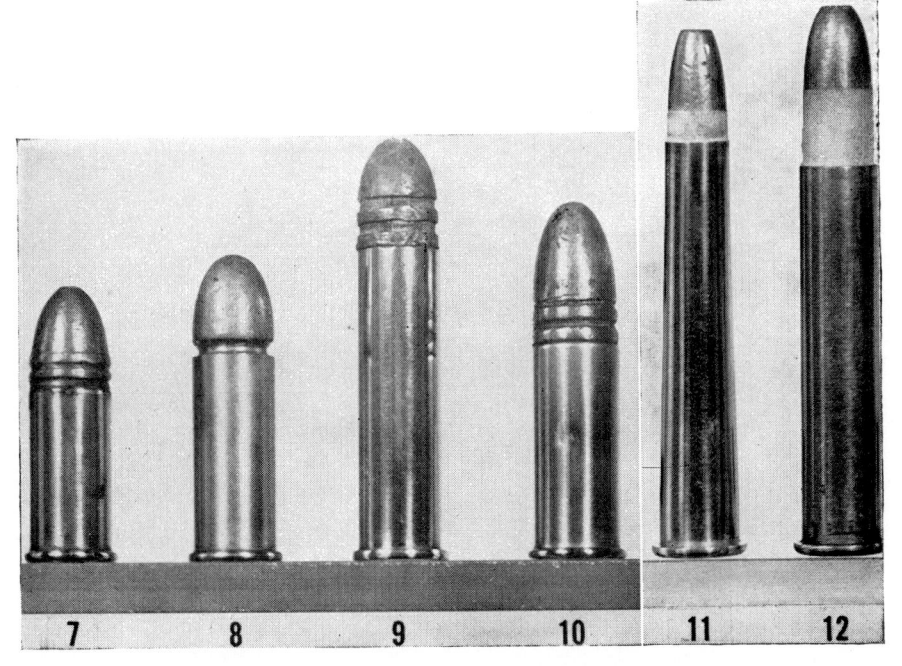

CARTRIDGES USED IN BALLARD RIFLES

1. .32 Long rim-fire
2. .32 Long center-fire
3. .32 Extra Long center-fire
4. .38 Long rim-fire
5. .38 Extra Long rim-fire
6. .38 Extra Long center-fire
7. .44 Rim-fire
8. .44 Center-fire Ballard
9. .44 Extra Long center-fire Wesson
10. .46 Rim-fire
11. .32/40/165 Paper-patch
12. .38/50/250 Everlasting Paper-patch

CALIBER	BARREL LENGTH	WEIGHT	PRICE
.32 Long	28-inch	8½ lbs.	$22.00
.38 Long	28-inch	8¾ lbs.	22.00
.44 c-f.	30-inch	9 lbs.	22.00

No. 3 GALLERY RIFLE. Octagon barrel.

BARREL LENGTH	WEIGHT	PRICE
24-inch	7½ and 8½ lbs.	$21.00
26-inch	8 lbs.	23.00
28-inch	9¼ lbs.	25.00

No. 4 PERFECTION RIFLE. Octagon barrel, extra heavy wrought-iron frame, Rocky Mountain sights. Using Everlasting shells.

CALIBER	BARREL LENGTH	WEIGHT	PRICE
.38/50	30-inch	9½ lbs.	$25.00
.40/63	30-inch	10 lbs.	25.00

No. 5 PACIFIC RIFLE. Octagon barrel, double-set triggers, cleaning rod under barrel, with brush and swab. Rocky Mountain sights.

CALIBER	BARREL LENGTH	WEIGHT	PRICE
.40/63 Everlasting	30-inch	10 lbs.	$30.00
	32-inch	11½ lbs.	32.00
.40/90 Everlasting	30-inch	10½ lbs.	30.00
	32-inch	11½ lbs.	32.00
.45/100 Everlasting	30-inch	11 lbs.	30.00
	32-inch	12 lbs.	32.00
.45 Government	30-inch	10 lbs.	30.00
	32-inch	11 lbs.	32.00

No. 5½ MONTANA RIFLE. Same style and finish as No. 5, weighing 14 lbs., rifle or shotgun butt.

BARREL LENGTH	PRICE
30-inch	$32.00
32-inch	34.00

This is a new style just introduced, suited to the Territory trade where a heavy arm is required.

No. 6 SCHUETZEN RIFLE. Octagon or half octagon barrel, double-set triggers. Marlin short vernier midrange peep and windgauge sights. Swiss pattern, handmade, polished, selected stock, nickel-plated butt plate. Full checquered. Finest finish. Using Everlasting shells.

CALIBER	BARREL LENGTH	WEIGHT	PRICE
.38/50	30-inch	13 lbs.	$70.00
.38/50	32-inch	15 lbs.	70.00

CARTRIDGES USED IN BALLARD RIFLES

13 .38/55/255 Paper-patch
14 .40/63/330 Paper-patch
15 .40 case head showing shallow Berdan primer pocket
16 .40/65/330 Ballard Everlasting
17 .40/70/330 Ballard Paper-patch
18 .40/85/370 Ballard Paper-patch

No. 6½ Pistol Grip Offhand. Rigby barrel, midrange vernier peep and windgauge sights. Fine English walnut stock, modified Swiss pattern, pistol-grip, Farrow butt plate, exactly fitting the arm. Finely engraved, and every part highly finished. Using Everlasting shells.

CALIBER	BARREL LENGTH	PRICE
.38/50	28- and 30-inch	$70.00

No. 4½ A-1 Mid Range Rifle. Half octagon barrel. Fine English walnut stock. Marlin's improved vernier peep sight graduated to 800 yds., windgauge front sight, bead, and aperture disks. Finely engraved frame,

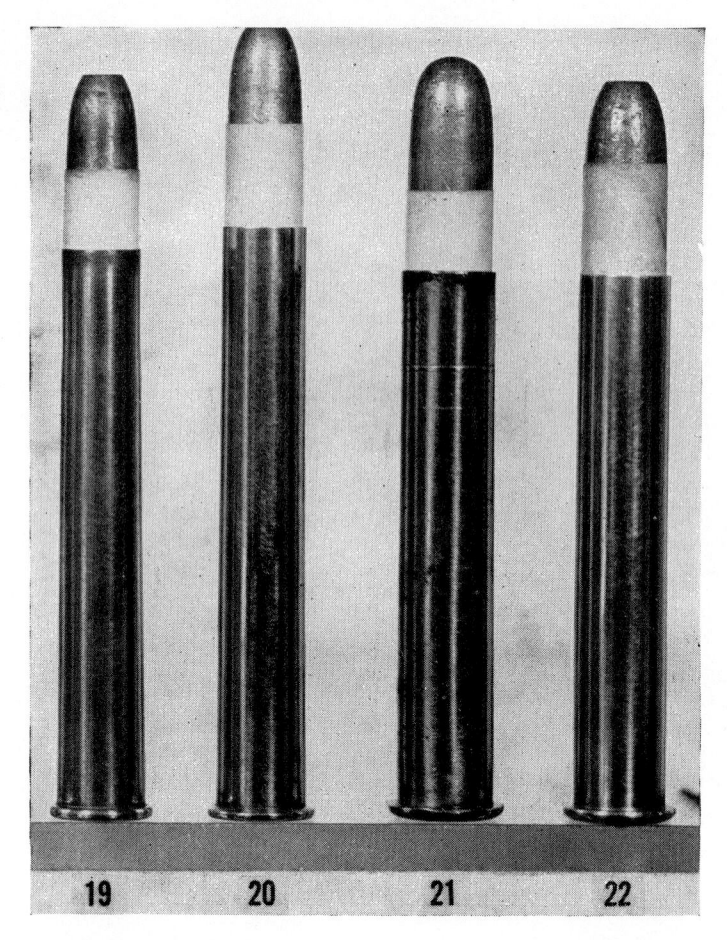

CARTRIDGES USED IN BALLARD RIFLES

19 .40/90/370 Ballard Paper-patch
20 .40/90/370 Ballard Ideal Everlasting
21 .44/100/530 Ballard Everlasting
22 .45/100/550 Ballard Everlasting

rubber butt plate, every part finished in the best manner. Using Everlasting shells.[6]

CALIBER	BARREL LENGTH	PRICE
.40/63	30-inch	$65.00

No. 7 LONG RANGE RIFLE. Half octagon barrel 34 inches long. Marlin's improved vernier peep sight graduated to 1300 yards. Windgauge sight with spirit level, bead, and aperture disks. Morocco sight case, handmade

---

[6] No illustration of this rifle is shown in the 1882 catalog, nor is it shown in any later Ballard catalog I have examined.

pistol-grip stock, full checquered, regulation weight and pull. Using Everlasting shells. Caliber, .45/100. Price, $75.

No. 7-A-1 LONG RANGE RIFLE. Rigby barrel finely engraved. Extra handsome English walnut stock, rubber butt plate. Every part made with the greatest care and finished in the highest possible style. Using a new thin end Everlasting shells. Caliber, .45, 100 grains. Price, $90.

The No. 6½ Rigby Offhand is shown in this 1882 catalog with straight-grip stock and odd ring-type lever, heavy butt plate, sharp, high-comb cheekpiece stock. This is a duplicate of one in the author's collection, shown on page 7, Fig. N.

The No. 6½ Pistol Grip Offhand is shown in the catalog with the regular Farrow plate, cheekpiece, pistol-grip stock, and regular loop lever for single trigger. This No. 6½ is shown with scroll engraving—no animal scenes.

The No. 7 Long Range is shown in this catalog with a Rigby barrel and no engraving on receiver.

In this particular catalog all actions except numbers 6½ Rigby Offhand and 6½ Pistol Grip Offhand are of heavy flat-side barrel housing type. That is, there is no narrow rebated ledge on the frames shown except in the two offhand models listed above. Many of the early Pacific forged and cast Norway iron frames were made this way, but in Marlin Firearms Company Ballards this flat-side barrel housing is not encountered quite so often except in Long Range and Mid Range frames.

Of course the No. 6½ Rigby Offhand and No. 6½ Pistol Grip Offhand models were made to be used with the round Rigby barrels with raised, engraved lugs at the breech, which was the Rigby trademark, and so these frames, to be in keeping with the smaller round barrels, were rebated, or set back, along the top side, and the corners were usually ground off of the octagonal receiver ring. (Note close-up pictures of these actions on page 45.)

The plain vernier rear sight shown on the No. 6 Schuetzen in this 1882 catalog is the long-based, exposed spring type as pictured on the early No. 6 Schuetzen on page 7(L). A short-based, regular midrange staffed vernier is shown on the No. 6½ Rigby Offhand illustrated in this catalog.

The same short base as shown on the No. 6½ Rigby Offhand is shown with a long-staffed vernier on the Long Range No. 7-A-1. However, the regular short midrange vernier staff is shown on the common longer base on the No. 6½ Pistol Grip Offhand pictured in the 1882 catalog.

Numbers 1½, 2, 3, and 4 model rifles are shown in the 1882 catalog with the uncommon doubled-back finger lever (#2, page 11). This type lever is a hangover from the pre-Marlin Ballard, and it is not likely that many rifles with this lever were shipped from the factory in the early 1880s. No doubt these cuts were a holdover from those used in the 1881 catalog. They were probably those that were used in the earlier catalog to picture some J. M. Marlin models.

The lever shown on the Pacific Rifle No. 5 is the regular common Pacific ring type for double triggers (#6, page 11).

The No. 6 Schuetzen carries the same loop-and-spur lever as the later No. 6 models.

The No. 6½ Rigby Offhand has the odd ring lever for single trigger (#3, page 11). (This odd little ring lever seems to have been used on all single-trigger models for a brief series of serial numbers.)

The No. 7-A-1 is shown in the 1882 catalog with the lever that is usually seen on the Long Range and Mid Range models—a four-finger loop lever for single trigger.

The No. 6½ Pistol Grip Offhand in the same catalog sports the same four-finger loop lever for single trigger.

SHOTGUN BUTT PLATES FROM SINGLE-SHOT RIFLES

1 Horn butt plate used on Ballard Long Range No. 7-A-1 Special Extra.
2 Hard rubber butt plate used on Ballard Mid Range No. 4½-A-1.
3 Hard rubber butt plate used on Ballard No. 6½ and Union Hill models. (These plates were optional equipment on these models.)
4 Checked steel butt plate used on Ballard No. 5½ Montana Rifle, No. 4½ Mid Range and No. 7 Long Range.
5 Steel butt plate used on Remington Rolling Block Creedmoor Rifle.
6 Hard rubber butt plate used on Remington-Hepburn Creedmoor Mid and Long Range models.
7 Checked steel butt plate used on Sharps Model 1874 Creedmoor Rifle.
8 Checked steel butt plate used on Sharps Borchardt Military and Sporting models.
9 Hard rubber butt plate used on Sharps Borchardt Short and Mid Range Target models.
10 Hard rubber butt plate used on Sharps Borchardt Long Range Creedmoor models.
11 Hard rubber butt plate used on Stevens O44½ English model.
12 Hard rubber butt plate used on Bullard single-shot rifles—fancy grade.
13 Hard rubber butt plate used on Winchester single-shot rifles. (This plate and a smooth steel plate were special equipment.)
14 Steel butt plate used on Peabody-Martini Creedmoor rifles.

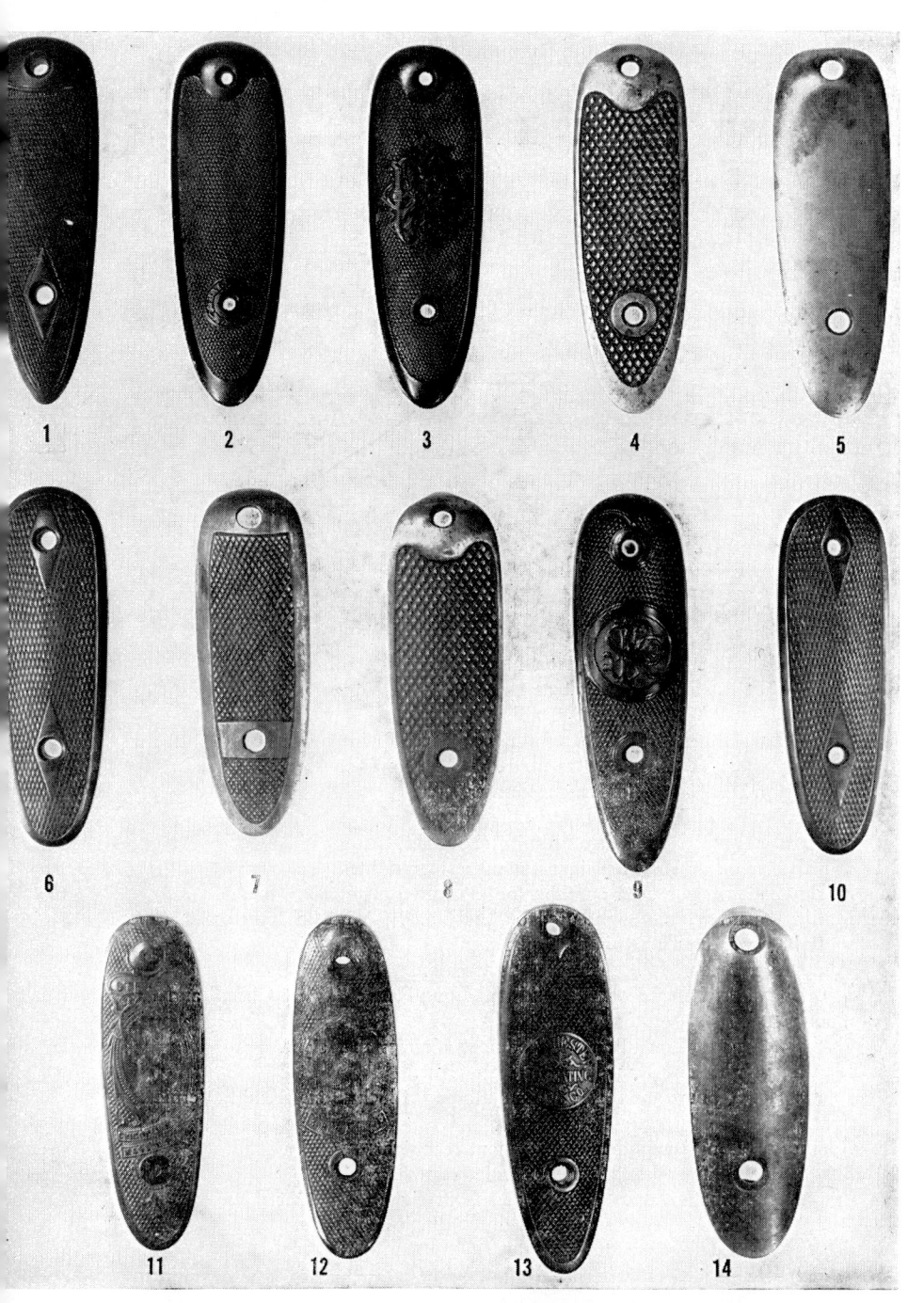

SHOTGUN BUTT PLATES FROM SINGLE-SHOT RIFLES

These loop levers on the Long Range, Mid Range, and early No. 6½ Ballards are all for single triggers; they do not have sufficient opening for double triggers.

Later on in the serial numbers of Ballards one finds some No. 6½ single-trigger Ballards with four-finger loop levers with opening large enough for double triggers. Evidently they were supplied this way so that a double-trigger block could be added later and the same lever utilized.

The following extra charges were made according to the January, 1882, catalog.

EXTRAS

All deviations from the regular styles and sizes cause a large outlay for hand labor, and when ordered will be subject to the following charges:

Engraving from $5.00 up. Full nickel plating, $5.00. Nickel-plated trimmings, $3.00. Fancy walnut stock, $5.00. Checking butt stock and forearm, $5.00. Shotgun butt rubber heel plate, $2.00. Double-set trigger,

SIGHTS USED ON SINGLE-SHOT RIFLES

1. Marlin Ballard Gallery tang sight.
2. Marlin Ballard tang sight used on No. 6 Schuetzen rifle.
3. Sharps Borchardt Vernier sight as used on Short Range Target model.
4. Marlin Ballard Mid Range adjustable tang sight.
5. Marlin Ballard Mid Range Vernier sight. (Marlin's improved peep sight.)
6. An early Maynard tang sight as used on the percussion sporting models.
7. Remington-Hepburn Mid Range Vernier sight.
8. Maynard rack and pinion adjustment sight.
9. Sharps Borchardt Mid Range Vernier rear sight.
10. Winchester Long Range plain adjustment rear sight.
11. Marlin Ballard sight used on the No. 4½ Mid Range rifle.
12. Marlin Ballard Vernier sight used on the No. 4½-A-1 Mid Range rifle. (Special short base was used on this particular sight.)
13. Winchester black Morocco leather sight case.
14. Vernier tang sight used on the Mid and Long Range "What Cheer" and Creedmoor rifles.
15. Sharps Borchardt Long Range Creedmoor Vernier rear sight.
16. Marlin Ballard Long Range Vernier rear sight.
17. Remington-Hepburn and Remington Rolling Block Long Range Vernier rear sight.
18. Remington Long Range plain adjustment rear sight.
19. Sharps side hammer Long Range Vernier rear sight.
20. Stevens combination open and hooded front sight for pocket rifles.
21. Beach combination front sight used on all single-shot rifles.
22. Stevens hooded front sight.
23. Winchester hooded front sight.
24. Remington-Hepburn windage adjustment front sight.
25, 26, 27 Windage adjustment front sights with and without spirit level slides

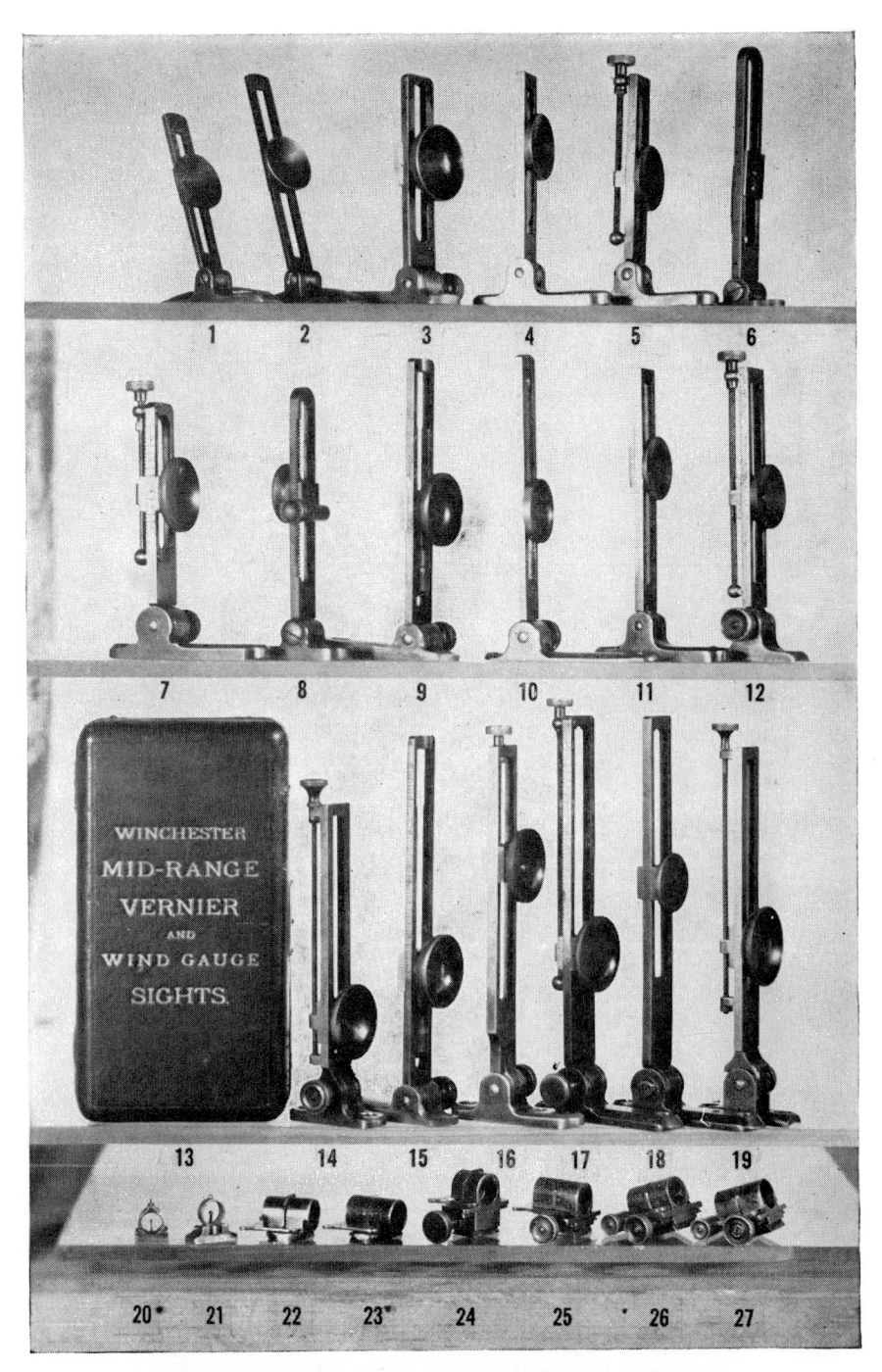

SIGHTS USED ON SINGLE-SHOT RIFLES

$5.00. Casehardening, $1.50. Swivels and sling (fitting same, extra 50¢), $1.50.

Price list of component parts for rifles numbered 1½, 2, 3, 3F, 4, 4¼-A-1, 5, 5½, 6, 6½, 7, 7-A-1 are shown in this catalog.

The price list of Marlin sights was as follows:

Rocky Mountain Rear Sight, $1.00. Rocky Mountain Front Sight, 50¢. Windgauge Sight, with spirit level, $8.00. Marlin's Improved Long Range Vernier Peep Sight, $10.00. Mid Range Vernier Peep Sight, $7.50. Mar-

SIGHTS USED ON SINGLE-SHOT RIFLES

28 Lyman tang sight for Ballard.
29 Lyman click adjustment windage and elevation sight for Ballard.
30 Stevens plain adjustment windage and elevation rear sight used on the tip-up series of rifles.
31 Stevens plain adjustable windage and elevation tang rear sight.
32 Stevens Vernier adjustment windage and elevation rear sight with Stevens 5-hole eye piece.
33 Stevens Vernier rear sight used on the Ideal No. 44 rifles.
34 Remington elevating sight used in connection with the usual Rocky Mountain rear sight. (Peabody-Martini Kill Deer and Rough and Ready Sporting rifles used a very similar sight with an open notch thus requiring no open rear barrel sight.)
35 Lyman rear sporting sight.
36 Lyman rear sporting sight.
37 Stevens-Pope windage and elevation adjustment rear sight.
38 Winchester Single Shot Vernier rear sight with circular holding spring.
39 Winchester Single Shot Vernier rear sight. The later type with flat spring in base holding staff upright.
40 Stevens-Pope telescopic sight front mount. The split ring type of mount clamping into circular milled recesses in the barrel.
41 Stevens-Pope telescopic sight rear mount.
42 Stevens rear scope mount, mounting on dovetail blocks.
43 Stevens front mount to match No. 42 rear mount.
44 Malcolm rear scope mount. Elevation is contained in rear mount.
45 Malcolm front scope mount. Windage is obtained by adjusting the opposing screws in the front mount.
46 A special rear telescope mount, mounting on the tang of the Ballard in place of the rear tang sight. The rifle is cleaned through the large hole in mount. This mount was made to be used with a long Malcolm telescope, in connection with the usual Malcolm windage adjustment front mount.
47 Sharps Borchardt removable top tang with integral sight base used on target models.
48 Sharps Borchardt sight base for heel of stock. Used when sight staff was moved to the heel for shooting in the Texas or other back positions.
49 Stevens rear sight, combination open or peep, used on pocket rifles and pistols.
50 Steel plate which was inlet in the heel of the Ballard Mid and Long Range stocks. The whole sight including base was moved to this plate and held in place with the regular tang screws.

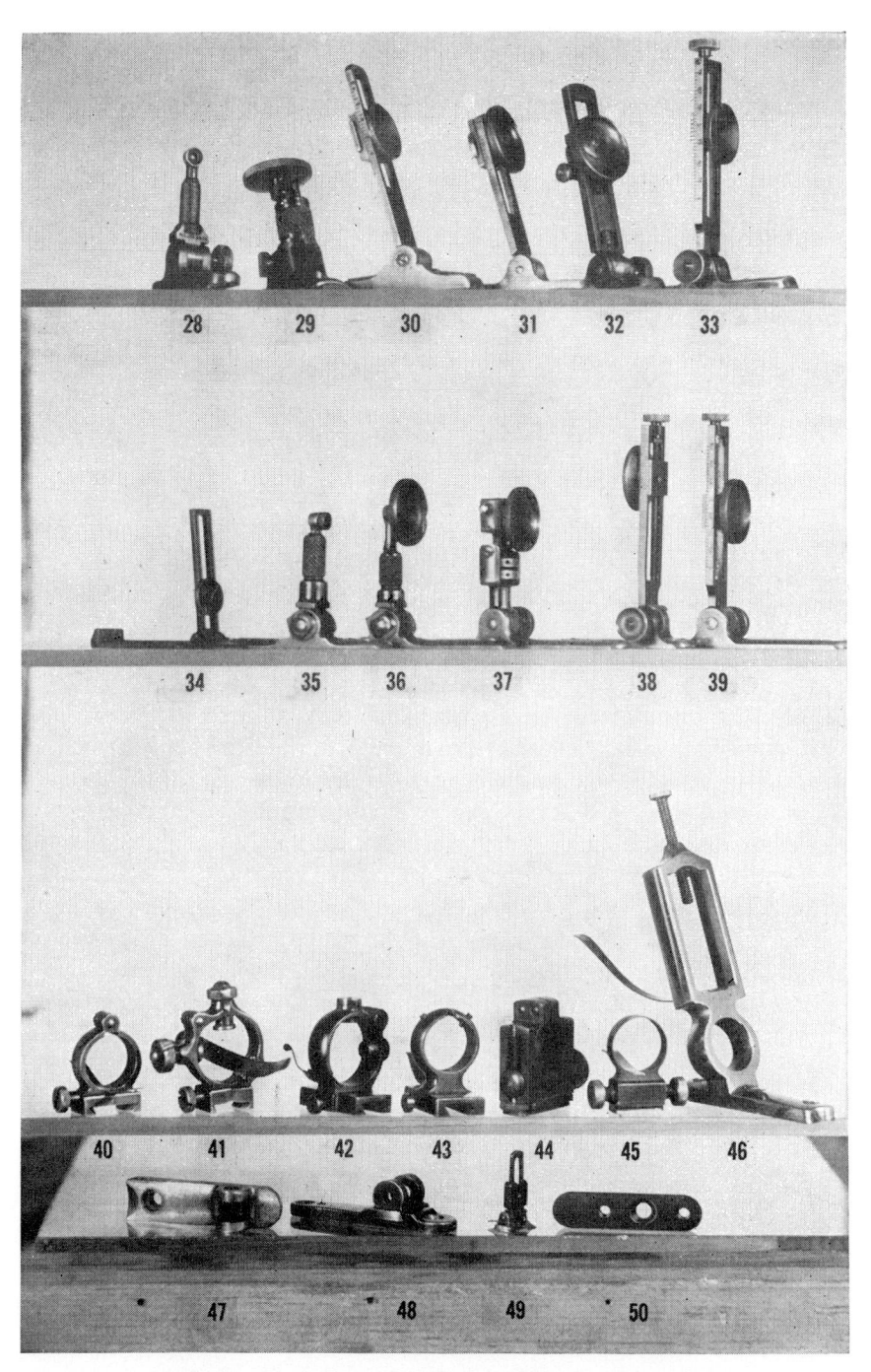

SIGHTS USED ON SINGLE-SHOT RIFLES

lin's Improved Graduated Peep Sight, $5.00. Interchangeable Discs for Windgauge Front Sights, $1.00. Beach's Combination Front Sight, $2.00. Lyman's Patent Combination Peep Sight, $5.00. Plain Globe Front Sight, $1.00. Peep Sight for Gallery and Sporting Rifles, $3.00.

ELEVATIONS FOR BALLARD LONG RANGE RIFLE

The scale is graduated in inches and twentieths of an inch. The slide has a vernier scale, by which hundredths of an inch can be measured. The bottom line of the scale is used in measuring elevations.

200 yds.	.20 in.	700 yds.	.90 in.
300 yds.	.32 in.	800 yds.	1.07 in.
400 yds.	.45 in.	900 yds.	1.25 in.
500 yds.	.59 in.	1000 yds.	1.44 in.
600 yds.	.74 in.	1100 yds.	1.65 in.

This is an average table when using 100 grains of FG Powder and a 550-grain bullet. Every trifling change in the circumstances requires a change in elevation; and experience alone can enable the marksman to properly adjust his rifle.

EVERLASTING CENTER FIRE SHELLS

The advantages of the Everlasting shells are numerous. There is less recoil than with a bottleneck shell; it is no trouble to clean them; they are exactly the same size as the bore, so that the ball lies in the grooves, as in a muzzle-loader. The rifle can be used as a muzzle-loader, one shell answering for hundreds of shots with the advantage of being able to see the condition of the barrel if desired, and having the cap covered, preventing blowing back, and having the cap and powder in close contact.

They are made of heavy metal, specially prepared, and a fine quality of powder can be used which would burst an ordinary shell and endanger the life of the shooter. There is no bother about reducing after firing. They are cheaper, as each shell will last for years.

.38/50—7¢ each; .40/63, .40/65, .44/75, .45 Gov't.—8¢ each; .40/90 and .44/100—9¢ each; .45/100—10¢ each; .40/63 is same size as .40/65 except that the edge is thin.

Directions for loading shells (Everlasting)

In loading shells for target shooting be sure that the charges are always the same; use a scale or cut off carefully with a Creedmoor flask. Fill the shell within $\frac{1}{16}$" of the top, settling it well, by tapping with some light article, or, which is better, pour slowly through a loading tube. Put the bullet in the shell with the ball seater, adjusting it so that it just goes home and does not crush the powder. In loading for hunting, use 8 or 10 grains less powder, place a wad over it and a lubricating disc over the wad. When grooved bullets are used, dip them in a melted lubricant, base end first, until the grooves are filled; place in the shell and dip quickly in the lubricant, which should be quite hot. Make a lubricant of clear tallow, four parts; beeswax, one part.

PRICE LIST OF BULLETS AVAILABLE

Grooved .38/250, .38/300, .40/285, .40/330,
.44/380, .45/405   Per 1000 $10.00

Patched .38/255, .38/330, .40/285, .40/330,
.40/370, .44/405, .45/420   Per 1000 $13.50

Patched .44/530, .44/555, .45/550   Per 1000 $15.00

Reloading implements, etc.

Reloading tools for grooved bullets, per set, $5.00; bullet moulds for grooved bullets, $2.00. Bullet moulds for patched bullets, to be used with swage, $1.50. Swage, made with great care, $5.00. Ball center, nickeled, $1.50. Re- and de-capper, $1.40. Wad cutter, $.40. Hawksley's Creedmoor Flask, 12 oz., 60 to 115 grains, $3.50.

Wilkinson's shell loader, $3.00. Loading tube 24" long, 50¢. Primers per M., $2.00. Wads per M., 30¢; lubricating discs, 60¢ per M. Farrow's lubricating material, in handled boxes, per box, 25¢. Cut paper patches per M., 50¢. Patch paper, per quire, 75¢.

[*Conclusion of 1882 Ballard catalog.*]

The Marlin catalog for fall, 1888, omits apparently the Ballards which were by this time, no doubt, discontinued. The models listed are not so varied nor are they so numerous as those described in preceding years.

In the introduction to this catalog the company called attention to the fact that Ballards were being offered chambered for regular ammunition as well as for Everlasting shells. They also made the statement that the Ballard was the only rifle being made at that time with double-set triggers; but this is obviously a misstatement.

The Ballard models offered in this 1888 catalog are as follows.

No. 2 SPORTING RIFLE. Octagonal barrel, chambered for .32 Long and .38 Long rim- and center-fire cartridges. Barrel lengths, 24, 26, 28, and 30 inches. Weights, from 7½ to 8¾ pounds. Prices, $15 and $16.

The .32 caliber could be chambered for the .32 WCF cartridge for $1.00 extra.

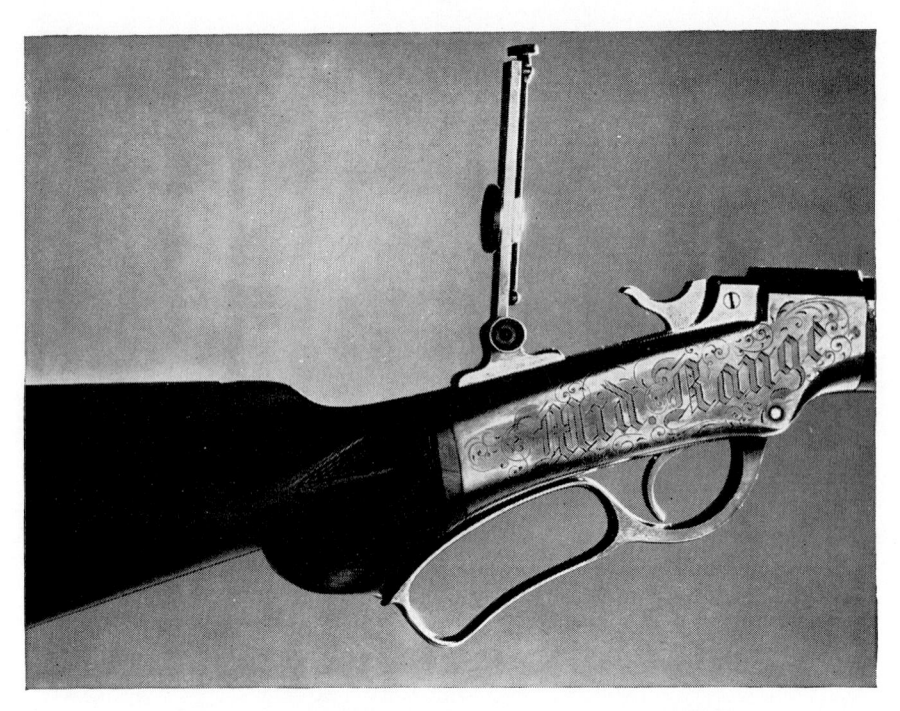

THE BALLARD A-1 MID RANGE RIFLE

The .32 and .38 calibers could be chambered for the Extra Long cartridges for 50 cents extra.

Nickel-plated frame, lever, and butt plate were 75 cents extra.

No. 3 GALLERY RIFLE. Octagonal barrel, chambered for .22 Short and .22 Long. Barrel lengths, 24, 26, and 28 inches. Weights, 7 to 8½ pounds. Prices, $15 and $17.

Could be chambered for Extra Long .22 rim-fire cartridge for 50 cents extra; or for new Extra Long center-fire cartridge (Maynard .22/10/45) for $1.00 extra; or for .22 WCF cartridge for $1.00 extra.

Nickel-plated frame, lever, and butt plate, 75 cents extra.

No. 4 PERFECTION RIFLE. Octagonal barrel, extra-heavy wrought-iron frame. Chambered for Everlasting shells or for factory ammunition in calibers .32/40, .38/55, and .40/63. Barrel length, 30 inches. Weight, 9½ pounds. Price, $17.

No. 3F FINE GALLERY RIFLE. Octagonal barrel, with pistol grip and "Improved" offhand nickeled butt plate. Uses same cartridges as No. 3 Gallery Rifle. The offhand butt plate exactly fits the shoulder, and the pistol grip gives a firmer hold so that much better average shooting can be done than with the plain rifle. Both these features add to the elegant appearance of the arm. Barrel length, 26 inches. Weight, 8½ pounds. Price, $22.50.

No. 5 Pacific Rifle. Regular Pacific style rifle in the following calibers: .38/55, Everlasting .40/63, Everlasting .40/85, WCF .44, .45/70, and Everlasting .45/100. Weights ran from 10 to 11½ pounds. Barrel lengths, 30 and 32 inches. Prices, $22.50 and $24.00.

No. 8 Union Hill Rifle. Half-octagonal barrel. Chambered for .32/40 and .38/55 calibers. Barrel lengths, 28 and 30 inches. Weight, 9¾ pounds. Price, $34.

With Mid-Range vernier rear and wind gauge front sights, $3.00 extra.

No. 9 Union Hill Rifle. Same as No. 8 except that it has a single trigger. Calibers, weights, and barrel lengths same as No. 8. Price, $30.

Mid-Range vernier and wind gauge front sights, $3.00 extra.

No. 10 Schuetzen Junior Rifle. Same pattern as No. 8 Union Hill except that it has a 32-inch barrel and vernier rear and wind gauge front sights. Chambered for .32/40 and .38/55 calibers. Weight, 12 pounds. Price, $42.50.

No. 6 Schuetzen Rifle. Part-octagonal barrel. Finely engraved animal scene frame. Chambered for .32/40 and .38/55 calibers.

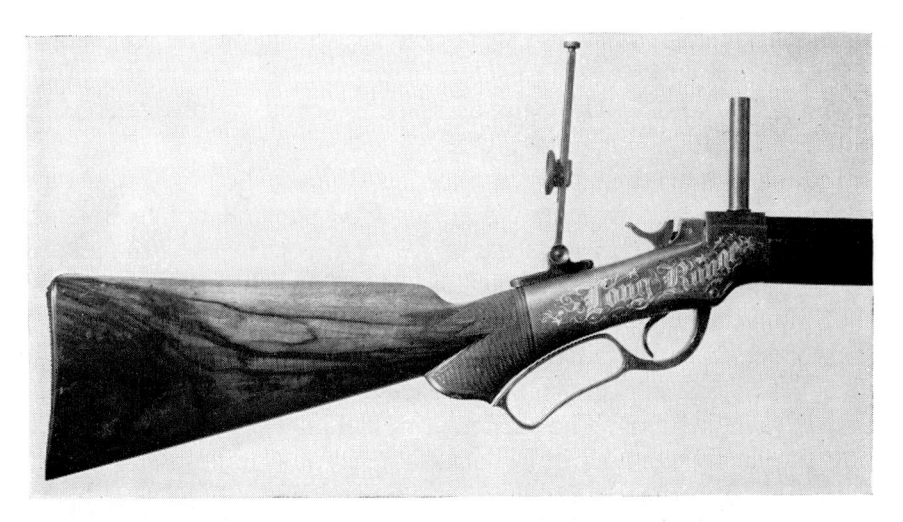

THE BALLARD A-1 LONG RANGE RIFLE
Cartridge on top of receiver ring is the .44/100 Ballard Everlasting.

Barrel length, 32 inches. Weight, 13 and 15 pounds. Price, $57.50.

No. 6½ OFFHAND RIFLE. Rigby round barrel. Finely engraved animal scene frame. Chambered for .32/40 and .38/55 calibers. Barrel lengths, 28 and 30 inches. Weight, just under 10 pounds; usually about 9¾ pounds. Price, $57.50.

This rifle could be furnished with shotgun butt and rubber heel plate, if preferred, at same price.

The 1888 catalog offered the same sights, extras, and spare parts as those described in the 1882 catalog, but by the later year the Ballard Everlasting shells in .38/50, .40/65, .40/90, .44/75, and .44/100 had become obsolete and were replaced by the Ballard .32/40, .38/55, .40/63, .40/85, and .45/100 shells. Consequently, the new types had come into popular use and the cases, tools, and bullets for these calibers occupied conspicuous place in the 1888 catalog.

The trend in these models is easily traced through the rifles as outlined in the preceding paragraphs. The Everlasting cartridge case is inseparably linked with the earlier model Ballards, and of course the later chambers would accept factory-loaded cartridges in most calibers, with the exception of the .44/100 and .45/100, which were always offered in Everlasting form only; in fact, there do not seem to have been many factory-loaded cartridges for these Creedmoor Ballard models. At least, they are rare today.

The actual basic models as collected by the author are shown on pages 3, 5, 7 and 9. The calibers for these models are discussed in detail in the following paragraphs.

FIGURE A is an early *Ballard Sporting Rifle* of the pre-Marlin type as made by the Brown Manufacturing Company. It has an outside, manual-operated extractor. It is chambered for the .44 rim-fire cartridge, and has a flat firing pin and also a nipple in the block, so that when the factory loads were exhausted, the case could be pierced and loaded from the muzzle, ignition being accomplished by means of a percussion cap on the nipple. This rifle has a full-octagonal barrel, 26 inches long. The particular model here shown has the stock bolt similar to late Marlin Ballards. The serial number is 22026.

FIGURE B is the *Ballard Hunter's Rifle No. 1½*. It has a heavy frame and a 28-inch round barrel. It is chambered for the .40/63 Ballard Everlasting cartridge, 2⅜-inch case, which was the Everlasting version of the .40/70 Ballard cartridge, adaptable to either grooved or patched bullets of 330 grains. This is a J. M. Marlin Ballard. Its serial number is 5684.

FIGURE C is the *Ballard Far West Rifle No. 1¾*. It is the same rifle as the No. 1½ rifle with the addition of double-set triggers. This is a J. M. Marlin model. Serial number is 947.

FIGURE D is the *Ballard Sporting Rifle No. 2*. It is chambered for the .38 Long rim- or center-fire cartridges, with reversible firing pin, details of which are shown on page 49.

FIGURE E is the *Ballard Gallery Rifle No. 3*. It is chambered for the .22 Long rim-fire cartridge and has a 30-inch full-octagonal barrel and nickel-plated frame (original). This model has the two-piece side extractor common to all .22 Ballard rim-fire rifles. Detail of this extractor is shown on page 49. This is a Marlin Firearms Company Ballard. Its serial number is 22896.

FIGURE F illustrates the *Ballard Gallery Rifle No. 3F*. It is chambered for the .22 rim-fire cartridge.

FIGURE G shows the *Ballard Perfection Rifle No. 4*. It has a full-octagonal, 30-inch barrel, and is chambered for the .40/63 Ballard Everlasting cartridge, 2⅜-inch case. This is a J. M. Marlin model. Its serial number is 5597.

FIGURE H shows the *Mid Range Ballard No. 4½*. Caliber .40/65 Ballard Everlasting Plain frame, no engraving. Marlin mid-range height staff, plain adjustable rear sight.

FIGURE I shows the *Ballard Mid Range A-1 Rifle No. 4½*, a model rare to find today. This specimen is all original. It is chambered for the .40/65 Ballard Everlasting cartridge with 2⅜-inch case. This model has the 30-inch half-octagonal barrel. The stock is of fine English walnut, with polished oil finish. It has the vernier midrange tang rear sight and windgauge front sight, with extra base on heel of stock for back position shooting. This model is engraved "Ballard A-1" on one side and "Mid Range" on the other. It is a J. M. Marlin model, serial number 2912.

FIGURE J is the *Ballard Pacific Rifle No. 5*. This rifle has the 32-inch full-octagonal barrel of about the #4 weight. It is chambered for the .40/90 Ideal Everlasting cartridge, with 3 1/16-inch case—an unusual caliber. It is a J. M. Marlin model, serial number 4370.

FIGURE K is the *Ballard Montana Rifle No. 5½*, with the shotgun butt plate stock. The caliber is .45 Sharps, with 2⅞-inch case. This is a J. M. Marlin model. Serial number is 9895.

FIGURE L is the early *Ballard Schuetzen Rifle No. 6*, with plain frame, pistol-grip type. But it has the early handmade Swiss pattern stock and special butt plate, spur-and-loop lever, and double-set triggers. The barrel is 30-inch full-octagonal. The caliber is .44/75 Ballard Everlasting, 2½-inch case. It is a J. M. Marlin model, serial number 1903.

FIGURE M is the later *Ballard Schuetzen Rifle No. 6*, with animal scene engraved on frame, spur-and-loop lever, double-set triggers, and 32-inch part-octagonal barrel. The caliber is .38/55 Ballard. It is a Marlin Firearms Company model, original throughout. The weight is about 12 pounds. Serial number is 28854.

FIGURE N is the early *Ballard Offhand Rifle No. 6½*. It has a scroll-engraved frame, single checkered trigger, and a ring lever. The stock is of polished Circassian walnut, with gold-plated butt plate. This has a 30-inch part-octagonal barrel, caliber .40/65 Ballard. (Rigby

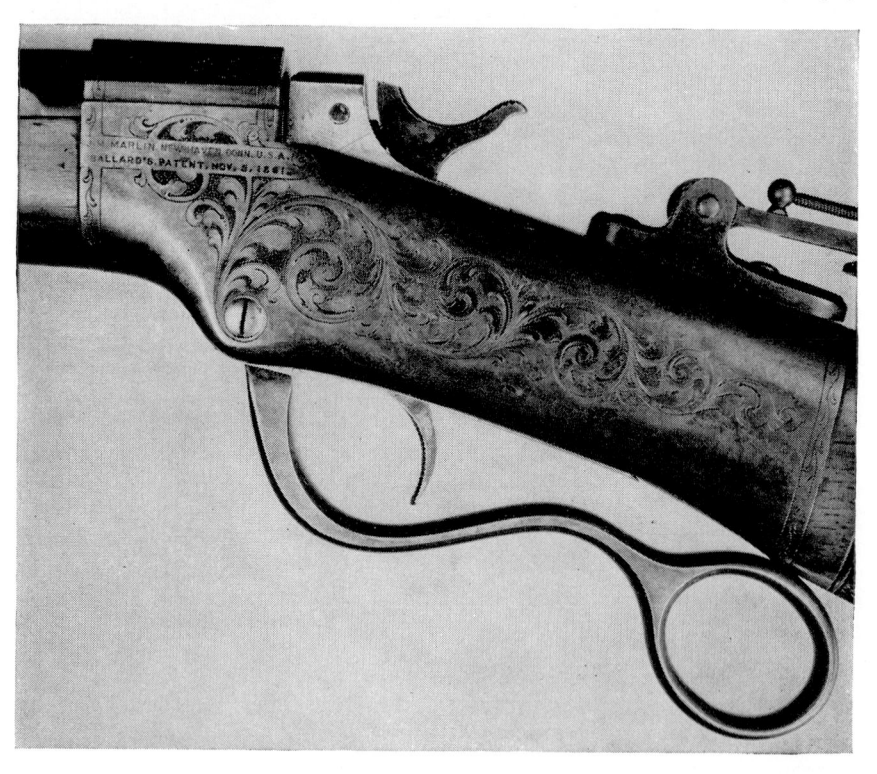

SCROLL ENGRAVED BALLARD OFFHAND NO. 6½ RIFLE, SERIAL NO. 4404

barrels were more common on this model.) This is a J. M. Marlin model, serial number 4404.

FIGURE O is the *Ballard Rigby Offhand Rifle No. 6½*, with Rigby 28-inch barrel. The model is original throughout, with single checkered trigger, loop lever, Circassian walnut cheekpiece, and pistol-grip stock. The grip tip has horn inlay, and the fore end is tipped with horn, as were most of the higher grade Ballards. The action is beautifully engraved with buffalo and deer. The caliber is .38/50 Ballard Everlasting, 1^{15}⁄$_{16}$-inch case. This is a rifle hard to find all original. It is a J. M. Marlin model, serial number 9178.

FIGURE P is a special custom Ballard, original throughout. It has a No. 6½ action, with lever and proper single checkered trigger. The beautifully figured Circassian walnut stock, however, is shotgun butt type with hard-rubber butt plate, and it is of much greater drop than the Creedmoor Ballard stocks. The barrel is a 34-inch Rigby. The caliber is .40/85 Ballard, 2^{15}⁄$_{16}$-inch case. This rifle has the tall vernier rear sight, but no base at heel of stock; the front sight is wind gauge. It is a Marlin Firearms Company model, serial number 27055. This beautifully engraved specimen I feel sure was a special order throughout.

FIGURE Q is a *Ballard Long Range Rifle No. 7*. The caliber is .40/90 Ideal Everlasting, 3^{1}⁄$_{16}$-inch case. It has a 34-inch part-octagonal barrel, vernier sights, with plate inlet into top of stock at heel so that the tang rear sight base may be transferred to this location for sighting in the Texas or other back positions. This action has no engraving. It is a J. M. Marlin Creedmoor Ballard model, serial number 8972.

FIGURE R is a *Ballard Creedmoor A-1 Long Range Rifle No. 7*. The caliber is .44/100 Ballard Everlasting, 2^{13}⁄$_{16}$-inch case. It has a 34-inch half-octagonal barrel, tall vernier rear sight and wind-gauge front sight. The action has the regular single checkered trigger, and is finely engraved—"Ballard A-1" on one side and "Long Range" on the other. The stock is Long Range pattern, with checkered steel butt plate and inlaid plate at heel for base of vernier sight. This stock is made of the most strikingly beautiful Circassian walnut of any Ballard I have ever owned. The wood, of a pale golden straw color, has dark umber streaks culminating in a swirl near the butt. It has the appearance of having been deliberately streaked with chocolate which ran down the wood toward the butt, forming a contrast with the golden yellow background that is beautiful beyond description. This rifle is the true Creedmoor Long Range Ballard in every detail. It is a J. M. Marlin model, serial number 1033.

FIGURE S is a rare model Ballard. It is the *Ballard Long Range 7-A-1 Extra Grade.* These were custom jobs, and made up to the buyers' specifications. They were designed to appeal to the discriminating rifleman who wanted a truly deluxe Creedmoor rifle. The action is specially engraved with animal scenes, in a different pattern, of course, from the more common No. 6 and No. 6½ Ballards. The barrel is a 34-inch Rigby, the caliber is .44/100 Ballard Everlasting, 2$^{13}/_{16}$-inch case. The stock is of beautifully figured Italian or Circassian walnut, with horn butt plate, and horn inlay on grip and fore-end tip. It has a base inlet in the top of the stock at the heel, for accepting the base of a long-range vernier rear sight when it was desired to shoot from that position. This is a truly magnificent rifle,

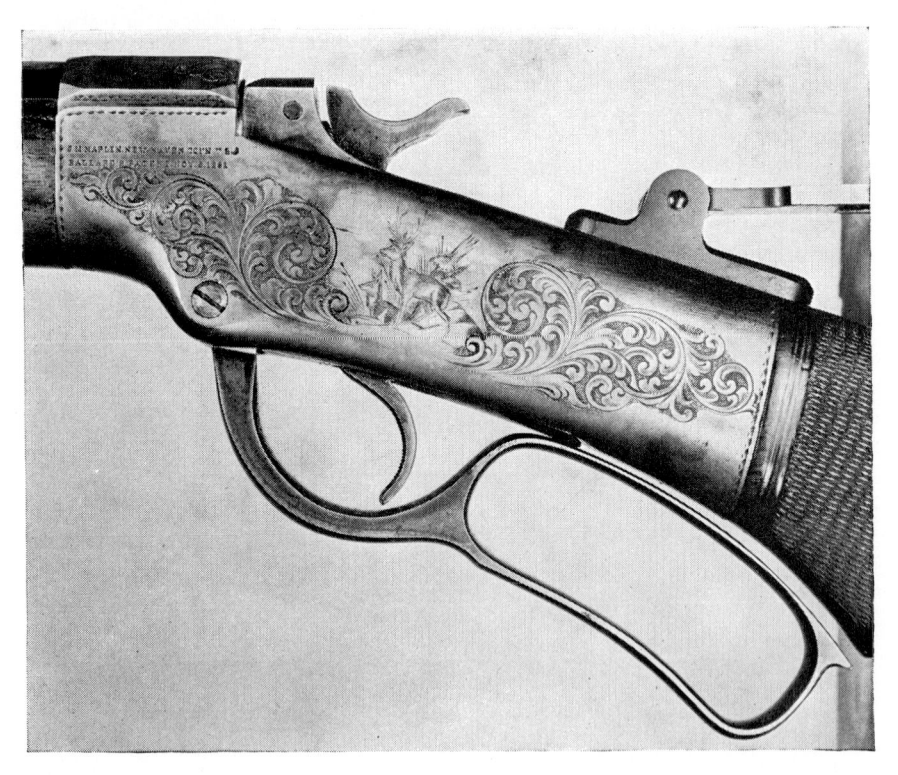

BALLARD NO. 7 A-1 SPECIAL LONG RANGE RIFLE
EXTRA GRADE

and the actual number of this particular 7-A-1 Extra Grade which were made must be very small. It is a comparatively early J. M. Marlin model, serial number 3409.

FIGURE T is the *Ballard Union Hill Rifle No. 8*, in .38/55 Ballard caliber. It is the regular standard No. 8 with all details correct—double-set triggers, loop lever, half-checkered grip, graduated adjustable tang rear sight and globe front sight. This particular rifle is a Marlin Firearms Company model, and the serial number is 33879.

FIGURE U is a *Ballard Union Hill Rifle No. 9*. The caliber is .38/55. It has the lighter weight, half-octagonal barrel, 28 inches long, and the regular loop lever and single trigger of this model. However, the stock and fore end are of specially selected American walnut, with a special checkering job. This was ordered with the rifle, as the wood, as well as the rifle, is original throughout; all numbers match. It is a Marlin Firearms Company model, serial number 25841.

FIGURE V shows a special *Ballard Perfection Rifle No. 4*. The caliber is .38/55. This was a specially ordered rifle, as it has double-set triggers and the Pacific lever. The frame is drop-forged type, so it may possibly be a special Pacific made with light barrel without ramrod thimbles. It is original throughout. This is a Marlin Firearms Company model, serial number 30808.

This completes the regular factory Ballard models with the exception of the *Ballard Schuetzen Junior Rifle No. 10*, which is identical with the No. 8 shown, with the addition of a heavier 32-inch barrel and the Marlin vernier sights.

Other Ballards not original throughout are shown and described in Chapter XIII.

SHOOTING THE OLDER BALLARD

I shoot all my rifles; the odder the calibers and the harder it is to find brass for them, the better I like 'em. For the early rim- and center-fire Ballards in .32, .38, and .44 Ballard calibers it is easy to find ammunition. All the specimen cartridge dealers have these sizes in quantity, and molds are still to be found occasionally. Originally these were all outside lubricated cartridges, of course, and usually they need to be regreased before shooting. The cases can be decapped and reprimed with almost any makeshift tool. You will find the Ideal tong type of many common calibers will accomplish this job.

and the bullets can be seated with the fingers and left uncrimped. Black powder must be used behind a soft lead bullet to upset properly and take the rifling.

The .32 Extra Long center-fire cartridge was used in some of the No. 2 Ballards, and these can be handled the same way as described in the preceding paragraph. I happened to find a 90-grain-bore size mold for my specimen, and I shoot this one with #80 powder, which makes a pleasanter shooting combination.

The .32/40 Ballard chambers accept the modern made cases of this caliber, of course, and a variety of bullets is available for this size. Mild loads of Dupont shotgun bulk smokeless powder or #80 and #4759 are the best powders for these guns. However, the load must be mild, for Ballard actions are designed for black powder and will open up just like a book if the load is excessive. Originally the .32/40 cartridge was used in the Ballards with 165- and 185-grain paper-patch bullets, with black powder. I have used these patched bullets but have never found the accuracy to be superior to a 165- or a 180- or even a 200-grain .319-size cast bullet with a mild load of around 8 to 10 grains weight of Dupont's shotgun smokeless, or #4759 powder. The Ideal handbooks give a great variety of loads for this caliber, of course, and it is too well known to go into much detail herein.

The .38/50 Ballard Everlasting case was used in the J. M. Marlin Ballards, and this was the forerunner of the later .38/55. The .38/50 case is 3/16 of an inch shorter than the .38/55, and of course it is heavier at the mouth, being the Everlasting type. I happened to get a small quantity of nickeled .38/50-1 15/16" cases with my No. 6½ Rigby Ballard and, taken care of, these have lasted a long time. I have used .38/55 cases in this chamber, cutting them off the necessary amount and seating the bullet in the breech, Schuetzen style. But inasmuch as the chamber is cut for the heavier case, the .38/55 case will not permit loading the .375-diameter bullet in the case mouth after firing, for the cases are much larger at the mouth after firing and will usually require a .40-caliber wad to hold the powder in the case. However, the .38/55 cases work perfectly, and they will, no doubt, be available for a long time to come. The regular bullets for the .38/50 caliber were 250- and 300-grain paper-patch bullets, but a .38/55 255-grain bullet sized to fit your barrel is very accurate, and this is what I have always used with success.

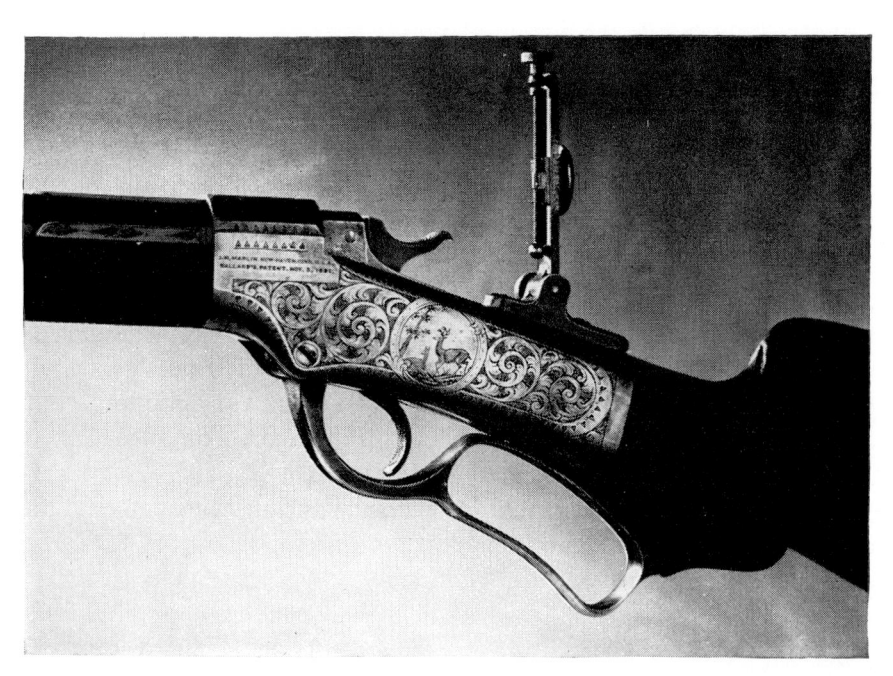

BALLARD ENGRAVING

BALLARD ENGRAVING

The .38/55 Ballard chamber, like the .32/40, will, of course, shoot with accuracy the regular case and bullet of this caliber. The .32/40 and the .38/55 Everlasting cases are not true Everlasting type, as they are the same size as factory-loaded ammunition, therefore interchangeable. They are a trifle heavier than the factory loaded in base or head, and usually they are unmarked; but the body of both case and mouth is thin, similar to the factory-loaded .32/40 and .38/55 ammunition. None of these cases should be crimped. Seat the bullet friction tight and you will then obtain the accuracy of which these finely made, deeply rifled barrels are capable. A warning of great importance to be heeded is: if you value your gun and your eyes and hands, don't shoot a jacketed, Hi-velocity, or Super-Speed .32/40 or .38/55 factory-loaded cartridge in a Ballard. These cartridges are designed and loaded for the lever-action Marlin and Winchester repeating rifles, and they have no part in the scheme of design of a Ballard target rifle.

The .40/65 Ballard Everlasting case is 2⅜ inches long, and it is seldom met with. My fine A-1 Mid Range engraved Ballard is in this caliber, and quite a supply of nickeled cases, a Ballard bullet seater, and recapper and decapper material came with the rifle. This cartridge case was usually made to take the odd, thin, and shallow Marlin-Berdan primer. The case has a central flash hole with a crater around it for the anvil, and I have never found any Berdan primers that fit it the way I thought they ought to. However, I have managed to ream out some of these cases to accept modern-size large rifle primers, and so have shot this fine rifle quite a bit. The case is a true Everlasting type, with thick mouth. With 60 grains of FG black or King's semi-smokeless powder and a 265-grain patched Winchester or 330-grain Ideal grooved bullet, it shoots very accurately up to 300 yards, the maximum distance I have targeted the rifle. The midrange height of staff on the vernier rear sight on this rifle is graduated up to 700 yards, and it has the base or the heel for back position shooting.

It is possible to use a .40/70 or a .40/63 Ballard brass case in a .40/65 chamber, as they are the same length—2⅜ inches; but it is impossible to get .40/65 Everlasting cases into a chamber cut for the .40/70 or the .40/63 case. They are not exactly interchangeable.

The .40/63 Ballard Everlasting is also a 2⅜-inch case, but it is the heavier version of the .40/70 Ballard factory-loaded cartridge. Most

LEFT AND RIGHT VIEW OF BALLARD ENGRAVING

.40-caliber Ballards made by the Marlin Fire Arms Company seem to be of this caliber, and brass is not particularly hard to find. The .40/63 is a heavy case, the same dimensions outside, of course, as the .40/70, with thin end case so that it will accept the .40-caliber bullet. Cases for the .40/63 can be made from .40-85 or .40/90 Ballard 2$^{15}/_{16}$-inch cases cut off and sized to fit. The .40/70 Sharps Straight 2½-inch cases can also be shortened a trifle and used. They will swell ahead of rim to fit, but most of them will remain intact.

There are many different .40-caliber bullet molds available, and no difficulty should be experienced in obtaining them. Size the bullets to fit your particular barrel, which is usually, in Ballards, around .403 to .408. The case mouths can be reamed slightly to accept the bullet if it is a trifle large to fit the case and is right for the barrel.

The .40/85 and the .40/90 Ballard cartridges are identical. In fact, they are the same cartridge. They are 2$^{15}/_{16}$ inches long, some are marked one way and some the other. The .40/90 is the older designation of this size. I use both cases in my Rigby Ballard No. 6½, with from 80 to 85 grains of FG ahead of 3 grains of Dupont shotgun smokeless powder behind the 330- or 370-grain bullet in grooved pattern. I have shot some paper-patch 370-grain Remington bullets in this barrel also with fine accuracy. However, these patched bullets require cleaning after every shot, and they are a lot of trouble, so I usually use the 370-grain Ideal bullet cast very soft, about 1-50 or 1-60. This is a pretty heavy load to shoot, and the 330-grain bullet offers a little less recoil.

The .40/90 Ideal Everlasting case is 3$^{3}/_{16}$ inches long. My Pacific Ballard No. 5 is chambered for this little-known case, and with the rifle came a quantity of used cases, a Ballard bullet seater, and a Ballard recapper and decapper. I managed to find a few more new cases in this caliber, so with care I shall be able to shoot this rifle for a long time to come. These cases that I have accept the modern large rifle primer, so that problem is easily solved. However, I have some cases in this size that were made for the odd Berdan type primer described under the .40/65 caliber (page 44). The load for this is essentially the same as for the .40/85 and the .40/90 Ballard cartridges described in the preceding paragraph.

For the .44/75 Ballard Everlasting caliber I have never been able to locate cartridges. I have the rifle, a fine, early Ballard Schuetzen No. 6, and the chamber says the case was 2½ inches long. The .44/75 is a straight case, not necked. A Schoverling and Daly list of

Ballards of about 1878 or 1879 shows a .40/60 Everlasting cartridge of 2⅛-inch length which was used in Ballard No. 4 and No. 4½ on the list. The No. 4 Perfection was also chambered for the .44/75. But all the shooting I have done with my .44/75 rifle has been with cases I made over to fit from some UMC solid-head Sharps .45-2⁶⁄₁₀″ cases, cutting them off and sizing and trimming them down until I could get them into the chamber. The bore of this rifle is a true .44 caliber, and the 405-grain .45/70 Government bullet sized down the necessary few thousandths of an inch in an Ideal hand die does the trick. I have never seen a specimen of this cartridge in any cartridge collection, but I am of the opinion that it was another of the special Marlin Everlasting cases similar to the .40/65, which took the odd, shallow Berdan-type primer.

The .44/100 Ballard Everlasting case is an extremely rare one today, also. I managed to get a few cases with my Long Range Creedmoor Ballard. Only two of them can be used with modern primers, the rest all take the same Berdan primer as the .40/65 case described in a preceding paragraph. (These case-head types are shown on page 23.) The .44/100 usually has a small raised ring near the mouth. Why this was so made, I have no idea. As a consequence, I have had to use just two cases for my shooting of these two rifles. However, if washed promptly after firing with the black powder, they should last indefinitely. It is not much bother to decap and reprime; just pour in the 90 to 95 grains of FG black powder, which I used, and seat with the fingers the 550-grain paper-patch bullet, or the 500-grain .45/70 bullet Ideal #457125 sized down to fit the barrel. I have some E. Remington & Son .44 caliber 550-grain patched bullets that came with a Remington Creedmoor rifle, and I have used these with good results also. These barrels when perfect—as the two in my possession are—will shoot very accurately. They must have been superb target weapons on the 1000-yard ranges at Creedmoor and elsewhere. The .44/100 and .45/100 cases may be made from Sharps .45-2⅞″ brass cases.

The .45/100-2¹³⁄₁₆″ is the same case as the .44/100, with this exception: the case mouth is counterbored, or reamed, to accept the .45-caliber bullet. These cases were used in the Marlin Firearms Creedmoor Ballards, and they are usually seen, if at all, with primer pockets for large rifle primers.

There is usually very little difference in the diameter of these old

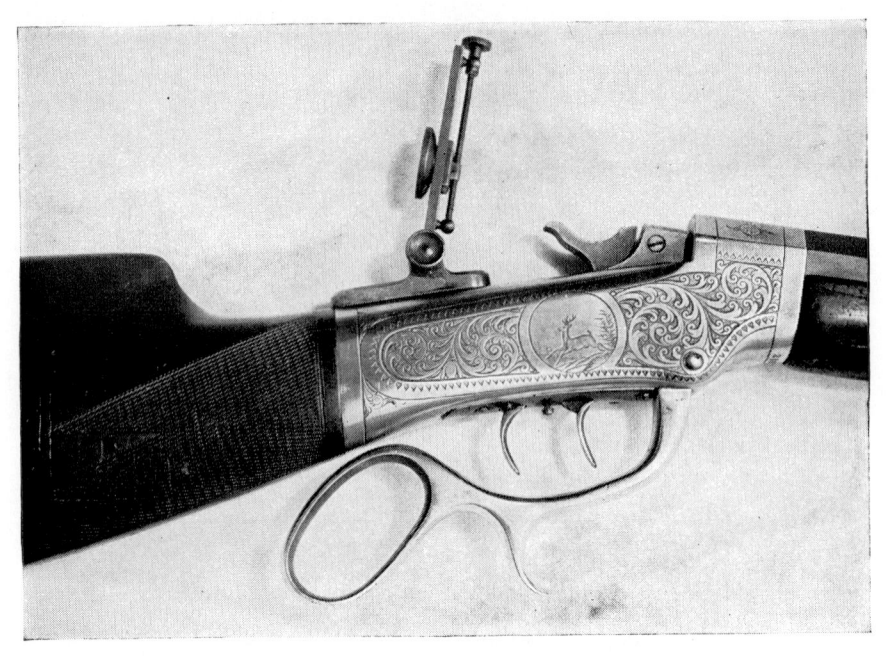

NO. 6 BALLARD ENGRAVING

.44- and .45-caliber Ballard barrels, and it is a simple matter to adjust the bullet size to the bore diameter.

The .45/70 Ballards will accept the regular black powder 405-grain bullet load and require no special shell. There were supposed to be a few Pacific Ballards chambered for the .45-2⅞" Sharps case, but I have encountered only one specimen in this caliber. I should not like to shoot one of these with more than 90 or 95 grains of black powder and a 500- to 550-grain bullet. The Ballard action, if tight, and with a good tool steel link installed, will hold these loads, of course; but they are pretty heavy, and in time they will require replacing of the link as well as possibly a few of the shooter's teeth, which will eventually become loose from this sort of blasting.

The Ballard cartridges, bullet seaters, recappers, and decappers, and other parts, are shown on page 152. Also here shown is a mold for the 370-grain patched .40-caliber slug, which is made exactly like Sharps Rifle Company molds, but this one is brand new and stamped Marlin Fire Arms Co. This leads me to wonder if possibly some third company, such as, for example, the Bridgeport Gun

Implement Company, had not made the molds for both companies.[7]

The Ballard butt plates are shown on page 27. Sight types are shown on pages 29 and 31. Close-ups of the various patterns and designs of engraving used on some Ballard rifles I have collected are shown on pages 34 to 48.

Such is the Ballard rifle—a great gun, and one of which I never tire. There is always something new and different to be found in Ballards even though their manufacture was discontinued many years ago. Almost every specimen is slightly unlike every other one, and each collection has some outstandingly different specimens.

There they are. They were made in grades and in qualities never dreamed of today by most riflemen, and they will never be made again. They are to be the more treasured because of that; and who can deny that we don't treasure them!

[7] The Billings and Spencer Company of Hartford, Connecticut, produced forgings for the Marlin Fire Arms Company consisting of Ballard receivers, breechblocks, levers, hammers, links, extractors, Ballard Creedmoor sight slides, etc.

BALLARD ACTION, TWO-PIECE EXTRACTOR, AND REVERSIBLE FIRING PIN

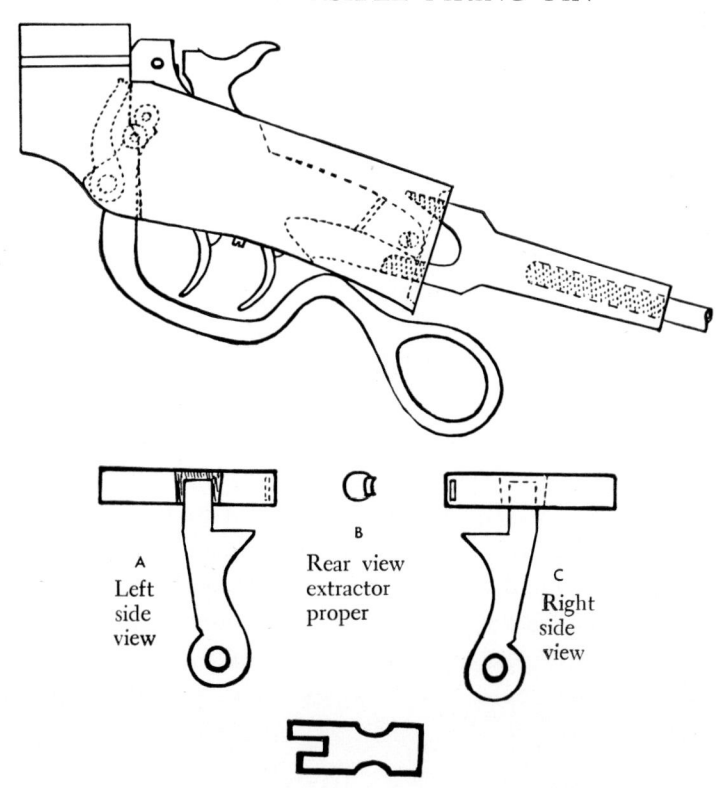

A — Left side view
B — Rear view extractor proper
C — Right side view

Firing pin enables use of either center- or rim-fire cartridges in same chamber.

II

Stevens Arms

THE J. Stevens Arms and Tool Company was established in 1864 and it is still in business, although it is now a division of a large arms corporation. It was prior to 1916, however, that the rifles to be described in this chapter were made. In fact, in that year the later, and famous, 44½ series was forever abandoned, much to our present discomfiture.

Next to the Ballards—possibly in some respects ahead of the Ballards—the Stevens rifle has appealed most strongly to me. If the reader will forgive a very bad pun, they are "Ideal," and my "Favorites."

Stevens rifles were for the most part target and small-game rifles. Of course there was the Stevens lever-action repeating rifle in high-power calibers, but we are not concerned here with a repeating rifle no matter what its excellence. In passing, however, let us say that the Stevens Model 425 repeating rifle produced in the .25, .30, .32, and .35 Remington rimless calibers was—and still is—an excellent mechanism. Stevens never made a military rifle, and this is one of the many reasons why this make appeals to me. There were boys' rifles in great variety—girls used them too. These were accurate, well-balanced hunting arms in a variety of calibers for woods loafers and small-game shooters. And there was an extensive line of beautiful target and Schuetzen rifles.

The justly famous 44½ series of target models was being manufactured later than any other make of single-shot rifle; up to 1916, in fact, the year in which all other important Schuetzen rifles were discontinued. They were abandoned then only because the world was in the throes of World War I, and war contracts were much more lucrative than the manufacture of single-shot target rifles.

Not to be overlooked or in the least slighted are the Stevens pocket, or bicycle, rifles. The company made an extensive line of these arms and was largely responsible for making popular the use of them.

A single-shot rifle collector and shooter should not be too enthusiastic about one particular make lest he thereby lay himself open to the accusation of sentimentalism, or of stressing one particular rifle overmuch. But in the case of the Stevens—especially the 44½ type Stevens—I must confess that this is the action that appeals to me especially as being the most symmetrical and, in the higher grades, the most beautiful.

For instance, the Walnut Hill Model 49-44½ and the Schuetzen Junior 52-44½ rifles, with their graceful Schuetzen stocks, long pistol grip and loop levers, and the quality of woods used, together with the engraved receivers, impress me as being the finest of the line. The Model 54, the Schuetzen Special, in a higher grade arm—in fact, the highest grade regularly made and in 44½ type action—was the only one with animal scene engraving, but because of its straight-grip stock and special lever it still does not appeal to me as being as symmetrical as the two previously mentioned models.

The 49 and 52 models are much more impressive in the 44½ type action than in the 1894 model, the 44 type action. The 44 action, with its sharply cut away side walls, is not nearly so symmetrical and attractive as the later model; nor, of course, is it in as much demand today as the strong falling-block 44½.

However, to discuss the 44½ Stevens series ahead of the models which preceded it would be like eating dessert before the less appealing courses, so we shall start with the tip-up barrel Stevens series of rifles. The models as offered in 1888 were as follows.

STEVENS TIP-UP SERIES

MODEL NO. 1. TIP-UP RIFLE. This was made in .32, .38, and .44 rim- and center-fire calibers, in 24-, 26-, 28-, and 30-inch full-octagonal barrels. These rifles weighed from 6½ to 8¼ pounds, and they were priced at $20, $21, $22, or $23, depending on the barrel length.[1]

MODEL NO. 2. GALLERY RIFLE. This was made only in .22 Short rim-fire caliber, with 24-, 26-, 28-, or 30-inch barrels. The rifles weighed from 6½ to 8¾ pounds. They had plain open sights, and were priced at $20, $22, $24, and $26.

MODEL NO. 3. TIP-UP RIFLE. This was the same rifle as Model

[1] This model, as well as models 2, 3, 4, 5, and 6, did not have a forearm.

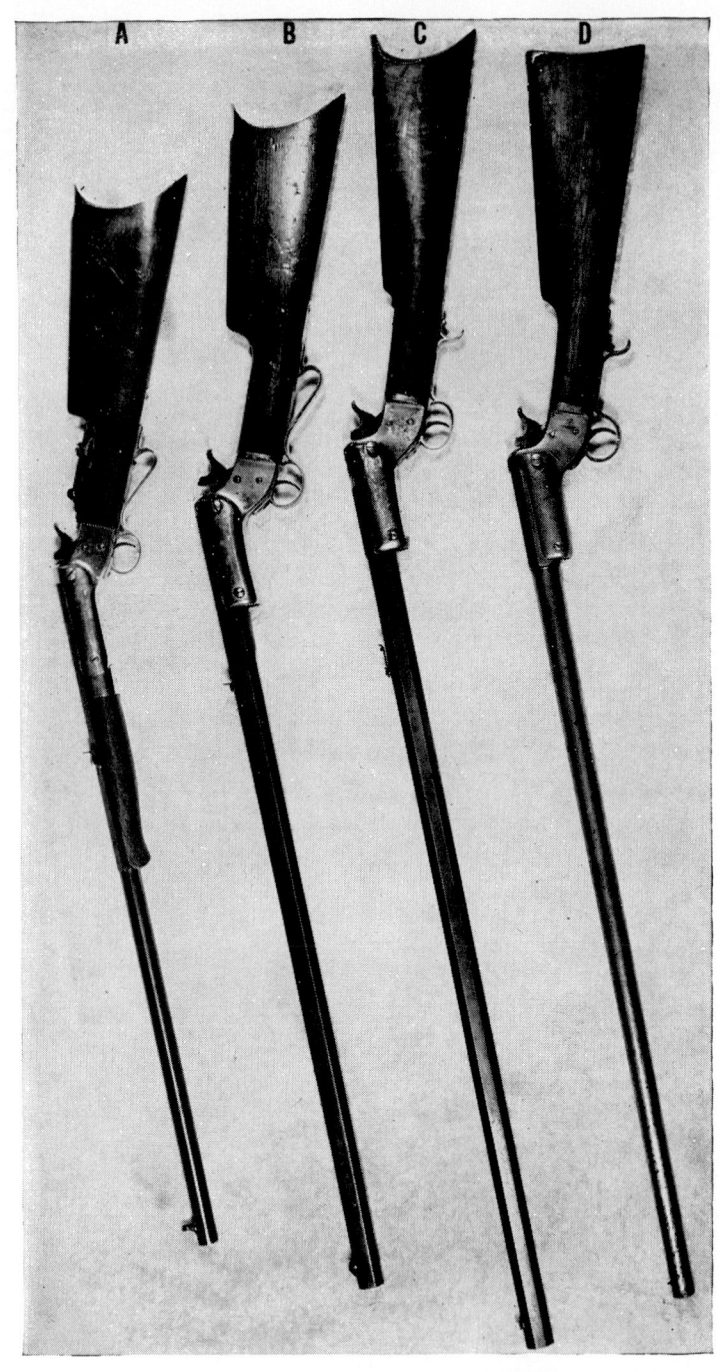

STEVENS TIP-UP RIFLES AND SHOT GUN
From the Allyn H. Tedmon collection

No. 1 except that it was offered in either half- or full-octagonal barrels, and with the Stevens combination open and peep sights. Prices were $23, $24, $25, and $26, an extra charge of $3.00 per rifle for the excellent sights used.

MODEL NO. 4. GALLERY RIFLE. This was the No. 2 Gallery .22 Short rim-fire model with Stevens combination sights. Because of these sights the price was $3.00 higher in each barrel length than the Model No. 2, with its open plain sights.

MODEL NO. 5. EXPERT RIFLE. This model carried a half-octagonal barrel in 24-, 26-, 28-, or 30-inch lengths. It had a Beach front sight, open rear barrel sight, and vernier peep sight on the tang. The stock was varnished, and the frame and rifle butt plate were nickel-plated. Cartridges used were .22 Short rim-fire, .32, .38, or .44 Long rim- or center-fire. Weights were from 6¼ to 8½ pounds, and prices were from $25 to $31.

MODEL NO. 6. EXPERT RIFLE. This was the same rifle as Model No. 5 except that it had a fancy walnut stock. Prices ran from $28 to $34, depending on barrel length.

MODEL NO. 7. PREMIER RIFLE. This model had a half-octagonal barrel, a Beach front sight, open rear barrel sight and vernier peep sight on the tang, a Swiss butt plate, nickel plates to match the frame, and a varnished stock and fore end. It was available in .22 Short rim-fire caliber in 24-, 26-, 28-, and 30-inch barrels. Weights were from 7 to 9 pounds. Prices were $29, $31, $33, and $35. This model was also made in .32, .38, and .44 rim- or center-fire calibers, in the same barrel lengths. The weights were a trifle less in each case, of course, because of the larger calibers. It was priced at $29, $30, $31, and $32.

MODEL NO. 8. PREMIER RIFLE. This model was the same as the No. 7 Premier but with the addition of a fancy grained walnut stock and fore end. Prices in .22 caliber were from $32 to $38, and in the larger calibers from $32 to $35.

EXPLANATION OF FACING PAGE

A Ladies Rifle No. 13. A deluxe rifle with original sights, weight 5½ lbs.
B Sporting Rifle No. 1, 28-inch barrel, caliber .32 rim-fire. Original sights.
C Target Rifle, 32-inch barrel, .38/55 caliber.
D Stevens Tip-up 12-gauge Shotgun.

Note that A has the special very light frame; C and D have the same extra large size frame. C was originally nickel plated while D was originally blued.

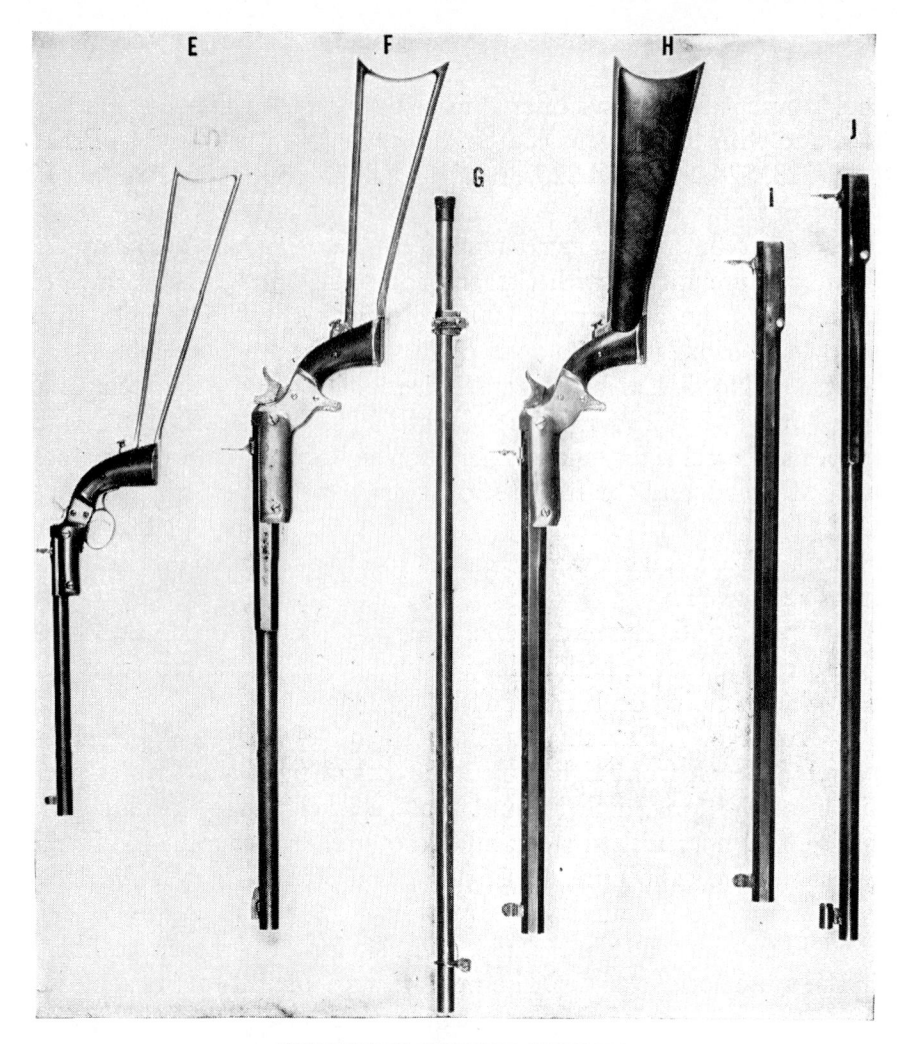

STEVENS TIP-UP RIFLES
E   Stevens Pocket Rifle, caliber .22 Long Rifle.
F   Stevens Hunter's Pet rifle, caliber .32 rim-fire.
G   Malcolm telescopic sight for the .25/20 caliber barrel marked J.
H   Stevens Hunter's Pet Rifle with full octagon .22 Long Rifle barrel.
I   Extra interchangeable barrel, caliber .32/20 for frame marked H.
J   Extra interchangeable barrel caliber .25/20 Single-Shot, for use with frame marked H.

Note that H has a .22 rim-fire caliber barrel bored eccentric at breech so that it will fit the center-fire breech piece. This three barrel Hunter's Pet outfit was apparently made up on special order at the Stevens factory. The breech piece and three interchangeable barrels all carry the same serial number. This outfit was carried in a leather trunk case with reloading tools and wiping rods. The wood fill-in was added by the original owner, possibly to balance the long barrels.

STEVENS ARMS 55

These No. 7 and No. 8 Premier rifles were regularly supplied in rim-fire version. The center-fire .32, .38, and .44 calibers were chambered to order only. None of these models were available in both rim- and center-fire with interchangeable firing pins.

MODEL NO. 9. NEW MODEL RANGE RIFLE. This model, a more symmetrical frame model, had a half-octagonal barrel, a wind-gauge front sight and vernier rear sight. The fore end and stock were varnished. The frame and a heavy Swiss butt plate were nickel plated. This was the most accurate tip-up model, being made especially for target use. It was offered in .22, .32, .38, and .44 calibers, but was especially adapted for the .22 Long rim-fire or center-fire cartridges and for the Stevens .32/35/165 taper cartridge, using patched or grooved bullets.

In .22 caliber the barrel lengths were 24, 26, 28, and 30 inches, and the prices were $31.50, $33.50, $35.50, and $37.50. In .32, .38,

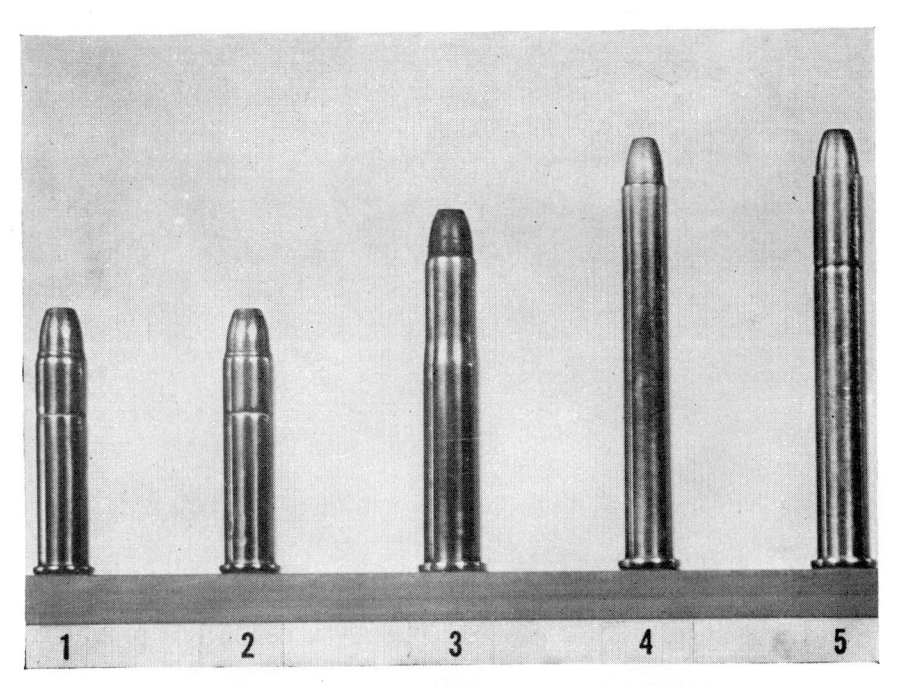

CARTRIDGES USED IN STEVENS RIFLES,
POCKET RIFLES AND SHOT GUNS

1 .25 Stevens rim-fire
2 .25 Stevens rim-fire high speed (Experimental)
3 .25/20 Stevens single-shot
4 .22/15/60 Stevens center-fire
5 .25/21/86 Stevens center-fire

and .44 rim- or center-fire calibers and in .32, .38, and .44 Stevens Everlasting calibers, the barrel lengths were the same as in the .22, but the prices were $31.50, $32.50, $33.50, and $34.50.

MODEL NO. 10. RANGE RIFLE. This model was the same rifle as No. 9, but with fancy figured stock. Prices were from $34 to $40, depending on calibers and barrel lengths. These rifles were specially chambered for the .22 Long rim-fire cartridge instead of the .22 Short. The .22 Extra Long center-fire Maynard cartridge was also offered in these models.

STEVENS LADIES RIFLES. These were a special model made up for ladies' use. The frame was a light, special tip-up design, nickel plated. The rifle had a walnut stock and forearm, with a metal joint on the rear of the fore end, which gives the frame a more finished appearance than any other Stevens tip-up model. The barrel was a light,

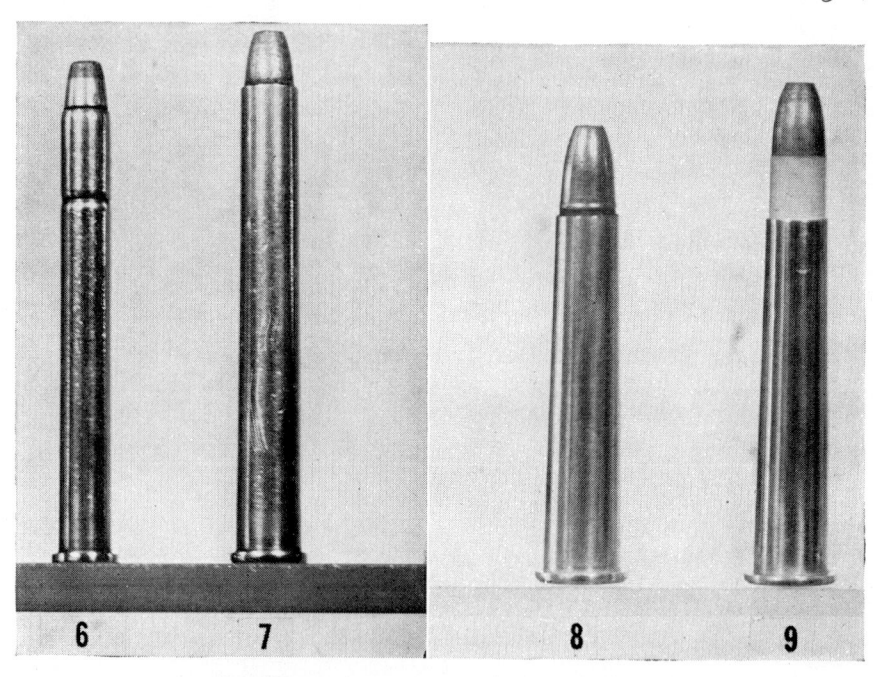

CARTRIDGES USED IN STEVENS RIFLES,
POCKET RIFLES AND SHOT GUNS

6 .25/25/86 Stevens center-fire
7 .28/30/120 Stevens center-fire
8 .32/35/153 Stevens taper
9 .32/35/165 Stevens taper paper patch

half-octagonal type, in keeping with the lighter, trimmer action. Calibers were .22 rim-fire and .22 center-fire, not interchangeable, of course. The details were as follows:

MODEL NO. 11. LADIES RIFLE. Plain open sights only.

  24-inch barrel Weight, 5½ pounds Price, $25
  26-inch barrel Weight, 5½ pounds Price, $27

MODEL NO. 12. LADIES RIFLE. Same as No. 11, but with extra fancy oiled stock.

  24-inch barrel Weight, 5½ pounds Price, $27
  26-inch barrel Weight, 5½ pounds Price, $29

MODEL NO. 13. LADIES RIFLE. Beach open and vernier sights.

  24-inch barrel Weight, 5½ pounds Price, $28
  26-inch barrel Weight, 5½ pounds Price, $30

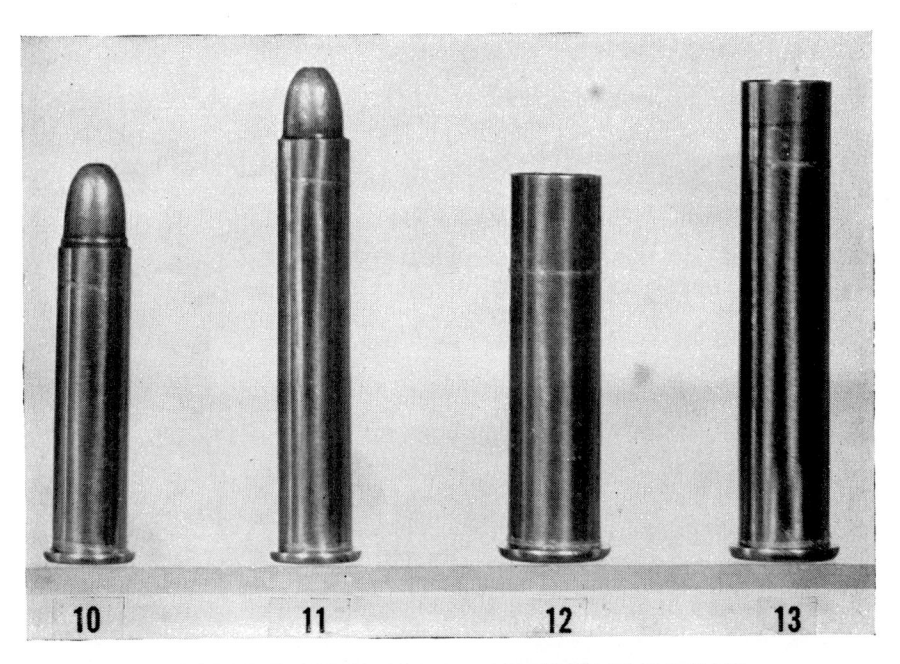

CARTRIDGES USED IN STEVENS RIFLES, POCKET RIFLES AND SHOT GUNS

10 .38/35 Stevens Everlasting
11 .38/45 Stevens Everlasting
12 .44/50 Stevens Everlasting
13 .44/65 Stevens Everlasting

(.44/50 and .44/65 were shot shells used in New Model Pocket Shot Gun No. 39)

MODEL NO. 14. LADIES RIFLE. Same as No. 13, but with extra fancy stock.

| 24-inch barrel | Weight, 5½ pounds | Price, $30 |
| 26-inch barrel | Weight, 5½ pounds | Price, $32 |

STEVENS TIP-UP SHOT GUN. This was a new style single-barrel breech-loading shotgun made up on a frame very similar to that of the rifles. These guns were offered in 10, 12, 14, 16, and 20 gauge, in 30- or 32-inch barrels of laminated steel. Twist or plain barrels were optional. They had a pistol-grip guard bow similar to the new

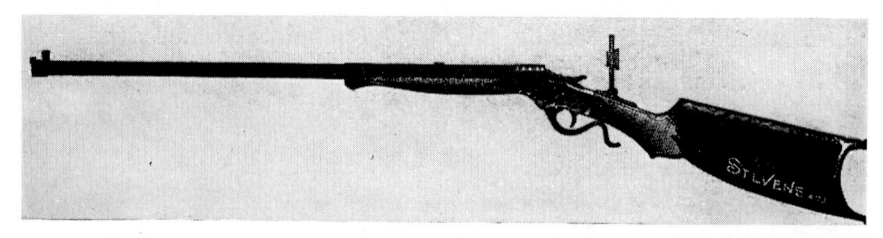

STEVENS MODEL 55 LADIES RIFLE

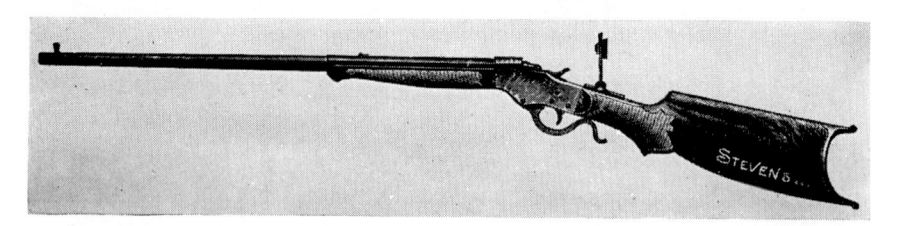

STEVENS MODEL 56 LADIES RIFLE

model Range rifle. They were available in nickel-plated or browned frame models.

Rifle barrels to interchange with the above shot barrels were also available at $11 and $12 in all lengths from 24- to 30-inch barrels, and they were chambered for all the cartridges offered in regular rifle models.

STEVENS HUNTER'S PET RIFLE. This was the first pocket rifle model. The frame was nickel plated, and it had a detachable shoulder stock. The barrels were half- or full-octagonal, with Stevens combination sights. Calibers offered in these Hunter's Pets were for .22 Short rim-fire, and .32, .38, and .44 Long rim- or center-fire cartridges.

Barrel lengths were 18, 20, 22, and 24 inches. Weights ran from 5 to 5¾ pounds. Prices were $18, $19, $20, and $21.

Hunter's Pet Shot Gun. These models were the same style and prices as the Hunter's Pet rifles, and were chambered for the Stevens Everlasting center-fire shells .38 and .44 calibers, or for the standard 20-gauge shell.

Combined Hunter's Pet Rifle and Shot Gun. The combined outfit with one rifle barrel and one shot barrel was priced at $28.

Stevens Vernier Hunter's Pet Rifle. This was the same as the regular Pet model except that a vernier tang rear sight was fitted to the frame just above the shoulder-stock attachment. This was the same sight staff as that used on the tip-up rifles, with a special base to fit the Pet frame.

The Stevens Everlasting center-fire shells were made in the following calibers and lengths:

Caliber .38/35; length 1⅝ in.   Caliber .38/45; length 2³⁄₁₆ in.
      .44/50; length 2 in.   .44/65; length 2½ in.

See page 57 for illustration of these four cases loaded with grooved bullets for this Range rifle. The same cases were used in the Hunter's Pet Shotgun loaded with shot instead of ball.

Reliable Pocket Rifle. This is the small pistol frame with 10-inch, slender, part-octagonal barrel chambered for the .22 Short cartridge only. It had globe and peep barrel sights. This model had the detachable shoulder rest, with just one rod attaching to the grip where it dovetailed into the bottom. With 10-inch black japanned shoulder rest, the price was $10.50; with 10-inch nickel-plated rest, the price was $11.

New Model Pocket (Bicycle) Rifle. This was the heavier pistol frame, with part-round barrel, Stevens combination sights, and detachable shoulder stock with regular two-rod construction. The frame and shoulder stock were nickel plated. It was the same style as the Hunter's Pet rifle but with a lighter frame. Calibers were .22 and .32 rim-fire. Barrel lengths were 10, 12, 15, and 18 inches. Weights were from 2 to 2¾ pounds. Prices were $12.25, $13.25, $15.00, and $16.50.

This model was also supplied in a vernier rear sight, Beach combination front sight, and open barrel rear sight version. These were priced at $3.00 more than the basic model. These latter models were

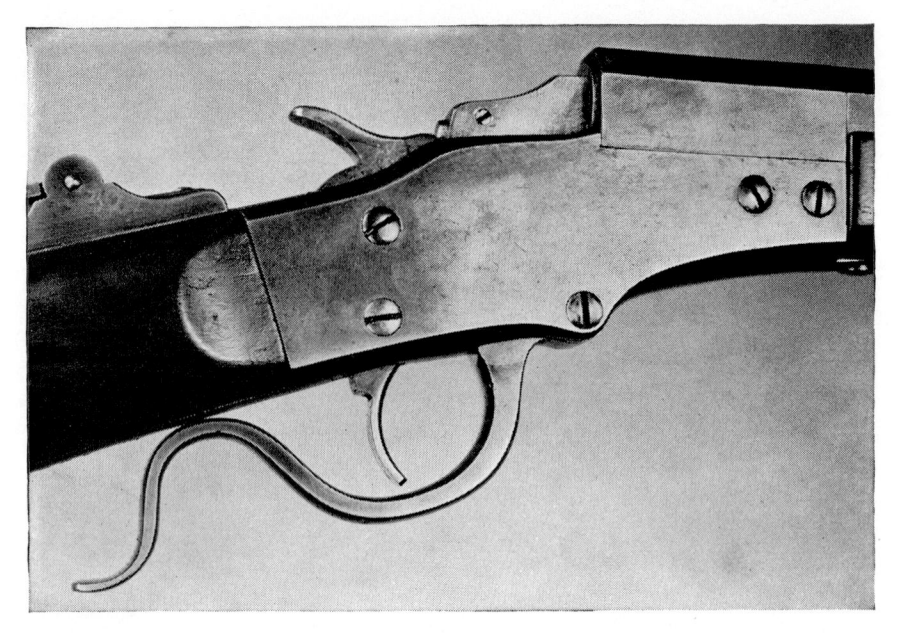

THE EARLY STEVENS ACTION WITH REMOVABLE SIDE PLATE, SERIAL NO. 152

supplied in the then new .22 Long Rifle caliber unless otherwise ordered.

The 1888 catalog also pictures Ballard wind-gauge front sights with spirit-level and vernier midrange tang rear sights at $4.00 each as being available for Stevens rifles. Evidently Stevens had not at this date developed their own vernier sights.

In the line of extras Stevens offered the following—

Extra length barrels at $1.00 per inch over standard.
Extra heavy barrels, round or octagonal, $2.00.
Checkering butt stocks, $4.00.
Fancy walnut stock and fore end checkered, $8.00.
Swiss butt plates $2.00 extra on some models. (On some models they were standard.)
Set screw placed on hammer to regulate pull of sear, $1.00.
Reversible firing pin for rifle, $3.50.
Reboring and chambering rifle, Hunter's Pet or New Model Pocket Rifle barrels to larger calibers, $3.00 and $3.50.

The cartridges for these early Stevens models were—

Caliber .22 Short, Long, and Long Rifle.
.32 Short, Long, and Extra Long rim-fire.
.38 Short, Long, and Extra Long rim-fire.
.44 Long rim-fire.
.22 Extra Long center-fire.
.32 Short Colt center-fire.
.32 Long Colt center-fire.
.32 Extra Long Ballard center-fire.
.32-20 Winchester center-fire.
.32 Smith & Wesson center-fire.
.32 Smith & Wesson Rifle center-fire.
.38 Short Colt center-fire.
.38 Long Colt center-fire.
.38 Extra Long center-fire.
.38 Smith & Wesson center-fire.
.44 Smith & Wesson center-fire.
.32/35 Stevens Taper center-fire.
.32/40 Ballard and Marlin.
.38/35 Stevens Everlasting.
.38/45 Stevens Everlasting.
.44/50 Stevens Everlasting.
.44/65 Stevens Everlasting.

The bullet molds and loading tools offered with these models were the Ideal line. Stevens evidently had no tools of their own design at this time.

In 1894 the Stevens Company began the production of the famous Stevens Ideal No. 44 rifle, which was a rolling-block lever action design. Also at about the same time the design of the equally famous Stevens Favorite rifle [2] was adopted, and within a year at the most all models of the Stevens tip-up rifles were discontinued. Thus passed into history the varied line of tip-ups.[3] They had served their purpose and served it well, but by 1894 and 1895 smokeless powders were beginning to be used to a certain extent, and with the resulting higher pressures the cast malleable iron frame of the tip-up models became obsolete.

[2] See page 65.
[3] There was also a "tip-up" pistol. This is described among pistol models on page 76.

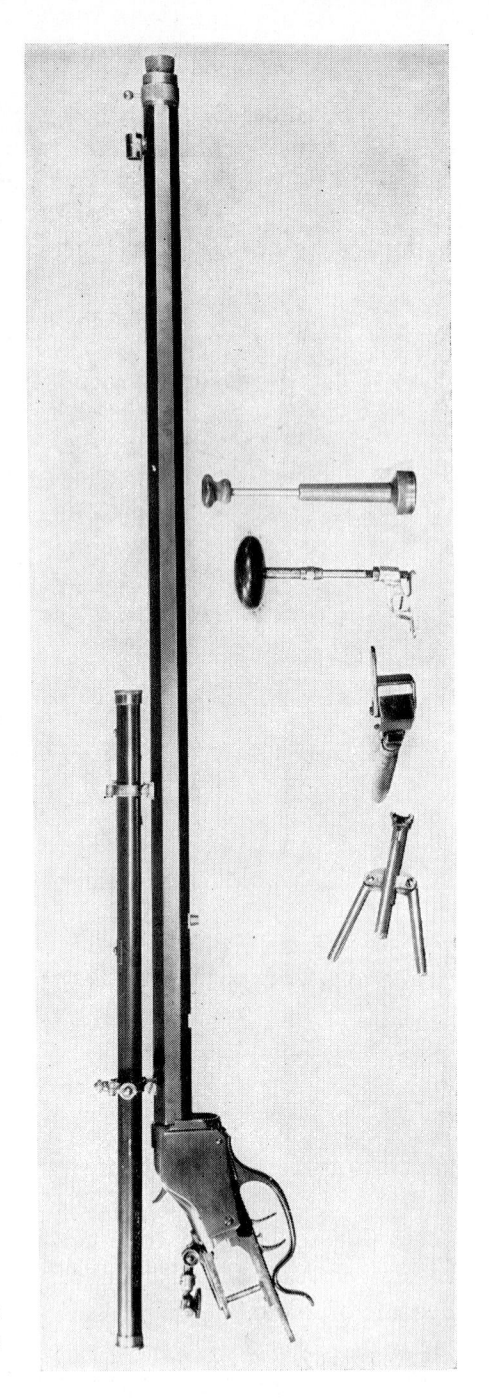

STEVENS-POPE BARREL
On Winchester single-shot action with accessories including Stevens-Pope clamp type scope mounts.

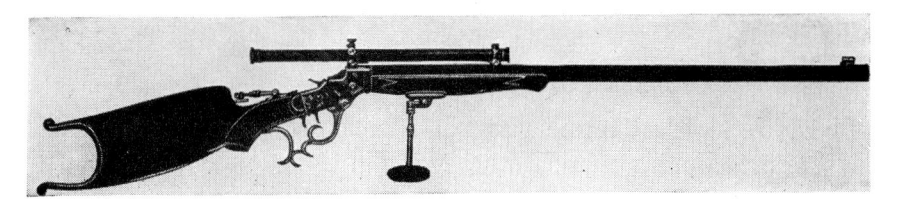

STEVENS-POPE SPECIAL RIFLE

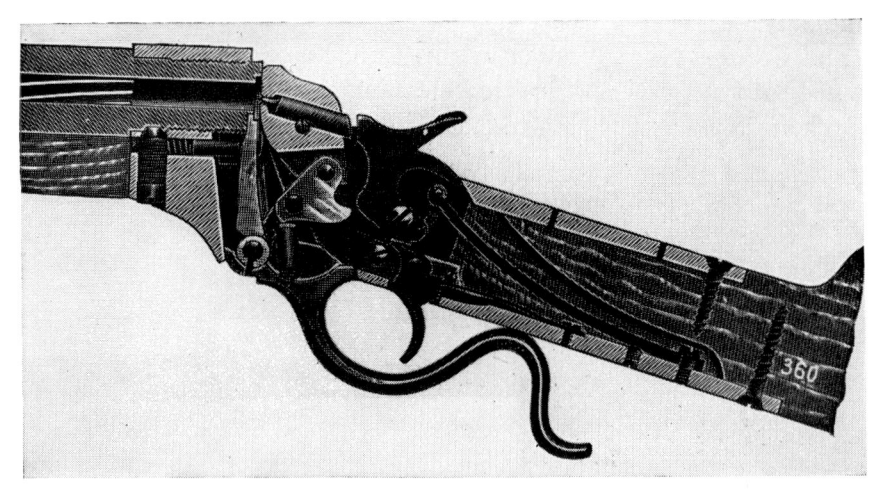

STEVENS IDEAL NO. 44½ ACTION

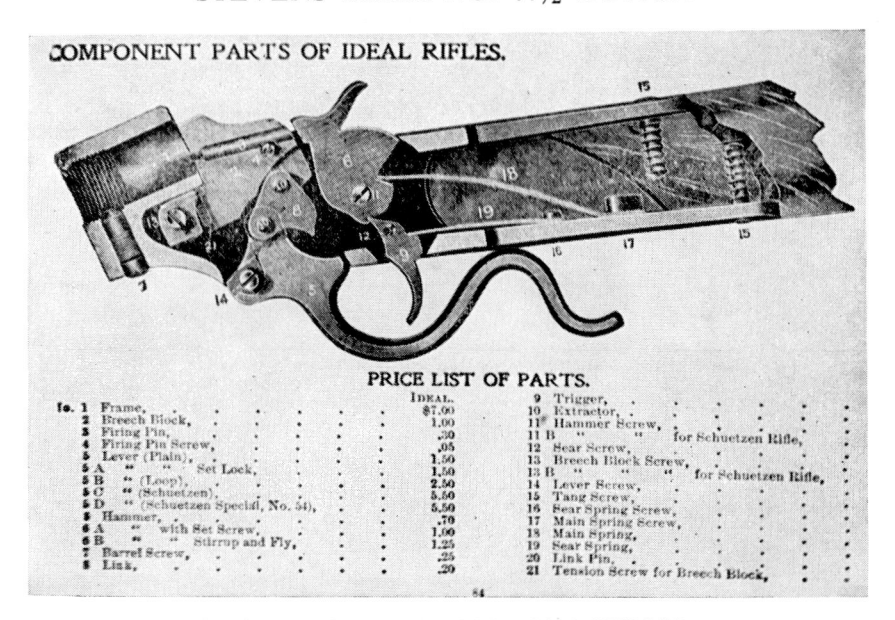

COMPONENT PARTS OF IDEAL RIFLES.

PRICE LIST OF PARTS.

No.		IDEAL.
1	Frame,	$7.00
2	Breech Block,	1.00
3	Firing Pin,	.50
4	Firing Pin Screw,	.05
5	Lever (Plain),	1.50
5A	" " Set Lock,	1.50
5B	" " (Loop),	2.50
5C	" " (Schuetzen),	5.50
5D	" " (Schuetzen Special, No. 54),	5.50
6	Hammer,	.70
6A	" with Set Screw,	1.00
6B	" " Stirrup and Fly,	1.25
7	Barrel Screw,	.25
8	Link,	.20
9	Trigger,	
10	Extractor,	
11	Hammer Screw,	
11B	" " for Schuetzen Rifle,	
12	Sear Screw,	
13	Breech Block Screw,	
13B	" " " for Schuetzen Rifle,	
14	Lever Screw,	
15	Tang Screw,	
16	Sear Spring Screw,	
17	Main Spring Screw,	
18	Main Spring,	
19	Sear Spring,	
20	Link Pin,	
21	Tension Screw for Breech Block,	

STEVENS IDEAL NO. 44 ACTION

IDEAL NO. 44 TYPE ACTION SERIES

The No. 44 Ideal frame was not a great deal stronger than its predecessors, and its manufacture was continued but a few years. During this time, however, it was widely used, and was made in higher grades than arms previously manufactured by the Stevens Company.

This Stevens No. 44 model was patterned along the lever action, single-shot type, which permitted cleaning and inspection from the breech, and it was very easy to load. The barrels were threaded with a coarse easy thread held in place by a set screw which permitted a quick interchange of barrels in a variety of calibers. It also per-

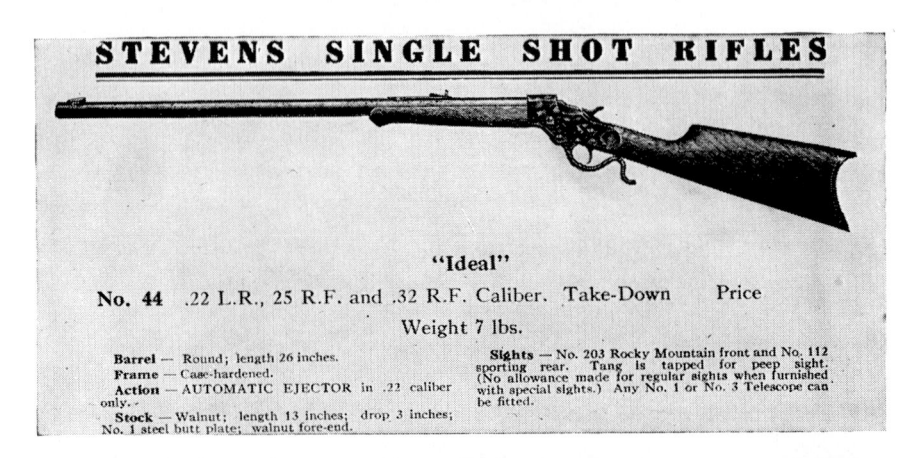

STEVENS SINGLE SHOT RIFLES

"Ideal"

No. 44   .22 L.R., 25 R.F. and .32 R.F. Caliber.   Take-Down   Price
Weight 7 lbs.

Barrel — Round; length 26 inches.
Frame — Case-hardened.
Action — AUTOMATIC EJECTOR in .22 caliber only.
Stock — Walnut; length 13 inches; drop 3 inches; No. 1 steel butt plate; walnut fore-end.
Sights — No. 203 Rocky Mountain front and No. 112 sporting rear. Tang is tapped for peep sight. (No allowance made for regular sights when furnished with special sights.) Any No. 1 or No. 3 Telescope can be fitted.

STEVENS SINGLE SHOT RIFLES

The Most Accurate Rifle.   "Armory" Model.

No. 414   Take-Down; .22 short or .22 L. R.   Weight 8 lbs.   Price

Barrel — 26 inches, round.
Frame — Case-hardened.
Action — Plain lever, AUTOMATIC EJECTOR.
Stock — Walnut; shotgun butt with steel butt plate; length 13 inches; drop 3 inches; long fore-end, large hand-hold. Fitted with strap loops.
Sights — Rocky Mountain front and Receiver rear sights, especially designed for this rifle. Special sights or any No. 1 or No. 3 Telescope fitted to order.

When ordering specify whether wanted for .22 short or .22 L. R.

STEVENS CATALOGUE REPRODUCTIONS

mitted easy storage of the taken-down rifle, as the pieces occupied very little space in case or trunk.

Like the Favorite rifle, this earlier No. 44 type used a side extractor which was very positive in action. This factor was continued until about 1901, when the newer central extractor was adopted.

The first models of this rolling-block type were designated under the numbers 107, 108, 109, 110. After a reorganization of the company in 1896, the model numbers adopted were 44, 45, 47, 49, 51, 52, 54, and 55.

The 1894 models utilized large screws to pivot the lever and breechblocks upon, but a few years later all models were changed

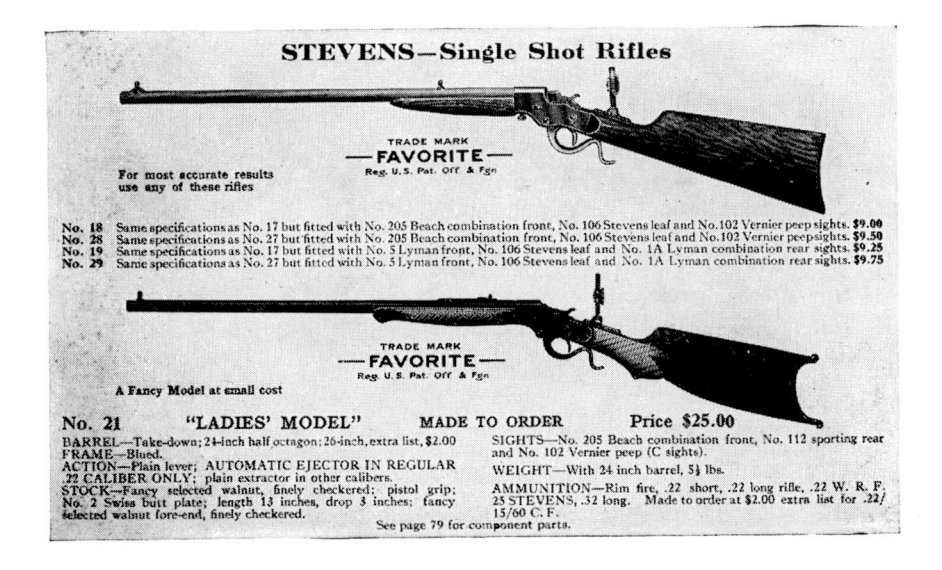

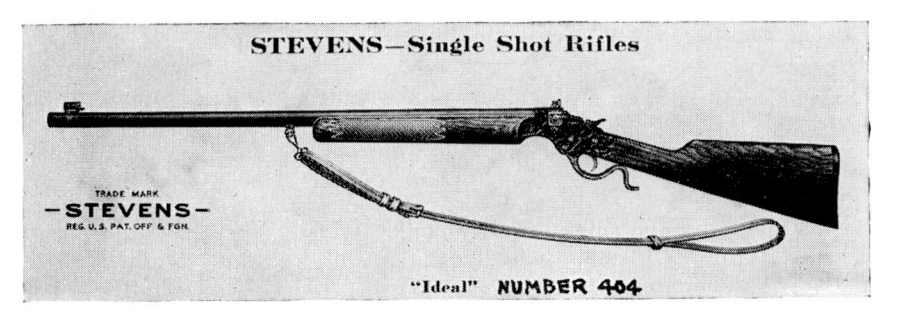

STEVENS CATALOGUE REPRODUCTIONS

to a different system. In this later system the breechblock and lever were pivoted upon bolts entering from the left side of the frame, and they were held in place by screws entering the ends of the bolts from the right side. The bolts were easily removed by turning out the screws from the right side, then pushing the bolts through. The bolts had squared projections under the heads, which engaged corresponding recesses in the frame on the left side, which prevented their turning during removal of the screws from their ends.

These Ideal models were made in several weights and sizes of frames. *The higher set-trigger grades all had removable lower tangs.* Several of the higher grades were made with lugs on the lower faces of the hammers which fitted into corresponding milled slots in the back side of breechblocks and under them, making these models very similar to the Remington-Rider block-and-hammer arrangement. This naturally increased the strength of the action and materially decreased the danger of the block rolling back under the impact of a heavy charge. The various models offered on the Ideal basic action are described on the pages following.[4]

IDEAL NO. 44 RIFLE. This is the plain basic model, the lowest priced grade. It was available, usually with half-octagonal barrel #2 weight, in 24-inch length in rim-fire caliber and in 26-inch length in center-fire caliber. A full-octagonal barrel could be bought for $2.00 extra. In the earlier No. 44 model, set triggers were also available at $6.00 extra. The stock was the plain walnut straight-grip type, with rifle butt plate, sometimes nickeled and sometimes casehardened in colors. (See page 64.)

The calibers offered in this model were varied. Among them were the following:

.22 rim-fire Short and Long Rifle .32/40 center-fire
.25 Stevens rim-fire .38/40 Winchester center-fire
.32 Long rim-fire .38/55 center-fire
.25/20 Stevens single-shot .44/40 Winchester center-fire
.32/20 Winchester center-fire

To special order the No. 44 was offered in:

.22/7/45 Winchester rim-fire .22/15/60 Stevens center-fire
.22 Extra Long center-fire

[4] Note extras for this 44 series as listed on page 74.

At an additional charge of $2.00 the No. 44 was also chambered for:

.25/21/87 Stevens   .32/35 Stevens taper
.25/25/87 Stevens   .32 Ideal
.28/30/120 Stevens

Sights on this model were plain Rocky Mountain blade front and plain sporting rear. All the "Special" Stevens and Lyman series of sights adaptable to the Stevens were available upon special order, of course.

This was the lowest priced No. 44 model, retailing for about $10, with plain sights.

IDEAL RANGE MODEL No. 45. This was the No. 44 model with a few refinements. The barrels were slightly heavier, and 28 inches was standard for center-fire calibers. The standard barrel is marked #2, but it varies in weight according to the caliber. The #1 and #3 barrels were also available, and at no increase in cost.

The standard stock and forearm were of varnished walnut with a Swiss butt plate. However, rifle butt or a rubber shotgun butt were

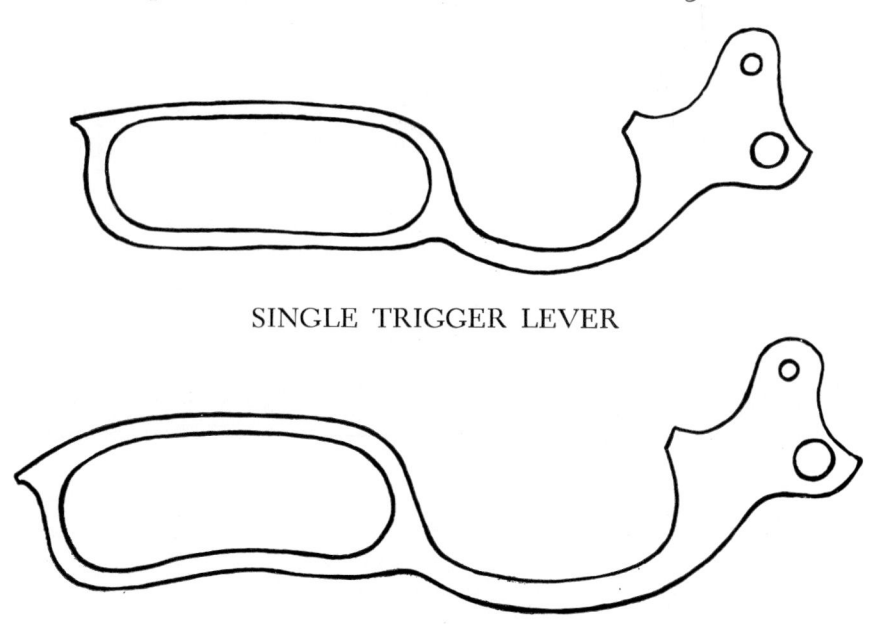

SINGLE TRIGGER LEVER

DOUBLE-SET TRIGGER LEVER
Comparison of two styles of finger levers used on Stevens Model 47 (44) rifles.

ENGRAVED STEVENS IDEAL MODELS
(TOP): Stevens Ideal Model 49 in 44 ½ type
(BOTTOM): Stevens Ideal Model 51 in 44 type. The heavy, with lug on hammer, 51-44 Schuetzen action.

offered at no increase in price. The single trigger was standard, but double-set triggers could be had for $6.00 extra.

The same calibers as in the basic No. 44 model were also offered in this No. 45.

Sights were Beach combination front with an open rear barrel sight and also a vernier peep sight on the tang. These were the standard sights for this model and were designated as "D" type sights. Other sights available were B, E, F, G, and H types. The specifications for these types will be found on page 75.

With the D sights this model was listed at $22 in rim-fire calibers and with 26-inch barrels. In the center-fire calibers and 28-inch barrel lengths, and with D sights, the price was also $22. Octagonal barrels were available for $2.00 extra.

IDEAL RANGE MODEL NO. 46. This was the same as No. 45, with the addition of a fancy-grained walnut stock in the same straight-grip pattern of the No. 45.

IDEAL MODERN RANGE NO. 47. This was the No. 45 rifle with the addition of a pistol-grip stock (uncheckered) and a loop lever. The standard butt plate was the #2 Swiss, same as on the No. 45. However, if a heavier barrel than the standard #2 was wanted, a heavier—a #3—Swiss butt plate was supplied.

The standard barrel was the #2 weight, and it was available in the same calibers as for the No. 44 rifle.

The standard sights were the D type. When sight combinations calling for front sights and vernier tang rear sight were ordered, there was no rear barrel sight slot cut.

The single trigger was standard, but upon payment of $6.00 extra, double-set triggers were provided. The standard loop lever was for single trigger, and it was rather short and did not follow the grip down very far. It is quite an odd-appearing lever. When the rifle was ordered with set triggers, however, a longer loop for double triggers was furnished. Thus in the earlier models there were two levers. (See page 67.)

The price of the standard No. 47 rifle was $5.00 more than the No. 45, or $27.

IDEAL MODERN RANGE NO. 48. This was the No. 47 rifle made with fancy walnut stock, checkered grip and fore end.

IDEAL WALNUT HILL NO. 49. The famous Walnut Hill was the lowest grade Stevens that was regularly engraved. As a matter of fact, the earlier No. 44 models were for the most part etched, not engraved. The designs varied greatly; no two were exactly alike. The frames usually had animal or hunting scenes thereon and were always different. Some had hunter and dog scenes; others, dogs and birds, dogs and deer, or bear. There is almost no limit to the animal figures that were used. As a rule these designs were well executed, but some specimens appear rather crude.

This Walnut Hill model had a varnished cheekpiece, pistol-grip stock, with checkered grip and fore end. The butt plate was the #3 Swiss type. The single trigger was still standard, but of course the double-set type was available as an extra. The barrels were the half-octagonal type, in 28- and 30-inch lengths. The calibers offered in this model were the same as in the plain basic No. 44; however, somewhere along between these models the .32 Long center-fire made its appearance and was offered in the "Extra Charge" series of calibers.

This model had as standard sights the H type, consisting of globe interchangeable front and vernier peep tang rear. There was, of course, no rear barrel slot with these sights. Any of the other types of sights were optional. This model was listed at $42 in the standard model.

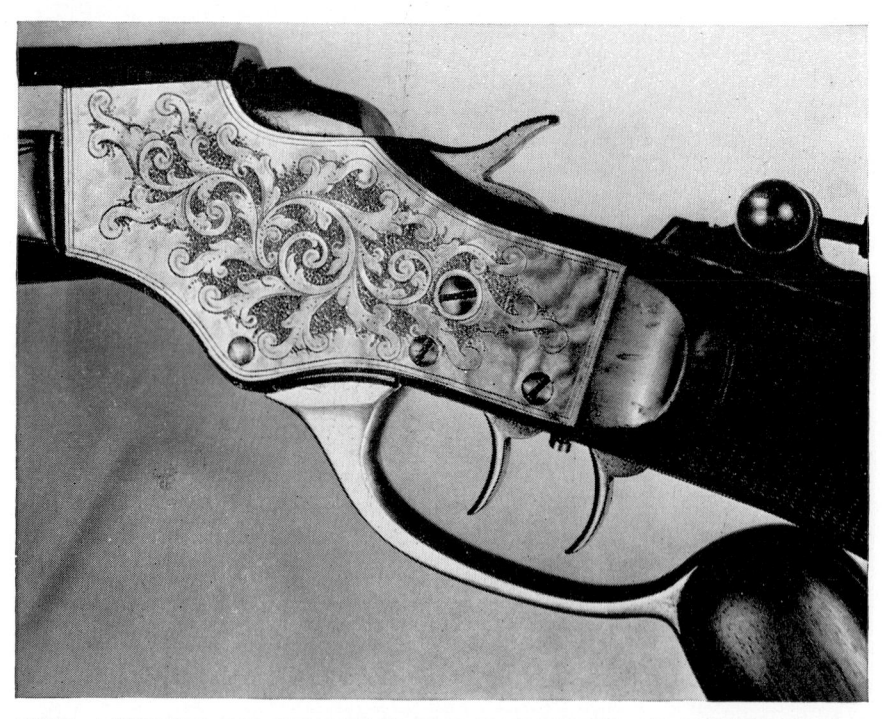

THE ACTION OF STEVENS IDEAL MODEL 52 IN 44½ TYPE
Usual lever was four-finger loop type

Gold-plated triggers are seen quite often on the No. 49, and the price for these is to be found in the table of extras.

IDEAL WALNUT HILL No. 50. This was the No. 49 with selected fancy walnut stock. In catalogs showing the earlier series of Stevens Ideal rifles the numbers 46, 48, and 50 were to be found, but in the later catalogs these models were dropped, and the fancy walnut stock, when ordered, was added as an extra to the No. 49 model.

IDEAL SCHUETZEN No. 51. This was a heavier action, usually seen with the lug on hammer fitting into and under the breechblock, and with straight-grip tang, cheekpiece, Schuetzen butt plate #4 stock, and fancy checkering on grip and fore end. Barrels made on this model were usually in #4 weight; however, all weights were available. The frames were engraved similar in design to the No. 49. The set triggers were standard, as well as the Schuetzen lever #5.

This model was highly finished, and it is usually seen in calibers .32/40 or .38/55, or chambered for one of the special target cartridges

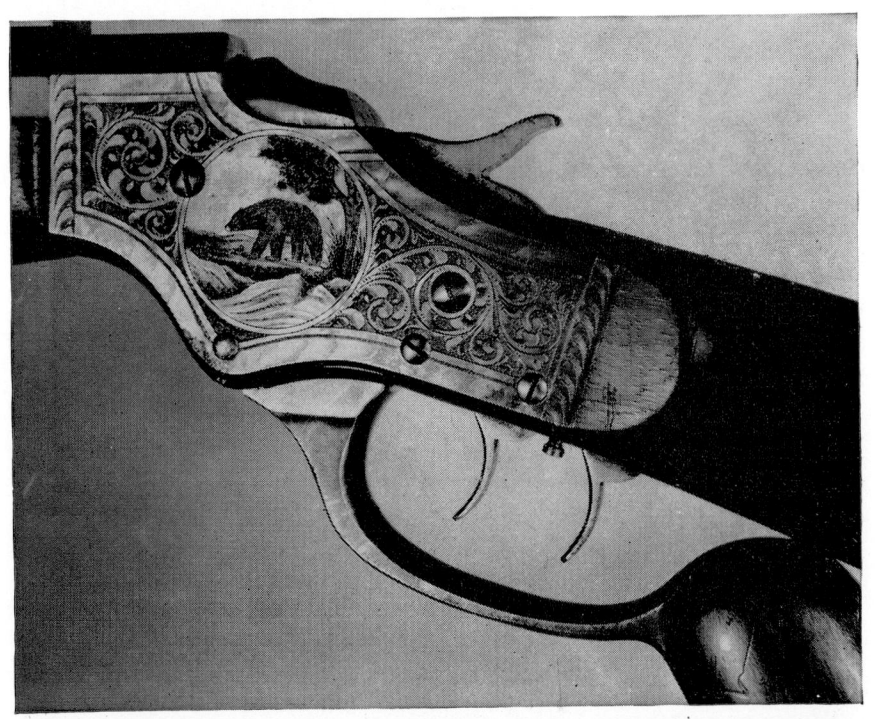

THE ACTION OF THE STEVENS IDEAL MODEL 54 IN 44½ TYPE

SPECIAL ENGRAVED 44½ STEVENS

offered by Stevens, such as the .25/21, .28/30, etc. However, it could be furnished in any of the calibers listed for the preceding models.

The weight of the No. 51, with 30-inch #4 barrel, was around 12½ pounds with the heavier Schuetzen frame, and 12 pounds with the regular lighter frame. The price with H sights was $58. Special sights and other extras were available, making the price of this rifle to vary from $58 on up as high as the buyer wished to go.

IDEAL SCHUETZEN JUNIOR NO. 52. This was very similar to the No. 51 model, but a higher-grade rifle. It had a pistol-grip frame and stock, a cheekpiece and heavy Schuetzen butt plate, and checkered grip and fore end. The wood used was usually fine American butt figured walnut, though occasionally the No. 52 and No. 54 are seen with imported walnut stocks.

Set triggers were standard on this model and also a loop lever (#4). The half-octagonal barrel in #3 or #4 weight was usually supplied. The 30-inch barrel weighed about 11 pounds, a little less than the No. 51 barrel. The frame was handsomely engraved in a pattern different from that of the No. 51. This model was also offered in two weights of frames, the regular and the extra heavy. Both utilized the lug-on-hammer principle. The H pattern sights were standard, and the calibers were the same as those of the preceding models.

The price of the No. 52 was $54, which was slightly less than that of the No. 51.

In my estimation the No. 52 is a more beautiful model than either the No. 51 or the No. 54, because of the graceful pistol-grip frame, the stock, and the loop lever. The wood in this model is usually finer than that in the No. 51.

IDEAL SCHUETZEN SPECIAL NO. 54. This was the highest grade regularly made by Stevens, and it is still about the highest grade offered to the shooting fraternity by any maker. It was a handsomely engraved arm and casehardened in colors, as were all these rifles. The type was a straight tang and grip model, with double-set triggers and a special Schuetzen lever (#6), that had a walnut grip fitted to the lever opening. The stock of selected walnut was finely checkered at the grip and also on the fore end, and it carried a special Schuetzen butt plate (#5).

These rifles were available in all calibers and with half-octagonal barrels in 30- and 32-inch lengths. The sights listed as standard were the H type. With the 30-inch barrel the rifle weighed 11½ pounds. The heavy Schuetzen frame was also available in this model and with the same barrel raised the weight to 11¾ pounds. The price of the 54 with 30-inch barrel was $68.

IDEAL LADIES MODEL NO. 55. This was a fancy model made in light weight especially for ladies' use. It was a beautiful little rifle, well balanced, and graceful in appearance. The action was the Ideal type, with single trigger and plain #1 lever. The stock was pistol-grip type, of fancy walnut, with the light #2 Swiss butt plate. Grip and forearm were finely checkered. Barrels were half-octagonal, light weight, and 24 inches long.

This model was chambered for the following calibers:

.22 Short rim-fire	.25 Stevens rim-fire
.22 Long Rifle rim-fire	.32 Long rim-fire
.22/7/45 Winchester rim-fire	.22/15/60 center-fire

The D sights were standard. With the standard barrel and Swiss butt plate, the rifle weighed 5¼ pounds. There was also available

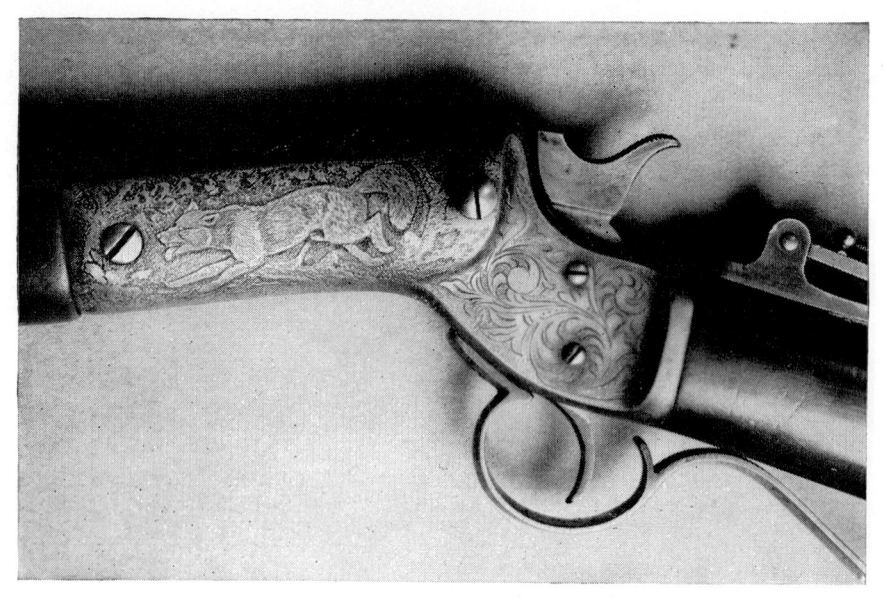

SPECIAL ENGRAVED STEVENS MODEL 10 RANGE RIFLE

upon special order—and for the same price—a shotgun butt plate. With this plate the rifle weighed about 5 pounds. (See page 58.)

This fine little rifle is a rather rare specimen to find today. When one with a perfect barrel is found, the accuracy of the model is quite surprising for such a light rifle.

IDEAL NO. 44 SERIES EXTRAS. The extras offered for the Stevens Ideal No. 44 series of rifles were as follows:

Full-octagonal barrels on all models	$ 2.00
Set screw in hammer (to regulate trigger pull)	1.00
Number 4 barrels	2.00
Number 5 barrels	5.00
Silver-plated frame, lever, and butt plate	4.00
Gold-plated frame, lever, and butt plate	15.00
Barrels up to 34 inches in length, per inch extra over standard	1.00
Palm rest	5.00
Extra interchangeable barrels with fore end	14.00 to 16.00
Extra breechblock and lever assembly, (price depending on lever type)	2.50 and up

The sight combinations were as follows:

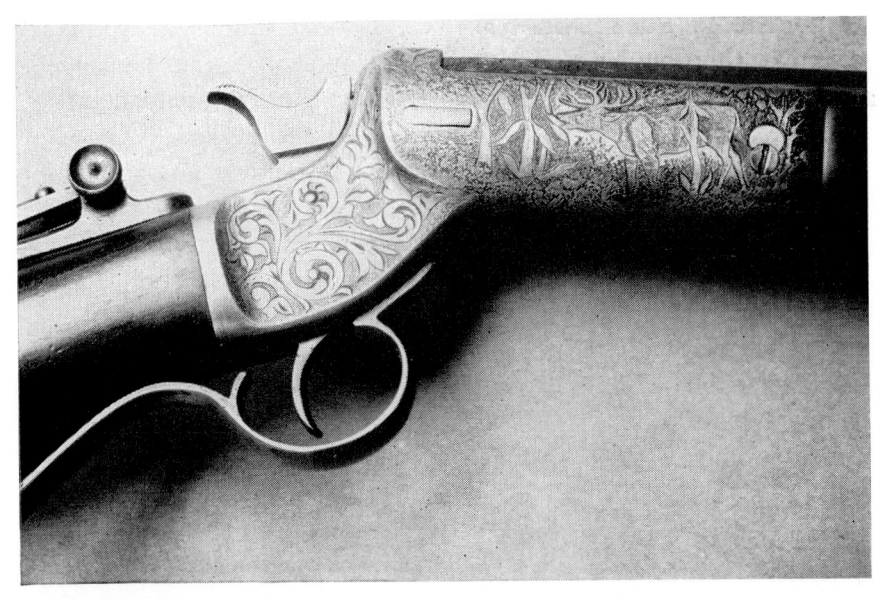

REVERSE SIDE OF STEVENS MODEL 10 RANGE RIFLE

B sights—Sporting rear and Rocky Mountain front
D sights—Beach combination front, sporting rear, and vernier tang peep
E sights—Lyman ivory combination front and Lyman combination rear
G sights—Windgauge front and midrange vernier peep
H sights—Globe interchangeable front and windgauge vernier peep, with adjustable eye cup

OTHER EARLY STEVENS MODELS

STEVENS FAVORITE MODEL. These little rifles were made at the same time the No. 44 series of models was at its greatest popularity, but they are too well known to describe at length here.

There was also a special fancy Favorite, with pistol-grip stock of fancy walnut, checkered grip and fore end, that was listed at $18, which was $12 more than the regular plain Favorite.

A special canvas case to carry the Favorite rifle, taken down, was listed at $2.00.

STEVENS POCKET (BICYCLE) RIFLE. The various models of this rifle were continued into the Ideal No. 44 series era, and were practically the same as the rifles made during the era of the Stevens tip-up series. The principal difference between the later series of these models and the earlier models is the addition of a trigger guard to all models.

NEW MODEL POCKET SHOTGUN No. 39. This model was the later version of the popular smooth-bored job in .38/35, .38/45, .44/50, and .44/65 Stevens Everlasting shot calibers. For factory-loaded shot cartridges it was chambered for the .38/40 and .44/40 WCF shot cartridges. These shotguns had 15- or 18-inch barrels, smooth bored and choked. They could be obtained in cylinder bore at the same price. The removable nickeled stock was standard.

Price with 15-inch barrel was $11.25; with 18-inch barrel, $12.50. Chambered for the .38/40 WCF and the .44/40 WCF shot cartridge the price with 15-inch barrel was $15.25; with 18-inch barrel, $14.50.

NEW MODEL POCKET (BICYCLE) RIFLE No. 40. This model was offered as follows:

| 10-inch barrel, | $ 9.25 | 15-inch barrel, | $11.25 |
| 12-inch barrel, | 10.00 | 18-inch barrel, | 12.50 |

Sights on this model were Stevens combination front and rear. The frame was nickel plated, as was the detachable shoulder stock. The barrel was octagonal to the end of the frame, and round the remainder of the length.

Calibers were .22 Long Rifle rim-fire, .25 Stevens rim-fire, and .32 Long rim-fire. A special-to-order caliber in .22/7/45 WRF was supplied for an extra charge of $2.00. Weight was from 2 to 2½ pounds.

STEVENS VERNIER NEW MODEL POCKET PISTOL No. 40½. This was the same as the No. 40, just described, except that a vernier rear sight was mounted on the grip above the removable shoulder stock, and there was a Beach combination front sight.

The price of this model ranged from $11.50 to $14.50, depending on the barrel length.

STEVENS TIP-UP PISTOL No. 41. This is the common and popular little Stevens pistol with 3½-inch barrel. It has a nickel-plated frame, a blued barrel, and a walnut grip. It also has the sheath-trigger. It is made only in .22 Short rim-fire, and is priced at $2.50.

STEVENS RELIABLE POCKET RIFLE No. 42. This is the light-frame later pocket rifle model, with lighter, removable, nickeled shoulder rest. Sights were globe front and peep on rear of barrel. It was offered in .22 Long Rifle in 10-inch barrel length, and was priced at $8.25.

STEVENS DIAMOND MODEL PISTOL NO. 43. This is another sheath-trigger model pistol with either a 6-inch or a 10-inch barrel, in .22 Long Rifle caliber only. It was made with globe front and peep rear barrel sights, also with open sights. Prices ranged from $5.00 to $8.50, depending on barrel length and sights.

STEVENS TARGET PISTOLS. These heavier pistols—Stevens Lord No. 36, Stevens Gould No. 37, Stevens Conlin No. 38—were made in the following calibers:

.22 Long Rifle	.32 Long rim-fire
.25 Stevens rim-fire	.38 Long Colt center-fire
.22/7/45 WRF	

They were all 10-inch barrel lengths, and were listed as follows: No. 36, $16.50; No. 37, $15; No. 38, $15. If desired, 12-inch barrels were available for No. 37 and No. 38, and these were priced at $16.

STEVENS-POPE SPECIALTIES

The Stevens No. 51 catalog has the following statement regarding the Stevens-Pope barrels:

On April 1, 1901, we purchased the tools and special machinery belonging to Mr. H. M. Pope, then of Hartford, Connecticut, and engaged his services to continue the manufacture of his barrel which, from that time on has been known as the "Stevens-Pope."

Mr. Pope has built up a national reputation as a manufacturer of high-grade rifle barrels, and, combining the best features that he was in possession of, together with ours, we have been able to produce the most perfect rifle barrels that it is possible to make.

The vast superiority of this barrel was shown on July 11, 1903, at Bisley, England, when the American team won the Palma trophy with a score of 1570, their nearest competitor being the English team, with a score of 1555.

In the United States the 50-shot record of 467 points out of 500 on the Standard American target, offhand, at 200 yards, is held by our Mr. Pope, and was made at Springfield, Mass., on March 21, 1903. The 100-shot record of 908 points out of 1000, at 200 yards, offhand, is also held by Mr. Pope, and was made January 1, 1903, at Springfield, Mass. Mr. Pope uses in his shooting a .32/40 Stevens rifle fitted with a Stevens-Pope barrel.

Associated with Mr. Pope at the Stevens factory is Mr. F. C. Ross, a marksman of international reputation. After the most careful manufac-

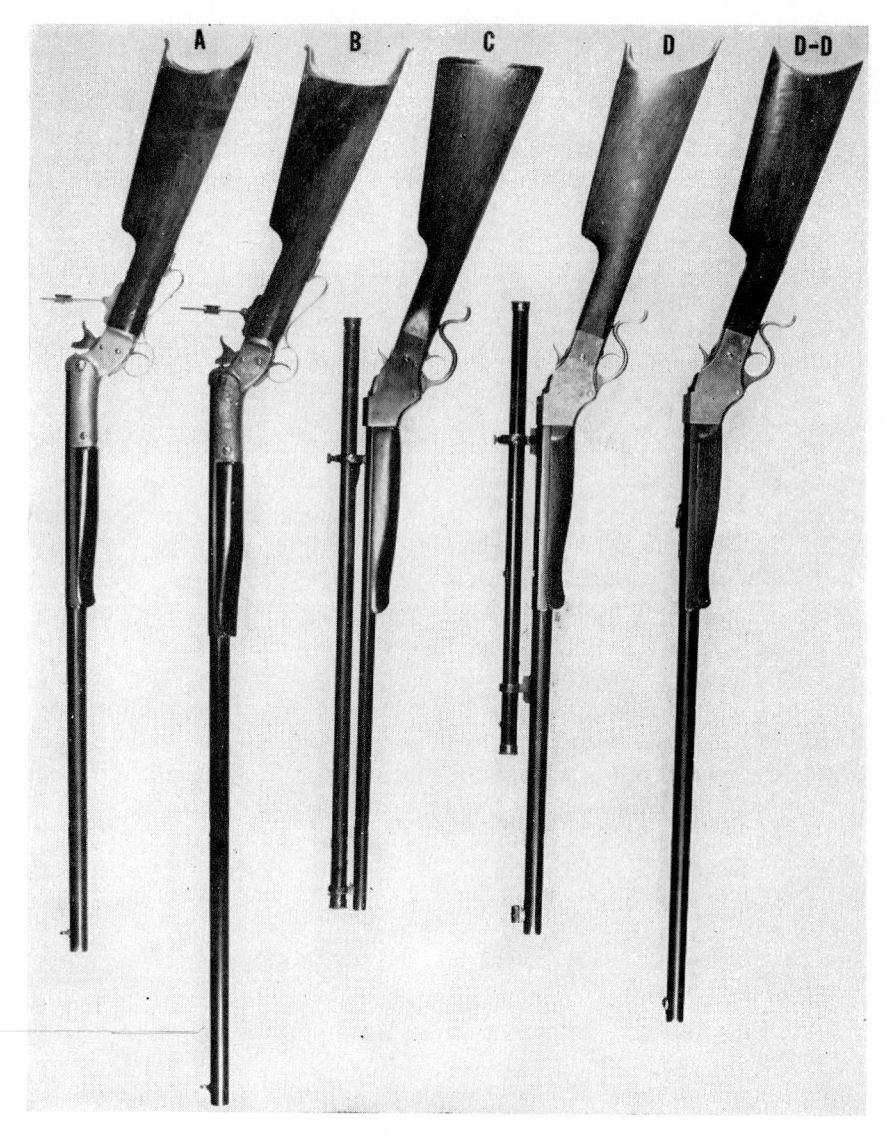

STEVENS RIFLES
(See page 112 for explanation)

ture, inspection, and fitting of a barrel, it is shot for accuracy by Mr. Ross, who is able to demonstrate the perfection of these barrels in a way which will satisfy the most exacting marksman.

At the time Mr. Pope went into the Stevens factory, in 1901, the 44 type action was the main Stevens action; consequently, most of

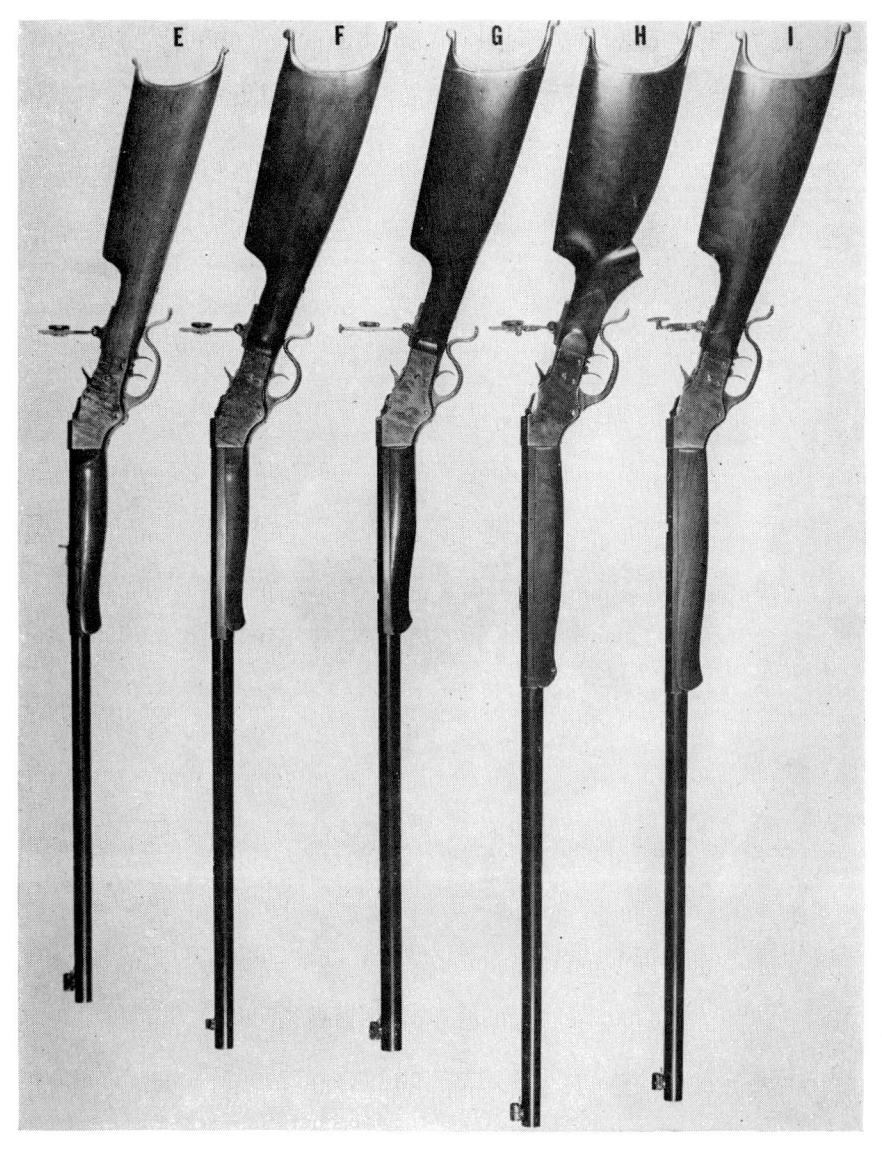

STEVENS RIFLES
(See page 112 for explanation)

the genuine Pope-made Stevens-Pope barrels were fitted to this type action. However, I have it direct from Mr. Pope himself that he worked on barrels up to about the 1200 serial number only. Since the Stevens-Pope name and system of rifling were continued for

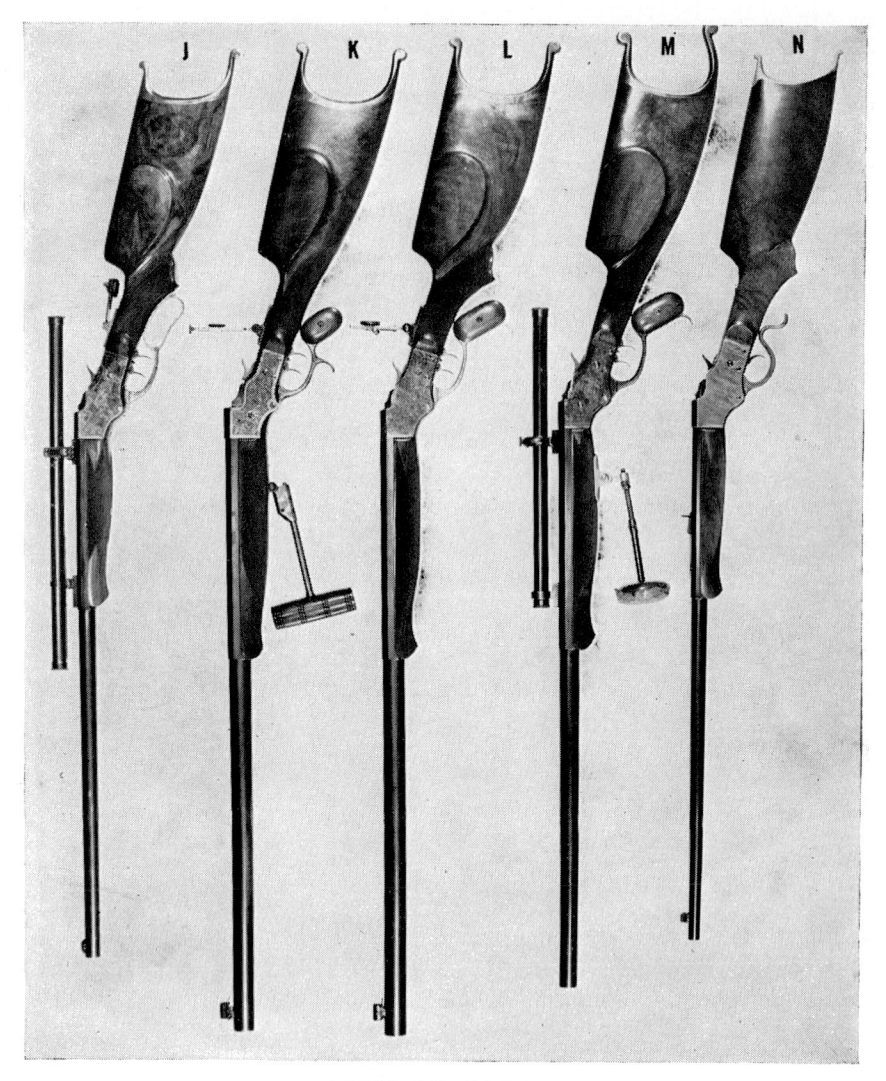

STEVENS RIFLES
(See page 112 for explanation)

several years, there are a great many of these rifles which were not made under the supervision of Mr. Pope himself. The 44½ type of action replaced the 44 type sometime in 1903, and of course many of these barrels are marked Stevens-Pope also. Stevens barrels, however, as furnished on the 44 series of rifles were super-accurate barrels themselves, and in most cases need take a back seat to no other barrels ever turned out at the Stevens factory, or at any other factory for that matter.

The Stevens Model 51 in .32/40 and .38/55 calibers in regular Stevens barrels were tested before shipment from the factory, and to pass inspection they had to make groups of 10 shots in 4 inches at 200 yards.

These figures were for regular black-powder-loaded cartridges, and of course the barrels were capable of much closer grouping than this. With the proper combination of smokeless and black powder load and breech-seated bullet of the proper weight and temper, these barrels are fully and easily capable of much smaller groups if in perfect condition as regards bore.

It is true beyond question that the Pope muzzle-loading system, with all the proper and balanced accessories, is unbeatable with black powder. But with smokeless powder the barrels as made by Stevens, Ballard, and any of the old custom barrelmakers, and breech loaded, are fully as accurate.[5] No doubt there are many experienced riflemen who will take exception to this statement, but let them obtain one of these old Stevens rifles in .28, .32, or .38 caliber, and with a perfect barrel, and see for themselves.

The Pope muzzle-breechloading system is adapted to black powder only, for maximum efficiency; or to a priming charge of smokeless powder and the balance in black powder. This is because the shock of exploding black powder is needed to upset the tapered bullet and thus expel it in an accurate manner. To use a full smokeless load in this system is not conducive to accuracy unless a bullet made for breech seating is used.

A "Stevens-Pope Special Catalogue" issued in 1903, while Mr. Pope was still affiliated with the Stevens company, lists several special barrels, rifles, and accessories peculiar to this type of performance. The quoted matter following is from this catalog.

STEVENS-POPE SPECIALTIES

In presenting the "Stevens-Pope" barrel to your notice, we call your attention to the fact that although there are but few of these barrels in use in comparison with the hundreds of thousands of rifles of other makes, yet in the field for which they are principally made, two-hundred-yard

---

[5] H. M. Pope used a type of rifling which he adopted from the muzzle-loading rifle maker Schalke, a system first devised by William Hayes and George Schalke.

offhand shooting, they hold all the records on all the targets in ordinary use at this distance for all the numbers of shots usually shot for a score. This fact proves conclusively that they have no equal; and it is also a fact that everyone using these barrels improves his score.

Following are records made with these barrels:

Standard American target—10 shots, 98, J. E. Kelley; 50 shots, 467, H. M. Pope; 100 shots, 917, H. M. Pope.

German ring target—3 shots, 75, L. P. Hansen; 10 shots, 240, L. P. Ittel; 10 shots, 240, L. P. Hansen; 50 shots, 1154, Dr. W. G. Hudson; 100 shots, 2301, Dr. W. G. Hudson.

Columbia target—3 shots, 4, F. O. Young; 10 shots, 26, A. H. Pape; 50 shots, A. H. Pape; 100 shots, A. H. Pape.

One-half-inch man target—5 shots, 98, J. Rebhan; 3 shots, many scores of 60.

King target—200 shots, 395, A. Strecker.

All important gallery records have been made with the "Stevens-Pope" .22 caliber. . . .

The "Stevens-Pope" rifling has eight wide grooves, and has the corners rounded out so dirt is easily removed, and it is clean in use. This groove is cut just deep enough to clean the bore in center and gives a depth at corners of about .004 inches. The lands are very narrow (about one fifth to one sixth the grooves). The bullet is made with a base large enough to fill the grooves completely, and the body is of practically the same diameter as the bore. This gives a form that is gas tight, loads very easily (being assisted in this by the narrow lands and choke bore), and on upset, instead of the body of the bullet meeting only sharp lands, and these cutting into the body more or less unequally, it is immediately held to place by the nearly flat center of the broad grooves and swells out into the grooves equally and perfectly central; consequently, it is balanced and accurate.

In this system a false muzzle and starter are used, and the lubricated bullet is seated from the muzzle, the shell with powder being afterward inserted in the ordinary way. In doing this the labor is very light, as the shooter has to handle nothing over a few ounces in weight, the rifle standing in the loading stand. By the simple act of pushing the bullet home, the sharp flat base of the bullet cuts the dirt down behind it, and does so exactly alike, each time giving a uniformly clean barrel, without the labor of cleaning. This is also less labor than the ordinary way of seating a greased bullet in the breech, having to invert the rifle and generally sustaining its weight while so doing.

Other things being equal, the man who tires himself least does the best shooting in the long run, and if this is accompanied by increased accuracy of the rifle, he has a great advantage over his fellows who do otherwise. . . .

A properly made barrel loaded in this way will shoot 10-shot groups at 200 yards that will average under all weather conditions about 1¼ or 1½ inches less diameter than the same or an equally good barrel shot dirty, bullet seated from the breech; while one using bullets seated in the shell is so far out of the game as to have no chance whatever on a string of any considerable number of shots, if otherwise he is an even match for his competitors.

1¼ to 1½ inches does not sound much, but on the fine-ringed targets now in use it means points. We have before us a good muzzle loading group, .32 caliber 10 shots, 200 yards. On the German ring target it counts 250. Another group shot breech loading, bullet seated in breech, same load, is but 1 inch larger diameter and is one of the best groups we ever saw shot under these conditions; it counts 245. On the Columbia target the scores are respectively, 12 and 21; on the Standard American target, 120 and 115. The difference between average groups is still more marked, averaging fully 7 or 8 points on German ring target. On this no comment is necessary. . . .

The base band of our "Stevens-Pope" bullet is broad and sharp, and of full size; the starter centers it perfectly, and fits it to the rifling with a perfect base, the shape of the grooves holds it central upon up setting, and it delivers perfectly from the muzzle. No other method will do this. "Stevens-Pope" barrels are all (unless specially ordered) cut with a left-hand gain twist and are so bored and rifled as to have a slight but gradual taper from breech to muzzle. This, besides keeping bullet perfectly under control, in connection with the narrow lands (which cut through the bullet easily) makes loading very easy and very materially increases accuracy. A bullet pushed through from the breech is tight all the way; there are no loose places, and this result is attained by close, careful workmanship; the result is a barrel with a long life. Wherever practicable, we chamber and make all crosscuts before rifling; we then fit a bushing to chamber, and bore and rifle it with the barrel and false muzzle. As the rifling is then the last cut made in the barrel, we are absolutely certain that there can be no burrs across the grooves—a very common fault. All this work is done by hand by the most skillful workmen, and is personally finished by H. M. Pope. We can not compete in price with automatic machinery, but the results are such that the best is very soon the cheapest.

The advantages of the gain twist are three: 1st—The twist being less at the breech, gives less friction to the bullet; it therefore starts easier and quicker, giving the powder less time to burn on in front of chamber, which therefore fouls less than in a barrel of uniform twist at the same necessary muzzle pitch. 2nd—The slight change in angle of rifling, in connection with choke boring, effectually shuts off any escape of gas and prevents gas cutting, which is another cause of imperfect delivery. 3rd—It holds a muzzle loaded bullet in position much better than a uniform twist. . . .

The "Stevens-Pope" muzzle loading outfit consists of barrel, false muzzle, starter, ramrod, "Stevens-Pope" special muzzle loading mould, and lubricating pump. The false muzzle is reamed and rifled with the barrel, and fits the same perfectly. A perfect one cannot be made except with the barrel. Its object is to prevent wear of the muzzle, of the barrel, upon the perfect condition of which the accuracy of the barrel depends. The starter is made so that it fits the muzzle closely and is perfectly central with it, so that bullets so seated are in exact line with the bore.

Barrels will be furnished of almost any weight and length, within about 3 to 6 oz. limit of variation up to 8 pounds for a 32-inch No. 4 octagon, .32 caliber barrel; longer or heavier barrels, also barrels to exact weight specified, at special prices. We consider for offhand work, 200 yard work, a barrel of about 7¾ lbs., 30 inch octagon as the best adapted. This we consider our standard and recommend it as giving the best average results. For caliber for offhand work we prefer a .28, .32 or .33.

A "Stevens-Pope" muzzle loading barrel is at the same time the most perfect breech loader that it is possible to make. It can be loaded with fixed ammunition, the bullet seated in the breech of barrel from either muzzle in the regular way, or a shell with primer and priming can be inserted in the breech, the action half closed, and any desired amount of powder poured down the muzzle as in a true muzzle loader and the bullet seated from the muzzle. . . .

The price for this outfit includes fitting the barrel to your action and fitting it to your extractor, forearm and sights, where they can be used. If new ones are necessary they will be charged for extra.

   Muzzle loading barrel and outfit untested $40.00
   Testing at 200 yards, machine rest, extra   10.00

10-shot group, guaranteed as follows: .25 caliber, 3½ inches or better across centers; .28 caliber, 3 inches or better; larger sizes, 2½ inches or better. . . .

In these there is absolutely no difference in the quality of barrels or workmanship. If tested, you see what has actually been accomplished with fine appliances and know exactly what load did it. If untested, you, unless very expert, can hardly expect to equal at once the results of our machine test, and may have to do some experimenting (when you are accustomed to the system, not before), to determine the best temper of bullets, etc. If weather is good, we get close groups; if weather is cold and wind tricky, they are not so good. It is perfectly obvious that we cannot guarantee for a fixed price to furnish as close a group as the barrel is capable of shooting, though we might happen to do so. We believe all our barrels are capable of shooting closer than 2-inch groups; with favorable conditions, they usually test closer than we guarantee. . . .

PRICE ON RECUTTING TO "STEVENS-POPE" SYSTEM

We recut rifles of other makes or smaller calibers to larger sizes with the same outfit and guarantee as for a new barrel:

Recutting with muzzle loading outfit, untested	$30.00
Testing at 200 yards, machine rest, extra	10.00

10-shot group guaranteed as follows: .25 caliber, 3½ inches or better across the centers; .28 caliber, 2 inches or better; larger sizes, 2½ inches or better.

Recutting for breach loaders, untested	12.00

The following calibers were offered in the "Stevens-Pope" system:

Caliber	Shell	Powder	M/L Bullet	B/L Bullet
.25	.25-25	27 grs.	100 grs.	86 grs.
.28	.28 Stevens	37 grs.	118 & 136 grs.	108 & 125 grs.
.32	.32/40 Marlin	46 grs.	180 & 200 grs.	165 & 185 grs.
.33	.32/40 Marlin	46 grs.	195 & 218 grs.	. . . . . .
.33	.33 Special	47 grs.	195 & 218 grs.	190 & 215 grs.
.38	.38/55	52 grs.	277 & 305 grs.	255 grs.
.38	.38/72 Special	77 grs.	305 & 330 grs.	255 to 330 grs.
.39	.38/55	52 grs.	290 grs.	. . . . . .
.39	.38/72 Special	77 grs.	343 grs.	. . . . . .

The weight of the powder charges given above is the average weight of the drawn shell even full. It will vary a little with different shells. Powder can be decreased by using Special or Everlasting shells, or by a moderate air space. It can be increased by first inserting the shell with priming charge, then loading any desired amount from the muzzle. The weight of breech loading bullets given are those intended to be seated in the shell. Barrels are rifled with a twist correct for the bullet they are intended to use. Shorter bullets can be used in a barrel cut for the longer bullet, but not the reverse. It is often times better to use the lighter bullet.

Unless specially ordered, we will use our best judgment in cutting the barrel.

BREECH LOADING BARRELS

We cut barrels for breech loading in the same style as for muzzle loading. A mould for same bullet to be seated in the barrel is recommended as giving better results than the ordinary B/L bullet. The price for new barrel of same sizes and weights as given under the muzzle loading outfit, fitted to your action, and to your extractor, forearm, and sights is $20.00. Recutting, $12.00.

Testing and guaranteeing same prices as for muzzle loading, but the size of groups guaranteed is 1½ inches larger.

.22 CALIBER BARRELS

We are now prepared to furnish .22 caliber barrels, with the same quality of workmanship used on our muzzle loaders. These can be furnished for .22 short or long rifle cartridges, up to 30 inches in length, #3, weight about 6 to 7 pounds.

Price, fitted to your action, etc., and tested at 25 yards $20.00
#4 barrel, $2.00 extra; #5 barrel, $5.00 extra.

THE "STEVENS-POPE" SPECIAL MUZZLE LOADING MOULD

As previously shown, a bullet with a perfect base is essential to the finest work. To meet this requisite a special mould was designed. It differs from all others in having a cut off with a bottom plate rigidly connected to it and swinging with it. These plates, with the joint pin and dowels, hold the two halves of mould perfectly in position; bullets from it average within .0005 inch of being round, which is practically perfect. No other mould does such work. The bullet is poured from the point, which brings imperfection to that end. When sprue is cut off, both plates swing entirely clear of bullet, which easily falls out. Great pains are taken to have each half of mould of equal depth, to avoid sticking. This mould is part of the muzzle loading outfit. It is also recommended as being the best for breech loading work, shooting dirty with bullet seated in the barrel ahead of case.

Moulds can be ventilated if desired. This consists of cutting air passages from each groove and from point and base in the mould to allow air to escape freely. It is a little advantage where one works so slowly that mould is apt to be too cool, but not otherwise.

All moulds are broken in, ready for use. Keep them dry and use no oil. Wax joints in use when necessary to keep them free.

We have a large number of cherries of various sizes and styles. Moulds can be made from any of these at regular prices. We make special sizes to order at $5.00 extra, retaining the cherry as our own property.

    Price of "Stevens-Pope" special mould, cutting off at point $4.00
    Price of moulds, cutting off at base 1.50
    Price of ventilating, extra .50

THE "STEVENS-POPE" LUBRICATING PUMP

This pump holds enough to grease 180 to 300 of our bullets, according to size. By its use, using grease cold, one greases bullets perfectly as fast as fifteen to 25 per minute, according to skill; rightly used, it just fills the grooves and no more, leaving the lands bare. This is essential for fine work, for if there be more grease on one side of the bullet than on the other, it displaces that bulk of lead upon upset, throwing the bullet out of balance. If the mould is round, as ours are, no wiping of bullets is necessary. Dies are made interchangeable, so any number of different ones may be had, each bullet requiring a different die.

This is an indispensable tool for the nicest work; it is included in the muzzle loading outfit. In ordering lubricating pump separately, send several samples of each size bullet it is intended to grease.

    Price of lubricating pump $2.50
    Extra dies, each .75
    Leopold's stick lubricant .05

THE "STEVENS-POPE" LOADING FLASK

[This] is designed to cover the range of charges of powder used in Stevens-Pope barrels and is adjustable for charge. It loads a nitro priming charge and black powder body or a full charge of black at one operation and is very quick and the most accurate flash made.

For the very finest work this flask is a necessity unless one wishes to take time to weigh charges. Price $6.00.

"THE STEVENS-POPE" PALM REST

[This] can be attached to any rifle and is made so the shank is easily unscrewed for carrying, without changing the adjustment. It swings away from the lever for loading, and from recoil. (Can be put on reversed if desired.)

The shank is adjustable for length by the telescoping tube and taper nut, a great advantage in shooting over different ranges when targets are not on the same level, and for position to or from the body, by changing the position of the check nuts on the shank, so as to allow the shank

THE "STEVENS-POPE" REAR WINDGAUGE AND ELEVATING SIGHT

Wind and elevation movements are entirely separate, so moving one can not disturb the other. One whole movement of either elevating nuts or wind screw equals 1 inch on 200 yard target (½ minute adjustments). A jam nut compensates for wear on this sight.

Price without base, fitted to any base sent us	$6.00
Price with base complete	7.00
Globe front sight, with interchangeable disc, one pin head and one aperture	1.25
Globe front sight with interchangeable disc, one pin head, one aperture, beveled edges	1.75

"STEVENS-POPE" RE AND DE CAPPER

This tool of special design is very light, extremely powerful, and subject to very little wear. It does not soil the hands as others do. Will be made in all sizes. Standard calibers are now ready. Price, plated, $1.50.

"STEVENS-POPE" SPECIAL TELESCOPE MOUNTS

These mounts are of the split clamping type. The feet of the mounts clamp into special milled slots in the barrel, and removing and replacing the scope with mounts does not change in any way the adjustment of windage or elevation.

This completes the catalog description of the special Stevens-Pope barrels and accessories. The barrel with accessories, Stevens-Pope wind gauge and elevation rear sight, recapper and decapper, and special Stevens-Pope scope mounts are shown on Plate 18.

The 1902 Stevens-Pope catalog lists the following stock models of rifles fitted with Stevens-Pope barrels:

IDEAL MODEL No. 45. Thirty-inch, half-octagonal #3 barrel; drop-forged and casehardened frame; varnished stock and forearm; Swiss butt plate; single trigger; "D" sights; Stevens-Pope muzzle-loading outfit of false muzzle, starter, ramrod, Pope special mold, and lubricating pump. Weight 10 pounds. Price, $47. No rear sight slot unless ordered.

IDEAL MODEL No. 47. Thirty-inch, half-octagonal #3 barrel; drop-forged and casehardened frame; single trigger; loop lever; varnished pistol-grip stock and forearm; Swiss butt plate or heavier "Interchangeable" butt plate similar to Schuetzen; "D" sights; Stevens-Pope muzzle-loading outfit. Weight about 10¼ pounds. Price, $52. No rear sight slot unless ordered.

IDEAL MODEL NO. 49. Thirty-inch, half-octagonal #3 barrel; drop-forged, engraved, and casehardened action; loop lever; pistol-grip stock with cheekpiece; stock and forearm varnished and checkered; Swiss butt plate; "H" sights; Stevens-Pope muzzle-loading outfit. Weight about 10½ pounds. Price, $63. No rear sight slot unless ordered.

IDEAL MODEL NO. 51. Thirty-inch #3 or #4 octagonal or half-octagonal barrel; drop-forged, engraved, and casehardened action; double-set triggers; Schuetzen spur lever; fancy walnut stock and forearm; finely varnished and checkered cheekpiece; Schuetzen butt plate; "H" sights; Stevens-Pope muzzle-loading outfit. Weight 12 to 13¾ pounds. Price, $75. No rear sight slot unless ordered.

IDEAL MODEL NO. 52. Thirty-inch #3 or #4 octagonal or half-octagonal barrel; drop-forged, engraved, and casehardened action; double-set triggers; loop lever; fancy pistol-grip stock and forearm finely checkered and varnished; Schuetzen butt plate; "H" sights; Stevens-Pope muzzle-loading outfit. Weight, 11 to 12½ pounds. Price, $72. No rear sight slot unless ordered.

IDEAL MODEL NO. 54. Thirty-inch #3 or #4 octagonal or half-octagonal barrel; drop-forged, finely engraved and casehardened action; double-set triggers; special #54 lever; extra fancy stock and forearm; finely checkered and varnished cheekpiece; special Schuetzen butt plate; "H" sight; Stevens-Pope muzzle-loading outfit. Weight, 11¾ to 13 pounds. Price, $81. No rear sight slot unless ordered.

SPECIAL POPE MODEL. Thirty-inch or 32-inch #4 octagonal barrel; drop-forged action, handsomely casehardened (no engraving) action; double-set triggers; fancy pistol-grip stock and forearm, Pope model; finely checkered and varnished cheekpiece set extra high and full so as to be tight against the face; special deep, snugly fitting butt plate; special three-finger lever; Pope sights; Pope palm rest; Pope muzzle-loading outfit. Length of stock, 13⅝ inches. Drop of stock, 3 inches. Weight, 12½ to 13½ pounds. Price, $82. Same rifle with plain walnut stock and without checkering, $75.

This rifle could also be fitted out with a Stevens-Pope 5-power telescope, 16 inches long. Price of telescope, mounted on barrel, with

Pope rib and Pope detachable sliding mounts, $24. Same without rib, $19.

EXTRAS

Set triggers	$6.00
Extra length of barrel, per inch	1.00
No. 4. barrels	2.00
No. 5 barrels	5.00
Octagonal barrels	2.00
Engraving, to any amount, upward from	5.00
Pope sights, rear windgauge and elevating rear, with interchangeable beveled disc globe front	8.75
"B" sights. Sporting rear and Rocky Mountain front	1.30
"D" sights. Beach combination front, open rear and vernier peep tang	4.80
"E" sights. Lyman Ivory Combination front and Lyman Combination rear #1	4.00
(For #2 rear with cup disc, add 50¢.)	
"F" sights. Globe interchangeable front and vernier peep	4.25
"G" sights. Windgauge front and midrange vernier peep	7.00
"H" sights. Globe interchangeable front and windgauge vernier peep with adjustable eye cup	7.25
Levers, plain	1.50
Lever, loop	2.50
Lever, Schuetzen, No. 51	5.50
Lever, Schuetzen, No. 54	5.50
Lever, 3-finger spur	5.00
(This is also made to order for Ballard and Winchester actions.)	
Changing dimensions of stock (special handwork)	5.00
Nickel-plated frame, lever, and butt plate	2.50

Smokeless barrels of high pressure still were offered for any suitable action in breech-loading type only, in .30/30, .30/40 U. S., .32 Winchester Special, .32/40, and .38/55. Price, round barrels only, $20.

"Special" Stevens-Pope Military barrels were made at the same price in .30/40 Krag caliber.

Armory barrels for the Krag in .22 rim-fire caliber which interchanged with the regular center-fire barrel were also priced at $20. These .22 "Special" barrels were bored and rifled the same as the

Ideal Levers and Butt Plates

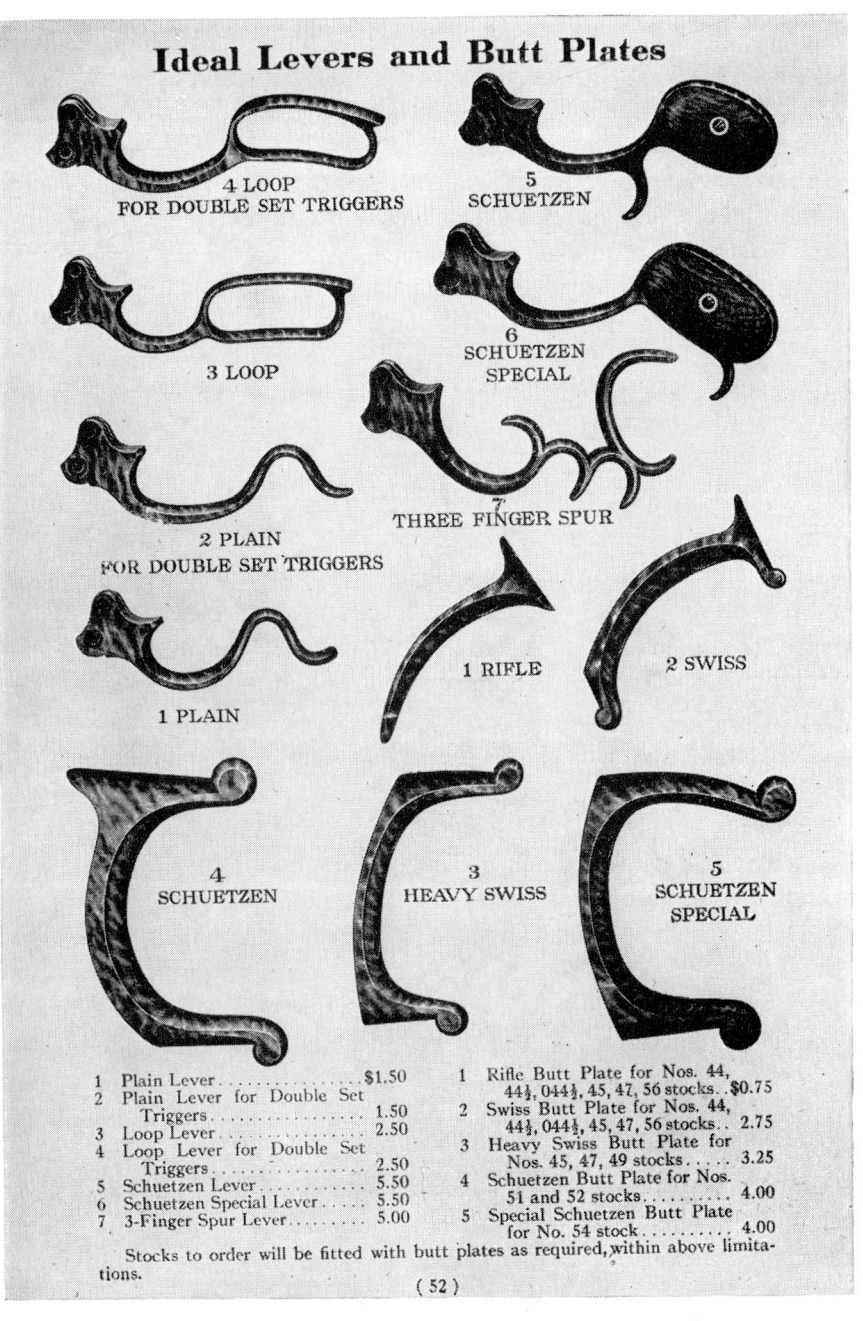

4 LOOP
FOR DOUBLE SET TRIGGERS

5 SCHUETZEN

3 LOOP

6 SCHUETZEN SPECIAL

2 PLAIN
FOR DOUBLE SET TRIGGERS

7 THREE FINGER SPUR

1 PLAIN

1 RIFLE

2 SWISS

4 SCHUETZEN

3 HEAVY SWISS

5 SCHUETZEN SPECIAL

1 Plain Lever	$1.50
2 Plain Lever for Double Set Triggers	1.50
3 Loop Lever	2.50
4 Loop Lever for Double Set Triggers	2.50
5 Schuetzen Lever	5.50
6 Schuetzen Special Lever	5.50
7 3-Finger Spur Lever	5.00

1 Rifle Butt Plate for Nos. 44, 44½, 044½, 45, 47, 56 stocks	$0.75
2 Swiss Butt Plate for Nos. 44, 44½, 044½, 45, 47, 56 stocks	2.75
3 Heavy Swiss Butt Plate for Nos. 45, 47, 49 stocks	3.25
4 Schuetzen Butt Plate for Nos. 51 and 52 stocks	4.00
5 Special Schuetzen Butt Plate for No. 54 stock	4.00

Stocks to order will be fitted with butt plates as required, within above limitations.

(52)

STEVENS LEVERS AND BUTT PLATES
Butt Plates 3 and 5 are shown upside down in this catalogue reproduction.

regular Schuetzen Stevens-Pope barrels. The Special Stevens-Pope Military barrel .30/40 caliber were 8-groove right-hand twist pattern unless specially ordered to be the same as the Schuetzen type of boring.

This covers the Special Stevens-Pope barrels and accessories as listed in the 1902 Special Pope Department Catalogue. The rifles shown therein—models 45, 47, 49, 51, 52, and 54—were the same as those illustrated in the regular #51 Stevens catalog, except of course that they were fitted with the muzzle-loading barrel and outfit. The action of these rifles at this time was still the 44 pattern, the 44½ type not being introduced until the year following, sometime in 1903. But when the 44½ type action was ready, the Stevens-Pope muzzle-loading outfit was available also for it in all model numbers, as it already was for the 44 type; however, the M/L barrels are mostly seen on the 44 type.

The "Special" Pope model rifle as described was not shown in the regular #51 catalog of this period; it was, of course, a "Special" model (see page 63) designed by Mr. Pope. This model was also available in the 44½ type action when this latter action became the standard in 1903. These "Special" Pope model rifles are marked "P" on the front end of the frame where the models were usually stamped.

IDEAL 44½ AND O44½ SERIES

In the year 1903—or about that time—the Ideal 44 type action was dropped and the new 44½ type action was introduced, and this latter became the standard action not only for new models but for all models that had been listed in the preceding catalogs. In other words, all model *numbers* such as 45, 47, 49, 51, 52, and 54 were retained, but the action used in these rifles was the new 44½ type action. The plain basic No. 44 rifle was continued along with the new series of rifles, as it was a popular model. The Ladies Model No. 55 was also continued for a year or so, but it was dropped as soon as a new Ladies Model No. 56, based on the new action, was ready. This changing of actions but continuing the same model number designations is rather confusing at first glance, and many persons seem to have difficulty in separating the two series of rifles. To clear up some of the confusion, the model number in both series —45, 47, 49, 51, 52, and 54—is sometimes stamped on the lower tang and sometimes on the front end of the action, visible when the forearm is removed; sometimes it is in both locations. Neither series is stamped with the action type number except in the case of the basic rifles in each action. The plain basic 44 type action rifle is usually stamped 44 on the action; the basic 44½ type action is usually stamped 44½ on the action; and the English version of this rifle, the O44½, is stamped O44½ on the frame. As already stated, these basic models are the only ones of these actions that are so stamped. It is really not hard to tell whether a model is made up on the 44 or the 44½ type action provided one takes more than passing interest in the two actions as illustrated on page 63. In fact, it is really very simple, the mechanical differences in the actions being readily apparent, and the model number, whether present on the frame or not, being apparent in the physical make-up of the complete rifle. As a matter of fact, some specimens are unmarked as to model numbers, so the best and only positive method of identifying the particular model your specimen happens to be is by comparing it with the catalog descriptions cited in this chapter.

Some Stevens 44½ type specimens are stamped in a rather haphazard manner; one is likely to find almost any model number stamped on the frames. It seems they were downright careless about this in certain instances, as some are even unmarked. Some actions are mismarked, though this is rarely the case. The name and other data as stamped on the barrels was sometimes stamped upside down, and I have one 44½ rifle—model 45, in .25 Stevens rim-fire caliber—with a high serial number that has the Stevens name stamped on the side of the action frame, and this is upside down.

Some of the lower grades in the 44½ series have an extra "O" stamped somewhere on the front of the frame separate from the regular model number, yet these are not O44½ actions. There is usually an "Ex" somewhere on these frames also; what is meant by this I have no idea, nor can I discover.

All these things lead me to believe that those who were responsible for marking some of these models were prone to look upon the wine when it was red—or perhaps they just didn't give a damn! At any rate, we forgive them, for these things are not important, and in some cases they are actually comical. These were fine rifles, and mismarked or unmarked they are appreciated by all Stevens enthusiasts. Would that they were still available!

IDEAL 44½ TYPE ACTION SERIES

The earlier editions of the Stevens No. 51 catalog were issued during the manufacture of the 44 type series in all models and at the time when this was still the standard action. There was a later No. 51 catalog, however, which is marked simply, "Catalogue No. 51, Reprint Edition."

In this catalog, evidently issued during or just after 1903, the new 44½ type action was then standard, for the 44 type action had by that time been abandoned in all higher grades. However, the illustrations of models 45, 47, 49, 51, 52, and 54 all show these rifles in the 44 type action, obviously because new illustrations had not yet been prepared. The text describing these models lists them all as being based on the "New Action" which was, of course, the 44½ type. The illustrations of the basic models 44½ and O44½, being new additions, carried new plates showing the 44½ action.

This catalog has the following to say regarding the discontinuance of the 44 type series of rifles:

The action used in the Stevens Ideal No. 44 rifle is the same that we have been incorporating in our Ideal rifles, models 44 to 54, since 1894 and has met with universal success throughout this country as well as abroad.

We have now decided to manufacture this arm to take only the following cartridges: .22 Long Rifle rim-fire, .25 Stevens rim-fire, .32 Long rim-fire, .25/20 center-fire, .32/20 center-fire.

The above sizes, in different lengths of barrel, will be carried in stock, but under no consideration will we make the above rifle for any other sizes, with the exception of making it to special order to take the .22 Short rim-fire cartridge, at a $2.00 additional list. For larger and special sizes, see description of our new No. 44½ rifle.

The latest Ideal 44 rifle is now made with our new and improved central extractor.[6] [NOTE: The 44 model as continued had a lower tang integral with the frame; therefore set triggers were not adaptable.]

The same catalog introduced the Stevens Ideal No. 44½ series as follows:

This model is the outgrowth of many years' experience in the manufacture of rifles, aided by the suggestions of acknowledged expert riflemen.

---

[6] Earlier 44 models in all grades for a while used the side extractor, later changed to a central type.

This arm represents the highest development of modern rifle making. It contains the best quality of metal; embodies superior points as regards mechanism, according to the opinion of expert shots of today; is portable, and possesses the most perfect rifling mechanical ingenuity and the finest machinery is capable of producing.

Since smokeless powder has come into such general use, it became necessary for us to devise and perfect a model that we could guarantee without any hesitancy and that would stand excessive charges of smokeless powder. In offering this new action, we are positive it is sufficiently strong to stand every test. We have experimented with the most extreme charges of high pressure, smokeless powder in this action, and have been unable in any way what so ever to affect its efficiency in the least.

In fitting barrels to this action, however, we use the regular stock steel that we have used in our other models, and this is sufficiently strong for all ordinary charges of regular, low pressure, smokeless powder. Where parties are desirous of obtaining barrels made of special smokeless steel we can supply them at an extra list of $3.00 over the regular price.

Our new action is of the well-known, sliding-bolt type, but in its application it is a radical departure from anything as yet put on the market. The bolt or block slides vertically in the frame. In loading: after the cartridge is inserted, and the lever started, the bolt has what we call a rocking motion; that is, it starts forward and upward at the same time, seating the cartridge in the chamber, then sliding vertically upward to place. We claim for this action that it is easier and quicker of manipulation than any yet brought out, and furthermore, it is an impossibility to buckle the shell—an easy matter in other actions that have a sliding breechblock.

The take-down system that has been applied to our regular Ideal rifles in the past has been retained in the new model, and all of our rifles from No. 44½ to No. 54, will have the new action whether so specified or not.

In this action, we are also manufacturing what we call our O44½, or in other words, an English Model. This is made with a light weight tapered barrel and the English shot gun stock and is a rifle that has been called for repeatedly by the American trade, one which we believe will meet with a ready sale on account of its light weight.

This quotation from the catalog tells the story of the new 44½ action concisely and, it would seem, rather modestly. In fact, collectors and shooters are much more enthusiastic about the 44½ Stevens than its makers appeared to be.

It is the only falling-block action patterned after the Sharps that actually does both rock the cartridge into its chamber and at the same time effectively lock the breechblock. The Sharps side-hammer, Sharps Borchardt, Winchester Single-shot, Remington Hepburn, and others, are all very strong and safe actions, but they require the cartridge to be pushed almost into its seat with the thumb before the breechblock will close. In contrast, the Stevens 44½ will seat the case when it is quite a way from being completely in. All the Stevens 44½ actions are drop-forged steel, and are much stronger than is generally realized. Some of the later ones made were proof-marked. One of my model 54-44½ rifles is so marked on the front of the action. A point to bear in mind regarding the 44½ Stevens actions is that they were made after 1902 and for *smokeless powder loads*.

At no place in the Stevens No. 51 or the No. 52 catalog—or in any other Stevens catalogs which I own or have examined—is the difference between the regular 44½ and the O44½ actions described. The standard 44½ action and the higher grades of this action— models 45, 47, 49, and 54—were made in a thickness of frame of about 1 3/16 inches. The models 51 and 52 were slightly heavier, usually about 1/32-inch thicker, and slightly deeper at the point of the barrel housing, or receiver ring. The O44½ action and the fancy version of the O44½ listed in the No. 52 catalog and on the model itself as No. 56 Ladies Model, were made the same as the regular 44½ except that the frame was only 1 inch thick, thus having a narrower breechblock and a narrower lever. The lower tang, however, was standard and would interchange in the regular 44½ frame. These O44½ and No. 56 actions were the same except that the O44½ had a straight-grip tang and the No. 56 had a pistol-grip tang. Both take small-shank #1 barrels. These barrel shanks are ¾ of an inch in diameter, in contrast to the ⅞-inch diameter of all other 44½ barrel shanks. Other than in these particulars, all dimensions of the O44½, the No. 56, and the 44½ actions are for all practical purposes identical.

The small-shank #1 barrels as used in the models O44½ and No. 56 were, of course, not chambered for cartridges larger in diameter than the .28/30 or the .32 Ideal, or other similar calibers for the reason that in larger calibers there was not sufficient steel for safety's sake.

Another noticeable difference between the 44 type series of models and the same models based on the 44½ type action is in the engraving. Most No. 49 and No. 51 rifles in 44½ type have simple open scrollwork, as shown on page 68. Model No. 52 has many variations; more, in fact, than most engraved models in this series, some being decorated with open scrollwork similar to No. 49 and No. 51, and others running to oak-leaf and floral designs (see pages 70 to 72). In all engraved models in all makes of rifles great variety of design exists, and one cannot expect to find very many specimens that are exactly alike. However, there is more uniformity among the No. 49 and No. 51 engraved frames than among any other make of single-shot rifles. As a rule, the No. 54 in the 44½ type action is the only one with animal scene engraving; on the other hand, this pattern is to be found on all models in the earlier 44 series of rifles, though it was usually etched rather than engraved, as noted previously.

The basic models as listed in the No. 51 catalog were as follows:

Stevens Maynard Jr. No. 15	$3.00
Stevens Maynard Jr. No. 15½, .22 smooth bore	3.00
Stevens Crack Shot No. 16	4.00
Stevens Little Krag (bolt action) No. 65	5.00
Stevens Favorite No. 17	6.00
Stevens Favorite No. 18	8.50
Stevens Favorite No. 19	9.00
Stevens Favorite No. 20, smooth bore	6.00
Stevens Favorite No. 21	6.00 to 9.00
Canvas Bicycle Case	1.50

FAVORITE RIFLE. This model was still offered in pistol-grip, fancy walnut stock at this date (1903) at $20. These Favorites were all made in rim-fire calibers only, and with the new central extractor.

STEVENS IDEAL No. 44. This rifle was offered in the plain model only, with both tangs cast in one piece with the frame, therefore set triggers for the No. 44 were no longer available, as formerly. It was made in the following calibers only:

.22 Long Rifle rim-fire .25/20 Stevens center-fire
.25 Stevens rim-fire .32/20 center-fire
.32 Long rim-fire

For larger calibers the buyer was referred to the No. 44½. This basic No. 44 was still priced at $10.

STEVENS IDEAL NO. 44½ RIFLE. This was the plain basic 44½ rifle which corresponded to the No. 44 model in the older—the 44 type—series. The barrel was half-octagonal, #2 weight, 24 inches in length for rim-fire and 26 inches for center-fire cartridges. The frame was drop-forged and casehardened; the action was the new 44½ type. This was a single trigger model, with plain oiled straight-grip stock, regular rifle butt plate, Rocky Mountain front and sporting rear sights. Calibers offered were as follows:

.22 Long Rifle rim-fire	.32/40 center-fire
.25 Stevens rim-fire	.38/40 center-fire
.32 Long rim-fire	.38/55 center-fire
.25/20 Stevens center-fire	.44/40 center-fire
.32/20 center-fire	

Made special to order at $2.00 extra were the following calibers:

.22 Short rim-fire	.25/25 center-fire
.22/7/45 WRF	.28/30/120 center-fire
.22/15/60 Stevens center-fire	.32/35 center-fire
.25/21 center-fire	.32 Ideal center-fire

The weight of this rifle was 7 to 7½ pounds. Price, $12.

STEVENS IDEAL ENGLISH MODEL NO. O44½. This model had the thinner 44½ type frame and half-octagonal #1 barrel, in 24-inch length in rim-fire caliber and 26-inch length in center-fire. Full-octagonal barrel was offered at $2.00 extra, but this is rarely seen today. This English version was made in most of the 44½ model calibers, but in none larger than .28/30/120 and .32 Ideal. The trigger was single. The stock was straight-grip type with hard-rubber shotgun butt plate. The sights were bead front and sporting rear. The weight with 24-inch barrel was 5¾ pounds; with 26-inch barrel, 6 pounds. The price was $12.

STEVENS IDEAL RANGE NO. 45. This was the same as the basic 44½ model except that the stock had the #2 Swiss butt plate with #2 barrel standard. Barrel lengths were 26 inches long in rim-fire caliber and 28 inches long in center-fire. If preferred, the #1 or #3 barrels were furnished at the same price as the standard #2. The stock and forearm were varnished. Single trigger and plain lever were standard. Rifle or hard-rubber shotgun butt plates were also optional on this Model 45. Calibers offered were the same as with the No. 44½ except that the .25/21 was on the regular list, and the .32 Long center-fire was added to the extra-charge list.

The sights were Beach combination front, open rear, and vernier tang peep (D sights). Weight with 26-inch barrel was 7½ pounds; with 28-inch barrel, 8 pounds. Both these weights were with standard #2 barrels. Price was $22.

STEVENS IDEAL MODERN RANGE NO. 47. This was the same rifle as the No. 47 offered in 44 type action except, of course, that the action was the new 44½ type. The standard barrel was the #2, and the weights were 7¾ and 8¼ pounds. Calibers offered were the same as with the basic 44½ model. The same pattern of unchecked pistol-grip stock as that on the 47-44 was still standard. Lever was loop type, and single triggers were standard. Sights were D type. Price was $27.

When this No. 47 was ordered with #3 or heavier barrel, the #2 Swiss butt plate was replaced at no extra charge with the heavier #3 Schuetzen butt plate (interchangeable type).

STEVENS IDEAL WALNUT HILL NO. 49. This model had the scroll engraved frame in 44½ type. It also had a loop lever, single trigger, cheekpiece, pistol-grip checkered stock, varnished and with Swiss butt plate. Calibers were the same as with the preceding models. Sights were globe interchangeable front and wind-gauge vernier rear, with adjustable eye cup. There was no rear sight slot with G and H sights.

Half-octagonal barrels in 28- and 30-inch lengths were offered. Weights and prices were:

28-inch barrel, #2 type, 8¾ pounds;	
#3 type, 10¼ pounds	$42.00
30-inch barrel, #2 type, 9¼ pounds;	
#3 type, 10½ pounds	43.00
With D, E, or F sights, 28-inch barrel	39.00
With D, E, or F sights, 30-inch barrel	40.00
False muzzle and bullet starter, extra	15.00

STEVENS IDEAL SCHUETZEN NO. 51. The frame of this rifle was drop-forged, engraved, and casehardened. Action was 44½ type. The stock was extra fancy Swiss pattern, with cheekpiece. Stock and forearm were of fancy walnut fully checkered and highly finished. Length was 13 inches; drop, 3½ inches. This model was made for all cartridges as listed previously. Double-set triggers and H sights were standard, and there was no rear barrel slot. Lever was spur loop type #5.

Weights and prices were:

30-inch barrel, 12 pounds; with G or H sights	$58.00
32-inch barrel, 12½ pounds; with G or H sights	60.00
34-inch barrel, 12¾ pounds; with G or H sights	62.00
Palm rest, extra	5.00
False muzzle and bullet starter, extra	15.00

STEVENS IDEAL SCHUETZEN JUNIOR No. 52. This rifle was drop-forged, engraved, and casehardened. Action was 44½ type, of course. The lever was loop type, and double-set triggers were standard. The stock was cheekpiece, pistol-grip type, of fancy walnut, varnished and checkered. The butt plate was special heavy Schuetzen type #4. This model was made in all calibers as listed in previous models. H type sights were standard.

Weights and prices were:

30-inch barrel, 11 pounds	$54.00
32-inch barrel, 11½ pounds	56.00
Palm rest, extra	5.00
Extra interchangeable barrel, up to 30 inches long, with fancy forearm checkered, globe front sight and interchangeable disc	18.00
Extra lengths of barrel over 30 inches, per inch	1.00

For Stevens-Pope equipment the buyer was advised to see the official Stevens-Pope catalog.

STEVENS IDEAL SCHUETZEN SPECIAL No. 54. This was the highest grade Ideal listed, with animal figure engraving on the 44½ type frame. The stock was of extra fancy walnut, straight-grip style with cheekpiece and special heavy Swiss butt plate, casehardened. Lever was the special #6, and double-set triggers were standard. Stock and forearm were finely checkered and highly finished. This model was made in all calibers as described previously. H sights were standard equipment.

Weights and prices were:

30-inch barrel, 11¼ pounds	$68.00
32-inch barrel, 11¾ pounds	70.00
False muzzle and bullet starter, extra	15.00
Palm rest, extra	5.00

For Stevens-Pope equipment the Special Stevens-Pope catalog was suggested for this model also. About this model the No. 51 catalog states:

This model was designed to meet all the requirements of riflemen who want the best. No expense has been spared to attain this end. The best points of the most approved models have been adopted, making this the most complete rifle ever made for the style of shooting in vogue among German riflemen. Every rifle is carefully tested from a machine rest, and a 3½-inch group of 10 shots must be made at 200 yards, using the .28/30, .32/40, or .38/55 cartridges to pass inspection.

STEVENS IDEAL LADIES MODEL No. 55. This was still listed in the No. 51 catalog as being made on the 44 type of action. It had a 24-inch half-octagonal barrel in .22 Short rim-fire, .22 Long Rifle rim-fire, .22/7/45 WRF, .25 Stevens rim-fire, .32 Long rim-fire, and .22/15/60 Stevens center-fire (its only center-fire) calibers.

The stock was pistol-grip style, in fancy selected walnut, highly finished and finely checkered, with #2 Swiss butt plate, casehardened. A rifle butt plate or a rubber shotgun butt plate were also available at no extra price. Sights were D type as standard. Weight with standard barrel and Swiss butt plate was 5½ pounds. Price with 24-inch barrel was $25; with 26-inch barrel, $27.

This was a fine, light-weight, graceful ladies' rifle, or a model pleasing to anyone wishing a rifle of this weight and finish.

This completes the entire line offered on the 44½ type action at this time. The Stevens pocket, or bicycle, rifles were continued with the exception of the Model No. 39, the New Model Shotgun, which was discontinued. The Stevens Gould No. 37 and the Conlin No. 38 were also discontinued in the No. 51 catalog.

The extras for the Stevens Ideal No. 44½ series of models were, with almost no exceptions, the same as those listed for the earlier No. 44 models.

The Stevens No. 52 catalog listed all the models previously described as in the No. 51, and it also carried the new No. 56 Ladies

Model on the same thin O44½ action as the English Model. This was a deluxe model, with pistol-grip stock of fancy walnut, checkered grip and fore end in a fancy pattern, highly finished, and with a #2 Swiss butt plate, casehardened or nickeled, as ordered. The barrel was the same #1 weight, half-octagonal, small-shanked type as was carried on the O44½ English model, and it was listed in the same calibers as the English model. The barrels were 24 inches long in rim-fire caliber and 26 inches long in the center-fire sizes. Standard sights were the D type, and the price was $30 in the standard model. The weight with #2 Swiss butt plate was 6½ pounds; with the rifle butt or hard-rubber shotgun butt plates, which were optional, the weight was slightly less.

In the No. 52 catalog the No. 55 Ladies Model as made on the 44 action was not listed, having evidently been dropped from the line.

Two new models for prone gallery shooting were introduced in this catalog, however, and they are the following.

IDEAL ARMORY MODEL NO. 414. This was a 26-inch round-barrel model made up on the 44 type action for .22 Long Rifle gallery or club shooting. The regular plain No. 1 lever was used on this model, as was also the automatic ejector. The stock was straight-grip type, with hard-rubber shotgun butt plate. The forearm was semi-beavertail type, with a band and swivel for a sling strap. A swivel on the butt stock was also provided. The fore end extended beyond the swivel to within a few inches of the muzzle, but there was no band at the tip. The sights were Rocky Mountain front and Lyman receiver, the latter made especially for this model. This rifle weighed about 8 pounds with sling, and was listed at $12.

STEVENS IDEAL SEMI-MILITARY MODEL NO. 404. This rifle was made up on the regular 44½ type action, with automatic ejector, round 28-inch barrel made for the .22 rim-fire caliber only. The stock was straight-grip type uncheckered, with shotgun butt. The length was 13 inches; the drop, 3 inches at the heel. The forearm was large type, 12 inches long, and checkered. The swivel base for the snap swivel was mortised into the under side of the barrel about 2 inches ahead of the end of the forearm. The sights were No. 210 globe interchangeable front and No. 42 Lyman rear mounted on the side of the action frame. This model was made only in .22 Short or .22 Long Rifle, and it weighed about 8 pounds. It was priced at $27. (See page 65.)

REBORING BARRELS

The Stevens No. 51 catalog offered the following reboring services:

We make a specialty of reboring old and worn-out barrels, of our own and other makes. When a rebored barrel leaves our shop it is guaranteed to shoot as well as a new arm using the same cartridge.

We cannot rebore repeating rifles, Floberts, Stevens Reliable Pocket rifles, and Diamond Model pistols.

Rifles of .32 rim- or center-fire and the .32/20 can be bored up to the .32 Ideal.

Rifles of .38 rim- or center-fire can be bored up to the .38/55, as the diameter of the latter is greater.

Both of these can be bored up to the .38/40, which has the greatest diameter of any .38 caliber.

Prices for reboring Stevens barrels:

Boring up .22 caliber rim-fire rifles, Nos. 1 to 16; Hunter's Pet or Ideal, to Stevens .25 rim-fire; .32 or .38 Long rim-fire, including browning and refinishing barrel which is necessary, $3.50.

Same work on New Model Pocket Rifle, $3.00.

Same work on Lord, Conlin, and Gould pistols, $3.00.

Stevens rim-fire rifles, Nos. 1 to 16, bored to, and firing pin changed for, the .25/20, .25/21, .25/25, .28/30, .32/20, .32 Long, .32/40, .32 Ideal, .38 Long, .38/55, or .38/40. This requires replating of frame. $6.00.

The same work on Hunter's Pet to take either of the .25 caliber, .32 Long, .32/20, .32 Ideal, or .38 Long center-fire cartridges, $6.00.

Stevens .22 rim-fire Ideal rifles rebored to any of the above center-fire cartridges; also for the .40/70 Ballard 2⅜-inch Straight shell, when weight of barrel will permit. This necessitates a new breech block. $6.00.

Boring up center-fire Stevens, Nos. 1 to 16, Hunter's Pet or Ideal, to any of the above center-fire cartridges for which weight of barrel is suitable, $3.50.

Reboring Stevens gallery pistols, $3.00.

Rifle barrels can be turned down to lighten them.

Price of turning down, rebrowning, and cutting sight slots, Stevens rifles, $3.00.

Other makes, $4.00.

REBORING RIFLES OF OTHER MAKES

Rim-fire .22 caliber rifles of other makes than Stevens, bored up to Stevens, .25 rim-fire or .32 Long rim-fire (except Ballard rifles, the chamber of which it is necessary to bush, if bored larger than .25 Stevens rim-fire, which will cost $2.50 extra), $7.00.

Rim-fire rifles of other makes than Stevens, bored to, and firing pin changed for, any of the .25, .32 and .38 caliber center-fire cartridges mentioned on preceding page, for which barrels are heavy enough, $10.00.

(.22 Ballards when brushing of chamber is necessary, $2.50 extra.)

Many Ballard rifles are fitted with "reversible" firing pins. Such rifles can be bored for center-fire cartridges at the regular charge of $7.00; no extra charge for changing firing pin.

Center-fire rifles of other makes than Stevens, when barrels are heavy enough, rebored to any of the following cartridges: .25/20, .25/21, .25/25, .28/30, .32 Ideal, .32/20, .32/40, .38/40, .38/55, .40/70 Ballard 2⅜-inch shell, .44/40, $7.00.

Maynard rifles that are center-fire and have sufficient metal in barrels can be bored for any of the different sizes of cartridges enumerated above, $7.00.

NEW BARRELS

New barrels, 24 to 34 inches in length, bored for any of the following cartridges, will be fitted to center-fire actions, in Ballard, Sharps hammerless, Remington and Winchester single-shot actions, using old fore ends: .22 Short, .22 Long Rifle, .25 Stevens rim-fire, .32 Long rim-fire, .38 Long rim-fire, .25/20, .25/21, .25/25, .28/30, .32 Long, .32/20, .32/40, .32 Ideal, .38/55, .38/40, .40/70/330 Ballard center-fire cartridges, $12.00 to $17.00, depending on length and weight.

SPECIAL STEVENS CARTRIDGES

The Stevens company was responsible for introducing many fine cartridges in the target and small-game category. The earliest of these were, of course, the .38/35, .38/45, .44/50, and .44/65 Stevens Everlasting cases as first used in the tip-up model rifles and pocket model shotguns.

The .38/35 and .38/45 may have been loaded in lead bullet style at one time, but they and the .44/50 and .44/65 are best known as shot shells for the pocket shotgun. These cartridge cases are quite rare today. They are pictured on page 57 along with other special Stevens sizes described further on in this chapter.

The Stevens company is also given credit by most authorities as having introduced the .22 Long Rifle cartridge.[7] They also designed

---

[7] Townsend Whelen in the *American Rifle* writes: "When the enterprising Stevens Arms and Tool Company, aided by the Union Metallic Cartridge Company,

and introduced the .32/35 Stevens taper cartridge as used in the early tip-up models. This cartridge was also adopted and used extensively by the Maynard rifle manufacturers.

The famous .25 rim-fire is another Stevens cartridge, and it is still quite popular.

The .25/20 single-shot cartridge was probably first obtainable commercially in the 44 Ideal and tip-up rifles. For a complete history of the development of this particular cartridge see H. A. Donaldson's article in the *American Rifleman* magazine for January, 1936.

The very fine series of straight-cased cartridges such as the .22/15/60 Stevens, .25/21/86 Stevens, .25/25/86 Stevens, .28/30/120 Stevens, and .32 Ideal were all first obtainable in the Stevens rifles. These cartridges were not all designed by the Stevens company, but to it credit is generally given for them. At any rate, this company no doubt did quite a lot of pioneering and engineering on these cartridges and produced fine, accurate rifles for them.

A detailed discussion of these Stevens cartridges as I have known them may not be amiss at this point.

THE .22/15/60 STEVENS CARTRIDGE. This little .22 center-fire cartridge was designed by Mr. Charles H. Herrick of Winchester, Mass., and was introduced in Stevens model 44 rifles in 1896. The case is 2 inches long and straight inside and nearly so outside, having very little taper. It takes the small rifle primer and was originally primed with the #1½ brass primer.

After collecting a succession of Stevens model 44 rifles I finally obtained a model 45/44½ with 28-inch #2 half-octagonal barrel, perfect inside, and with single trigger. At first I had no 60-grain .226 bullet mold, so used the .228 45-grain WCF bullet, and with #6½ Remington primers and 5-grains weight of #80 powder behind the 45-grain bullet *unsized*, this 45/44½ model shot into dime-size groups at 50 and 75 yards; in fact, many groups were even smaller. And there was no more recoil or report than with a .22 Long Rifle hi-speed cartridge. This became a very favorite hunting rifle with me for small game, and accounted for many squirrels and crows and other so-called varments. I recapped and decapped the cases on a Belding and Mull Model 26 tool, and seated the bullets with a bul-

originated the .22 Long Rifle cartridge, it was necessary to quicken the twist in the rifles in which this cartridge was shot from one turn in 25 inches to one turn in 16 inches."

let seater which this firm made up for me. Later I obtained a set of Ideal adjustable tong type tools and a 60-grain bullet mold for the standard #22636 bullet; and this bullet ahead of 5½ or 6 grains of #80 powder was a more accurate load at 100 yards than the 45-grain .22 WCF, but of course not quite so speedy a load, and I really prefer the 45-grain bullet. My barrel measures .225 and has the standard 12-inch twist for this caliber; however, some of these barrels were made with a 14-inch twist especially for the 45-grain bullet.

I also own a Stevens Ideal No. 56 Ladies Model in this .22/15/60 caliber, and as it weighs just 6 pounds, it is a very light, handy little rifle for woods rambling.

THE .22 EXTRA LONG CENTER-FIRE CARTRIDGE. This was the old Maynard cartridge, and it was used for the most part in that rifle. However, there were some Stevens Ideal rifles chambered for it, and I have an English Model O44½ in this caliber with 26-inch #1 barrel.

These cases are very small at the head, and although most of them will accept the small rifle-size primer, there isn't much brass left, and consequently primer pockets stretch quite a lot and the webs of the cases give way quite often. This cartridge was made originally with the No. 0 primer. Cases and cartridges are not particularly hard to find in this size; the hard job is to locate a rifle with a good barrel for them.

I was never able to buy Ideal or Maynard tools for this case, but recapped and decapped my cases with the Ideal No. 2 tool, holding the cases with a new cradle which a machinist friend made for me. Bullets were seated with the fingers, and the case, of course, was uncrimped.

My barrel measures .227 and I use the 45-grain .22 WCF bullet with #6½ or #116 Winchester primers and 4 or 4½ grains of #80 powder. I have also used the same weight charges of #4227 with sometimes better results, sometimes inferior results. Maynard catalogs state that this case was loaded with from 8 to 10 grains of powder.

This cartridge seems to be rather erratic when loaded with smokeless powder; at least, it proved to be so in my rifle. Although I dislike black powder in these small sizes, I loaded some cartridges with 7 grains of FFFG black and the 45-grain bullet cast 1-40 and had somewhat better results. However, I still have much more experimenting to do with this particular cartridge before I am to be thoroughly satisfied.[8]

Some of the Maynard .22 Extra Long center-fire cartridges were loaded with a paper-patch bullet, but I have always felt that .22 cast bullets were tedious enough to cast and lubricate without driving myself completely loco trying to patch .22 caliber bullets, even if I had a mold for them.

This cartridge case is 1$\frac{5}{32}$ inches long.

THE .25/21/86 AND .25/25/86 STEVENS CARTRIDGES. The .25/25 Stevens was first made up by the Ideal Manufacturing Company and introduced in Stevens rifles.

The older Ideal handbooks have the following to say regarding these sizes:

> Not being satisfied with either of the above .25 calibers [.25/20 single-shot and .25/20 repeater], Captain W. L. Carpenter of the 9th U. S. Infantry called on our Mr. Barlow, who made for him, from a solid brass rod, the first model shell, which has since become famous as the .25/25 Stevens; so called because the Stevens Arms Company made the first rifle for it. There is now another modification of it called the .25/21 Stevens, which is the same shell shortened and loaded with 21 grains of powder instead of 25 grains. Both of these cartridges use the same bullets as the .25/20 cartridges.

My .25/25 rifle is a model 47-44½ Stevens with a special order #3 32-inch barrel and double-set triggers. This barrel has a perfect chamber, and therefore extracts perfectly, which many specimens in this long .25 caliber do not. I used the standard Ideal bullet #25720 in my .2565-inch diameter barrel with #6½ primers and 7-grains weight #80 powder for fine accuracy at 100 and 125 yards. These are the longest distances I have shot this caliber, and at these distances, it is superbly accurate. These standard 86-grain bullets were cast about 1-16.

I later obtained a perfect .25/21 barrel which I use interchangeably on this action, the same extractor serving for both cases, of course. In the .25/21 barrel this 7-grain load shoots well but not to so small a group as the .25/25. Also I found that #1204 powder

---

[8] Most writers of the '80s and '90s state that this was a far more accurate cartridge at 200 yards than the .22 WCF size.

seemed to be better suited to it. I have never tried #4227 powder but believe it should be even better.

To recap and decap these .25/21 and .25/25 cases I used an old Ideal #2 tool which was made in these sizes. Bullets were seated friction tight in the mouth of uncrimped cases with Belding and Mull die-and-plunger type bullet seaters. None of these Stevens straight cases should be crimped.

For maximum accuracy in the .25/21 and .25/25 cases, the bullets should be seated $\frac{1}{32}$-inch to $\frac{1}{16}$-inch ahead of the case in the breech, and the case mouth closed with a felt wad. I used wads cut from an old felt hat with a wad cutter supplied by Belding and Mull.

The length of the .25/21 case is $2\frac{1}{16}$ inches, and that of the .25/25 is $2\frac{3}{8}$ inches. The .25/25 case may, of course, be cut off the necessary amount and used in .25/21 chambers.

THE .28/30/120 CARTRIDGE. This cartridge was also designed by Mr. Charles H. Herrick of Winchester, Mass., and was first introduced by the Stevens company in their rifles. The case is 2½ inches long, and straight inside, as the rest of the Stevens straight cases were. I have never seen this case made for any but the large rifle primer, and believe they were all made that way.

This was an extremely popular cartridge and an exceptionally accurate one. It was a favorite cartridge with H. M. Pope and other barrelmakers. This .28/30 case and the .25/21 case were used in a great many fine target barrels made by these custom rifle makers.

My .28/30 Stevens rifle is a model 45-44½, with 30-inch #3 half-octagonal barrel, perfect inside, and with double-set triggers. It uses the standard 120-grain Ideal bullet #285221 and 8 or 9 grains of Dupont's shotgun smokeless powder, with a card wad over the powder. The bullet is seated in the breech of the barrel ahead of the case. With muzzle and elbow rest, at 100 yards the group will average 1 inch or smaller, consistently. The sighting equipment used was usually a Malcolm 8x scope.

This is an easy cartridge to load and light in recoil, and the results are always amazing when care is used in assembling its component parts.

I have a mold for the sharp pointed Ideal bullet #285222, which is a small-game bullet, but I have never tried this cartridge on game. It was, however, at one time a very popular woodchuck and small-game caliber.

The other .28/30 rifle I have is a Remington Hepburn #3 with double-set triggers and 28-inch #2 full-octagonal barrel. This rifle was originally a .22 WCF caliber, but was recut and rifled to the .28/30/120 cartridge years ago by the Stevens company when they were doing work of this kind. This barrel is not quite so perfect inside as the No. 45 Stevens barrel, for the reason that some previous owner failed to take the best care of it. However, with #80 powder, which it seems to prefer, it shoots almost as well as the perfect Stevens barrel. I usually load the bullets in the case with an Ideal tool in this caliber, and use this as a hunting rifle, which purpose it fills admirably, being of lighter weight than the Stevens No. 45 job.

These .28/30 Stevens cases are 2½ inches long. They are becoming more scarce every year, and I have not been able to find any other size case that may be adapted to my rifle.

THE .32/35 STEVENS TAPER CARTRIDGE. This particular cartridge was, of course, a Stevens caliber originating in the tip-up series of rifles. It was an extremely accurate cartridge and, as a consequence, popular with riflemen. Many of the Maynard rifles were chambered for this size. In my Stevens Premier tip-up rifle chambered for this .32/35 I have always used some Everlasting shells that came with the rifle and FFG black powder, 30 grains behind the Ideal #3117 153-grain bullet, which is the standard bullet for this cartridge.

My tip-up barrel measures .309 in the grooves, and the bullet as cast seems to be about perfect for it. This cartridge was formerly used either with the patched or grooved bullet, but I have never obtained just the right size patch bullet mold to try it this way.

The .32/40 smooth ball is, of course, too large to be used in this .32/35, which falls really in the .30-caliber class.

I looked for years for a Stevens 44½ rifle in this caliber before finding one, though in the meantime I did run across several 44 Stevens models. The No. 51 catalog lists this caliber as being made in the basic 44½ model, and eventually I located a Model 45-44½ with double-set triggers and the standard #2 28-inch barrel in new condition. This rifle is in beautiful condition and, being in the 44½ type action, is naturally strong enough for smokeless loads. Ideal tools came with the rifle.

My most accurate load in this barrel was the regular, or Everlasting, case with #6½ Remington primers, 9-grains weight of Dupont #80 powder, and the 153-grain bullet seated in the breech ahead of the case about ⅟₃₂-inch. I have also used Dupont's shotgun smokeless with fine results. The .32/20 Standard 115-grain bullet is also adaptable to this caliber, being also .311 diameter, and for ranges up to about 100 yards it is sufficiently accurate.

This barrel measures .310 in the grooves, so I use the regular .3117 Ideal 153-grain bullet without sizing, cast 1-16.

My Maynard No. 16 rifle in .32/35 Stevens caliber measures .3095, and although a perfect barrel, I have never been able to obtain quite as good results from it as from the Model 45-44½ Stevens; possibly one reason is because of the fine Stevens set triggers and fine target sights.

This old .32/35 Stevens taper cartridge is a nice one to reload. It is very accurate and has a very mild recoil compared to the .32/40 and the .38/55. Also it is fully as accurate as these larger sizes. This case length is 1⅞ inches.

THE .32 IDEAL CARTRIDGE. Many Stevens Ideal and Winchester single-shot rifles are found today chambered for this .32 Ideal cartridge. After acquiring a series of Winchester single-shots and Stevens Ideals with not too good barrels, I finally found a nice Model 45-44½ Stevens with 28-inch #3 half-octagonal barrel that was almost perfect in the bore. With the rifle came an Ideal combination tool and mold for this cartridge, and a quantity of cases.

So after experimenting for some time I eventually had the outfit shooting with fair accuracy. I used the Remington #6½ primers, and usually had the best results with 7 to 8 grains of #80 powder. The 150-grain bullet cast 1-15 was seated in the case with the Ideal tool, and of course uncrimped. It seemed to give no better accuracy with the bullet seated in the breech ahead of the case and a card wad over the powder, unless Dupont's bulk shotgun smokeless powder was used. With this powder, using from 8½ to 9 grains, and the bullet seated ahead, it gave slightly better accuracy but not, however, as good as should have been expected.

About this time a friend was using a Winchester high-side with 28-inch #3 barrel for the .32 Ideal cartridge, and this particular rifle would not group with anything we tried in it. We used bullets of 75 grains, 100 grains, 125 grains, and the regular 150-grain .32 Ideal bullet, all cast in an Ideal Perfection adjustable mold, with a great variety of powder charges. But for some reason or other this particular barrel would not give more than accuracy of about 2 to

2¼ inches at 100 yards. The barrel was of correct bore size and 18-inch twist, the same as my Stevens No. 45 barrel, but the Stevens with plain trigger outshot the set trigger Winchester consistently.

The early Ideal handbooks have the following comments to make concerning this .32 Ideal cartridge:

> The shell and bullets shown here are new ones designed by our Mr. Barlow and first made for us by the Union Metallic Cartridge Co., who are always ready to help the crank with any new cartridge that can be proved to have merit in it, or that may appear to have a future for it. The shell is 1¾ inches long, is straight inside and outside, has a solid head and strong pocket equal to the everlasting shells. Round bullets or the lighter grooved bullets cast in Perfection mold may be seated down upon the powder within the shell, a desirable feature not obtainable with the common bottle necked shells. For description of bullets for this shell, and rifles adapted to this size see those illustrated and numbered .323 etc. The Standard .32 Ideal shell as made by the U. M. C. Co. is this shell with 25 grains of powder, and 150 grain bullet seated to cover all grooves and no crimp. The diameter of the bullet is .323 which fills a niche that has long been vacant, namely:—a desirable center fire, inside lubricated cartridge that the thousands of .32 caliber, short, long and extra long, rim- and center-fire rifles that have been shot out or rusted, may now be rebored, rifled and chambered for the .32 Ideal cartridge (also .32/20 barrels): thus converting a discarded and useless weapon into an Ideal rifle. Those who have arms of any caliber to be rebored, rifled and chambered, we would respectfully refer to the J. Stevens Arms and Tool Co. of Chicopee Falls, Mass., who are prepared to do this work in a satisfactory manner and as reasonable as possible.
>
> The .32 Ideal cartridge has now become a popular one for the Stevens and Winchester single shot rifles.

Stevens rifles were, of course, made for other and larger cartridges than these described. They were made in .32/40 and .44/40 WCF and in many other calibers, but these sizes are much too common to necessitate going into detail here. The special Stevens sizes are the ones we are interested in now.

Stevens had no reloading tools or molds of their own manufacture—that is, unless you would consider the Stevens-Pope accessories as such—and so the Ideal Manufacturing Company furnished their excellent tools and molds especially adapted for all Stevens sizes.

The early Ideal Handbooks give invaluable data on loading these cartridges and should be studied assiduously.

PHOTOGRAPHS OF STEVENS RIFLES

Actual photographs of most of the Stevens models are shown on pages 78 to 80.

FIGURE A. Stevens Premier #8 rifle .22 rim-fire caliber.

FIGURE B. Stevens Range Model rifle .32/40 B and M caliber. This rifle is specially factory engraved.

FIGURE C. Stevens Ideal English Model O44½, caliber .22 Extra Long center-fire. Stevens full-length telescope.

FIGURE D. Stevens Ideal No. 44½ rifle, caliber .22 rim-fire, with #2 Swiss butt plate. Below D is shown the later 44½ in .25/21 caliber with rifle butt plate.

FIGURE E. Stevens Ideal No. 45 rifle, caliber .32/35. This has the regular #2 barrel and #2 Swiss butt plate; also double-set triggers.

FIGURE F. Stevens Ideal No. 45, caliber .22/15/60, with #3 barrel and #3 Swiss butt plate.

FIGURE G. Stevens Ideal No. 45, caliber .32 Ideal.

FIGURE H. Stevens Ideal No. 47, caliber .25/25 and extra barrel for .25/21 cartridge. This is the regular model 47 with extra length barrel, 32 inches, double-set triggers, and #2 lever.

FIGURE I. Stevens Ideal No. 45, caliber .28/30/120. This rifle has a 30-inch barrel, #3 Swiss butt plate, and double-set triggers.

FIGURE J. Stevens Ideal No. 49 Walnut Hill, .25/20 single-shot caliber, engraved frame.

FIGURE K. Stevens Ideal No. 51 Schuetzen on the heavy Schuetzen 44 action, with Stevens pre-Pope palm rest, etc., .32/40 caliber. Model 51 in 44½ type is made on the same pattern as this specimen.

FIGURE L. Stevens Ideal No. 52 Schuetzen Junior, with 30-inch #5 Stevens-Pope barrel, .32/40 caliber.

FIGURE M. Stevens Ideal Schuetzen Special No. 54 rifle with Stevens-Pope palm rest and Stevens 3x telescope, .22 Long Rifle, with extra barrel for the .22 Short. Animal engraved frame. This specimen is one of the very last made in 44½ type with the automatic extractor in .22 rim-fire caliber, necessitating an extra screw through the frame for a spring plunger base.

FIGURE N. Stevens Ideal Ladies Model No. 56 in .22/15/60 Stevens caliber.

This collection represents all the models in 44½ type, the only 44 type being Figure K, the Model 51 Schuetzen.

The English Model, Figure C, and the Ladies Model, Figure N, are both on the O44½, or thin 44½, type action. The four engraved models as regularly made at the factory are shown in Models 49, 51, 52, and 54, figures J, K, L, and M. Close-ups of the engraving on these models will be found on pages 68, 70 and 71.

The special Stevens cartridges will be found on pages 55, 56 and 57.

The various levers and butt plates as supplied on the Ideal 44 and Ideal 44½ series of models are shown on page 91.

This concludes the story of Stevens rifles as I can tell it. I believe all the models that interest serious collectors and shooters will be found to be described sufficiently and so illustrated on page 63 that they may be readily identified.

There were many Stevens rifles made to order, of course, as there were models of other makes so constructed, but we are concerned herein with models as offered in the catalogs.

The fact that the 44½ type action was ever discontinued is certainly to be bemoaned by all who are interested in these rifles. If made with just a trifle heavier side walls and a better firing pin retractor than the one used on some models, and with blued heat-treated finish instead of the casehardened finish, we should have actions that are capable of standing up to almost any modern cartridge we wished to use in them. As it is, they are amply strong for most of the small game and varment cartridges in favor today, and I have one plain 44½ action that was barreled in .30/30 caliber and it handles this cartridge in perfect safety.

The 44½ action is so much easier to load under a low-mounted scope than other actions—such as Winchester and Sharps Borchardt —that there is no comparison between them.

On some 44½ actions the tip or spur of the hammer interfered somewhat with the cleaning rod, but not many are so found, and this is, of course, easily remedied.

Some men object to the Stevens Ideal action because of the slant of the firing pin or because of some screw slots in the heads being off center, but we cannot condemn the design for these reasons, and the off-center slots in screw heads are usually found only on the plain basic models which sold for $12.

III

Remington Single-shot Rifles

ROLLING-BLOCK RIFLES

REMINGTON single-shot rifles have played a very large part on the target ranges and in the game fields of this country. They are the product of the Remington Arms Company, the oldest firearms house in continuous existence in the United States. The firm was founded by E. Remington in 1816, and the story of its growth to the present size and importance of the company reads like a novel. The rifles described in this chapter were early models, appearing about the years 1873 and 1880.

The Remington-Rider rolling-block rifle was first made by E. Remington & Son at Middletown, Connecticut. This was the split-breech rim-fire type patented in 1863. The rolling-block action design is shown on the page opposite.

These models were at first all made in military pattern, of course, and it was not until the year 1873 that the main line of sporting and target rifles appeared.

The rolling-block 1871 pattern of rifle was made at the Springfield Armory and also at the Remington factory in Ilion, New York. My specimen of this 1871 model was made at the Springfield Armory in 1871. It has a 36-inch round barrel with three grooves and lands, and is .50/70 Gov't.-1¾" caliber. It has the special safety feature found on some of these rifles, in which the hammer slides down to a safety notch when the breechblock is rolled shut upon a cartridge. The hammer must be again moved back to full cock before it may be released by the trigger to fire the rifle.

No. 1 SPORTING RIFLE. This seems to have been the first sporting rifle to appear in any quantity on the rolling-block action. It was introduced about 1869 or 1870, and was made in frames of several sizes and in a great variety of calibers. It was discontinued around

1889. L. D. Satterlee in *A Catalogue of Firearms for the Collector* lists the No. 1 Sporting Rifle as made in the following special calibers:

.22 Long rim-fire
.22 Extra Long rim-fire
.32 Long rim-fire
.32 Extra Long rim-fire
.32/20 WCF
.32/40/150 Remington
.38 Short and Long and Extra Long rim-fires
.38/40 WCF
.38/40/245 Remington straight
.40/45 Sharps and Remington straight 1⅞-inch case
.40/50 Sharps bottleneck
.40/70 Sharps bottleneck
.40/65 Remington straight [which of course was the .40/70 Sharps Straight case 2½ inches in length]
.44 Short and long rim-fire
.44 Long center-fire
.44 S & W American center-fire
.44/77 Sharps bottleneck
.44/40 WCF
.45/70 Gov't.
.46 Long rim-fire
.58 Gov't. rim-fire
.50/70 Gov't. rim-fire
.50/70 Gov't. center-fire

Satterlee also lists the No. 1 Sporting Rifle as introduced in .45 Peabody Sporting center-fire in 1871 under the name of *Adirondack Model*.

REMINGTON DEER RIFLE. This was introduced in 1872, in .46 Long rim-fire, with a 24-inch barrel weighing 6½ pounds. [Satterlee]

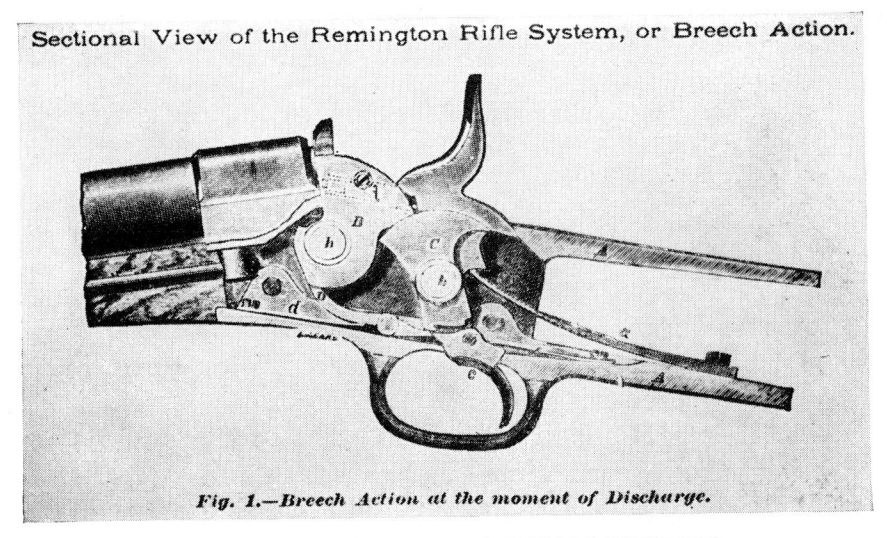

Sectional View of the Remington Rifle System, or Breech Action.

Fig. 1.—Breech Action at the moment of Discharge.

REMINGTON-RIDER ACTION DESIGN

REMINGTON BUFFALO RIFLE. Introduced in 1872. This is a heavier model than the Deer Rifle, in .40/50 Sharps bottleneck, .40/70 Sharps bottleneck, and .50/70 Gov't. center-fire calibers, with a 30-inch round or octagonal barrel. This model enjoyed a mild popularity with the buffalo runners on the plains. [Satterlee]

REMINGTON BLACK HILLS RIFLE. Introduced in 1877. This was in .45/70 caliber with 28-inch round barrel. Weight of this model was 7½ pounds. [Satterlee]

These models are comparatively rare today and I have not been fortunate enough to find all of them as so described.

I have one No. 1 Remington Sporting or Buffalo Rifle, with the heavy octagonal receiver ring which has a heavy full-octagonal 30-inch barrel in the .50/70 Gov't. caliber; however, the customary E. Remington & Son stamp on the barrel is lacking. The only mark on this barrel is the serial number—which, incidentally, is the same as that on the action—and the word "Slotter," which is stamped on the left barrel flat from the top at the breech just ahead of the receiver.

This rifle has a plain straight-grip stock and fore end of plain walnut—in rather poor condition—and plain sporting sights. There has been a tang rear sight at one time but this is now missing.

My 1883 E. Remington & Son catalog lists the following models.

REMINGTON MILITARY BREECH-LOADING RIFLE. In rolling-block pattern. To quote from page 6 of the catalog: "Adopted by nine different governments; unequalled for simplicity, strength, durability and rapidity of fire." This model is shown with both angular and saber bayonets, in calibers of .43, .45, .50 and .58 center-fire. The carbine was listed as being made in .43 and .45 center-fire and .50 center- and rim-fire.

Page 7 of the catalog gives a "List of Military Rifles" as follows.

EGYPTIAN RIFLE. Caliber, .433 (11mm.). Saber bayonet. Weight without bayonet, 9 lbs. 4 oz.; with bayonet, 10 lbs. 14 oz. Barrel length, 35.2 inches. Length of rifle, 50.2 inches.

SPANISH RIFLE. Caliber, .433 (11mm.). Made for Spanish .43 cartridge. Angular bayonet. Barrel length, 35.2 inches. Gun length, 50.2 inches. Weight without bayonet, 9 lbs. 4 oz.; with bayonet, 10 lbs. 4 oz.

CIVIL GUARD. Made for Spanish .43 cartridge. Angular bayonet. Barrel length, 30.34 inches. Gun length, 45.35 inches. Weight, with bayonet, 10 lbs. 4 oz.

UNITED STATES MODEL. Caliber .50. Angular bayonet. Barrel length, 32.5 inches. Gun length, 47.5 inches. Weight without bayonet, 9 lbs. 1 oz.; with bayonet, 9 lbs. 15 oz.

SPRINGFIELD MODEL CALIBER .58. Angular bayonet. Barrel length, 36 inches. Gun length, 54.75 inches. Weight without bayonet, 9 lbs. 11 oz.; with bayonet, 10 lbs. 9 oz.

SPRINGFIELD MODEL CALIBER .58 SHORT. Angular bayonet. Barrel length, 36 inches. Gun length, 51.75 inches. Weight without bayonet, 9 lbs. 8 oz.; with bayonet, 10 lbs. 6 oz.

CARBINE. Caliber .50 and caliber .433. Barrel length, 20.5 inches. Carbine length, 35.5 inches. Weight, 7 lbs.

Page 15 of this 1883 catalog shows the following.

LONG RANGE CREEDMOOR RIFLE. Rolling-block action. Price list:

A—Pistol-grip stock, vernier and wind-gauge sights, spirit level, and 2 extra discs	$ 80.00
B—Same as A except rubber tip and butt and checkered fore end, including spirit level and 2 extra discs	100.00
C—Same as B except curly, polished stock and extra finish throughout	125.00

Spirit level extra when not mentioned above, $3.00
Wind-gauge sight discs, extra, each, $1.00

This action shown on the Creedmoor rolling-block type has a heavy type frame, octagonal receiver ring, and full-octagonal barrel, and shotgun butt stock.

SPORTING RIFLE No. 1. To quote from the catalog: "Sporting or target rifles using cartridges of the following sizes: .22, .32, .38, .40, .44, .45 and .50 calibers, either rim or center fire as may be adapted to same."

Sporting stock, open sights, 26-inch barrel	$20.00
For each 2 additional inches length of barrel	1.00

SHORT RANGE RIFLE No. 1. Using the following cartridges:

    .38 Extra Long center- or rim-fire
    .40 caliber, 50 grains, center-fire only
    .44 caliber, S & W, center-fire only
    .44 Extra Long rim- or center-fire
    .46 rim-fire only

A—Sporting stock; sights, combination peep and open rear, and Beach front.
    Price: 26-inch barrel length $24.00
           28-inch barrel length   25.00

B—Sporting stock; sights, tang peep rear and Beach front.
    Price: 26-inch barrel length   25.50
           28-inch barrel length   26.50

C—Creedmoor pistol-grip stock; sights, tang peep rear and Beach front.
    Price: 26-inch barrel length   30.50
           28-inch barrel length   31.50

D—Creedmoor pistol-grip stock; sights, vernier rear and Beach front.
    Price: 26-inch barrel length   37.00
           28-inch barrel length   38.00

E—Creedmoor pistol-grip stock; sights, vernier rear and wind-gauge front.
    Price: 26-inch barrel length $39.00
           28-inch barrel length   40.00

MID RANGE RIFLE No. 1. Using the following center-fire cartridges: .40/70, .44/77, .45/70, .50/70. This rifle was made in the same five grades as the Short Range.

Following are the prices in the two barrel lengths:

	28-inch	30-inch
A	$25.00	$26.00
B	26.50	27.50
C	31.50	32.50
D	33.50	34.50
E	40.00	41.00

REMINGTON SINGLE-SHOT RIFLES 119

This rifle was also made in grade F with Creedmoor pistol-grip stock, vernier rear and wind-gauge front sights, rubber butt and tip, and checkered fore end. Barrel lengths and prices were:

28-inch	$45.00
30-inch	46.00

SPORTING RIFLE No. 2. Catalog states: "This rifle cannot be used with set triggers. (Please note that in the manipulation of these rifles, throwing down lever, tipping up barrels is entirely avoided.)" The stock was plain finish; sights were plain; calibers were .22, .32, .38, and .44 rim- or center-fire. Weight was 5 to 6 lbs. Barrel lengths and prices were as follows:

24 or 26 inches	$20.00
28 inches	21.00
30 inches	22.00

For tang peep and Beach front sight, extra, $5.50

To quote the catalog: "These rifles are specially adapted for small game and gallery practice, note the large reduction in price."

The illustration shows full-octagonal barrel with a shorter barrel housing ring with round receiver top. On this model the barrel is inlet into the forearm very shallowly. The stock is plain straight-grip type, with Remington type rifle butt plate.

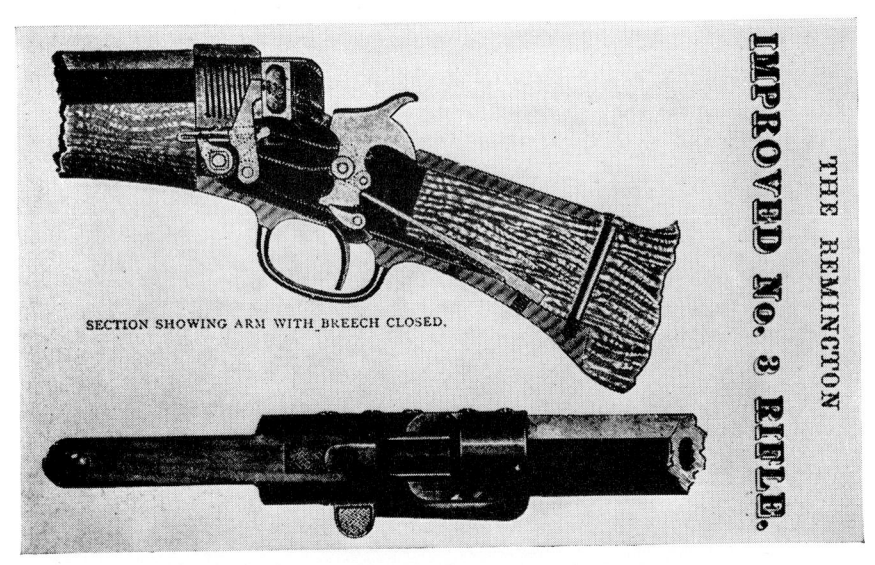

REMINGTON HEPBURN ACTION DESIGN

REMINGTON IMPROVED CREEDMOOR RIFLE. This is listed in the catalog as "Hepburn's Patent: Number 3 Sporting and Target Rifle." The illustration shows the regular Hepburn action, with tall vernier tang rear sight and a checkered pistol-grip stock.[1]

REMINGTON IMPROVED NO. 3 RIFLE. To quote the catalog:

This rifle is designed especially for long range target shooting and for general use as a sportsman's and hunter's rifle, being constructed with a special reference to the use of a reloading shell. It has a solid breechblock with direct rear support, side lever action, and rebounding hammer so that the arm always stands with the trigger in the safety notch thus rendering premature discharge impossible and is believed to be the best in use for the purpose described. They are all made with pistol-grip stocks, which heretofore have been furnished only with the higher priced rifles, and are chambered for the straight .38, .40 and .45 caliber shells using either a patched or a cannelured bullet.

The cartridges these early Creedmoor Hepburns were chambered for were probably the .38/40 Remington, .38/50 Remington, .40/70 or .40/65-2½" Straight, and .45 Sharps cases in various lengths.

Again quoting from the catalog:

Directions for taking the Remington Hepburn Rifle No. 3 apart: Remove the upper screw in the left hand side and the breechblock may be taken out. To take out the hammer, remove the next upper screw and slip the hammer forward into the breechblock hole. To take out the extractor, remove the forward screw on left-hand side.

The lever which operates the breechblock passes through the rocker sleeve with a square stud and is held in place by a set screw directly under the fore stock which must be removed if it is ever desired to take off the lever.

If necessary to remove the guard it can be done by taking off the butt stock and taking out the side screws in the usual way.

The barrel should not be unscrewed from the frame except by experienced hands and with proper appliances.

When necessary to unscrew the frame, the extractor should be taken out and the breechblock, and guard put back in place before putting on the wrench.

[1] These Hepburn models are included here as they appear in the 1883 catalog along with the rolling-block models; otherwise, the continuity of the models is lost. For the later Remington-Hepburn models see page 139.

NOTE—If at anytime the primer should be driven back into the firing pin hole, so as to make the breechblock open stiffly, it can be relieved by snapping the hammer against the firing pin.

LONG RANGE CREEDMOOR. Price list as given in catalog:

   A—With vernier rear and wind-gauge front sights, and with spirit level and 2 extra discs $ 80.00
   B—Rubber butt and tip, checkered fore end, fine selected stock   100.00
   C—Rubber butt and tip, checkered fore end, extra fine stock   125.00

This rifle used the .44 caliber 2$\frac{4}{10}$″ straight shell with 90 to 100 grains of powder. This was the Sharps 2$\frac{4}{10}$″ case.

The catalog illustration shows the Hepburn Creedmoor rifle with shotgun buttstock, half-octagonal barrel, long-range vernier rear sight and with extra base on the heel of stock.

REMINGTON HEPBURN CREEDMOOR RIFLE

HUNTER'S OR SPORTING RIFLE No. 3. This is the regular, plain Hepburn model shown with half-octagonal barrel, open sights, and the earlier Remington rifle butt plate. The catalog describes this No. 3 rifle as using .38 caliber 1$\frac{3}{4}$″ case, .40 caliber 1$\frac{7}{8}$″ and 2$\frac{1}{2}$″ cases, and .45 caliber 2$\frac{4}{10}$″ Straight shell. All these rifles have pistol-grip stocks.

HUNTER'S OR SPORTING RIFLE. Plain open sights, American walnut stock, oil finish.

   With 26-inch barrel $25.00
   For each additional 2 inches in barrel length, extra, $1.00
   Double-set triggers, extra, $3.00

SHORT AND MID RANGE RIFLE. Combination peep and open-rear sights, Beach front sight.

With 28-inch barrel	$29.00
With tang peep and open rear and bead front sights	31.50
With Creedmoor stock, rubber butt and tip, vernier rear and wind-gauge front sights	50.00

"These rifles," the catalog states, "of weights varying from 8 to 10 pounds, are kept in stock. When made up to special order, an additional charge of $5.00 will be made for special styles of rifles with any of the extras designated on page 14 and the corresponding price thereon stated."

MATCH RIFLE. Vernier rear and wind-gauge sights, spirit level, Swiss butt and cheekpiece.

26-inch barrel	$55.00
28-inch barrel	56.00
30-inch barrel	57.00

"We make these rifles," the catalog states, "to use the .38-1¾" special cartridge or the .40-1⅞" and .40-2½", as may be ordered. This rifle is intended to take the place in short range shooting that the Creedmoor takes in long range."

The catalog illustration of this model shows the Hepburn action with Swiss butt plate, cheekpiece stock, checkered grip and fore end, and short vernier rear sight. (See H, page 143.)

REMINGTON BREECH LOADING SHOT GUN. "Fine quality barrels, 32 inches long. Single barrel. Full length, 48 inches. Weight, 6½ lbs. Remington rifle system [rolling-block action]." The catalog illustration shows the single-barrel gun made on the rolling-block action, with plain straight-grip stock and front sight only.

Price of 32-inch No. 16 B gauge plain barrel	$14.00

Extras offered in the 1883 catalog are the following:

Set triggers for the rolling-block action	$ 2.50
Set triggers for the Hepburn action	3.00
Loops or swivels	1.50
Vernier sight, rear, long	10.00
Vernier sight, rear, short	7.50
Vernier sight base	3.00

Pistol-grip stock, checkered, if furnished with gun	$5.00
Pistol-grip stock, checkered, if furnished separately	9.00
Checkering butt and tip stocks, ordinary	3.75
Checkering butt and tip stocks, extra fine	6.00
Varnishing or oil polishing stock and forearm	4.00

REMINGTON HEPBURN LONG RANGE MILITARY CREEDMOOR RIFLE. This model was evidently added sometime in the late 1880s and is described as follows: "Remington Hepburn long-range rifle, NRA pattern. Length of barrel, 34 inches; total length of gun, 49¼ inches. Weight, 9¼ lbs. This model has a straight-grip, shotgun buttstock; military type long fore end with two bands and wiping rod under the barrel; long-range tall vernier rear sight, and blade front sights."

REMINGTON HEPBURN SPECIAL MILITARY CREEDMOOR RIFLE

An illustration of an actual specimen of this rare model Hepburn may be seen in Fuller's *The Breech Loader in the Service*, page 171, Figure V, Plate IX. Fuller does not list the caliber of this model, but I believe it was made only in the special Remington straight shell, .44/90 or .44/100 in 2⁶⁄₁₀" case. This cartridge is very rare today, and is listed on some cartridge dealers' lists as both .44/90 and .44/100. An illustration of an original box of these cartridges in the author's collection, may be seen on page 187.

The Remington Arms Company catalog of 1904-1905 lists the following models.

REMINGTON NO. 4 RIFLE. New model take-down, rolling-block action. Weight, 4¼ lbs. New design open sights. Prices in various calibers were as follows:

.22 Short and Long rim-fire, 22½-inch barrel	$8.00
.22 Long Rifle rim-fire, 22½-inch barrel	8.00
.25/10 Stevens rim-fire, 22½-inch barrel	8.00

.32 Short and Long rim-fire, 22½-inch barrel $7.50
.32 Short and Long rim-fire, 24-inch barrel   8.00

EXTRAS

Gallery or peep sight $2.50
Beach combination front sight   1.00
Sporting stop rear sight   .75

REMINGTON NO. 6 TAKE-DOWN RIFLE. This is a modified type of the rolling-block rifle. Open rear and front sights and new tang peep rear sight.

Calibers (rim-fire) were .22 Short black, .22 Short smokeless, .22 Long black, .22 Long Rifle, .32 Short, .32 Long.

Cartridges adapted to this rifle were CB caps smokeless, BB caps, BB caps smokeless.

Barrel length was 20 inches; weight, 3½ to 4 lbs.; price, $4.00.

REMINGTON NO. 2 RIFLE. This was the heavier rolling-block action. It was made in a number of calibers, as follows:

Rim-fire calibers: .22 Short; .22 Long; .22 Long Rifle
    Barrel lengths: 24, 26, and 28 inches
    Weight: 5½ to 6 lbs.
    Prices: $10 to $12, according to barrel length
Stevens center-fire calibers: .25/20; .25/21; .25/25
    Barrel lengths: 26, 28, and 30 inches
    Weight: 5¾ to 6 lbs.
    Prices: $10, $11, $12, according to barrel length
Stevens rim-fire .25/10 caliber; WCF .22 caliber; .22 Extra Long center-fire caliber
    Barrel lengths, weights, and prices same as Stevens .25/20
Rim-fire .32 caliber
    Barrel lengths: 24, 26, 28, and 30 inches
    Weight: 5¼ to 6 lbs.
    Prices: $10, $10, $11, and $12, according to barrel length
Center-fire .32 caliber; .32/20 WCF; .32 Long
    Barrel lengths: 26, 28, and 30 inches
    Weight: 5½ to 6 lbs.
    Price: $10, $11, and $12
WCF .38 and .44 calibers
    Barrel lengths: 28 and 30 inches
    Weight: 5½ to 6 lbs.
    Price: $10

Remington No. 7 Target and Sporting Rifle. Quoting the catalog: "This rifle is our latest model, and its attractive lines, balance, and fine finish will appeal to all interested in target and sporting rifles. It is bored and rifled and chambered with the utmost accuracy, under the most improved scientific methods. Each rifle is carefully sighted and target sent with it."

This No. 7 rifle was made up in .22 Short, .22 Long Rifle, and .25/10 Stevens rim-fire calibers. Barrel lengths were 24, 26 (standard), and 28 inches. Weight was from 5 to 6¼ lbs. Price, $24.

This model was also made to order in the same calibers as the No. 2 rifle, with half-octagonal barrel, polished imported walnut stock of special design, adapted to snap and target shooting. It had a checkered grip and forearm, and a rubber pistol-grip cap and butt plate. The sights were special Lyman combination rear, and Beach combination front. Trigger was checkered. The trigger pull was uniform and durable. It was adjustable to weigh 2½ lbs.

Extras: When ordered on the rifle these were priced as follows:

Swiss Butt plate	$2.00
Windgauge front sight	2.00
Windgauge spirit level	1.00

This is the special target rifle made up on the Remington rolling-block army pistol frame. Illustration is shown on Plate 36.

Remington No. 5 Special Rifle. This is an arm adapted to high-power smokeless ammunition. It has a round special smokeless steel barrel, oiled walnut stock, casehardened frame and mountings; also sporting front and rear sights. Following are the calibers, barrel lengths, weights, and prices:

Calibers:
    .30/30 Smokeless   .32/40 High Pressure
    7mm.   .32 Winchester Special
    .30 U. S. Army   .38/55 High Pressure
    .303 British

Barrel lengths: 24, 26 (standard), and 28 inches
Weight: 7 to 7¼ lbs.
Price: $18
    Extra: Single-set trigger, to order, $2.00

REMINGTON NO. 3 RIFLE (HEPBURN ACTION). Quoting the catalog:

The New Model No. 3 Remington rifle is especially designed for long-range hunting and target purposes, requiring the use of heavy charges. It has a solid breechblock with direct rear support, convenient side-lever action and rebounding hammer so that the arm always stands with the trigger in the safety notch, rendering premature discharge impossible. Chambered for the standard black powder cartridges mentioned below. Half octagon or full octagon barrel, oiled walnut stock, pistol grip, checkered. Rebounding hammer, casehardened frame and mountings. Knife blade front and buck horn rear sights.

Following are calibers, barrel lengths, weights, and prices of this rifle:

Calibers .22, .25, and .32:
   .22 WCF
   .22 Extra Long center-fire
   .25/20 Stevens center-fire
   .25/21 Stevens center-fire
   .25/25 Stevens center-fire
   .32 WCF
   .32/40 Marlin and Ballard center-fire
   .32/30 Remington center-fire
   .32/40 Remington center-fire

Barrel lengths: 26, 28, and 30 inches
Weight: 8 to 9 lbs.
Price: $15

Caliber .38:
   .38 WCF
   .38/40 Remington center-fire
   .38/50 Remington center-fire
   .38/55 Ballard and Marlin center-fire

Barrel lengths: 28 and 30 inches
Weight: 8½ to 9½ lbs.
Price: $15

Caliber .40:
   .40/60 Ballard and Marlin center-fire
   .40/60 WCF
   .40/65 Remington Straight center-fire
   .40/82 WCF

Barrel lengths: 28 and 30 inches
Weight: 9 to 10 lbs.
Price: $15

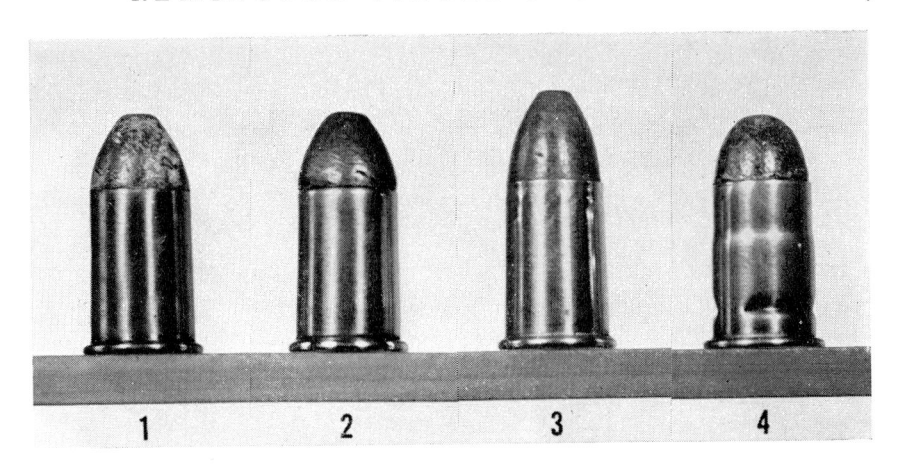

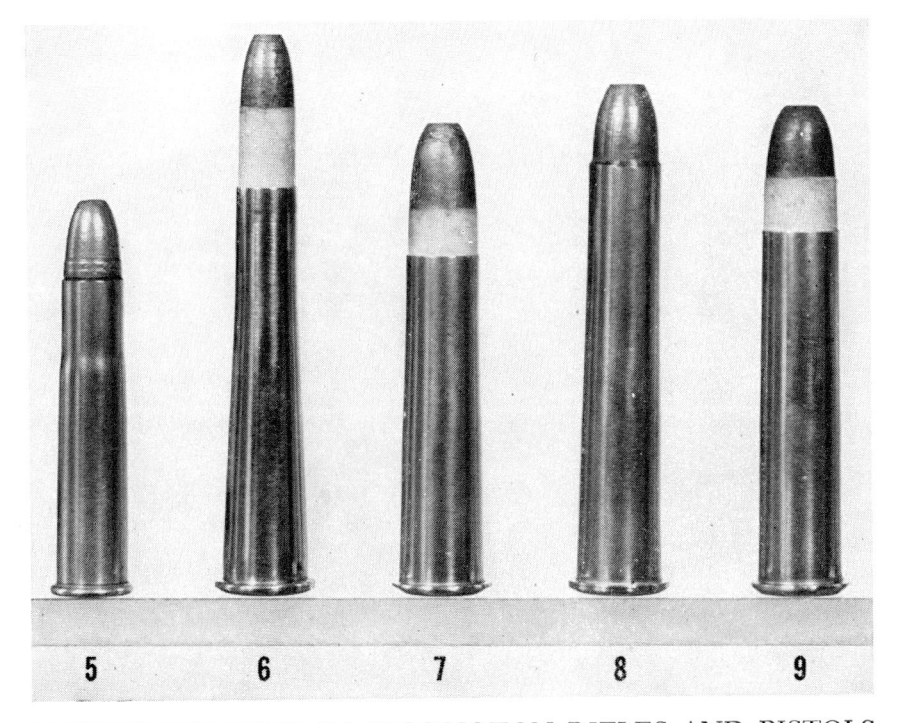

CARTRIDGES USED IN REMINGTON RIFLES AND PISTOLS
1 .50 rim-fire, Remington Navy pistol
2 .50 center-fire, Remington Navy pistol, Winchester loading
3 .50 center-fire, Remington Navy pistol, UMC loading
4 .50 center-fire, Remington Army pistol, inside primed
5 .32/30 Remington   6 .32/40/150 Remington paper-patch
7 .38/40/245 Remington paper-patch   8 .38/50/265 Remington, paper-patch
9 .40/45/265 Remington straight, paper-patch

Caliber .45:
   .45/70 Gov't. center-fire   .45/90 WCF

Barrel lengths: 28 and 30 inches
Weight: 9 to 10 lbs.
Price: $15

In addition to the sizes noted, this rifle could be made to order in any of the following calibers:

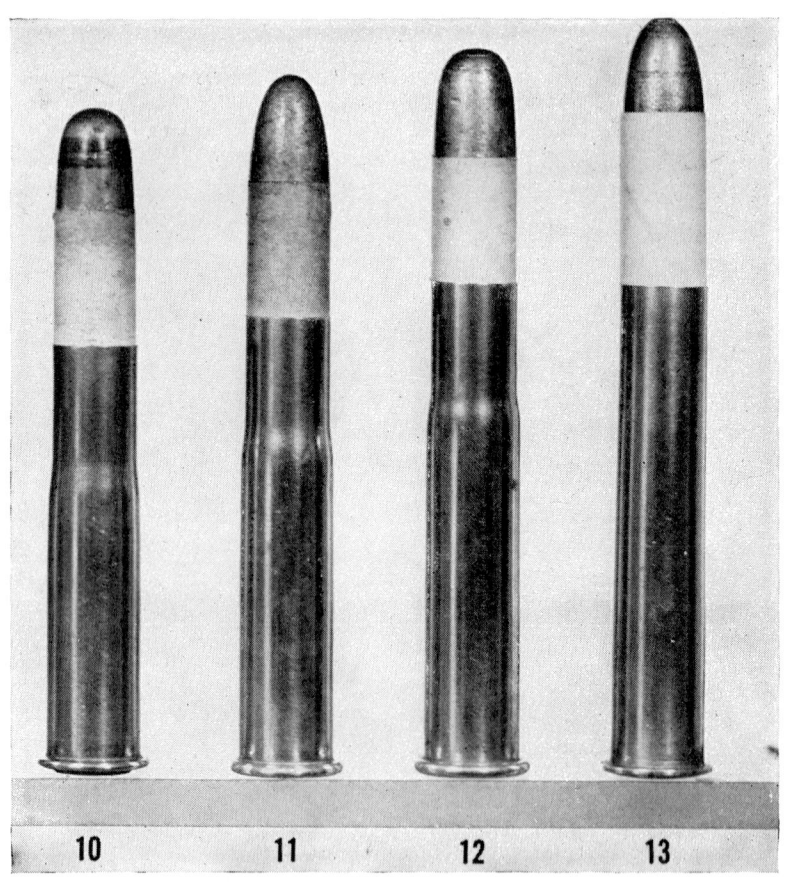

CARTRIDGES USED IN REMINGTON RIFLES AND PISTOLS
    10   .44/77 and .44/90 Remington and Sharps 2¼-inch case
    11   .44/90/520 Remington Special Match 2⁷⁄₁₆-inch case
    12   .44/105/520 Remington and Sharps Special 2⅝-inch case
    13   .44/100/550 Remington Creedmoor 2⁹⁄₁₀-inch straight

Remington bottlenecked, .40/50, .40/70, .40/90, .44/77, .44/90, .44/105
Gov't. .50/70
Sharps Straight, .50/90
  Extras: Double-set triggers to order, $3.50

REMINGTON NO. 3 HIGH POWER RIFLE. A sporting and target model. To quote from the catalog: "The continued demand for our single-shot No. 3 rifle for high-power ammunition has induced us to adapt this celebrated rifle to the high pressure cartridges by substituting the improved breechblock, using the necessary small firing pin and special Ordnance steel barrel." Therefore this rifle was made with round ordnance steel barrels. It had a rifle butt plate, case-hardened frame and mountings, open hunting sights, and checkered pistol-grip walnut stock.

The following calibers were carried in stock:

Gov't. .30/30	.32/40 HP
Gov't. .30 (.30/40) [2]	.38/55 HP
.32 Special HP	.38/72

Barrel lengths: 26 (standard), 28, and 30 inches
Weight: 8 lbs.
Price: $20
  Extras: Double-set triggers, to order, $3.50
      Shotgun butt, to order, $2.00

REMINGTON-SCHUETZEN MATCH RIFLE (NEW SPECIAL MODEL). This is the special under-lever Hepburn model (see page 137). Quoting from the catalog:

This model is made to meet the demand for a Match rifle of the most improved expert design of high-class workmanship, material and finish, and of extreme accuracy. It is nearer popular expert requirements than any Schuetzen rifle made in this country. The action is a modification of our No. 3, with under lever and sliding breechblock so arranged as to force home a shell partly inserted in the chamber. . . .

New design finger lever, fancy walnut stock with cheekpiece, finely checkered, new, improved and carefully adjusted double-set triggers. Special rear windgauge vernier sight and hooded front sight with interchangeable pin head and aperture discs. Specially designed Swiss butt plate.

[2] Today .30 Gov't. means .30-'06 and .30 Army means .30-40.

The prices given were as follows:

Barrel, 30 or 32 inch, half octagon, Weight from 11 to 13 lbs.	$60.00
Remington Walker barrel, breech loading, *extra*	12.00
Palm Rest, *extra*	5.00
Remington Walker barrel, muzzle loading with patent muzzle, starter, wooden rod, lubricator, sizer and bullet mold, *extra*	15.00
Testing for guaranteed group within 2¼-inch circle at 200 yards	8.00
Total	$100.00

REMINGTON NO. 3 MATCH RIFLE. Quoting from the catalog:

We are now furnishing the No. 3 Remington Match Rifle which has gained such popularity in short and midrange matches for any of the central fire cartridges mentioned on pages 62 and 63. . . .

This rifle is expressly made for fine target shooting at from 200 to 500 yards, and the fact that it is used in most of the rifle clubs after severe and careful tests is sufficient evidence of its super quality.

The catalog shows an illustration of this basic No. 3 rifle with the later rifle butt plate, which is different from the early Hepburn plate. This model is also shown without the metal fore-end tip that was used on the earlier Hepburn. (See A, page 141.)

The *No. 3 Match Rifle A Quality* is described as having "half octagon barrel, rebounding hammer, oiled walnut stock, pistol grip, checkered, Swiss butt plate, casehardened frame, Beach combination front and tang graduated rear sights."

This rifle was chambered for the following calibers:

.25/20, .25/21, and .25/25 Stevens center-fire
.32/40 Remington Straight
.32/40 Ballard and Marlin
.38/40 Remington Straight
.40/65 Remington Straight center-fire

Barrel lengths were 28 and 30 inches; weight was 8½ to 10 lbs.; price was $25.

The *No. 3 Match Rifle B Quality* is described as having "half octagon barrel, rebounding hammer, fine selected walnut stock, with cheekpiece, pistol grip and forearm checkered. Swiss butt plate, case-hardened frame. Short vernier peep and windgauge sights with spirit level."

Calibers were:

>.25/20 Stevens center-fire
>.32/40 Ballard and Marlin
>.32/40 Remington Straight center-fire
>.38/40 and .40/65 Remington Straight

Barrel lengths were 28 and 30 inches; weight was 9 to 10 lbs.; price was $42.

The catalog carries an illustration of the Special No. 3 B Grade, showing the match stock, with small Swiss butt plate and metal tip on forearm nickeled. These higher grades of Hepburns, such as the Match and Creedmoor patterns, were made with checkered forearms.

The *No. 3 Mid Range Creedmoor Rifle* is described as having "half octagon barrel, rebounding hammer, selected walnut stocks, pistol grip, checkered grip and fore end, rubber butt and tip. Short vernier graduated and wind-gauge sights with spirit level; adapted for 200 to 600 yards."

Calibers were .40/45 and .40/65 Straight center-fire.

Barrel lengths were 28 and 30 inches; weight was 8½ to 9 lbs.; price was $34.

Extras: Double-set triggers, to order, $3.50. Barrels for high-pressure cartridges, $5.

REMINGTON NEW MODEL SMALL-BORE MILITARY RIFLE AND CARBINE. This rifle was of the rolling-block type, and was made for South and Central American armies. The caliber was 7mm. for smokeless powder. It was also made in .30 Gov't. (.30-40 Krag), 7mm. Spanish and Brazilian Mauser models, and .303 British calibers.

The Model of 1902 rifle had a 30-inch barrel. The weight without bayonet was 8½ lbs.; with bayonet, 9½ lbs. Price was $20.

The bayonet was $4.00 extra, and the bayonet scabbard was $1.00 extra.

Carbine: Barrel length, 20 inches; total length, 36 inches. Weight, 7 lbs. Price, $18.

The catalog notes that "Over 1,600,000 of the celebrated Remington Military rifles have been sold."

SPORTING RIFLE No. 1

These Rifles, of weights varying from 8 to 12 lbs., are kept in stock. When made up to special order, an additional charge of $5 will be made.

SPORTING OR TARGET RIFLES.

REMINGTON ROLLING-BLOCK NO. 1 RIFLE

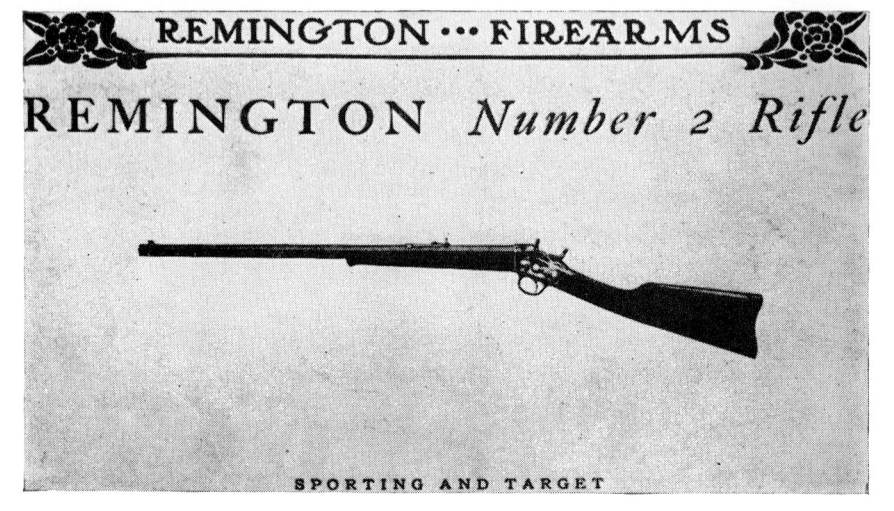

REMINGTON ··· FIREARMS

REMINGTON Number 2 Rifle

SPORTING AND TARGET

REMINGTON ROLLING-BLOCK NO. 2 RIFLE

Illustrations show these two models with wood hand guard and steel military type butt plate. The rifle has sling swivels, a ramrod under the barrel, and two barrel bands. The carbine has a wood hand guard, a swivel ring on left side of frame, and one barrel band.

REMINGTON MILITARY RIFLE, CARBINE, AND LIGHT "BABY" CARBINE. Quoting the catalog: "Military rifle .43 and .50 caliber. The .43 caliber was standard arm of Spain, Cuba, Argentine Republic, and the majority of South and Central American Governments. . . . The .50 calibers have been used largely throughout the Southern and Central American republics."

Rifle calibers were .43 and .50; total length was 50 inches; weight, 9 lbs.; price, $15.

Carbine calibers were .43 and .50; total length, 35½ inches; weight, 7 lbs.; price, $13.25.

The "Light 'Baby' Carbine" was designed for sporting, police, and saddle use. The frame was the same as that of the regular carbine. The caliber was .44 center-fire (WCF .44). Barrel length was 20 inches; total length, 35½ inches. Weight was 5¾ lbs., approximately only double that of any army revolver. Price: blued, $13.25; nickeled, $14.

REMINGTON SINGLE-SHOT TARGET PISTOL. Quoting the catalog: "New model for target and gallery practice. Stock and tip of selected walnut finely checkered. Ivory bead front sight; adjustable, wind-gauge rear sight. . . . Half octagon 10-inch barrel, carefully bored and finished. . . . Trigger pull of 2¼ to 3 lbs."

Calibers were .22 Short rim-fire; .22 Long Rifle rim-fire; .25/10 Stevens rim-fire; 44 S & W Russian center-fire. Weight was 2½ lbs. Price, $16.

The following items were also listed in the 1883 Remington catalog.

REMINGTON AUXILIARY RIFLE BARREL. These barrels extend the full length of the shotgun barrels and are held in place by a thumb nut at the muzzle. They shoot accurately up to 500 yards, and can be inserted into any shotgun, and taken out with perfect ease, thus making the most desired combination shotgun and rifle. Weight about 2 pounds. These barrels are not adapted for high-pressure smokeless cartridges.

Price of auxiliary rifle barrel in 28", 30" and 32" lengths for any 10-, 12-, or 16-gauge shotgun, and rifled and chambered for any center-fire black powder cartridge mentioned in our list, $10.00.

RELOADING TOOLS. .43 Spanish, .45/70 Marlin, .45/70 and .50/70 Gov't. complete, consisting of bullet mould, ball seater, recapper, decapper, powder measure and wad cutter, per set, $3.00.

Remington Recapper and Decapper 10- 12-, 16- and 20-gauge, 60¢.

A detailed list of reloading implements is also quoted:

Grooved Bullet Mold for the following—

.22/45	.32/165	.38/330	.45/405
.25/67	.32/175	.40/265	.50/450
.25/86	.38/245	.40/330	.50/465
.32/125	.38/265	.40/370	.50/565
.32/150	.38/306	.43/390	

Price, $1.10

Ball seater with base, $1.00
Recapper, .25, .32, .38, and .40 calibers, 50¢
Decapper, .25, .32, .38, and .40 calibers, 35¢
Recapper and Decapper, .43, .45, and .50 calibers, 60¢
Wad cutter, 40¢
Powder measure, 10¢

The last pages in the 1904-1905 Remington Arms Company catalog list the following cartridges for which rifles could be chambered. In some cases these calibers were special for the model rifle:

.22 Short rim-fire	.30/30
CB caps	.30 U. S. Gov't.
BB caps	.303 British
.32 Short rim-fire	.38/40 WCF
.32 Short smokeless	.38/40 Remington Straight
.22 Long Rifle rim-fire	.38/50 Remington Straight
.25/10 Stevens rim-fire	.38/55 Ballard & Marlin
.41 Short	.40/60 Ballard & Marlin
.32/20 WCF	.40/60 WCF
.32 Long center-fire	.40/65 Remington Straight
.32 Long rim-fire	.40/82 WCF
.25/20 Stevens single shot	.43 Spanish
.22 Extra Long center-fire	.45/70 Gov't.
.22 WCF	.45/90 WCF
.25/21 Stevens	.50/70 Gov't. SH
.25/25 Stevens	6mm. U. S. Navy rimless
.32/40 Remington Straight	7mm. Spanish Mauser
.32/40 High Power	7.65mm. Belgian Mauser
.32 Winchester Special	

The Remington Arms Company catalog for 1903-1904 shows all the models and other data as listed in this 1904-1905 catalog with the exception of the Remington-Schuetzen Special rifle with under-lever Hepburn action.

REMINGTON-RIDER. This rolling-block action rifle was one of our most popular single-shot rifles and was dropped from the Remington line only a few years ago—in 1935—when the light .22 caliber version was discontinued. The heavier action, made up into military types, was discontinued in 1917. During the many years this action was made, it was available in practically every popular caliber that was on the market in rifles of other makes as well as several special Remington calibers. It was made in various size frames and in various grades, from the plain sporting rifle to fancy target grades engraved upon order (see page 147).

Double-set triggers were optional on the earlier models at $2.50 extra, and are seldom seen today. The single-set trigger version is much more common, and in all specimens of this type I have owned or examined the triggers were good, and capable of fine adjustment. In fact, I would go out on a limb and state that these were probably

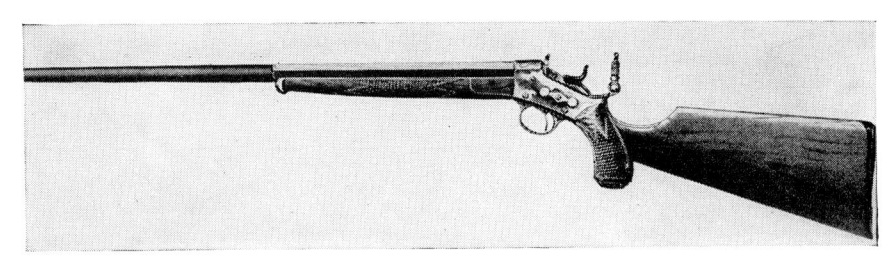

REMINGTON NO. 7 RIFLE

the best of the single-set triggers available on American single-shot rifles.

CREEDMOOR REMINGTON RIFLES. These rifles, made up on the rolling-block action, were among the most accurate and popular long-range target models of their day, and they were used by such famous riflemen as Fulton, Bodine, and others who were top-flight marksmen of that day. Probably next to the Sharps, these Creedmoor Remingtons were the most popular rifles used on the Creedmoor range, though in other sections of the country the Remingtons may have had the edge on the Sharps.

The action is extremely simple, and rarely is one seen that will not operate as smoothly as when it was first made. It is impossible in this type to cause the hammer to fall until the breechblock is completely closed, thus making it one of the safest of arms.

The military rifle as made by Springfield Armory in 1871 pattern has an extra safety device, in that when the breechblock is closed on this cartridge, the hammer automatically follows it to a safety notch just ahead of the full-cock notch, from which it must be brought to full cock when ready to fire.

The Creedmoor style of rifle usually had a half-octagonal 34-inch barrel chambered for the .44 caliber case in 2¼-inch length. This was first loaded with 77 grains of powder, as was the Sharps in this size; but a little later it was loaded with 90 grains.

Later these rifles were chambered for the Sharps .44/90 and .44/105 cartridges loaded in 2⅝-inch necked cases. There is also a special Remington .44/90 cartridge in 2⁷⁄₁₆-inch necked case. When this cartridge was first introduced, I have been unable to determine. Whether it was Remington's answer to the Sharps 2⅝-inch case, or whether it was due to their efforts to find a case more suitable for 90 grains of powder than for the then standard .44/77 or 2¼-inch case, is a matter for speculation.

It is possible that this cartridge was really introduced by Sharps; at least it was available in Sharps rifles (see the chapter on the Sharps). However, I believe it was a Remington development. It was evidently used for a not very long period of time, as few rifles, in either Remington or Sharps manufacture, are seen today chambered for this particular .44/90 case. This cartridge is shown with the other special Remington sizes, on page 128. No information on this special Remington .44/90-2⁷⁄₁₆″ cartridge is available in the files of the Remington Arms Company, so it will always remain one of the little-known cartridges of this era.

A few Creedmoor Remington rifles were made up with full-round barrels, especially in the later days in which this type of rifle was made. Possibly the Sharps influence was to a certain extent responsible for this. One of my Creedmoor Remington rifles in .44/105-2⅝″ bottleneck caliber has a full-round 34-inch barrel which is marked on top in the usual manner, E. REMINGTON & SONS. Under the forearm or under the side of the barrel, L. L. HEPBURN is also stamped in two places. Mr. Hepburn was Remington's special barrel man, among his other duties, and he made many of the special Creedmoor barrels. I have seen one other round barrel marked in this manner.

The early heavy Remingtons in the plain hunting grades are hard to find today in good condition. Eventually I found one in Colorado in .50/70 Gov't. caliber that has a full-octagonal barrel 30 inches long in very good condition inside. This barrel is very heavy and extends beyond the action at breech about ⅛ of an inch, and is on the heavy frame. This particular rifle had been used as a hunting

REMINGTON ··· FIREARMS
REMINGTON - SCHUETZEN
Match Rifle

NEW SPECIAL MODEL

REMINGTON HEPBURN UNDER-LEVER RIFLE

weapon for many years, and may have accounted for a great many head of buffalo and other large game.

The outside of this rifle shows a vast amount of wear, but no abuse. It has plain open sights, straight-grip stock, of course, and weighs 14½ pounds. The workmanship on these Remington rolling-block rifles of all grades was of the best, and the finish of the higher grades was equal if not superior to all other single-shots of that period.

No. 7 Sporting and Target Rifle. This is one of the most fascinating and unique models of the decidedly unique Remington line. According to Mr. Frank J. Kahrs, of the Remington company, this model was first made in 1903 and was discontinued in 1911. It was made up on the Remington Army pistol action, with a special full pistol-grip stock of extremely comfortable design (see page 135).

The actions used on this model may have been converted from surplus Army pistols remaining at the Remington factory, though no one there today seems to know about this. But the rifle is a far cry from a crude military arm.

The stock was of imported walnut, with fancy grip cap, and butt plate of hard rubber. This is the best-balanced little rifle I have ever shot, and one of the most accurate.

I have not as yet found one with the original Remington barrel in fine condition, though several which had been relined have turned up. My specimen of this model had a nice Stevens .22 Long Rifle barrel fitted to it when I got the rifle, and as it was a fine job of fitting and shot very accurately, I have never removed the barrel. It is the correct size and, being half-octagonal, does not look out of place on this action.

REMINGTON SINGLE-SHOT PISTOLS. These pistols on the rolling-block action are fairly plentiful in .50 caliber, though lately many of them have been remodeled to other calibers, such as .22 rim-fire, .22 Hornet, and others.

The target pistols in calibers .22, .38 and .44 are well finished, and are sometimes seen in deluxe grades, being engraved and otherwise embellished.

The first model pistol was evidently the Navy model, with sheath trigger in .50 rim-fire pistol caliber. The later model in the Navy version has a round grip and a trigger guard, and is chambered for the .50 Navy center-fire cartridge.

The Army model has an 8-inch barrel instead of the 7-inch furnished on the Navy pistol, a trigger guard, and also an improved grip with hump at the top of frame. It is chambered for the .50 Army pistol cartridge, which is very similar to the Navy cartridge. These cartridges are shown on page 127.

My Remington pistol is the Army type, and I shoot it a great deal. The original cartridges, except in Berdan primed type, are rather scarce today and not too strong even for black powder loads in a handgun. I use .45/75 WCF or .50/70 Gov't., with cases cut off to ⅞-inch length. Thus a strong solid head case is easily made for these pistols.

Some of the bullet mold manufacturers of today will make special molds for this caliber upon order, and the 300-grain mold for the .50/95 Winchester cartridge can be used. Not having an original Remington or Ideal mold for this size, I have used the 300-grain .50/95 bullet with good results, casting the bullets of almost pure lead and using 20 grains of black or semi-smokeless powder. Good results were also obtained with bullets from a .50 caliber Maynard mold. I have never used smokeless powder in my pistol; however, a mild load could undoubtedly be used. Possibly ¼ shotgun smokeless and ¾ black would be much cleaner than straight black loads. This pistol is an interesting plaything and also very handy for digging post holes with no effort whatever.

Certain cartridge dealers are still listing cartridges for these pistols loaded with shot in wooden ends. All I have seen in shot loads, however, are loaded in the Berdan primed case, and while they usually will fire, these primed cases are thin and hard to find primers for in any quantity today. The .45/75 cases and cartridges are plentiful and can be trimmed off to the correct length with very little labor. Being solid-head type usually, they are quickly reprimed with #2½ or large pistol or rifle primers of current manufacture in almost any tool that will accept the case.

REMINGTON HEPBURN RIFLES

THE Remington Hepburn action is quite old, being patented in 1879 and first introduced to the rifle-shooting fraternity around 1880 (see page 121). It was designed by Lewis Lobell Hepburn, who was employed by E. Remington & Sons at Ilion, New York.

In his earlier years Hepburn was engaged in the manufacture of percussion target rifles, I believe, and later was employed by the Remington firm, and it was during this later period that he designed the action that bears his name. He was a specialist in the target barrel department. Some barrels made by him, and which bear his name on the under side of the barrel beneath the forearm, are seen today.

The Hepburn action is today not so popular as some other single-shot actions; however, the possibilities of this type are overlooked by many gun-conscious persons. It has certain advantages that no other action can offer; among these are the rebounding hammer, the simplicity of the design itself—its few parts and the type of extractor employed.

Naturally, having no under-lever and link mechanism to cam back the hammer to the safety notch, the rebounding hammer was used. The moving parts are few in number, consisting of only the lever, tumbler, breechblock, extractor, and hammer and trigger. There is no link to wear and require replacing at periodic intervals, and the parts are well hardened; thus the problem of wear is negligible. The Hepburn frames are among the hardest of all the old single-shot frames.

The side lever is conveniently located, and a simple flip of the thumb opens the breech. When the original wide lever spring is still in place, it carries the breechblock down quickly and operates the extractor with a sudden push that usually causes the fired case to come tumbling out clear of the action. In this respect it is superior to many of the single-shot designs, particularly those which necessitate clawing around in the narrow breech opening to remove the partly extracted case.

The hammer spring on the Hepburn is stiff, and the hammer fall is short and quick, making for the best ignition.

The cartridge must be pushed almost entirely in, to prevent its being hit by the ascending breechblock. But in this respect the Hepburn is not quite so bad as the Borchardt, which must have the case entirely seated before the block will close.

The Hepburn action is not so beautiful as some actions, because the tangs set on the frame at rather awkward angles and the sharp drop behind the block-supporting walls are not conducive to smooth, pleasing lines. Beauty is, however, as beauty does, and certainly no one can find fault with the strength and soundness of the Hepburn action.

All Hepburns—except the Creedmoor Military and under-lever models—had long pistol-grip frames with round pistol-grip tips, and they were checkered in all grades, even the plain hunting models. The forearms of the lower grades were plain, without checkering unless specially ordered; but on the higher grades these were finely checkered to match the fine checkering of the grips.

A few Hepburn stocks are seen with pistol-grip caps instead of the usual round snobble, but these are very unusual.

The earlier hunting rifle fore ends had hardened metal tips, and this was changed to a plain end tip in later ones made. In most cases these were inlaid on the bottom side of the tip with hard rubber or horn.

The match grades, however, carried the hardened or nickel-plated tips up to the last rifles of this type made, unless of course they were the grades that carried a full horn or rubber tip to match the pistol-grip cap.

The sights used on the Hepburn rifles were the same as those offered with the rolling-block models, with the exception of the special rear vernier tang furnished on the under-lever Hepburn. The Remington target sights are shown on page 29.

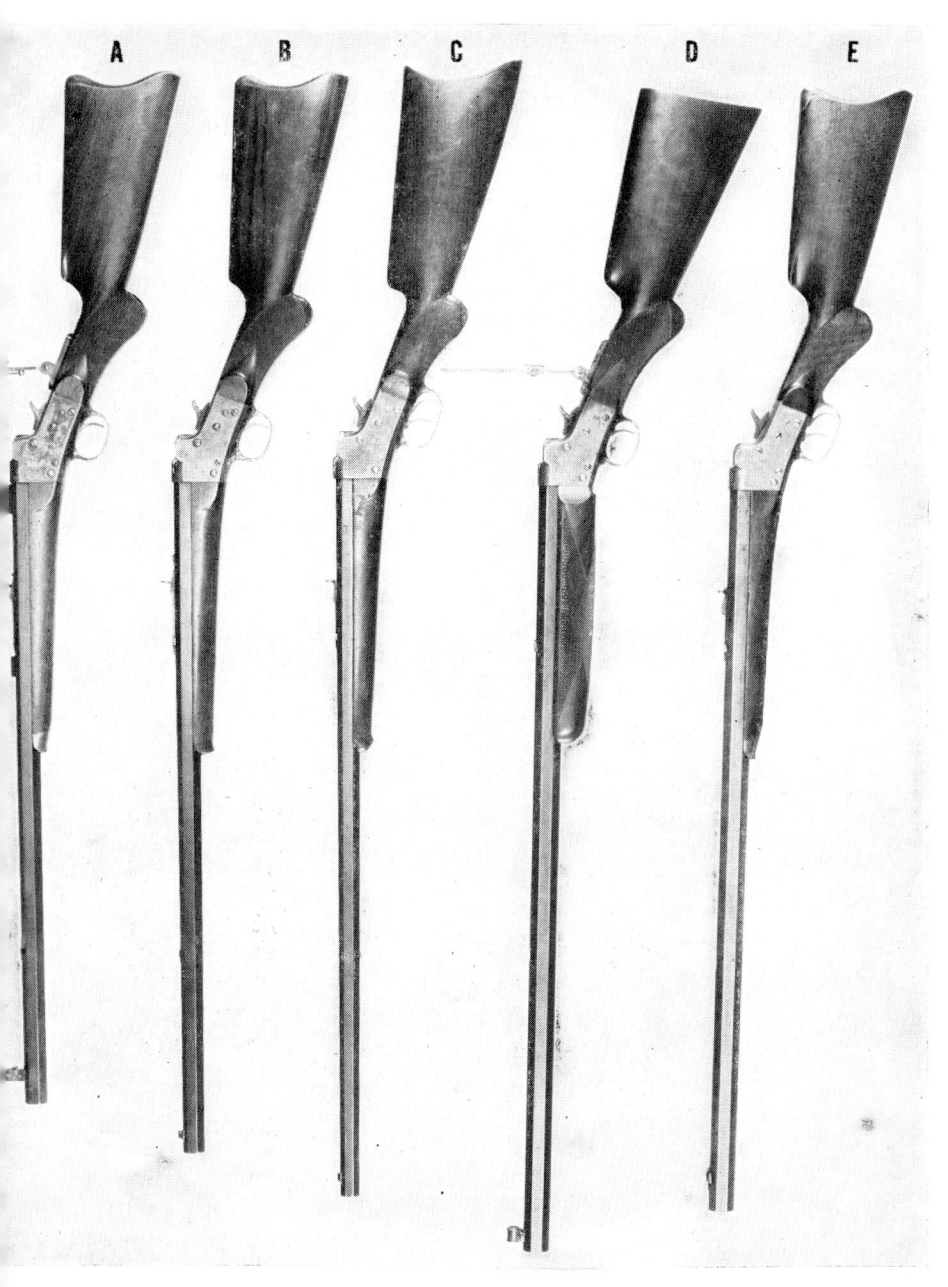

REMINGTON RIFLES
(See page 159 for explanation)

The Hepburns were available with double-set triggers of three distinct types—four types counting the under-lever Hepburn trigger. In the earlier models these were priced at $3.00 extra, and in the later series at $3.50 extra. There seems to have been a steady improvement in double-set triggers. This probably accounts for there being three types of them. The price of $3.50 was certainly reasonable, and no doubt it accounts for the many Hepburns seen so equipped.

I do not believe these rifles were ever fitted with single-set triggers, as were so many of the rolling-block models.

The earliest type of trigger among my specimens is on a .32/40/150 Remington rifle. The next improvement is seen on a .28/30 Remington Hepburn rifle. The last type is represented on the No. 3 Special Match B Grade trigger.

The triggers used on the Special Schuetzen Model of under-lever pattern are the finest of the triggers seen on Hepburn rifles, and they are really the only type of Remington-Hepburn set triggers that can be compared with Sharps, Ballard, or Stevens triggers. The earlier triggers are of such a pattern that the sensitive adjustment is very hard to obtain. Then, too, both triggers were crowded into a trigger guard which was very little larger than the single trigger guard.

The Remington Hepburn rifle had the caliber stamped in a rather odd place. It is found on the under side of the barrel, several inches ahead of the forearm tip. Why they were marked in this particular place is hard to understand, but at least they were marked, and some contemporary rifles of other makes were not marked at all. The caliber is usually—but not invariably—stamped on the extractor, and it may be seen when this piece is removed. However, since there are many cartridges that have the same head size, this is not an infallible method of identifying the caliber.

Many of the early Creedmoors and Hepburns have no caliber stamping on them whatever, and very seldom is the caliber found on the barrels furnished on the under-lever type of Hepburn. Those that are marked in the accustomed place as described are usually marked in the regular manner of the designation of that caliber if the caliber is another manufacturer's cartridge. For instance, the .38/55 Ballard & Marlin caliber is marked simply 38/55; and the .32/40 Ballard & Marlin is marked the same way, 32/40. When the caliber happens to be one of the many Sharps cartridges for which

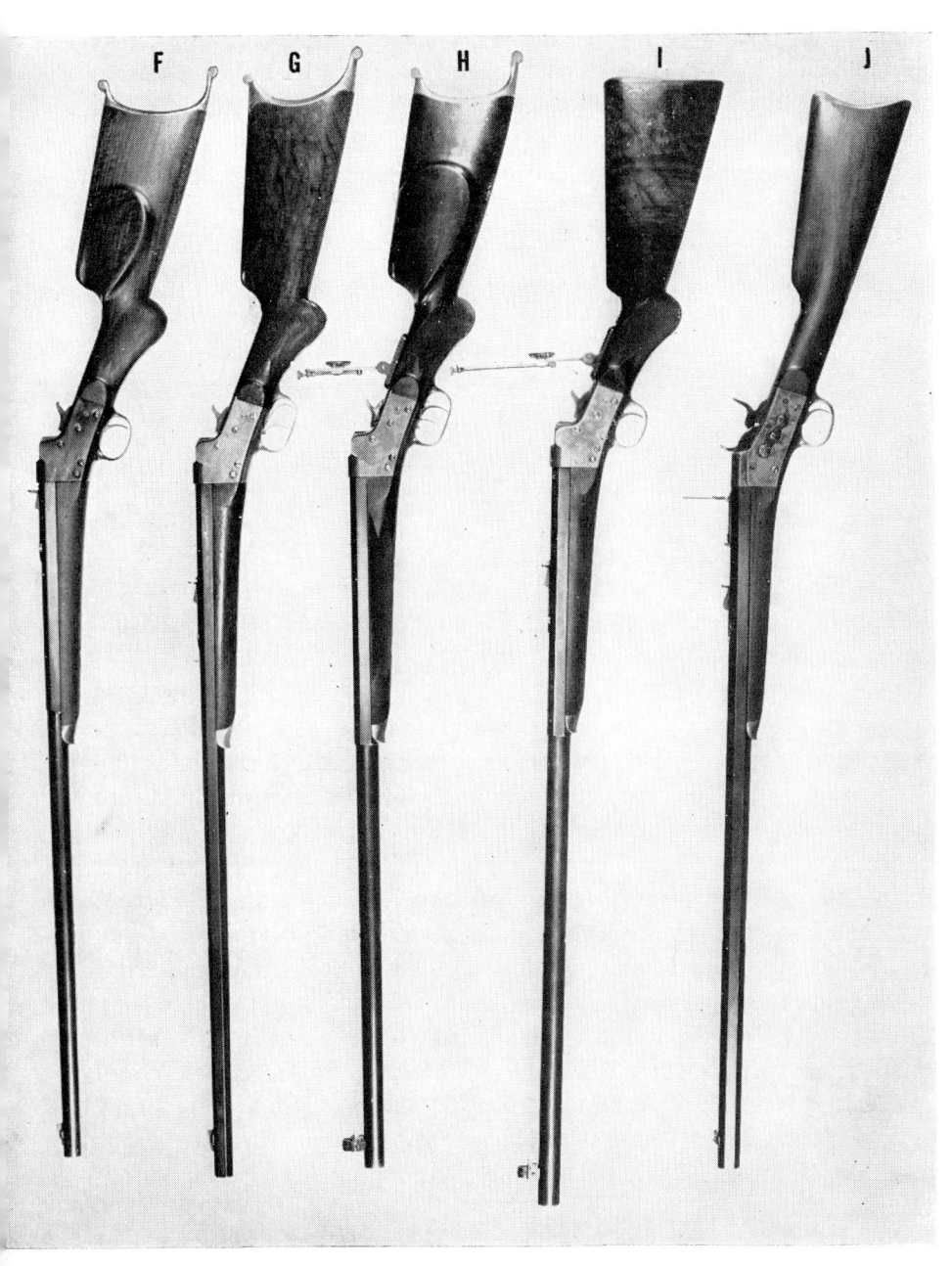

REMINGTON RIFLES
(See page 160 for explanation)

Remington rifles were available, the marking is 44/90 S., 40/90 S., 40/70 S., etc., when the case is the bottleneck type. When the rifle is calibered for a straight case of Sharps persuasion, the mark is usually 40-1⅞ for the .40/50 Straight, and 40-2½ for the .40/70 Sharps Straight. However, the two Remington Hepburns I own in .40/90 SS-3¼" caliber are marked simply, 40/90 S.

The .45/70 Gov't. and .50/70 Gov't. calibers were usually marked simply 45 Gov't. and 50 Gov't. It is when we get into the "Special" odd Remington calibers that the markings are likely to be confusing. For example, the .32/30/125 Remington is marked 32-1⅝; the .32/40/150 Remington Straight is marked 32-2⅛; the .38/40/245 Remington Straight is marked 38-1¾; and the .38/50/265 Remington is marked 38-2¼.

I have seen a few of the Remington rolling-block type chambered for the Special Remington .44/90 in 2⁷⁄₁₆-inch case, and they are marked simply 44/90 or not at all.

The one specimen of Hepburn Military Creedmoor rifle that I have seen chambered for the Special Remington .44/90 or .44/100-2⁶⁄₁₀" Straight case was unmarked. A Hepburn Creedmoor Target Model was marked in the usual place 44-2⁶⁄₁₀. But this is the only specimen I have seen so marked. Many of these "Special" Remington cartridges were very accurate; at least, as accurate as contemporary calibers. But they are almost unknown today because they were not available in rifles other than the Remingtons. Possibly this was the idea—to compel the shooter to buy a Remington if he wanted a rifle made for a special Remington caliber. Thus, many men were unacquainted with these calibers because they didn't happen to care for the rifle for which they were made; just as other men preferred a Remington to a Sharps, Ballard, Winchester, etc.

I have never seen a rifle of other than Remington manufacture chambered for a special Remington cartridge, but of course there may have been some so made upon special order. Some of the Farrow rifles were made in .32/40/150 Remington caliber. I do know that some of the custom barrelmakers of that day would make barrels for these cartridges.

Mr. A. W. Peterson of Denver, Colorado, told me that he had made many barrels for the .32/40/150 Remington cartridge, and he remembered at least one that he had made for the .32/30/125 Remington bottleneck cartridge. No doubt other barrelmakers would also make barrels for these similar sizes if they were so ordered.

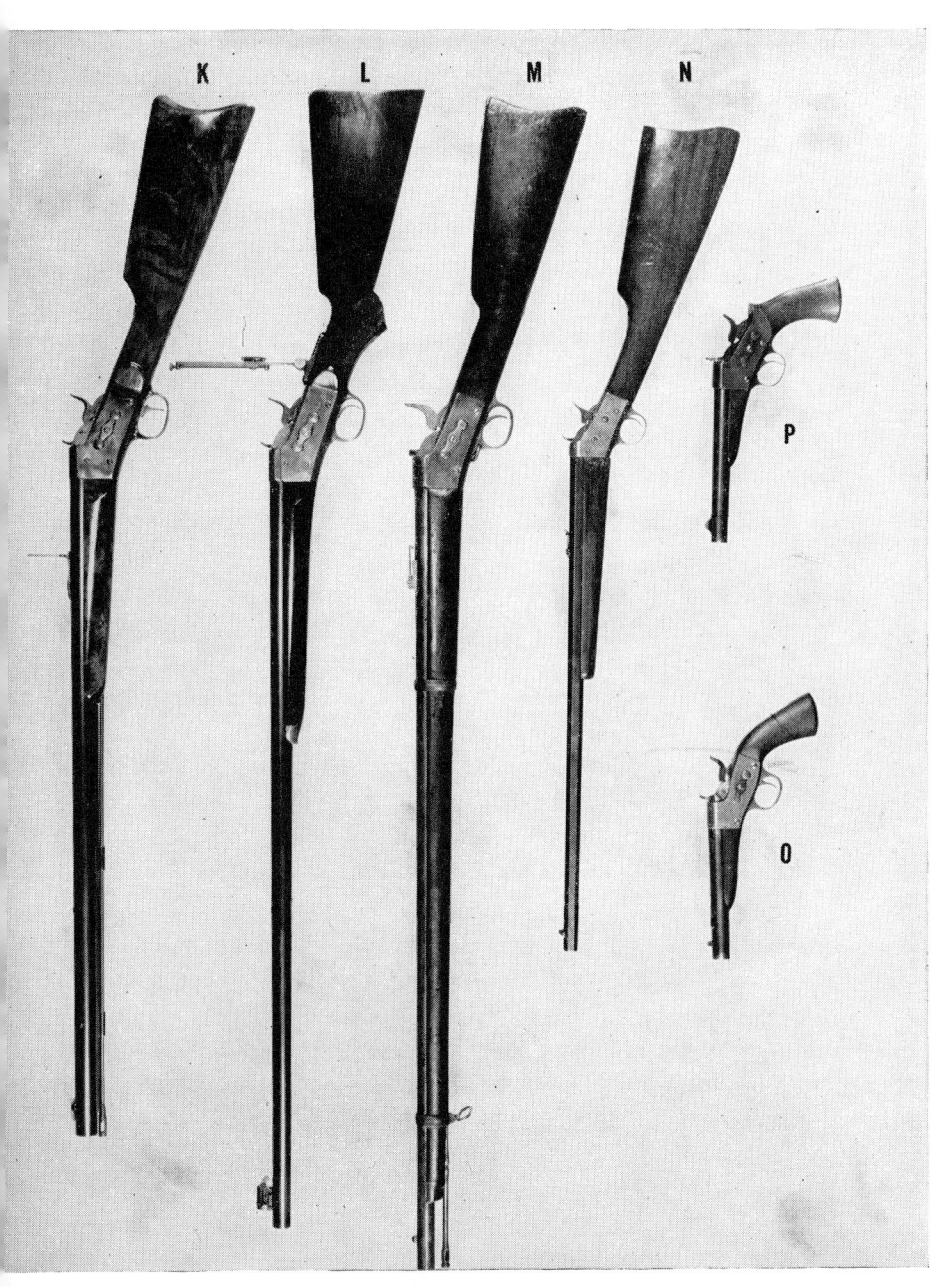

REMINGTON RIFLES
(See page 160 for explanation)

THE SPECIAL REMINGTON CARTRIDGES

The "Special" series of sizes introduced by Remington are deserving of specific mention, as they are very interesting; also they are unknown to many who are interested in single-shot rifles. Most cartridge collectors have specimens of all these cartridges—but what is the cartridge without the rifle!

The smallest of the Remington cartridges is the .32/30/125, which is a slightly bottlenecked case, 1⅝ inches long and, as the designation shows, loaded with 30 grains of black powder and a 125-grain bullet in grooved style. This cartridge may have been loaded with a patched bullet at one time, but I have never seen it in that style. The bullet was a .313-inch diameter, and as there were patched bullets available in that diameter, it could have been loaded with this bullet as well as with the regular grooved one. Mr. W. E. Witsil, of the Remington Arms Company, informed me by letter dated July 15, 1943, that after searching through all the old records at both Bridgeport and Ilion, he could furnish only the following information on this cartridge:

"This cartridge was first manufactured in November, 1884. A change in head construction was made July, 1891, to take advantage of the solid head design. The cartridge cases were primed with the #1½ primer, and were loaded with a powder charge of 30 grains of black powder. The bullet was the grooved style, weighing 125 grains. This cartridge was adapted to the Remington No. 3 rifle. The last production order was dated November 18, 1912."

This cartridge was evidently never very popular, and was too close in power and size to the Winchester .32/20 to really fill any definite need. I hunted for a long time for a rifle in this caliber and finally bought an almost perfect No. 3 plain Hepburn from Mr. N. H. Roberts, who had owned the rifle for years. It was one of his favorite target rifles, and since I have owned it, I have grown to share his enthusiasm for it. It has a 26-inch full-octagonal #3 barrel and the regular Remington Hepburn stock and butt plate. The barrel is excellent inside, and it shoots well enough to satisfy the most critical gun crank. The vernier Hepburn rear sight is on this rifle, but as it was drilled and tapped for Lyman scope blocks, I have used the scope in all my shooting with it.

I obtained with the rifle 50 folded head cases, unstamped, and 50

ENGRAVED REMINGTON ROLLING BLOCK RIFLE

solid head cases which have the head stamp; also an Ideal bullet mold for the 125-grain bullet #31114, which is just right for this barrel, as it is cast .313 in diameter. I use Mr. Roberts' load for this rifle, which is Remington #6½ primer, 6 grains bulk of Dupont Shotgun Smokeless as a priming charge, and 35 grains of Kings semi-smokeless powder, with a card wad over the powder. The bullet, cast 1-32, is seated in the breech ahead of the case about 1/16 of an inch. This load is for the folded head cases.

The solid-head cases are loaded with 8 grains weight of Dupont's #4759, and the bullet is seated in the case without crimping, or in the breech. Another load that gives good accuracy is 9 grains weight of Dupont's #4227, and the bullet breach seated. With these smokeless loads the bullets are cast about 1 part tin to 20 parts lead. The lubricant is Vaseline ¼ part, beeswax ¾ part, melted together in a double boiler. For the man who likes his rifles accurate—and who doesn't!—and his calibers odd, here is an ideal combination.

As yet I have had no occasion to make cases for this chamber, but I may have to one day. However, cases may be made in a pinch from .28/30 brass, I believe. An original from a box of factory-loaded cartridges in the .32/30 Remington is shown with the special Remington series on page 127.

The .32/40/150 Remington is another odd one. This is a slightly bottleneck taper case 2⅛ inches long. It is unlike the .32/40 Ballard & Marlin and the .32/40 Bullard, and the bullets are cast .308, so it is really a .30 caliber. These cases are not plentiful, but neither are they rare, and they may be found upon diligent search. It is possible to make cases from .30/40 Krag brass, but this requires a full-length die, a strong press or vise, and plenty of elbow grease.

My Hepburn in this caliber is an early No. 3 match rifle with fancy walnut stock and Swiss butt plate. This stock may have been a special order, as it is quite a bit different from the regular No. 3 match Schuetzen stock. It is shown on page 143, Fig. G.

This action has set triggers, and they are the earlier type, which are not so sensitive as the later ones used. The barrel is full-octagonal, 30 inches long, and about #3 weight. It "mikes"[3] .308, which for a change is the correct size for this cartridge, and I use the Ideal bullet #308241, which is a 154-grain bullet adapted to the .30/30 Winchester & Marlin. It is the correct weight and gives good results in this barrel.

I have another barrel in this caliber that as yet I have not fitted to an action, and this barrel measures .310 in one groove, .311 in another, and .3115 in another, so it is scarcely likely that this barrel will shoot at all; in fact, I have never had the desire to put it on an action and try it.

My best load in the .32/40 Remington case and with the #308241 bullet is 11 grains of Dupont's bulk shotgun smokeless with a greased wad over the powder and the bullet, cast about 1-18, seated in the breech of the barrel. I have never found Remington or Ideal tools or a mold in this caliber, so I use a Ballard recapper and decapper in .32/40 Ballard & Marlin caliber to recap and decap these cases; and the bullets have all been breech-seated ahead of the case, so no bullet seater to seat bullets in the case has been needed.

My .32/40/150 Remington cases have the rounded heads that are seen on so many cases made for the Hepburn action. These rounded case heads are, of course, so made to enable the breechblock to slide up over the case, which is not completely seated. They are also

---

[3] Among gun literati this slang word is used to indicate micrometer measurement.

often found in .38/40 and .38/50 Remington cartridges. These cases are usually marked .32/40 SH [4] and of course the shape always differentiates them from both the .32/40 Bullard and the .32/40 Ballard & Marlin, and none of the above .32/40 cartridges are interchangeable.

The .38/40/245 Remington is loaded in a straight case 1¾ inches long. It was loaded in paper patched as well as in grooved bullet types, and was a very popular size when these rifles were being made. These cases are found in both Berdan and solid-head type, of course.

My Hepburn in this caliber is a regular model No. 3, with 30-inch half-octagonal barrel, and plain sights front and rear. The stock has the common Hepburn round pistol grip (similar to a Belgian shotgun pistol grip) and the regular Hepburn rifle butt plate.

I have used for this caliber only the solid-head case with #1½ primer, 12 grains of #80 powder, and the regular Remington 245-grain bullet cast 1-15. This barrel "mikes" .3765 in the grooves, and I use the bullets as cast, which are .377 in this particular Remington mold.

I have also used with good results the 255-grain .38/55 Ballard & Marlin bullet, and the regular 217-grain bullet for the .38/90/217 Winchester Express. This latter bullet from a Winchester mold that came with my rifle in this caliber is .375 as cast and is my favorite bullet for the lighter loads in .38/40 Remington, and in the .38/55 Ballard & Marlin chambers also.

Remington tools in the .38/40 caliber turn up occasionally, but I seat the bullet with an old Ideal tong tool in .38/50 Remington caliber by screwing up the double adjustable bullet-seating chamber to the correct length for the 1¾" case. This, being a straight case, is easy to reload, and crimping is unnecessary; in fact, it is more accurate uncrimped. The barrel being in good condition, good accuracy may be expected.

With the plain open sights on my rifle, and using muzzle and elbow rest, the groups averaged around 4 inches at 100 yards. Using good aperture sights or a telescopic sight the groups will shrink accordingly. With this, as with all the old lead bullet loads, the proper bullet temper and lubricant and powder charge must be carefully balanced with each other in order to secure good results.

[4] Solid Head.

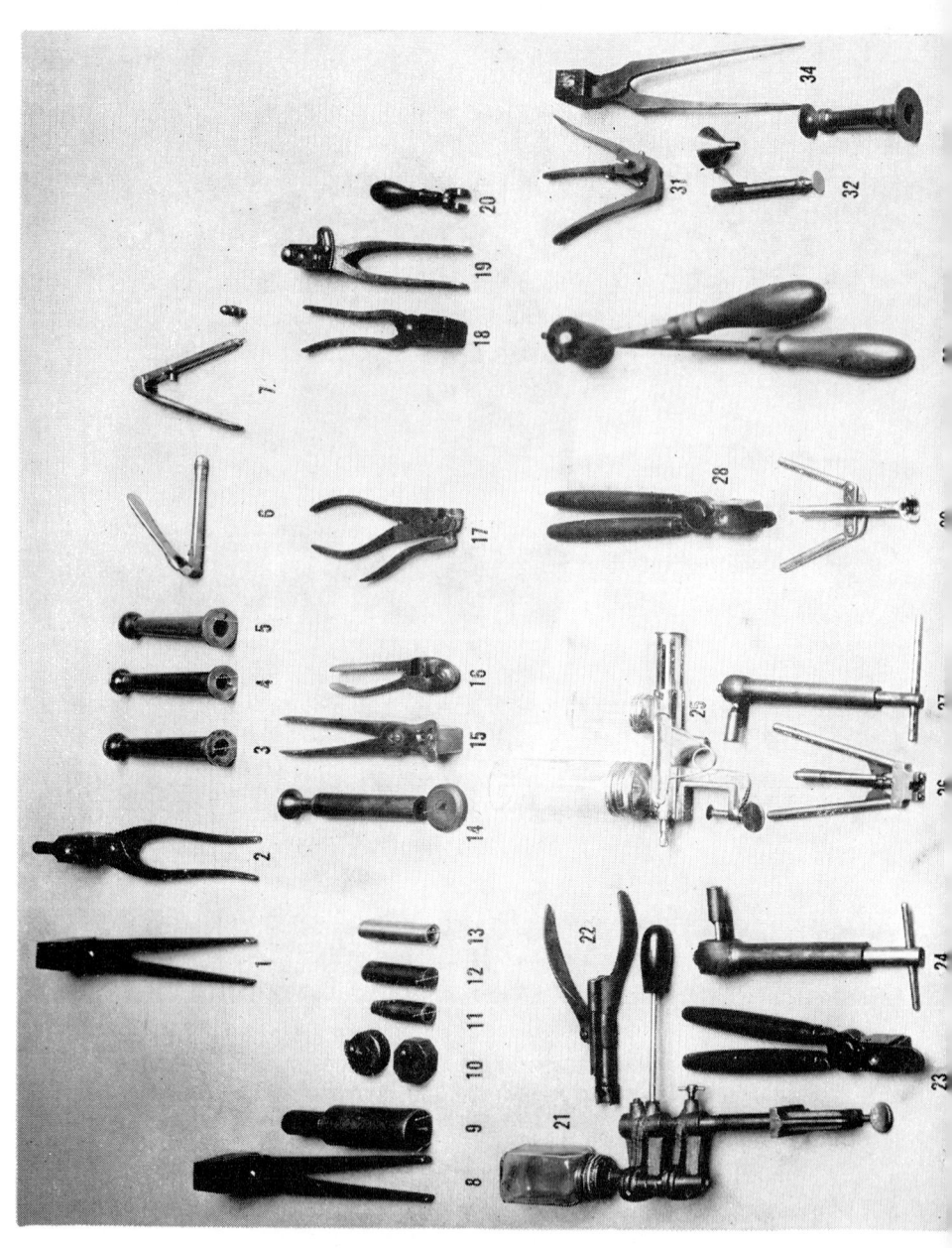

LOADING TOOLS, MOLDS AND ACCESSORIES
(Explanation on facing page)

LOADING TOOLS, MOLDS AND ACCESSORIES

1. Marlin Ballard .40 caliber paper patch, 370-grain mold.
2. Marlin Ballard .44 caliber, 500-grain mold.
3. Ballard bullet seater, caliber .40/90 Ideal Everlasting.
4. Ballard bullet seater, caliber .40/65 Ballard Everlasting.
5. Ballard bullet seater, caliber .38/50 Ballard Everlasting.
6. Ballard .38 caliber recapping and decapping tool.
7. Ballard .40 caliber recapping and decapping tool.
8. Sharps Rifle Co. 550-grain .45 caliber paper patch mold.
9. Sharps Rifle Co. swage for the .45 caliber, 550-grain slug.
10. Sharps Rifle Co. base and nose trimmers for paper patch bullets.
11. Sharps Rifle Co. .45 caliber wad cutter.
12. Sharps Rifle Co. bullet seater for the .40/50 single-shot cartridge.
13. Sharps Rifle Co. full length case resizer for the .45-2 4/10-inch cartridge.
14. E. Remington and Sons bullet seater and base for the .40/65-2½-inch straight cartridge.
15. E. Remington and Sons bullet mold .38 caliber.
16. E. Remington and Sons recapping tool.*
17. Berdan primer recapping and decapping tool.*
18. Maynard .44 caliber 430-grain single cavity mold.
19. Maynard double cavity .40 caliber mold.
20. Maynard decapping tool for the 1873 Berdan primed cases.
21. George C. Schoyen bronze powder measure.
22. George C. Schoyen bronze recapper and decapper for the .32/40 cartridge.
23. George C. Schoyen .32/40 caliber bullet mold.
24. George C. Schoyen bullet lubrication pump.
25. Schoyen and Peterson powder measure.
26. Peterson recapping and decapping tool for .28/30 cartridge.
27. Peterson bullet lubrication pump.
28. Pope bullet mold.
29. Pope recapper and decapper for .32/40 cartridge.
30. Brockway .44 caliber 550-grain paper patch mold.
31. German made recapper and decapper for Berdan type primers.
32. German black powder measure.
33. Bullet seater for the 10.5mm. German Martini cartridge.
34. Bullet mold for the 10.5mm. German Martini cartridge.

* These tools were made by the Bridgeport Gun Implement Company for the various rifle manufacturers. This company also made the molds shown in No. 1 and No. 8, although they are marked "Marlin" and "Sharps" respectively.

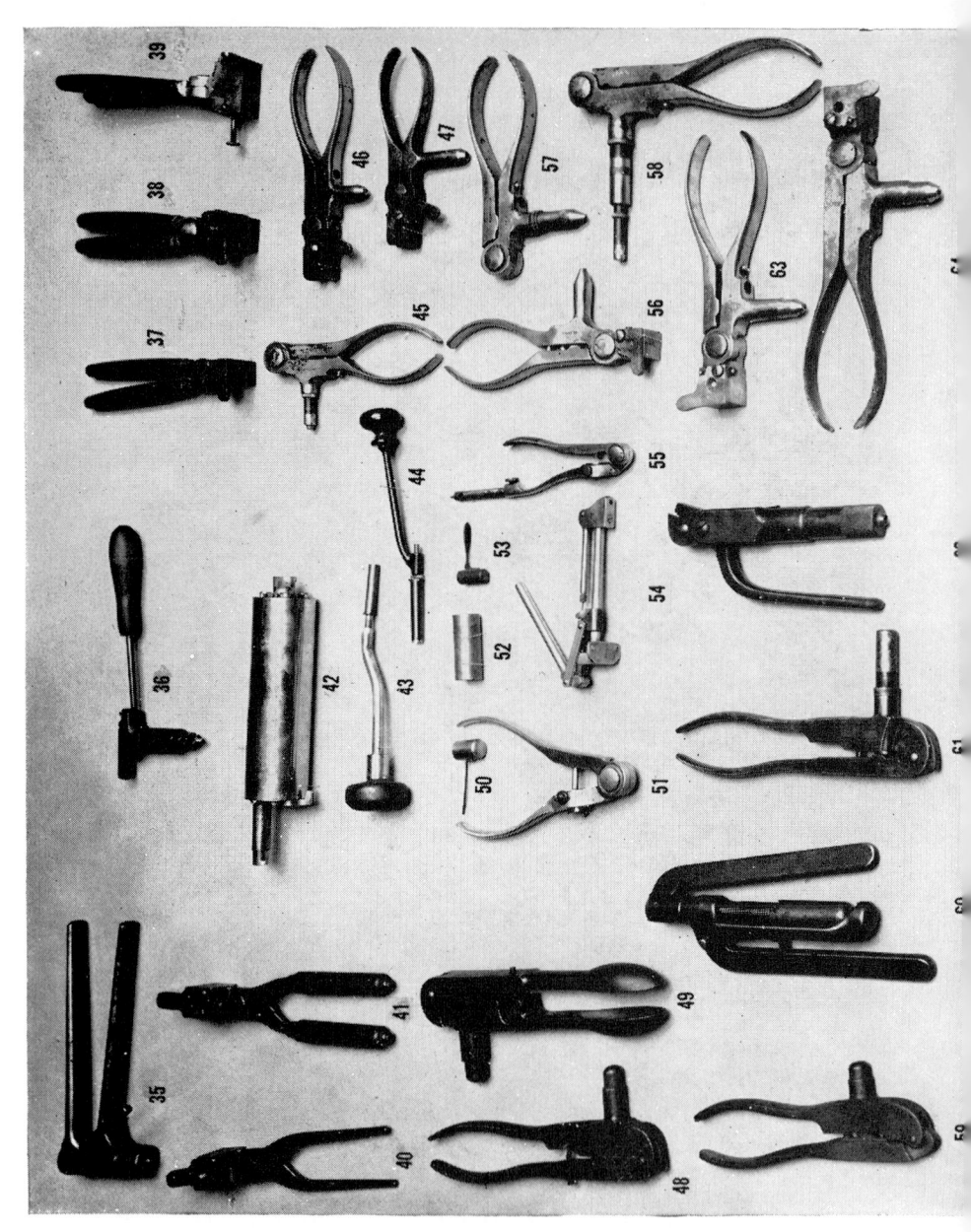

LOADING TOOLS, MOLDS AND ACCESSORIES
(Explanation on facing page)

LOADING TOOLS, MOLDS AND ACCESSORIES

35 Winchester loading tool patented March 17, 1891.
36 Ideal cylindrical adjustable mold for paper patch bullets. Patented January 10, 1893.
37 Early type of Ideal mold.
38 Ideal removable block type of mold.
39 Ideal Perfection adjustable mold for grooved bullets.
40 Winchester mold, early iron handle type.
41 The later walnut handled Winchester mold.
42 Ideal flask type of powder measure No. 1.
43 Ideal No. 1 bullet seater.
44 Ideal No. 2 bullet seater.
45 Ideal No. 3 loading tool for the .22/15/60 cartridge.
46 Ideal No. 1 loading tool and mold for the .32 Long C.F. cartridge.
47 Ideal No. 1 loading tool and mold for the .32 Extra Long cartridge.
48 Winchester loading tool, patented September 14, 1880, for .40/60 Berdan primed cartridge.
49 Winchester loading tool, patented September 14, 1880, for .45/75 Berdan primed cartridge.
50 Ideal black powder charge cup.
51 Ideal bullet sizing tool.
52 Ideal full length shell resizing die.
53 Ideal black powder charge cup.
54 Ideal No. 2 recapper and decapper.
55 Ideal No. 1 recapper and decapper.
56 Ideal No. 6 tool and mold for the 32 Ideal cartridge.
57 Ideal No. 3 tool with single adjustable chamber.
58 Ideal No. 3 tool with double adjustable chamber.
59 Winchester loading tool, patented Oct. 20, 1874, and Nov. 7, 1882.
60 Winchester loading tool, patented January 24, 1888.
61 Winchester loading tool, patented September 14, 1880, for the .40/110/260 Winchester Express cartridge.
62 Winchester loading tool, patented February 13, 1894, for the .45/70 cartridge.
63 Ideal No. 6 tool and mold for the .38/55 cartridge.
64 Ideal No. 6 tool and mold for the .32/35 cartridge. Mold casts 153-grain grooved bullet.

Bullets of lighter than standard weight will usually give better accuracy than bullets of heavier than standard weight, so if you haven't the proper mold, a little experimenting will usually enable you to use a mold that is available for some other cartridge. The .35 WCF and .30/40 Krag cases may be cut off and used as .38/40 cases in case the factory-made cases are not at hand. An Ideal Perfection adjustable mold in .38/55 caliber may be used if one is at hand.

The .38/50 Remington is another straight case, 2¼ inches long. All the cases I have seen in this size take the small rifle primer also, and have the case heads rounded off in UMC or Remington manufactured cases. These cases are not rare, by any means, and a small supply can usually be found.

If it is necessary to make cases in this size they may be made from .303 British cases by firing a mild load of powder to expand the neck; or the cases may be cut off at the shoulder and the bullet loaded into the breech of barrel ahead of the shorter cases. Also the .35 WCF brass can be worked over to fit .38/50 chambers.

The .38/40 and .38/50 Remington calibers were once quite popular, and many of these rifles with fine barrels are still found. My specimen in the .38/50 is a rather light, full-octagonal barrel job 28 inches long. This barrel is about a #2, while most of the .38/50s seen are usually heavier-barreled match rifles. In this barrel I use the 255-grain .38/55 standard bullets sized down to .375, in which diameter they fit the case mouths snugly without crimping. Most of the .38/55 molds cast the bullets several thousandths over the regular .375 diameter for this size, so they can be sized down to fit almost any barrel under standard. The regular weights of bullets used in the .38/50 case were 265 or 306 grains, and others up to 330 grains were sometimes used.

I have used some old E. Remington and Sons 330-grain patch bullets with fairly good results, but the best bullets I have found so far are smooth slugs cast in an old Ideal cylindrical mold for the .38/55 and similar cartridges. These molds being adjustable for length, almost any length and weight bullet wanted may be cast therein. I set the mold to cast a slug of 270 grains, and after patching with bond paper of the proper thickness to bring the bullet up to a size that will fit the case mouth, it gives fine accuracy with 3 grains of Dupont bulk shotgun smokeless powder as a priming charge, and then 47 grains of King's semi-smokeless powder, with a greased card

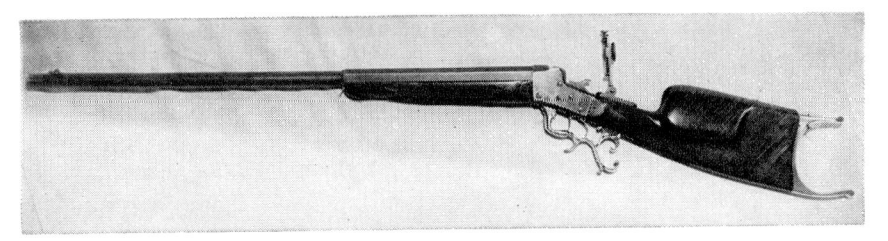

REMINGTON HEPBURN UNDER-LEVER SCHUETZEN RIFLE, CALIBER .38/55

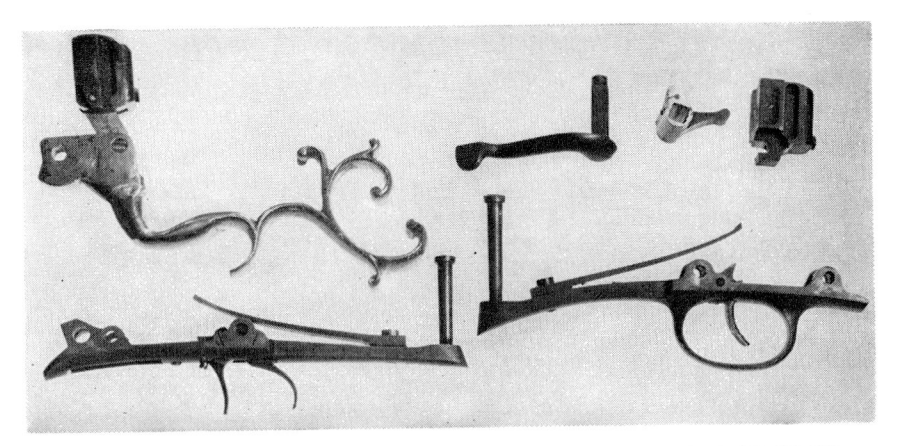

A COMPARISON OF PARTS OF THE HEPBURN UNDER-LEVER ACTION (LEFT) AND THE REGULAR SIDE LEVER MODEL (RIGHT)

wad over the powder, and the patched bullet seated lightly in the case with the fingers. This load in my .38/50 barrel gives fine accuracy, and under normal conditions will require no cleaning of the barrel between shots.

My barrel "mikes" .379, and the cases that fit the chamber are too small to accept bullets of this diameter. However, with black or semi-smokeless powder they will upset sufficiently if cast about 1-40 in the paper-patched form.

When using the .375 (.38/55) grooved bullets seated in the case, the accuracy is inferior, of course, to the above patched load, but with the same 255-grain bullet cast 1-20, sized .379, and seated ahead of the case $\frac{1}{32}$ or $\frac{1}{16}$ of an inch, and a load of 12 to 13 grains of bulk shotgun smokeless powder, it will shoot groups of 1½ inches on the average. This I consider fine accuracy for this light barrel, while a heavier #3 or #4 barrel carefully loaded should shoot into 1-inch groups consistently, as this cartridge is capable of such accuracy.

These cases I reload with an Ideal tool #3 that came with the rifle. The adjustable bullet-seating chamber had a crimping shoulder, but I had this reamed out as none of these cases should be crimped. With a single-shot rifle there is no need for this.

The Hepburn rifles were chambered for the .32/40 and .38/55 Ballard & Marlin cases, of course, and I have a pair of No. 3 Match Grade "B" rifles in these calibers. The .32/40 is just as described in the catalog, while the .38/55 has double-set triggers and a Walker-Remington breechloading barrel. The triggers on this particular rifle are very good, it being one of the later ones made. These two barrels are marked simply .32/40 and .38/55 in the usual place. They both have the handmade Swiss butt, the cheekpiece stock in the regular pattern for this model, and are finely checkered on grips and forearms. These fore ends have a nickeled tip to match the nickeled Swiss butt plates. They are marked with the name C. GIDDINGS stamped in the wood under the top tangs—evidently the name of the stocker who made these fine stocks at the Remington factory.

One of the most accurate Hepburns I have at present is a No. 3 with double-set triggers and the later type rifle butt plate. This has a full-octagonal #2 barrel, 30 inches long, which is marked ".22 WCF." However, this barrel has been recut and rechambered to .28/30/120 Stevens caliber and apparently was so altered at the Stevens factory when they were accepting work of this kind. It has the Stevens style of rifling, and I have found it to be most accurate with 8 grains of #80 powder and the 120-grain bullet cast 1-16.

My Hepburns in .40/50 or .40/45-1⅞" and .40/65-2½" I load with Sharpshooter powder to avoid the mess of black powder, as these actions will, of course, stand the heavier charges.

These calibers are quite common in the Hepburn rifles. Remington usually called the .40/50 Sharp Straight the .40-1⅞" or the .40/45; and the Remington .40/65 Straight is, of course, the .40/70 Sharps Straight in 2½-inch case. Some cases of E. Remington make are marked .40/65, while others are stamped .40/70 SH (Solid Head) and other trade signs.

I have always used grooved bullets in these two Hepburns, and while the barrels are not perfect, they deliver good practical accuracy and require far less work and care than the paper-patched cartridge.

My Hepburn .40-1⅞" will handle 265-grain bullets from a Remington iron mold very well, but no other size. In the .40-2½" rifle the same bullet shoots much better than 330-grain bullets from a Winchester mold.

In the Creedmoor midrange Hepburn with 32-inch half-octagonal barrel for the .40-2½" case, I have used almost entirely 370-grain UMC patch bullets, of which I have a good supply. The load is, of course, black or semi-smokeless powder, being a charge of 72 or 75 grains, with a card wad over the powder and the bullet seated fairly well out of the case.

With the long-range vernier rear and wind-gauge hooded front sights on this rifle, it is capable of fine shooting, and as 200 yards is the length of my range, I have not tried it at any longer distance at this writing.

This is a popular caliber for the midrange rifle, and it was also used to a certain extent for ranges of over 500 yards. However, the long-range models seen are practically all .44/77, .44/90, or .45 caliber. These rifles have a shotgun butt stock of almost no drop. In fact, in some cases the stock is sometimes lower at the comb location by ⅛ to 3/16 of an inch than at the heel of the stock. These stocks were designed for long-range prone shooting in the back or Texas grip positions, and they are well suited for that type of work.

In the Hepburn with 32-inch #4 full-octagonal barrel for the .40/90 SS-3¼" cartridge, I use one case, reloading it for each shot, as these cases are getting quite rare and one case will last quite a while. I reprime with a #2½ Remington UMC primer and 3 grains of FFFG black powder, then the main load of 85 grains of FG black powder.

The bullets used are mainly 370-grain grooved bullets from a Winchester mold, cast about 1 to 30 or 1 to 32. This is a pretty stiff load, and not many shots are needed to shake a few teeth loose and cause the shooter to seek a less strenuous pastime.

I have never as yet used a smokeless load in this caliber, but I intend to work up one some day, as the mentioned charge of black powder will cake quite badly on dry hot days. Possibly the same charge of King's semi-smokeless powder would be much cleaner. I haven't tried that, as yet. I had quite a supply of black FG, and finding that this long case eats up powder fairly fast, I stuck to what I had. Even with these heavy loads in the long 3¼-inch case, the fired case comes tumbling out with ease when the Hepburn side lever spring throws the block down and taps the extractor.

One advantage of the Hepburn in these calibers is that there are more of them, and in finer condition, than of the old Sharps in the same calibers. Then, too, the Hepburn will accept heavy charges of smokeless in its stride, which one should avoid in the Sharps side-hammer action.

The Remington barrels were made with great care, and a properly balanced load will give accurate results.

The Remington .44/90 or .44/100-2⁶⁄₁₀" Straight case is, of course, different from the Sharps case in the same length. It was made for the Creedmoor Hepburn in the Military Creedmoor pattern, and possibly it was used in some other models in the Hepburn and Rider actions upon special order.

I have seen only two rifles chambered for this cartridge and never shot either one, so my experience with it is decidedly limited.

I do have a couple of boxes of the cartridges, and they are the rounded head, small primer type, loaded with 100 grains of FG black powder, and they have no wad over the powder. The 550-grain patched ball is seated very shallowly, being inserted in the case only about ⅛ of an inch. If a wad were used over this powder charge, the seating depth would, of course, be insufficient to hold the bullet in the case.

The box, together with the covers, is pictured on page 187. It is marked as follows:

Solid Head Metallic Cartridges, Mfg. by
E. Remington and Sons, Ilion, N. Y.
Adapted to the
Remington Military Creedmoor Rifle
Special .44 caliber, Straight shell 2⁶⁄₁₀ inch

Many Remingtons are found chambered for the Sharps .45 in 2⁴⁄₁₀-inch and 2⅞-inch Sharps cases, but I have never seen one chambered for the 2⁶⁄₁₀-inch Sharps. However, no doubt they were so made.

The specimens I have observed for the 2⁴⁄₁₀-inch and 2⅞-inch cases were marked simply, 45 S. Fairly satisfactory cases for the

REMINGTON BREECH-LOADING SHOT GUN.

Fine Quality Barrels, 32 inches long.

SINGLE BARREL.

FULL LENGTH 48 INCHES. WEIGHT 6¼ POUNDS.

REMINGTON RIFLE SYSTEM.

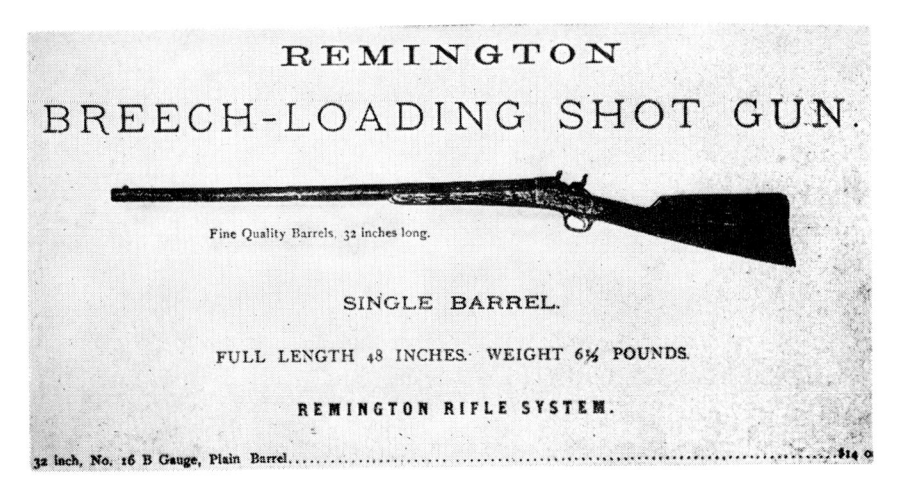

32 inch, No. 16 B Gauge, Plain Barrel...$14.0

REMINGTON SHOT GUN ON THE ROLLING BLOCK ACTION

.44/60 bottleneck and .44/77 bottleneck, Sharps and Remington chambers may be made from .43 Spanish cases. Cases for the special Remington .44/90-2$7/16$" chambers may be made by cutting off and sizing down .44-2⅝" bottleneck cases. After firing, they are then the correct shape.

As far as I am aware, this covers the special Remington cartridges, and the actual specimen cartridges will be found illustrated on pages 127 and 128.

The recapper and decapper shown on page 150 was furnished with certain Remington rifles. It is for Berdan type primers, of course, and was made by the Bridgeport Gun Implement Company.

The actual specimen rifles are shown on pages 141, 143 and 145, and they are described as follows:

FIGURE A. This is the plain basic No. 3 Hepburn rifle with 26-inch full-octagonal barrel, type #3 weight. Caliber is .32/30/125 Remington. Wind-gauge front and vernier rear sights. The early type rifle butt plate.

FIGURE B. This is the same basic No. 3 model as in Figure A, but in .38/50 Remington caliber and with 28-inch #2 barrel. This stock has the early, and commoner, Hepburn butt plate.

FIGURE C. Shows a double-set trigger Hepburn, with the more recent rifle plate and 30-inch #2 full-octagonal barrel, in .28/30 caliber.

FIGURE D. This is a plain Sporting No. 3 rifle, with the full-octagonal #4 barrel, 32 inches long, in .40/90 Sharps Straight caliber, and with custom-made stock and forearm.

FIGURE E. The heavier #4 full-octagonal barrel, 30 inches long, caliber .40/90 Sharps Straight, 3¼-inch case. This rifle is entirely original.

FIGURE F. This is the No. 3 rifle with 28-inch half-octagonal #3 barrel, in .38/40 Remington caliber, 1¾-inch case.

FIGURE G. This is a double-set trigger No. 3 early Schuetzen, or Match Grade A rifle. Barrel is full-octagonal, 30-inch length, #3 weight. Caliber is .32/40/150 Remington Straight. This rifle has a Swiss butt plate and fancy walnut stock, but it is without cheekpiece, and the dimensions are not the same as those of the later No. 3 Schuetzen, or Match.

FIGURE H. Remington Hepburn Match Grade B Rifle, a later version of Figure G, with Remington-Walker .38/55 breech-loading barrel. Wind-gauge front and Remington vernier rear sights.

FIGURE I. Remington Hepburn Creedmoor Mid Range Rifle. Caliber .40/70 or .40/65 Sharps Straight, 2½-inch case. Wind-gauge front and tall vernier rear sights; 32-inch part-octagonal barrel.

FIGURE J. Remington Rolling-block No. 1 Sporting Rifle. Caliber .44/77 necked, with open rear barrel sight, also elevating staff rear barrel sight.

FIGURE K. Remington Rolling-block Buffalo Rifle, caliber .50/70 Gov't. center-fire, with 30-inch round barrel. A custom-made job, as it has an iron ramrod under the barrel and a silver plate inlet into the top of the barrel, with the name R. F. Dodge, U. S. A., thereon. Single-set trigger and open sights.

FIGURE L. Remington Rolling-block Creedmoor Rifle. Caliber .44/90 necked, 2⅝-inch case. 34-inch round barrel, marked "L. L. Hepburn" on under side. Wind-gauge, spirit-level front sight, tall vernier rear sight.

FIGURE M. Remington Rolling-block Military Rifle. Caliber .50/70 Gov't. center-fire. Marked "Springfield, 1871." Barrel length 35 inches.

FIGURE N. Remington Rolling-block #4 Takedown Rifle. Caliber .22 Long rim-fire.

FIGURE O. Remington Navy Pistol. Caliber .50 center-fire; 7-inch round barrel.

REMINGTON NO. 6 RIFLE

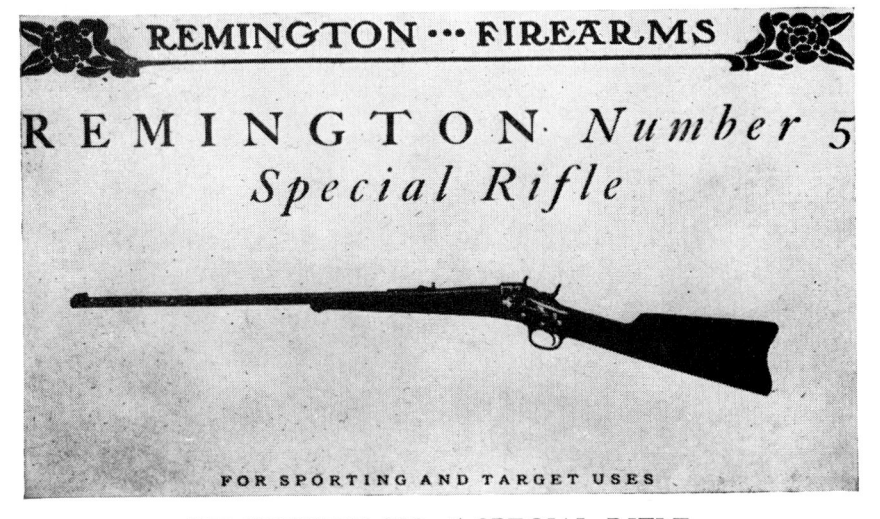

REMINGTON NO. 5 SPECIAL RIFLE

FIGURE P. Remington Army Pistol. Caliber .50 center-fire; 8-inch round barrel.

An unusual rolling-block Schuetzen rifle with engraved receiver and 30-inch half-octagonal #4 barrel is shown on page 147. The caliber is .38/55. The trigger is a single-set type, and the stock and forearm are of original Remington manufacture. The sights are vernier mid- or short-range rear, and globe wind-gauge front.

The rare under-lever Special Schuetzen model is shown on page 155. This particular rifle has a 30-inch half-octagonal Remington-Walker breech-loading barrel, #3 weight. The caliber is .38/55 Ballard & Marlin. The action is the under-lever type, and the stock on these special models was a Special straight-grip, with a cheekpiece of heavy type and a heavy Schuetzen butt plate. The grip and forearm are finely checkered. The walnut used on this rifle is a superb piece of American butt walnut.

The lever shown is the original Special type used only on this model.

The details of the lower tang and breechblock as compared with the common Hepburn parts are shown on the same page.

This model used the same frame as the regular Hepburn action, but a special lower straight-grip tang was installed. The under-finger lever operates the breechblock with a link very similar to other under-lever falling-block pattern rifles such as Sharps, Winchester, Stevens, and others. The under-lever Hepburn action is, however, the smoothest of them all, and requires for opening and closing no effort whatsoever. It was adopted late in the life of the Hepburn series, and was designed especially for Schuetzen shooting. As can be seen in the illustration, the breechblock was rounded off more at the top, to facilitate seating the case.

The greater number of these actions made were no doubt fitted with the Walker Special Schuetzen barrels chambered in the popular Schuetzen rifle calibers—.32/40, .38/55, etc., in breech-loading or muzzle-loading types. (See the catalog description of this model.) The set triggers used on this model are the best of all the triggers used on Remington rifles. They are as sensitive as the fine Ballard and Stevens set triggers.

There is a great deal of speculation among single-shot enthusiasts concerning this rare model, and very little is actually known about these rifles as so few of them were made. Some authorities claim that only about 100 actions were so manufactured by Remington. My own specimen has a very low serial number—below 20; and both of the two other specimens I have seen in collections were numbered well below 50. These three are all marked with a large "W" in front of the number.

One of these rifles, which is in a friend's collection, has the Walker muzzle-loading barrel of #4 weight, full-octagonal, and the complete loading outfit. This rifle has the regular pattern stock lever and other parts as the one shown on page 155.

The other rifle I have seen on this action is a plain hunting or sporting rifle. It has a straight-grip sporting stock, with rifle butt plate, double-set triggers, and a plain lever without the usual finger roost scroll work. The barrel on this particular rifle is a #3, 30-inch, which was originally chambered for the .32/40/150 Remington cartridge but has been rebored and chambered to accept the .32/40 Ballard & Marlin cartridge. So they were not all made in Schuetzen rifle style, as this specimen proves.

This special under-lever modification was designed by Mr. L. N. Walker, who was employed by E. Remington and Sons as a tool-room supervisor and special workman. Mr. Walker worked for the Remington company from 1870 until the time of his death, on March 1, 1918. There is absolutely no record at the Remington plant today which gives any information on the actual number of rifles that were made on this special style of action.

Regardless of how many were actually made, this is a fine model, and probably the finest made in Schuetzen style by any company. The lines of this action are, of course, not an improvement over the regular Hepburn, so it was not a symmetrical, beautiful target arm such as the Ballard and Stevens rifles were.

The mechanical excellence and the quality of wood and finish used were the best obtainable. For that matter, the precision with which all the Remington target models were made is superior to many. The parts are always of the finest material, and the hardening of parts is comparable only to those found in the Ballard. The barrels were as accurate as any made. The Hepburn action was discontinued in 1911, according to Mr. Frank J. Kahrs of the Remington Arms Company.

The rolling-block and the Hepburn systems were both unique, in that in an era of under-lever single-shots, neither one was of that pattern. They are unique not alone in this respect but also in many other features, and they are among the most desirable of all collection pieces today.

If you have a Hepburn or a rolling-block Remington rifle in one of the old calibers listed in this chapter, think twice before you rebarrel it or otherwise remodel the arm, as you may be overlooking a vast amount of pleasure in using the gun as is. If it is one of the little-known and odder calibers, the search for cases, molds, etc., may also prove to be part of the pleasure of possession. At least, my specimen has so impressed me.

Many times I have spent as much time and effort—not to mention cash—in running down the proper cases or cartridges and tools or molds for a rifle as I did in locating the arm in the first place. In some instances I have even started with a cartridge first and then hunted a rifle to fit it. The .32/30/125 Remington was such a case, for I started with one cartridge I bought from a specimen cartridge dealer and then expended a great amount of effort to locate a rifle and more cartridges. Needless to say, the personal satisfaction that results from such a chase is great; but you can take it from me, this is the hard way to do it.

When you find the one rifle for which you are looking, load it mildly, and don't try to duplicate present-day cartridge velocities and trajectories. They were not intended for that, and your pleasure will be appreciably decreased when you are attempting to pick pieces of frame, hammer, and breechblock, out of your face.

If you want modern high-velocity performance, the best way to get it is to go down to your nearest sporting goods dealer and buy a modern rifle such as the superb Winchester Model 70 or a Remington 30-S or 720, and have done with it.

By all this I do not mean to imply that the Remington single-shots are inferior in strength to any of our other single-shot target rifles, because of course they are not; but after all, these fine old rifles are of another, a more golden, era; one in which speed was something to be avoided rather than sought.

Get yourself a Remington "Heartburn!"

IV

The Sharps Rifle

No VOLUME of single-shot rifles would be complete without a chapter on the famous Sharps, the granddaddy of them all. This rifle and its makers have been the subject of so many fine articles by a host of authorities that there is very little that is new or that has been unsaid left for me to include in these pages.

To Mr. Winston O. Smith we are particularly indebted for his volume *The Sharps Rifle,* for he has therein presented for the first time under one cover all the data on the Sharps in historical and chronological manner. His discussion of the early military models should and will make these varied types even more appreciated than they have been in the past.

For an intelligent discussion of the mechanical principles and functions of the Sharps rifles I would refer you to J. V. K. Wagar's article in the *American Rifleman* for February, 1940.

For a perusal of the original catalogs as issued by the different Sharps companies I recommend the 1859, 1864, 1875, 1876, 1877, 1878, 1879, and 1880 catalogs as reprinted in facsimile by Mr. L. D. Satterlee in his book entitled, *Fourteen Old Gun Catalogues,* published in 1941. These are all the Sharps catalogs that are known to exist, and the data as shown therein is invaluable to the collector.

There is, however, in the Sharps models—as there is in all these old single-shots—a wide variation, and possibly a discussion of the actual specimens as I have them or have seen them will be acceptable here. I have confined my Sharps section of the single-shot collection strictly to the cartridge models, particularly the Sharps Borchardt. I shoot all my rifles—I wouldn't care for them unless I could do so— and so possibly there is room here for what data I can supply on this phase of the Sharps and the Sharps Borchardt.

As already stated—and as all Sharps fans know—the variations in the models as they exist today are many and amazing. With the exception of certain of the military models, there are hardly any two specimens that are alike. Whenever I have found, for example, a sporting rifle that conformed to the catalog specifications of that particular model, I have always felt more elated than when it turned out to be another variation or a special model. In most makes of single-shot rifles we usually are more interested in the odd or unusual custom-made specimens, but in the Sharps line it always seemed to me, at least, that I had one that was more valuable when it conformed to what I thought it should. This may, no doubt, seem odd, as perhaps it is. All gun cranks and collectors are a trifle "teched," and possibly I just abuse the privilege. But I realize that the reader did not invest in this book to discover my weaknesses but to see what I could dig up on his, I hope, favorite subject.

The main part of my experience with the early percussion Sharps rifle has been with a fine engraved sporting model, the slanting breech specimen shown on the next page. This has the 1852 pattern action so ably described by W. O. Smith in his book cited. The Lawrence pellet primer mechanism is intact and in fine working condition. This action is finely engraved all over with scroll designs. The hammer, patch-box cover, steel butt plate, and barrel breech are also nicely and tastefully engraved. There is also some scroll work around the barrel flats at the muzzle. The fore end tip appears to be of silver, and has line engraving thereon.

This rifle has double-set triggers of an odd pattern, and the adjustment screw instead of being flat-headed and slotted has a ball with hole through it so that adjustment can be obtained by inserting a pin or piece of wire to turn the screw. The action is casehardened, as was common with these rifles. The stock and forearm are of fancy walnut, uncheckered.

This rifle has a full-octagonal 26-inch barrel of about #3 weight or slightly heavier, and it is browned, not blued. The bore measures .339" in the grooves, and is rifled with eight grooves.

The sights are the regular Sharps sporting front, fixed rear barrel, and an unusual tang plain adjustment type that is different from any I have observed on other rifles—and I believe it to be original with this particular specimen.

This is a beautiful, well-balanced arm, and it is the only percussion Sharps I have ever really enjoyed owning. My aversion to military

THE SHARPS RIFLE

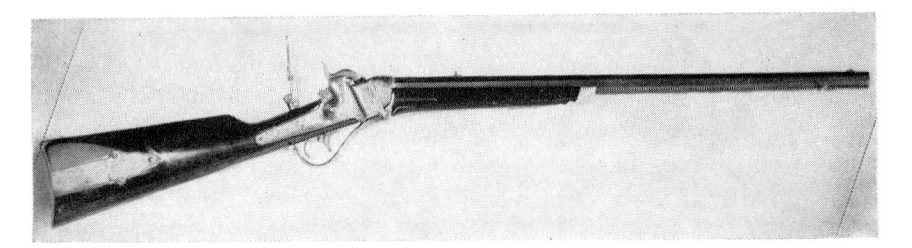

ENGRAVED SLANTING BREECH SHARPS RIFLE

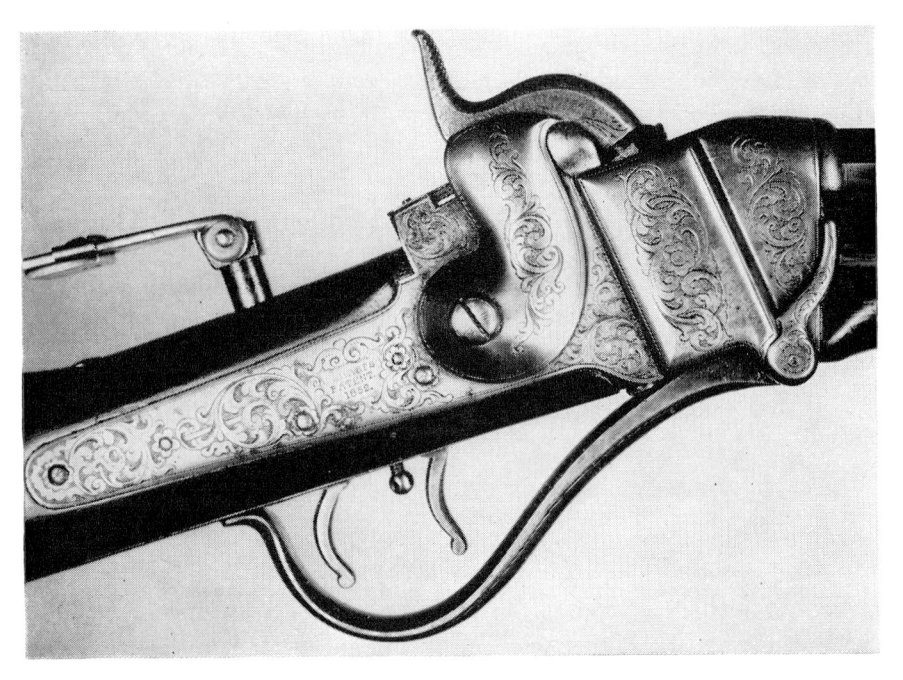

SHARPS SLANTING BREECH RIFLE

arms has kept me from experiencing the delights (?) of any Sharps percussion model except this particular one. It has satisfied all my curiosity concerning what makes these mechanisms tick and shoot.

In shooting this rifle I have used a conical bullet with two grease grooves, weighing 265 grains, and sized to fit the bore. I never made the paper or cellophane cartridges as described by Mr. Smith, but merely seated the bullet in the breech with a homemade bullet seater, poured in from 40 to 55 grains of black powder, and used a musket cap on the nipple, the pellet primer mechanism being disconnected, of course.

The barrel of this Sharps of mine is perfect inside, and I mean to keep it so. The accuracy was rather mediocre at first, until I got some pure lead and made bullets from that; then it improved to the point that I could keep 10-shot groups down to about 3¼ to 3½ inches, which I considered fairly satisfactory for this particular model.

Incidentally, King's semi-smokeless powder gave better results and less fouling and caking in my particular climate (northwestern Ohio) than regular black powder. I detest black powder in a mechanism of this kind, however, as it necessitates dunking you, your clothes, and the rifle in the bathtub in order to get all three thoroughly clean.

The Lawrence pellet primer mechanism on this rifle is a really efficient device. It will feed and flip those little pellets out there on to the nipple in perfect synchronization with the descending hammer.

I tried disks made of aluminum and of other metals that were of different weight from the original Sharps pellets and none would land in the right place at the right time. Some of the lighter ones were flipped quite a distance from the rifle. This was done merely for amusement purposes, to see what would happen. None of the Sharps pellet primers I have would fire, of course, and I always used percussion caps for the actual firing of the rifle.

THE CREEDMOOR SIDE-HAMMER SHARPS RIFLE

My experience from a hobby standpoint has been almost entirely with the side-hammer and hammerless Sharps rifle. Of this type the Creedmoor side-hammer Sharps specimens always appealed to me much more than the heavy, clumsy hunting rifles. I prefer the long, beautifully tapered, full-octagonal barreled models, with their checkered single triggers, pistol-grip shotgun buttstocks of fine walnut, usually nicely checkered. The true Creedmoor models weigh just under 10 pounds, of course, to conform to the rules of their era, and they are the highest grade and finest finished of the side-hammer Sharps models.

While I have seen full round-barreled models, these rifles usually have 30- or 32-inch octagonal or half-octagonal tapered barrels. In the higher grades 32 inches was usually the standard; 34-inch barrels were, of course, used to a certain extent.

The sights on these models were of the finest, consisting of the Sharps vernier rear and wind-gauge front, with spirit level.

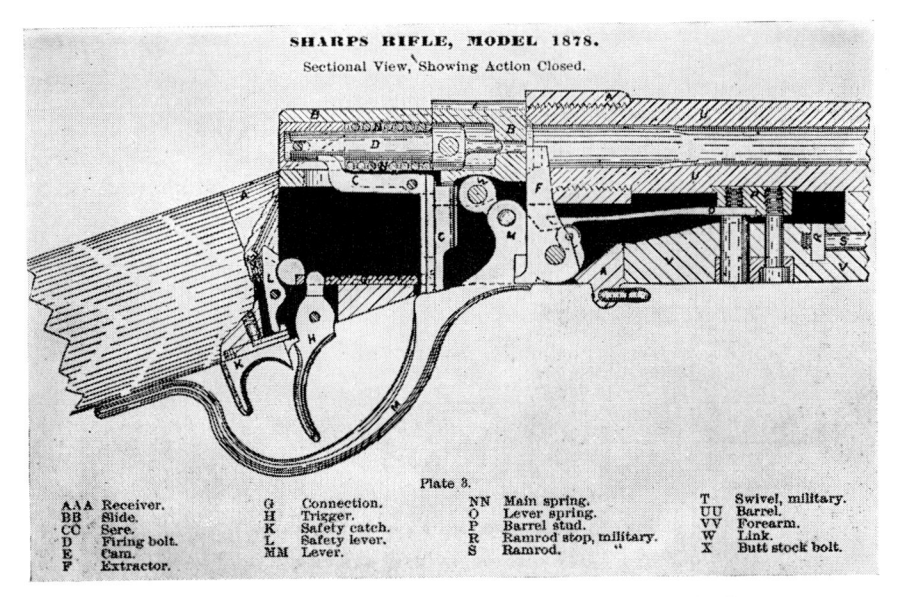

SHARPS RIFLE, MODEL 1878.
Sectional View, Showing Action Closed.

Plate 3.

AAA	Receiver.	G	Connection.	NN	Main spring.	T	Swivel, military.
BB	Slide.	H	Trigger.	O	Lever spring.	UU	Barrel.
CC	Sere.	K	Safety catch.	P	Barrel stud.	VV	Forearm.
D	Firing bolt.	L	Safety lever.	R	Ramrod stop, military.	W	Link.
E	Cam.	MM	Lever.	S	Ramrod.	"	X	Butt stock bolt.
F	Extractor.						

SHARPS-BORCHARDT ACTION DESIGN

Some of the rifles made on the Creedmoor pattern were supplied for hunting purposes and have double-set triggers. The true Creedmoor was obligated to a single trigger of 3 pounds pull, and these triggers on the Creedmoor grades are usually finely checkered. The earlier Creedmoor Sharps have straight grip stocks.

The caliber used in the earlier Creedmoor Sharps seems to have been first the .44/77-2¼" case necked. Later this case was loaded with 90 grains of powder, and also about this time the 2⅝-inch bottlenecked .44/90 case was used. The powder charges were increased to 100 and also to 105 grains in this same 2⅝-inch case, to give more push to the heavier paper-patch bullet being used at the long ranges.

A few of these side-hammer Sharps Creedmoors are also found chambered for the special Remington .44-2⁷⁄₁₆" bottlenecked case loaded with 90 grains of powder.

The greater number of the Creedmoor pattern rifles found today seem to be chambered for the various .44 caliber bottlenecks; however, once in a while one turns up in .45-2.6" Straight caliber. I have never seen these later side-hammer Creedmoor Sharps chambered for the .45-2.4" case, but I imagine there were some so made. I have seen this rifle chambered for the .45-2⅞" case in several instances.

I have never yet seen a true Creedmoor rifle chambered for the .44/60 Sharps-Berdan case, but of course there may have been some so made. However, I am inclined to the opinion that this size case was used for the most part in the shorter range target models, and possibly in some sporting rifles. The earlier sporting models were made in several calibers and, of course, in many styles.

The higher grade mid- and short-range target models are as finely made as the Creedmoor rifles. These usually have the shorter staffed vernier rear sight, and they are in less powerful caliber, the .40/50 bottlenecked, .40/50 Sharps Straight, .40/70 bottlenecked, .40/70 Sharps Straight, .40/90 bottlenecked being very popular. I believe all the bottlenecks appeared on the scene first, the straight case with the same powder charge coming along later.

The heavier sporting rifles were regularly available in weights up to 16 pounds, but I have seen two specimens that tipped the scales at 18 pounds, one a .50 caliber chambered for the 3¼" case, the other a .45 caliber for the .45-2⅞" case.

The common calibers in the earlier specimens of this type seem to have been .44 and .40; the .45 caliber coming later, of course.

I have one Sharps side-hammer plain hunting rifle, caliber .45, with 30-inch octagonal barrel, that weighs 14 pounds. This barrel is chambered for the special 3¼-inch case. The barrel is marked simply ".45 cal.," with no case length indicated.

It is in the sporting, plain rifle pattern that we find the great majority of Sharps rifles today, the fine target and sporting models being far in the minority, of course. The condition of some of these old hunting rifles is appalling, but they are found mostly in the West, where of course they were used and just worn out completely. The finer specimens of the hunting rifle and, of course, most of the Creedmoor and midrange target models are found in the East, and they are usually in fine condition. The circumstances under which they were used were naturally very different from those of the hunting models, and accordingly more conducive to better care and less actual use.

One otherwise fine and mint-condition Sharps Creedmoor I own, however, has had scope blocks mounted on the barrel by some former owner. This rifle has the 32-inch full-octagonal barrel, .44/90-2⅝" caliber, and I have often wondered if the man who put the modern scope on this rifle was using it to hunt squirrels with! Need-

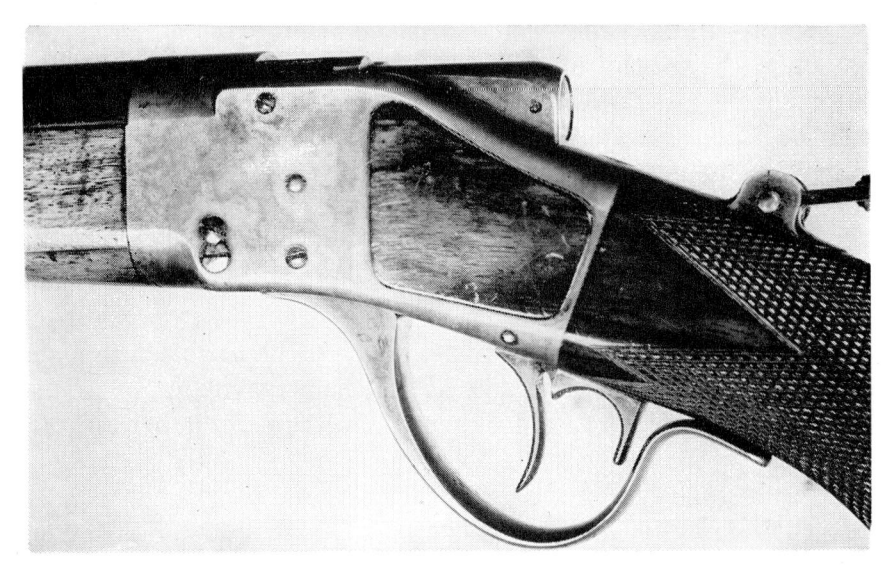

SHARPS-BORCHARDT LONG RANGE RIFLE ACTION

less to say, I plugged the holes and blued the spots so they would not show. One man I know cut off a fine 30-inch full-octagonal Sharps barrel in .40/90 Sharps Straight caliber to 24 inches because there were a few very minor pits near the muzzle!

I have owned several Sharps in .44/77, .44/90, and .40/70 and .40/90 bottlenecked calibers and enjoyed shooting all of them. However, the only ones I retained are the specimens which have excellent barrels, and in the better grades.

To me, the heavy, clumsy Sharps sporting rifles are too much in the nature of ordnance to be interesting; but I know many Sharps fans will disagree here.

Once in Denver, Colorado, I obtained from a collector some Sharps rifles and parts that had come from the J. P. Lower sporting goods store when this stock was sold. J. P. Lower was the distributor of Sharps rifles in the early day, and his name is found stamped on many Sharps barrels. Among the items I obtained from this store was a brand new Sharps barrel, full-octagonal, 30 inches long, and weighing 9 pounds. The bore was perfect, of course, being unfired, and it was chambered for the Sharps .45-2⅞" case. The barrel was completely threaded and chambered, but the extractor cut had not been made. The barrel was in the white.

Evidently these barrels were carried in stock to a limited degree by Lower, though this may have been just an extra barrel that had been ordered for someone and never fitted to his action. Someday I hope to find the right sporting action and have the barrel fitted to it. This should then make a fine shooting rifle, as the barrel has never been used.

The set triggers as used on the Sharps side-hammer models are very fine and of sound construction. Very seldom are a set of these triggers found to be out of order.

One fault, outside the firing-pin troubles in this action, is the fact that many tumblers that carry the side-hammer are found to be broken on the inside of the lock plate, and these are rather difficult to make.

All in all, the Sharps were rugged rifles, and it is small wonder that the name Sharps is so well known today, even among men who are not single-shot rifle conscious. However, the great Sharps is more than just a single-shot rifle; it is an institution.

THE SHARPS BORCHARDT RIFLE

Of the two types of Sharps, the hammerless, or Borchardt, is my choice. This trim, symmetrical model appeals to me more, by far, than the clumsy outside hammer model.

We find in the Borchardt series a little more uniformity than in the earlier models. The military Borchardts are almost identical, with very minor differences. On the later ones made, the improved rear sight is used;[1] also the serial numbers are usually stamped on the side of the frame below the Sharps name, which is stamped on the last models made. Also, the later military models are usually blued receiver types.

I believe that the later series of military models have the serial numbers on the side instead of on the under side of the frame because of the fact that the frames of most of these later Borchardts, both military and sporting models, were milled ahead of the trigger slot, to accept set triggers if so ordered. This extra slot is filled with a small block held in place by a pin through the frame. When set triggers were ordered, it was a simple matter to install them, as the

---

[1] The wind-gauge bar used on the later Sharps Borchardt Military rifles was devised by Mr. F. M. Barnes of Michigan.

3/16"

Rear view of trigger tumbler

Front trigger 1/4" thick

Pivoted 9/16" ahead of rear trigger

Strong spring plunger

Side view of trigger tumbler

Spring plunger

Trigger-sear connector piece.

1/4"

7/16"

5/16"

9/16"

5/8"

Upper part of trigger slotted to accept small tumbler shown above. Both parts are held in place by trigger pin

Pull adjustment screw

Trigger-slot in frame

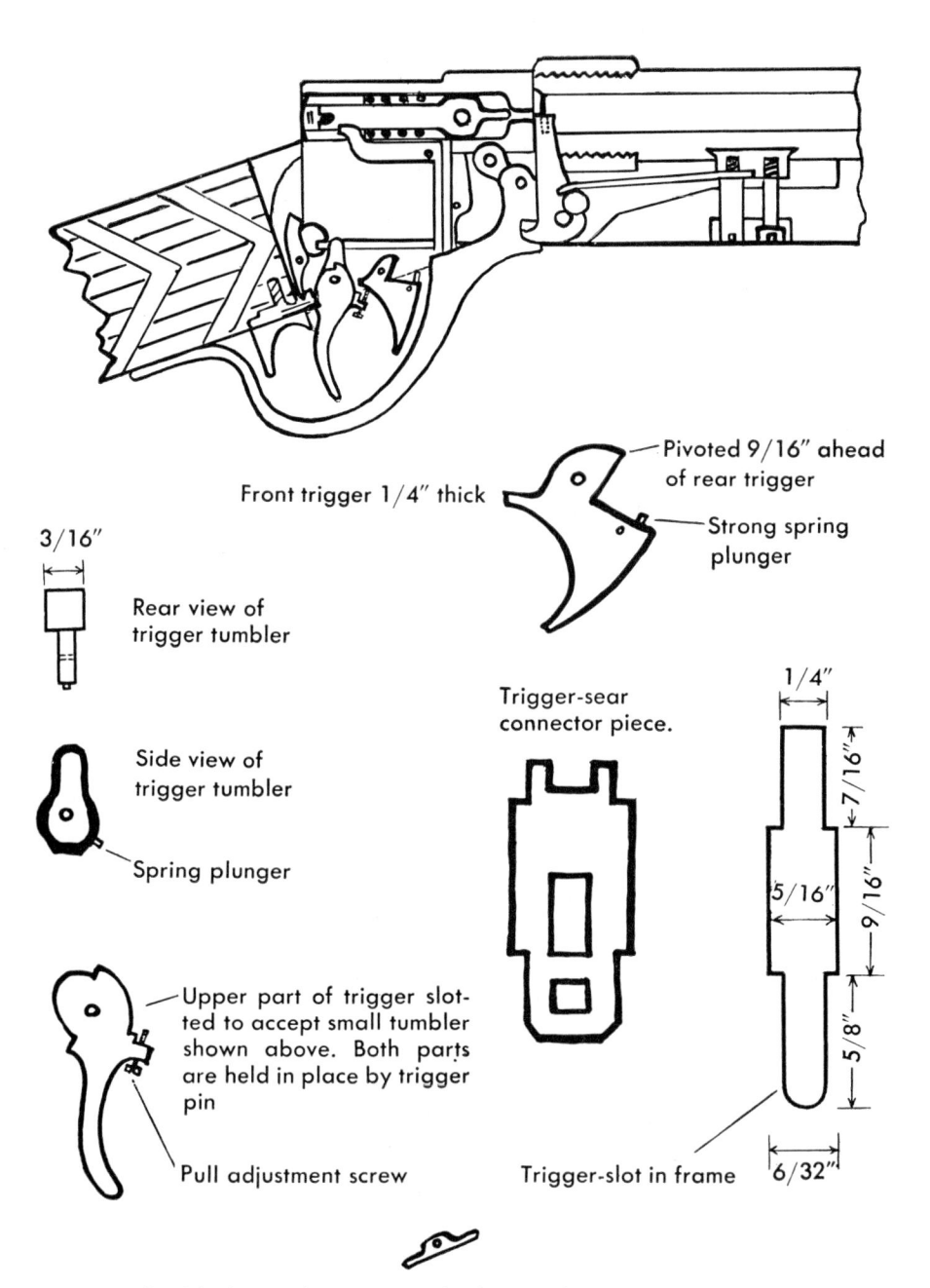

6/32"

Filler block—used in space in the frame when set trigger was not ordered from the factory. This block is held in the frame opening by traverse pin through holes in frame. 9/16" ahead of regular trigger pin holes.

SHARPS RIFLE CO. SET TRIGGER FOR BORCHARDT ACTION

SHARPS-BORCHARDT EXPRESS RIFLE, CALIBER .45 2⅞-INCH SHARPS

26-inch full octagon barrel, top flat full length matted

SHARPS-BORCHARDT OFFICERS RIFLE, PANELED RECEIVER, CALIBER .45-70, 32-INCH BARREL

frames were so milled. Many sporting frames have these blocks in place, but not so many military frames are seen.

I have never seen the sporting frames in the blued finish but only in the casehardened style; but of course there may have been many so finished. The sporting models have a neater frame than the military model, because the barrel housing and the bottom of the frame at the front are rounded and finished off much better.

This military Sharps Borchardt was made only in .45/70 Gov't. caliber, so far as I know. It is a very neat and trim rifle for a military rifle, with the nicely tapered 32-inch round barrel, well-designed steel shotgun buttstock, and other good features.

Why this rifle was not adopted by the U. S. Army instead of the clumsy, obsolete, trap-door Springfield is still a mystery to the admirers of the Borchardt. The absence of the large outside hammer was no doubt partly responsible; obtuseness of the military mind was possibly the rest of the story. The Sharps catalog for 1878 mentions on page 23 that the Manual of Arms should be written for the model rifle used by the Army and not vice versa. Of course, the fact that the Borchardt had no firing-pin retractor and also that the common cartridge case was primed with the large soft Berdan type of primer, figured in the decision to a certain extent.

All the military Borchardt that I have examined had firing pins which projected through the breechblock almost ⅛ of an inch, and were almost that size in diameter and square in profile. It is not necessary that the pin be this shape to fire the Berdan primer, and if the pin were shortened slightly and of smaller diameter, with the nose well rounded off, the likelihood of its hanging on large primers is greatly reduced. These military breechblocks could also have been drilled with one small hole in the top to enable the soldier to insert a wire or a nail or some similar implement into the hole and thus pry back the firing pin from the primer if it hangs up. This was done quite often when the Borchardt was rebarreled by some of the old Schuetzen barrelmakers, and it is still good policy when modern varment calibers are used in this action.

The set triggers as supplied by the Sharps Rifle Company on order at $4.00 extra are not too good. To counteract a special design frame, they used a design in which the one trigger was reversed, and was of rather flimsy construction compared with the rest of the action. Very few Borchardts are seen today with these original Sharps set triggers, and fewer of these that still function. (See page 173 for details of this trigger.)

The fact that in order to trip the sear the knock-off on a set trigger design for this action must fly forward instead of upward, as in most single-shot designs, complicates the matter, of course. Many Borchardts are seen today, however, with set triggers that were installed by Zischang, Pope, and other designers, and these are, of course, very fine, sensitive triggers. All these triggers were installed by milling out the rear of the action and fitting an extra tang in place which carried the triggers. The safety lever in these instances is, of course, done away with. A. W. Peterson of Denver, Colorado, altered two or three Borchardt frames for his own set triggers, and he told me that it was a terrible job. He was not interested in so altering any more Borchardts, he said.

The Borchardt action was really Mr. Peterson's favorite for a match or a Schuetzen rifle, and he has won many medals and trophies with it. Practically all the photographs in his shop today, showing Mr. Peterson, include a fine Sharps Borchardt by his side.

A. O. Zischang, the famous barrelmaker, of Syracuse, New York, also preferred the Sharps Borchardt, and some of his alterations on these actions are very fine.

Of the sporting Borchardts in the higher target grades, almost all had removable upper tangs held in place by one screw. This was done so that an extra tang with the base for a tang rear sight could easily be installed and removed if so desired. This removable tang is shown on page 31. The plain sporting Borchardt hunting rifle usually had a top tang forged in one piece with the rest of the frame.

Practically all the Borchardt actions have round barrels and round receiver rings. There are two exceptions: one is the plain Sporting Rifle, Model of 1878, which was supplied with either round or octagonal barrels. When fitted with the round barrel, the receiver ring is round on top, as is the case in the military and higher grades. When this Sporting Rifle was ordered with octagonal barrel, the receiver usually supplied—but not always—was octagonal in shape, to conform to the shape of the barrel. I have also seen this model having an octagonal barrel and a round-top receiver. You figure it out; I give up.

The other model supplied with octagonal barrel is the Express Rifle, Model of 1878, which has a 26-inch full-octagonal barrel, the top flat of which is full length matted. This model also has the octagonal-shaped receiver ring, and I have never seen this model with the rounded receiver ring.

The models which regularly carried round barrels were the following: Military Rifle, Carbine, Hunter's Rifle, Business Rifle, Short Range Rifle, Mid Range Rifle, and Long Range Rifle.

The better grades of the Borchardt were sometimes paneled with fancy walnut, hard rubber, horn, and other hard material (see page 171). These panels are set into milled recesses in the receiver, and they are held in place by a pointed-end screw which enters at the rear. The stock must be removed to allow these screws to be backed out and the panels removed. When the actions were furnished in paneled style, the Sharps name and address, which was usually stamped on the left side of the frame, was, of course, omitted. As a rule, the only markings on these paneled models are "Sharps Rifle Co., Bridgeport, Conn." and "Old Reliable," which is stamped on the barrel. Also the serial number is found on the under side of the frame between the trigger and the block opening. My Long Range Creedmoor paneled models are so marked, while the Short Range model, being made without panels, has the name and serial number on the left side of the receiver.

ENGRAVED PANELED SHARPS-BORCHARDT RIFLE

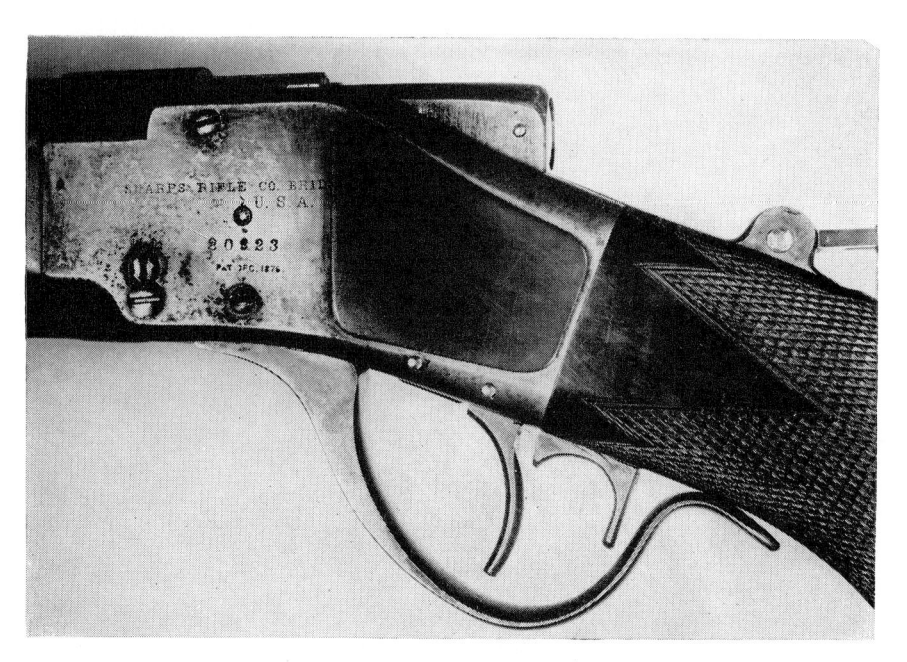

HARD RUBBER PANELED SHARPS-BORCHARDT MID
RANGE RIFLE ACTION

These rifles were available upon special order, paneled and engraved both. The 1878 and 1879 catalogs state that special engraving was available at charges from $5.00 up to any amount the customer wished to pay.

I have one target grade Borchardt, a midrange .40/70 SS caliber that has hard rubber panels let into the side, evidently after the Sharps name was stamped on the side. Part of the name and address are apparent, but some of the letters were obliterated when the milling out for panels was done. This was, no doubt, done at the Sharps factory, as it is finely executed and is of exactly the same dimensions as other paneled models I have. This action was evidently rehardened after this remodeling work was done, as it has the same finish as other paneled actions (see page 177).

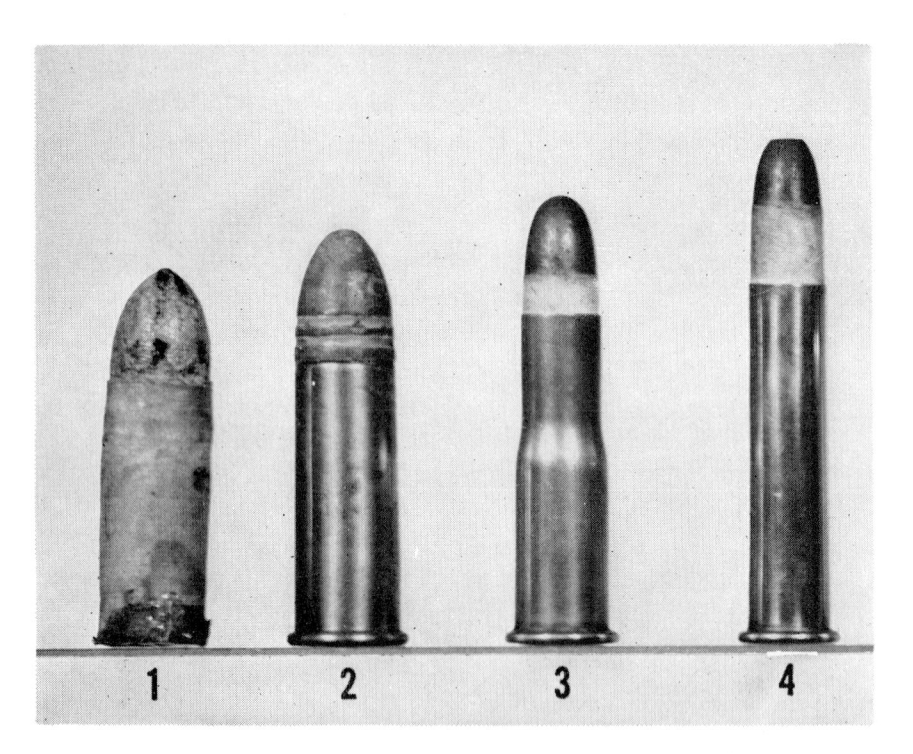

CARTRIDGES USED IN SHARPS RIFLES
1   .52 Sharps linen
2   .52/70/405 Sharps rim-fire (copper case)
3   .40/50/265 Sharps necked
4   .40/50/265 Sharps straight

The man from whom I obtained this rifle said it had belonged to his grandfather, who had bought a plain sporting rifle originally. After using it for some time he sent it back to the Sharps factory, where it was paneled, a new barrel and stock were installed, and the completely remodeled rifle returned to him. I am more inclined to believe that the frame was already stamped with the name and then paneled and finished before it ever left the factory in the first place.

The improved vernier tang rear sights as used on the Borchardts

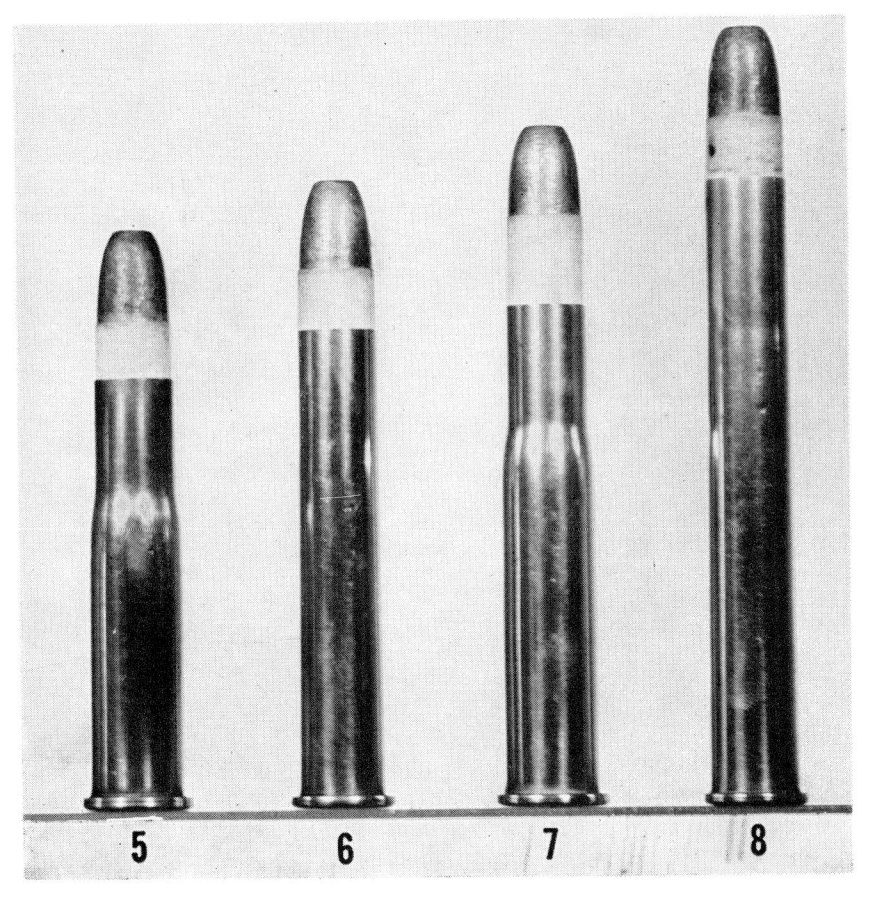

CARTRIDGES USED IN SHARPS RIFLES
5   .40/70/330 Sharps necked
6   .40/70/330 Sharps straight
7   .40/90/370 Sharps necked
8   .40/90/370 Sharps straight

were a big improvement on the type used on the side-hammer models, as there was no long, delicate adjusting screw to become bent or damaged. The micrometer adjustment device on these sights is also a clever idea. With this system, finer adjustments are possible than with any other vernier rear sight. The adjusting of this type sight is described in the catalog as follows:

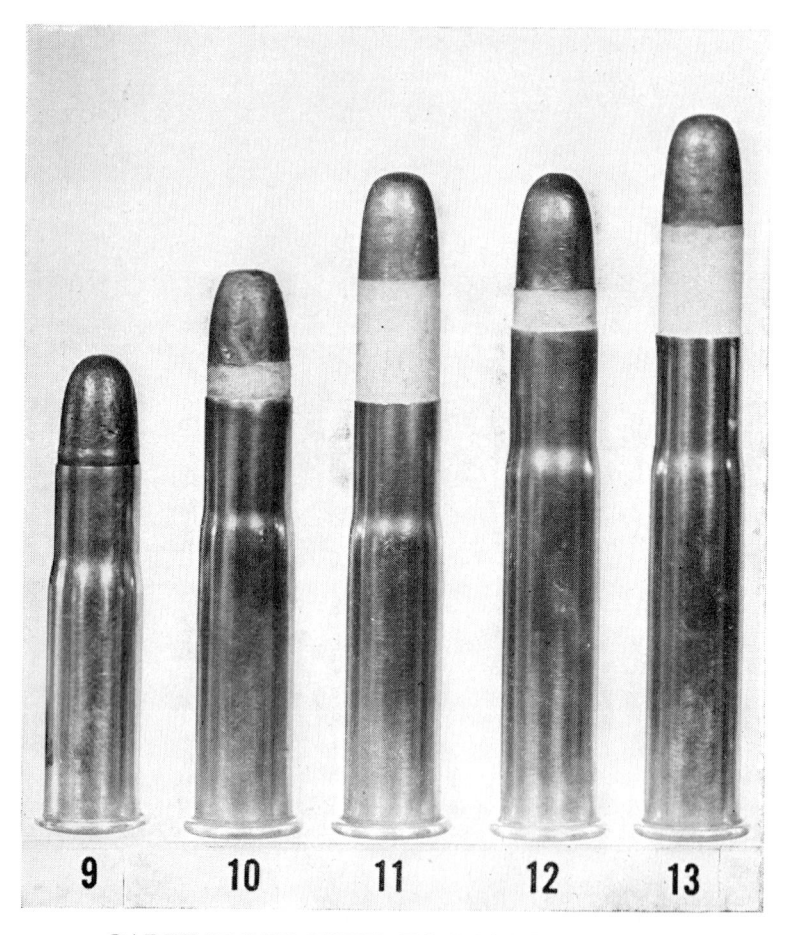

CARTRIDGES USED IN SHARPS RIFLES
9 .44/60/395 necked
10 .44/77/380 necked, 2¼-inch case
11 .44/90/405 necked, 2¼-inch case
12 .44/90/500 necked, 2⅝-inch case
13 .44/105/520 Sharps and Remington special, 2⅝-inch case

THE SHARPS RIFLE

DIRECTIONS FOR MEASURING ELEVATIONS BY THE VERNIER SCALE

Elevations for Sharps Long Range Rifles are measured by inches, marked 1, 2, 3, etc. (On some of the old model guns the scale is marked in half inches.) These are sub-divided into twentieths of an inch, each

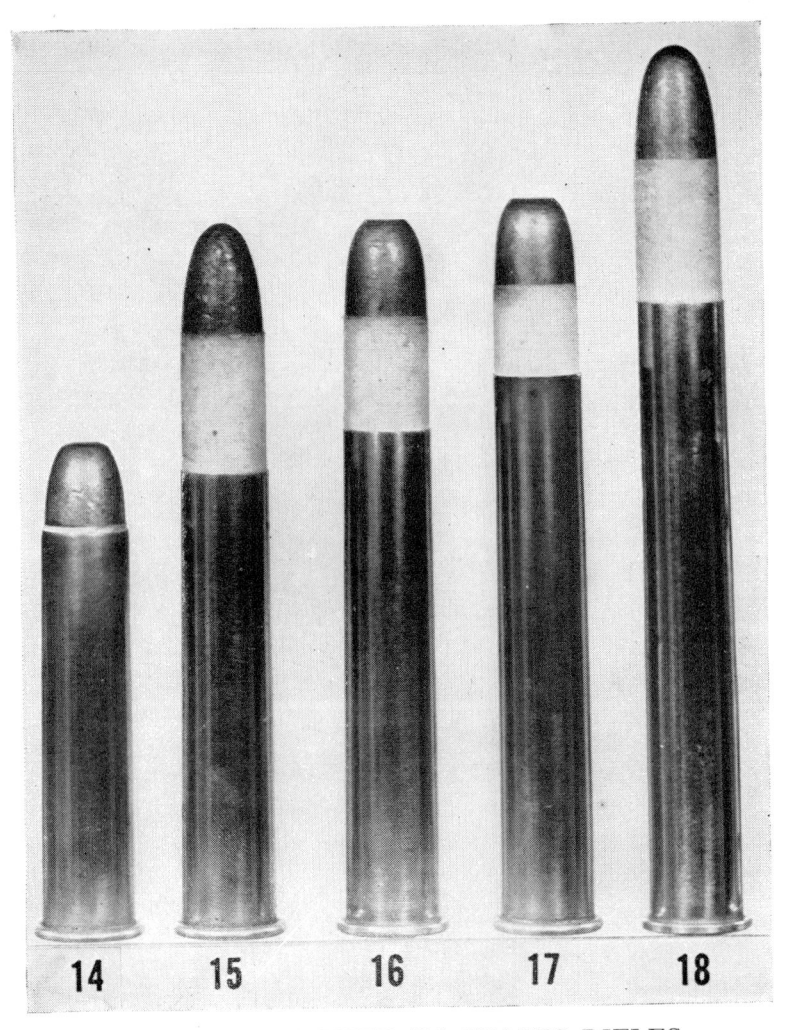

CARTRIDGES USED IN SHARPS RIFLES
- 14 .45/75/420 Sharps straight, 2 1/10-inch case
- 15 .45/90/550 Sharps straight, 2 4/10-inch case
- 16 .45/100/500 Sharps straight, 2 6/10-inch case
- 17 .45/100/500 Sharps straight, 2 7/8-inch case
- 18 .45/120/550 Sharps straight, 3 1/4-inch case

mark on the main scale representing five one-hundredths (more commonly called points). If the bottom line of the short sliding scale be set opposite the line marked 1 on the main scale, it shows one inch elevation. To add $1/100$ (or one point) to this, we set the second line from the bottom on the short scale, to the line on the main scale above it.

To add $2/100$ (or two points) we move the third line from the bottom on the short scale, to the line above it. To add $3/100$ move up the fourth

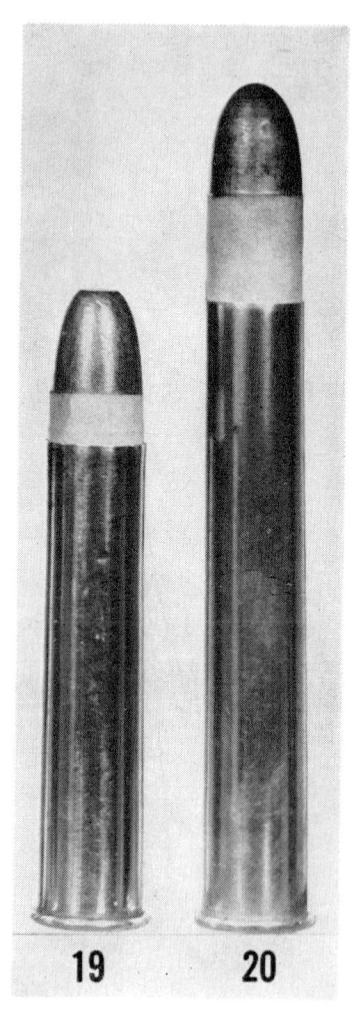

CARTRIDGES USED IN SHARPS RIFLES
19   .50/90/473 Sharps straight, 2½-inch case
20   .50/140/700 Sharps straight, 3¼-inch case

line, and for $\frac{4}{100}$ the fifth line, then to get the $\frac{5}{100}$ the bottom line is now moved up to the first line above the inch mark, and we have $1\frac{5}{100}$-inch in elevation or as more commonly called one hundred and five points. Proceed in the same manner for any number of points required.

TO MEASURE FRACTIONS OF A POINT BY THE NEW VERNIER

On the lower half of the screw that moves the sliding scale will be observed grooves cut diagonally across the threads at regular intervals. Move the screw the width of one of these, and it changes the elevation one-tenth of a point, or one one-thousandth of an inch, two of them two-tenths, etc.

On the center of the screw will be observed the figures 0, 5, 10, 15, 20 at regular intervals. From 0 to 5 changes one-half a point; 0 to 10 changes one point; turning it entirely around changes two and one half points. The new vernier scale is an invention recently patented by the Sharps Rifle Company, and it can be used on no other rifle. The numerous advantages it possesses over the old one will be greatly appreciated by expert riflemen. Besides the old scale measurement, it has an additional Vernier by which any decimal of a point, $\frac{1}{10}$ (one-thousandth of an inch), $\frac{2}{10}$, $\frac{3}{10}$, etc., can be moved in elevation with accuracy. The slender screw, which gave so much trouble when bent, is done away with, and the rifleman can be certain when he fixes his elevation at any point that it will not be found at some other point after the peep cup be tightened.

The short-range, midrange, and long-range Sharps Borchardt sights are shown on page 29.

THE SHARPS CARTRIDGES

Today a great deal of interest is centered in the Sharps cartridges, and some sizes of these are almost impossible to find in any quantity. The cartridges as put up by the Sharps company itself were practically all Berdan primed types; therefore there are few left that can be reloaded many times. However, UMC and Winchester both loaded all these sizes, and for the most part with the Winchester type of anvil-contained primers, so there are some of these still available, and they are much to be desired as far as the reloading is concerned.

The Sharps cartridges as made at Hartford, Conn., were put up in white-label boxes, and these are much more rare than the Bridgeport-made numbers, which have green labels.

Sharps tools for reloading their cartridges were very simple, consisting of an awl to pry out the old Berdan primer, a recapper, and a simple one-piece bullet seater. The molds as furnished by Sharps are of the iron-handle type, with nipper jaws on the end, to cut off the sprew. These molds are an abomination when it comes to casting bullets, as the handles, unless covered with wood or some other material, soon become too hot to hold. In the larger, longer bullet sizes it is quite a job to get perfect bullets with these molds. If a swage to swage the paper-patched type of bullet is available, good bullets may be made, but otherwise you will spend most of the time cursing the mold, the makers, and yourself for ever getting fouled up in such a thankless job.

After the bullets are cast and swaged, it is rather a simple matter to patch them, using a thickness of bond paper to bring the bullet to the correct size so that it may be seated in the case snugly without tearing. As long as it fits the case mouth properly and can be inserted in the chamber, black powder and ballistics will take care of the rest.

The barrels that were made for paper-patch bullets are easily identified because of the very shallow grooves, while the deeper grooved barrels were, of course, bored and rifled especially for grooved bullets. They can, however, be used interchangeably, with fairly good results.

For an informative article on loading and patching the Sharps cartridges, the shooter should read Frank Mayer's articles in the September, 1934, and October, 1934, issues of the *American Rifleman* magazine; also J. V. K. Wagar's article in the same magazine for March, 1941. The Sharps catalog for 1864 contains complete instructions for making the paper or linen cartridges.

The earlier side-hammer Sharps were chambered mostly for .44 caliber bottlenecks, .50/70 Gov't., .50/95 Sharps-2½", .40/50, .40/70, and .40/90 bottlenecked and straight cases, and the .45 caliber straight cases in 2ⁱ⁄₁₀, 2⁴⁄₁₀, 2⁶⁄₁₀, and 2⅞ inches. Upon special order they were also chambered for the 3¼-inch cases in .40, .45 and .50 calibers. However, there is no reference to these longer sizes in the Sharps catalogs. They were made, we know, as we have the cases and the rifles so chambered to show for it.

There were, no doubt, a few Sharps rifles also chambered for certain Everlasting case sizes of other makes. The only one I have seen so chambered was an 1877 side-hammer rifle which was specially chambered for the .40/90 Ideal Everlasting case, 3³⁄₁₆ inches

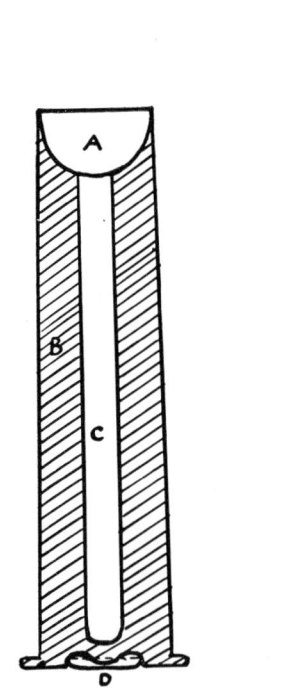

SHARPS 45 2 1/10-INCH
SHARPS 40 2 1/2-INCH

SECTIONAL VIEW

A Cavity for round ball
B Solid steel shell
C Powder chamber
D Berdan Primer

CASE DIMENSIONS

.45 caliber 2 1/10-inch		.40 caliber 2 1/2-inch
Diameter at head	.505	.451
Diameter at mouth	.4795	.421
Diameter of rim	.601	.5515
Thickness of rim	.0625	.0627

Berdan No. 1 Primer .255 inch diameter
Approximate size of .45 cal. powder chamber at mouth, .248

The Sharps Rifle Co. solid steel shells for gallery use with round balls and 12 grains of black powder. Made in the 2 sizes shown.

long. While this caliber is found quite often in the Ballard rifles, that was the only Sharps I have ever seen made for it. The barrel was stamped merely "40 cal.," no case length being indicated. However, there are many Sharps made in Sharps calibers that are unmarked.

The 1879 Sharps catalog makes the following statement regarding Everlasting cases:

> We have made exhaustive experiments with the so-called "Everlasting" shells and have failed to find the advantages claimed for them. The "Everlasting" is drawn like other cartridge shells, in a press, from cold metal, and seldom can brass of sufficient ductility be found to stand the enormous strain to which it is subjected, in drawing such a thickness, without so disintegrating the grain of the metal that the thick shells become brittle, and split or break after a few discharges. The most durable cartridge shells in use are reinforced or strengthened by a cup of brass, which is placed inside the completed form, thus allowing the body to be drawn of comparatively thin material. Our experiments have proved ordinary shells to outlast the "Everlasting" which cost 4 times as much. We are prepared to chamber any of our arms for these heavy shells to order but do not recommend them to our customers, believing that they cannot be made to average well for durability.

Well, we all have our opinions, it seems; but a lot of us would be out of luck if it were not for Everlasting shells in some of the old Ballard and other calibers, for if all shells were made in the style the Sharps cases were made—i.e., of thin brass and in Berdan type—we should not be shooting them much today. There is no question but that the Everlasting case is the most durable it is possible to make of brass. The walls are so thick that there is practically no give to them; and the cases, being mostly of the solid, thick-headed type, are in fact almost "Everlasting." The only reason there are not more of these in existence today is because many were neglected and the black powder residue was not washed out promptly.

The same catalog that contains the statement quoted regarding the Sharps opinions concerning the Everlasting type of case, also contains the following:

> We are now prepared to furnish hardened steel cartridge shells, holding about 12 grains of powder, and using No. 1 Berdan primers with dropped bullets, 50 to the pound (obtainable at any gun store) for gallery and short range practices with our military, or other styles of rifles of .45

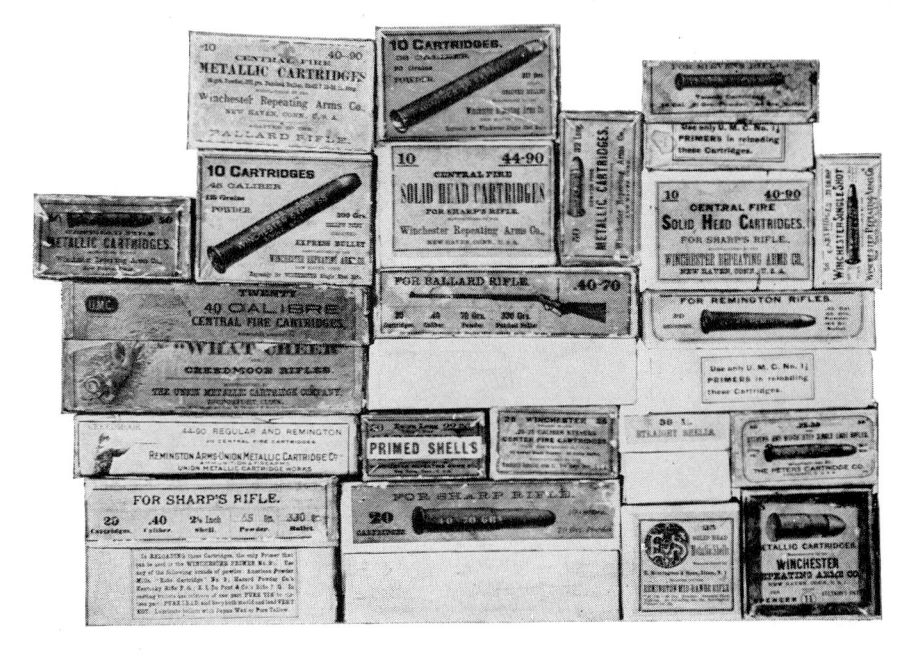

HOW CARTRIDGES FOR SINGLE-SHOT RIFLES
WERE PACKAGED

caliber. As fine results can be obtained with them at short ranges as with the best gallery .22 or .32 caliber rifles, and at a trifling cost for ammunition. Their use in military rifles accustoms the soldier to his arm, and will perfect him in marksmanship as rapidly as practice with regular military cartridges. With ordinary care after using, to prevent rust, these shells will prove, we think, practically indestructible. It is not believed that nickel plating will add to their endurance or prevent corrosion from the effect of the fulminate of the primer.

Straight .40 caliber, 2½-inch hardened steel shells, holding 12 grains of powder, using dropped bullets, 70 to the pound, can be furnished at the same cost. Price each, 75¢.

When ordered in lots of 100 or more, a discount of 25 per cent will be made to the list price.

Well, possibly I am wrong again; but if these were not "everlasting" shells, what were they?

I have some of the .45 caliber steel shells as described in this catalog which are made for the .45-2 $\frac{4}{10}$" chamber, or the .45/70, but I have never found any of the ones made to fit the .40/70 Sharps Straight 2½" chambers. Since a photograph of this type case will not show the construction, a drawing is given.

Really, the only proper way to designate the different Sharps cartridges is by caliber and length such as .45-2 $\frac{4}{10}$" or .40-2 $\frac{5}{8}$", as the powder charges and bullet weights of most of these cartridges were changed from time to time, and it means very little in describing, for instance, a .45-2 $\frac{7}{8}$" cartridge as ".45/100 Sharps." This case was loaded with from 90 to 120 grains of powder at different times, and the .45-2.4" and .45-2.6" cases were also loaded with 90 grains and 100 grains at different times.

The barrels were usually stamped with the case length as well as the caliber, although this is not always the case.

The Sharps Borchardt military rifles are generally marked "45 cal. 2.1," which was the .45/70 Gov't. cartridge, of course. In Sharps loading, it was .45/75 Sharps, as due to the thinness of the brass and folded head case construction more powder room was available.

Sharps cartridges in actual specimens are shown on pages 178 to 182.[2]

I have seen on specimen cartridge dealers' lists from time to time

---

[2] The .44/90 in 2 $\frac{7}{16}$-inch case and the .40/90 in 3 $\frac{1}{16}$-inch Everlasting will be found on other pages.

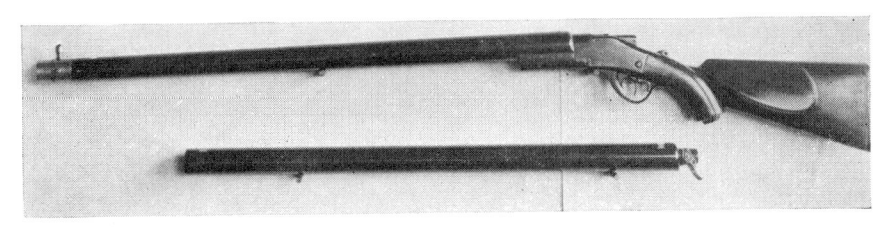

SHARPS-BORCHARDT RIFLE WITH SHARPS RIFLE CO. FALSE MUZZLE BARREL, .45 CALIBER

The lower barrel was made by E. Remington & Sons and is .32 Ideal caliber. This barrel fits the above action. The butt stock shown is not original Sharps Rifle Co. The action has Sharps set-trigger.

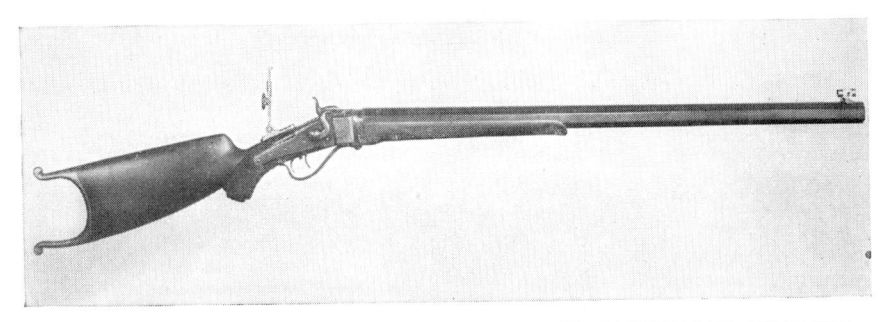

SHARPS SIDE HAMMER RIFLE WITH OFFHAND STOCK
From the Lloyd Bender collection

a cartridge described as Sharps .45-2²⁄₁₀″ case. I hardly believe this is a Sharps cartridge, but that it is the .45 Wolcott cartridge which is described in an old Hartley and Graham cartridge catalog as .45/75/475.

All the .45-3¼″ and .50-3¼″ cases I have seen were unloaded cases, new, and made by Winchester or UMC. On page 187 may be seen a box of the .45-3¼″ as put up by Winchester.

Most of the .50/70 and .45/70 or .45/75 Sharps rifles will accept and fire satisfactorily these sizes as made by all companies; and neither of these two cartridges is by any means rare, as yet. Tools and molds for the .45/70 are abundant, but the tools and molds for the .50/70 are not quite so plentiful. However, I believe the Lyman Gun Sight Corporation can still make this size to order.

The .50/90 Sharps cases 2½ inches long may still be obtained in limited quantities from cartridge dealers who make a specialty of obsolete ammunition. One way of getting around the case problem in these .50/90 chambers is to have the barrel cut off and set back, then rechamber for the .50/70 Gov't. case. However, I should never do this to a Sharps barrel, and doubt if many others would. The .50/100 and .50/110 WCF cases are 2$\frac{4}{10}$ inches long and can be used, though they are a trifle short. It is, however, a simple matter to just seat the bullets out of the case a little farther than normally, and there you are!

The bullet molds for these .50 caliber Winchester cartridges in 300- and 450-grains weight will work satisfactorily when sized to fit your particular barrel. The regular 450-grain .50/70 Gov't. bullet can also be used, of course. In my .50/90 Sharps rifle I have used with satisfactory results bullets from the Ideal mold, casting the 500-grain bullet designed for the New York State Guard rifle team when they were using the .50/70 Remington rifle. This is a round-nosed bullet similar to the .45/70/500 Ideal #457125.

I have never shot the .50 caliber using the 3¼-inch case, and I cannot say that I would enjoy this too much. To judge from Elmer Keith's description of this cartridge in the *American Rifleman* for June, 1940, I am afraid this is pretty much along the line of heavy ordnance.

The 45-2⅞" Sharps cases can still be obtained from some dealers and if obtained in the solid-head type as made by UMC, they will last a long time.

The .45-2$\frac{6}{10}$" Sharps are rather rare today and hard to find in even small quantities. However, the .45-2⅞" cases can be cut off.

The .45-2$\frac{4}{10}$" Sharps are a little more plentiful yet, and may be found by searching. Also, they may be made by cutting off the .45-2⅞" cases as above. However, the .45/90 Winchester case is 2$\frac{4}{10}$ inches long, and in most Sharps chambers is just right. Since most Sharps cartridges were made of thinner brass than our later Winchester, UMC, and other like cases, the .45/90 WCF cases may be a little tight at the mouth in some chambers. However, they are easily sized down with an Ideal tool and die of the proper size. If too thick at the mouth, the inside of the mouth may be reamed to accept the proper diameter bullet for your barrel, or the bullets may be breech-seated ahead of the case, and the case with a card wad used as in the Schuetzen rifles.

In my Creedmoor Sharps Borchardt .45-2$\frac{4}{10}$" caliber rifle, the new .45/90 WCF cases are just right and will accept the paper patch or grooved bullets I use in this barrel. However, most of the shooting I do with this rifle is with #80 or Sharpshooter powder behind the 405-grain .45 caliber bullet, and the fixed ammunition is loaded with an Ideal tool in .45/90 caliber.

The .44/77 and .44/90 Sharps cartridges are comparatively common and easy to find. The Berdan primed cases are easily decapped with an awl, and a new primer may be seated with a Winchester .45/75 1880 tool. There are several other size tools which will work here also.

The bullets used in my rifles of this size have always been paper-patch factory-made, as I have a large quantity of these. I seat them with the fingers, but an old loading tool can easily be converted to handle this size. The .45/70/405-grain bullet can be sized down to fit most of these .44 caliber barrels, which are almost .45 caliber. There is not much difference between the early .44 and .45 caliber barrels.

Cartridges in the .40/70 and .40/90 Sharps bottlenecked sizes are easy to find; much easier, in fact, than the .40/70 and .40/90 Sharps Straight. These two latter sizes in the 2½-inch and 3¼-inch cases were very common just a few years back, but they are now getting more and more rare.

The .40/70 Sharps Straight case can be made of .40/72 WCF, .38/72 WCF, and .35 WCF cases. However, there is nothing that I know of that is 3¼ inches long that can be used for the .40/90 Sharps Straight.

I happened to get good quantities of both these sizes with Remington Hepburn rifles of these calibers, as well as bullet molds and Remington straight-line bullet seaters, so I have had cases to use in my Sharps rifles of these sizes. These cases may be decapped with a punch made to fit the flash hole in the case, and there are a dozen sizes of Ideal tools which will serve to recap them. Bullet-seating chambers may be made up for these sizes to fit Ideal handles if they are the adjustable chamber type.

The .40/90-3¼" cases and cartridges are becoming so rare lately that I have, when shooting this size, taken just one case and decapped and recapped it after every shot. The powder may be measured by a powder measure taken with you to the range, or by measuring the charges before you leave for the range and putting them in small paper envelopes. In this way one case will serve for many days of shooting, and it is not too much trouble to reload between shots. Besides, it gives you time to cogitate upon the beauties of nature, the girl friend, or upon the vagaries of human nature that cause a man to want to play with one of these old charcoal burners instead of hanging it on the wall.

The .40/50 bottlenecked and .40/45-1⅞" Straight are still available in certain quantities. A few years ago I bought of Bannerman—and at that time they had thousands of them—a lot of .40-1⅞" cases, new, taking the small rifle primer as made by E. Remington & Sons. The .40-1⅞" cases may be made from .30/40 Krag cases.

The .40/50 bottlenecked cases may be made from .45/70 cases with a .40/50 full-length die—provided you can get someone to make the die. I have never found reloading tools in either of these calibers in Ideal make, but I do have the Remington bullet seaters for the .40/45 Straight, and the Sharps bullet seater and case resizers that came with my Sharps Borchardt Short Range .40-1⅞" rifle. I shoot the Sharps Borchardt Mid Range .40/70 Sharps Straight rifle and the Borchardt short-range .40/45-1⅞" Sharps Straight rifle quite a lot. They are my favorite Sharps rifles, and with them I use only smokeless powders, Dupont's #80 or #4759 and Hercules Sharpshooter. These make a far cleaner charge and the cases do not require the care necessary when fired with black powder. All the Sharps Borchardt rifles I have in the higher grades have well-rounded, medium-sized firing pins, and of course the actions will stand quite a lot. I load these up with mild-to-stiff loads of smokeless, and get fine accuracy with all of them. In the .40/70 Sharps Straight I use the 330- or 285-grain grooved bullets from Winchester molds cast 1 to 10 or 1 to 15, and sized to just bore size. In the .40/50 Sharps Straight rifle I use the 265-grained grooved bullets from a Remington mold for this caliber.

I have cast and patched bullets for these rifles from Winchester 285-grain and Sharps 330-grain slug molds, but it is very hard to get perfect bullets this way, and without a swage for these sizes they are not so accurate. The Sharps paper-patch molds cast the bullet with a hollow base to twist the patch into, and the Winchester mold leaves the base flat. The Sharps hollow base is a little easier to twist the tail of patch into, thus disposing of the surplus paper. But when properly patched, the Winchester bullets are as accurate as the Sharps. At least they have proved to be so for me.

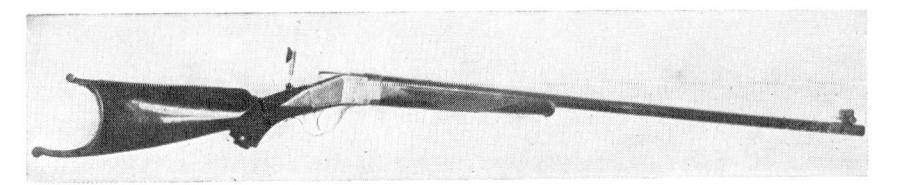

SHARPS-BORCHARDT WITH FACTORY ORIGINAL SCHUETZEN STOCK

The best paper-patch molds I have found are the Ideal cylindrical molds shown on page 152. These are the easiest to use and get the finished bullet out of in perfect shape. Being adjustable, they can be used to cast bullets of a great variety of weights in each caliber. They are hard to find in .40 or .45 calibers, though, being used in .32 and .38 calibers mostly, and so these are the ones commonly found. In my Sharps Borchardt Long Range rifles, calibers .45-2$\frac{4}{10}$″ and .45-2$\frac{6}{10}$″ cases, I have the original Sharps slug mold for the 550-grain patch bullet, and also the Sharps swage to swage these 550-grain 1$\frac{13}{32}$″ bullets. With the swage came trimmers to trim the nose and base of the bullets to a perfect shape and remove all burrs and other excrescences. These accessories are shown on page 150.

Casting and swaging and patching these bullets is quite a chore, so I usually use grooved bullets in these rifles and they shoot very satisfactorily at 100 and 200 yards, the distances I usually shoot them.

The following data on paper-patched bullets is quoted from *Modern American Rifles*, by A. C. Gould.

NOTES ON PATCHING BULLETS

Patches may be cut from bond paper of the proper thickness to bring bullet up to size. Bullet mfrs. formerly used Bank Note Bullet Patch Paper made in three thicknesses so bullets came thick, medium or thin patched. A special extra thin patch was also supplied at times. Two styles of bullet patch guides are shown.

Bullets were usually patched in factories by girls as their nimble fingers seemed better adapted to this work. A little paste was used sometimes to adhere end of patch to the bullet but soon discovered by expert riflemen that anything which caused the patch to adhere to the bullet after leaving the rifle was detrimental to accuracy so paste and glue was discarded by intelligent riflemen. Some placed the patches in water, the wet patch clinging to the bullet. This method is also questioned as patch will sometimes adhere to the bullet after leaving the rifle. Some others wet the tip end of patch with saliva and claim it patched satisfactorily. Others applied the patch dry which is the best method and if rolled in together and properly with end twisted and tucked in hollow base will give best results. Even then better results are sometimes secured if the patch is split with a knife before inserting in the chamber or mouth of shell. Many factory patched bullets still retain the patches after being found in the back stop and after going through the target. Some factory patched bullets will even support weight of bullet when suspended by the fingers. Some even will permit the patch to be torn away with the fingers in spots and retain the rest of the patch. Needless to say this will cause the bullet to be variable in flight.

The Chase method of patching is a simple rectangular or square patch of correct size to just meet around circumference of bullet without lapping. This is usually used by riflemen to make sure the patch parts from the bullet after leaving the muzzle. Usually patched at the range singly.

If the rifles were being used for the 1000-yard matches they were made for, it would be a different story, of course.

The Sharps company supplied for their Express Model Borchardt, and for use in all their .45 caliber rifles, an express bullet cast with a hollow point which would just accept a .22 rim-fire blank cartridge, rim end forward, for use on big game.

I have never seen a bullet mold as made by Sharps to cast this bullet. I am rather inclined to think that most men bought their bullets already cast and patched from Sharps or Remington, to avoid the terrific job of casting bullets in these old Sharps molds. They are certainly a contrast to the good Winchester and Ideal wood-handled molds.

None of the Sharps catalogs list a Sharps available with a muzzle-loading barrel. However, there was at least one so made.

On page 189 may be seen a Sharps Borchardt rifle with Sharps factory set triggers and a very heavy round barrel, caliber .45-2$\frac{4}{10}$″ case, with a false muzzle for the cross paper patch. That this barrel was made by Sharps, there is no question, as it has all the correct markings on it.

Shown with the rifle is a Remington Arms Company barrel bored and chambered for the .32 Ideal cartridge, the extractor for which is shown attached to the barrel. This barrel interchanges with the .45-2$\frac{4}{10}$″ barrel shown on the action. The rifle has been restocked

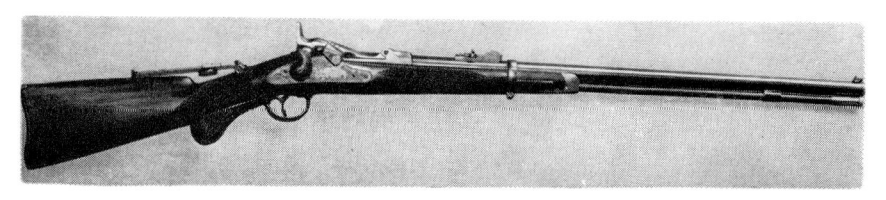

1873 SPRINGFIELD OFFICERS MODEL, SERIAL #196473, 26-INCH ROUND .45/70 CALIBER BARREL
Vernier tang sight adjusted for windage and elevation (original).

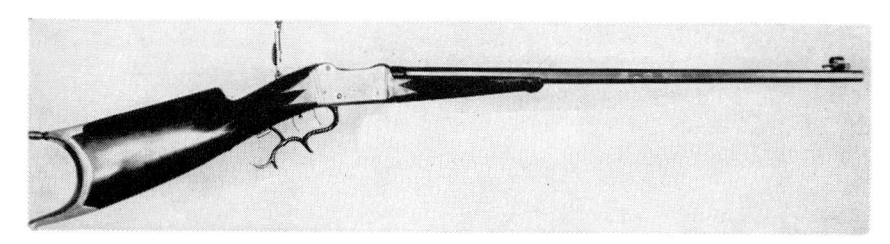

TOGGENBURGER MARTINI RIFLE, CALIBER .38-50 EVER-LASTING
Frederich Toggenburger, gunsmith, Chicago, Ill., imported Martini actions and made up rifles. Swiss born, he died about 1905.

J. RUPERTUS RIFLE, CALIBER .45-70
Philadelphia, Pa.; Patented November 12, 1878

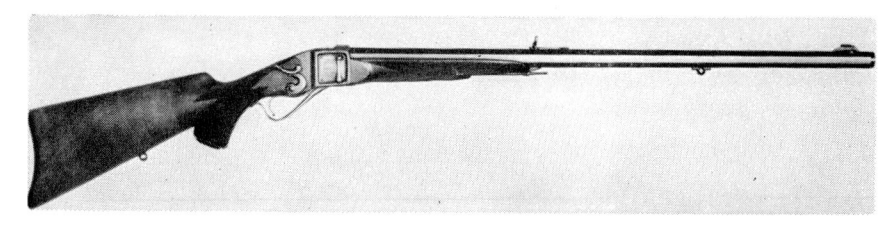

F. W. FREUND RIFLE, CALIBER .45 3¼-INCH SHARPS
Jersey City, N. J.; Patent Freund

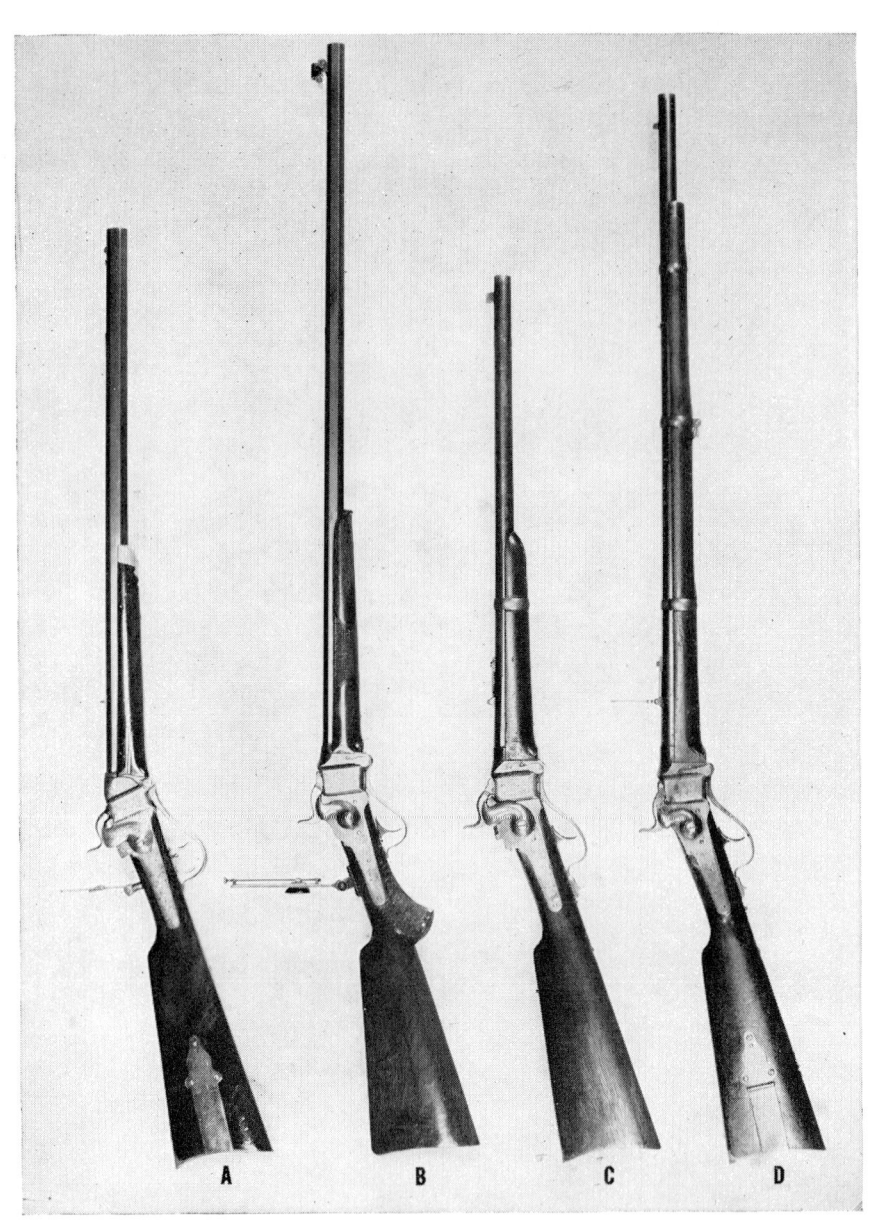

SHARPS RIFLES
(See page 198 for explanation.)

SHARPS RIFLES
(See page 198 for explanation.)

by an amateur at some time, as the stock shown is not, of course, original.

Dimensions of the .45 barrel are as follows: .45 cal. #20846, 30 inches long, 1⅜ inches diameter at muzzle, 1⅝ inches at breech.

Dimensions of the Remington Arms Co., Ilion, N. Y., .32 Ideal barrel are as follows: 29 inches long, 1⁹⁄₁₆ inches by 1²²⁄₃₂ inches.

Sharps Borchardt and side-hammer models were available in Schuetzen pattern, usually in the .40/45-1⅞" caliber. See page 189.

The Sharps catalog of 1879 lists under the "Extras" column the following:

    Schuetzen butt plates (nickel or silver plated) full
        German style $5.00 extra
    Schuetzen butt plates (nickel or silver plated) modi-
        fied Sharps style   5.00 extra

A fine little rifle made at the Sharps factory with Schuetzen stock is shown on page 193.

Many men are under the impression that the Sharps Borchardt rifles were available in .32/40 and .38/55 calibers. This is an impossibility, of course, as these target cartridges introduced by Marlin, in the Ballard rifles, were too late for the Sharps Rifle Company to have ever made barrels for them. These cartridges did not appear till early in the 1880s, the .38/55 Ballard came about 1883, and the .32/40 Ballard not until around 1885, and Sharps went out of business in 1880 or 1881 at the very latest. Many of these actions were of course rebarreled by custom barrelmakers in these calibers, but it is a chronological impossibility for the Sharps Rifle Company to have made them.

Actual specimens of the following Sharps models are shown on pages 196 and 197.

FIGURE A. Engraved Sharps slanting breech percussion model.

FIGURE B. Sharps 1874 Creedmoor Long Range Rifle, caliber .44/90 or .44/105 bottlenecked, 2⅝-inch case, 32-inch barrel.

FIGURE C. Sharps Military Carbine, caliber .50/70-1¾" case.

FIGURE D. Sharps Military Rifle, caliber .45-2⁷⁄₁₀" case.

FIGURE E. Sharps Borchardt Military Carbine, model 1878, .45 caliber, 24-inch round barrel, ring in receiver, carbine sight.

FIGURE F. Sharps Borchardt Military Rifle, 32-inch barrel, .45/70 caliber.

FIGURE G. Sharps Borchardt Short Range Rifle, .40-1⅞" caliber, 26-inch round barrel, short-range vernier sight.

FIGURE H. Sharps Borchardt Mid Range Rifle, 30-inch barrel, caliber .40/70 Sharps Straight, 2½-inch case. Midrange vernier rear sight. Receiver paneled in hard rubber.

FIGURE I. Sharps Borchardt Long Range Rifle, 34-inch barrel, caliber .45-2⁴⁄₁₀" Sharps. Tall, long-range vernier rear sight interchangeable at heel and tang; stocked and paneled in fine English walnut.

The butt plates as used on the various Sharps models are shown on page 27.

When the Sharps company failed, in the fall of 1881, this put an end to a beautiful rifle, the Borchardt. It was made over a very short period of time—1877 to 1881—and if it were not for the National Guard units of North Carolina and Michigan having adopted the military Borchardts as their official arm, no doubt there would be far fewer for us to collect today, as the fine sporting and target models were bucking the stiffening competition of the repeating rifles and so the sale of these models was certainly limited. Since Sharps had no repeating mechanism upon which to fall back, there was no question but that they would fail, especially after the disastrous British contract. The really serious and informed rifleman of those days was not satisfied with any of the repeating mechanisms as made at that time, and the passing of the Sharps must have been quite a serious blow to him. Of course the Ballard was continued for about ten years longer, and the excellent Winchester and Remington single-shots were still available. This may account for the great numbers of the rifles made by these two companies which are found chambered for the famous and efficient Sharps cartridges.

The old-time, long-range buffalo hunter found the precision accuracy of the single-shot mechanism to his liking, and even today the dyed-in-the-wool and really serious rifleman is satisfied with nothing but the superb accuracy obtainable with the single-shots. Colonel H. P. Sheldon summed up this conviction succinctly in the *American Rifleman* for June, 1943 (page 9):

The Ballards, Winchesters, Sharps Borchardt, the Remingtons and Stevens single-shots were, and are, very close to perfection from the mechanical point of view, and they were beautiful things, too. I question if today with all the advances in the science of ballistics, mechanics, and metals, we could turn out single-shot rifles much superior to these old reliables. If I were the only one to think so, I would not have the effrontery to say so, but I observe that many keen riflemen as they progress in the craft eventually acquire single-shot actions and become interested in the refinements of accuracy.

For those readers who are further interested in the Sharps Borchardt rifle from the standpoint of utilizing the military actions for remodeling, I have included more data on this action in the last chapter of this book.

V

Winchester Single-shot Falling-block Rifles

THE action used on the famous Winchester line of single-shot rifles was designed and first manufactured by John M. Browning in Ogden, Utah. Winchester acquired the patent rights and first made this model around 1885. It is a modified Sharps pattern action with many advantages over the Sharps system and certain disadvantages compared with other falling-block actions which also stem from the old Sharps. The rifles as made by Mr. Browning were few, and no doubt they were made to order.

My specimen of the Browning is illustrated on page 203. This rifle is marked on the top flat of the 30-inch full-octagonal #4 barrel: "Browning Bros., Ogden, Utah, U.S.A., caliber .45/70, Pat. Oct. 7, '79." The serial number is 488, and this number is stamped on the front end of the action. The lower tang is made integral with the frame, and so is not removable, as is the Winchester single-shot tang. The breechblock is round on top instead of having the channel of the Winchester blocks. The method of attaching the buttstock is inferior to that used on the Winchester, as there are no tenons extending into the frame, and the tangs and frame have a wedging action which prevents a stock from remaining tightly fitted for any great length of time. The lever used is, as the illustration shows, very similar to the Sharps lever. The trigger spring is slightly different in this action and is not positioned on the lower tang, as in the Winchester. The remainder of the parts are very similar to the regular later Winchester parts.

J. V. K. Wagar in the *American Rifleman* for April, 1940, gives a highly instructive analysis of the Winchester single-shot action, and since this is our most common American single-shot rifle, it is hardly necessary to go into a detailed description of it here. (See page 204.)

The first model made was the high-wall type, as was the original Browning action. This action was made over such a long period of time (1878-1920) that there are bound to be many variations of it. Some of these are seen with round receiver ring tops, and some with flat tops.

The high-wall action was made in three basic types. First we note the regular high-wall frame with either round- or flat-top barrel ring taking the regular size barrel shank of the #3, #4, or #5 barrels. These were made in both casehardened color finish and later in blued finish. The last ones made on this pattern, as typified by the Winchester-Winder muskets in .22 rim-fire caliber and other single-shots in larger center-fire caliber, were of heat-treated steel, were blued finish, and were proof-marked with the Winchester proof on both the barrel ring and the barrel.

Second, there is the high-wall action with receiver ring threaded for the smaller shanked #2 barrels which are usually seen only on the low-wall action. These actions for the smaller barrel shank are usually—though not invariably—thinner walled than the regular #3 action. They are not common, for when the lighter barrels for the smaller calibers were wanted, the low-wall action was furnished as standard.

The third, and heaviest, action made was the so-called "Express Action," in which the walls were left in their original thick condition and the sides of the frame were not milled out to the slightly thinner style of the regular #3 frame. These frames were used on the heavier caliber barrels, and they are quite a bit stronger than the milled concave side frames.

All these actions were available in straight-grip or pistol-grip tang style, with plain, single-set, double-set, or Schuetzen double-set triggers, and with several varieties of levers. They were made in all grades, from the plain, octagonal #3 barreled sporting rifle to the engraved frame target and Schuetzen models with fine American or imported walnut stocks, with #3, #4, or #5 barrels in all lengths, and in round or octagonal style, according to order.

The low-wall action was made in this style to facilitate loading short small cartridges of low to medium power. The cut-away side walls are much more convenient for this purpose. The first actions made in this low side-wall pattern had breechblocks that were very

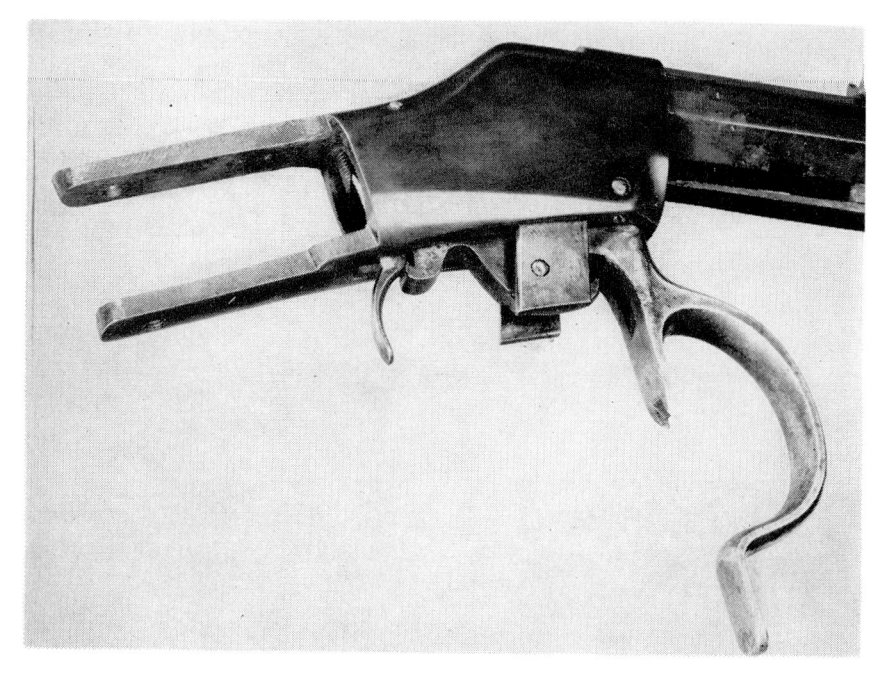

BROWNING SINGLE-SHOT RIFLE

similar to those used in the high-wall frame. Later, however, these were changed to a type which are milled down to conform to the sloping side walls.

I have heard two old-time barrelmakers claim the credit for first inducing Winchester to make this cut-away version of the high-wall action, but I imagine if the truth were known that the engineers and designers at the factory were aware of the need for a modification to accommodate the smaller cartridges.

The low-wall action was also made in plain, single-set, and Schuetzen double-set trigger types like the high-wall, but I have never seen this low-wall action with the regular Winchester close-coupled double-set triggers that are common on the high-wall action. The low-wall frames were also made in pistol- and straight-grip styles, and though I have not as yet seen one engraved, no doubt there are many such in existence. The levers on the low-wall actions were usually plain type; however, they could be had with Schuetzen spurs similar to the Winchester Schuetzen levers.

Both the high- and low-wall frames were made in take-down barrel version at one time, though the low-wall is seldom seen in this style.

This take-down system was the interrupted thread system as used on the Winchester repeating shotguns.

The famous Winder musket on the Winchester single-shot action was introduced by Winchester in 1905 at the behest of Col. C. B. Winder. This was made first in .22 Short caliber, and it established many gallery records. A little later, when the .22 Long Rifle cartridge became the standard small-bore cartridge, this model was chambered for the more accurate longer cartridge.

These Winder muskets were made with a plain straight-grip stock, and long, military type of fore end, the earlier fore end being held on with two bands and the later model having but one band (see page 206).

The barrel was full-round, 28 inches in length, and it had a front

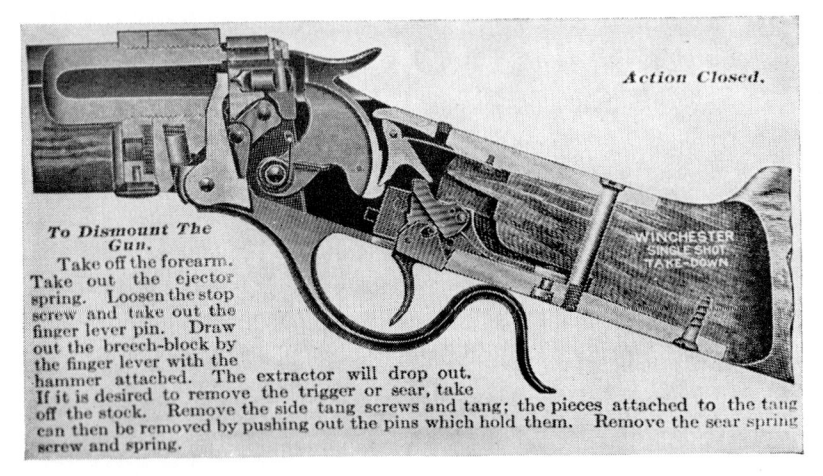

WINCHESTER TAKEDOWN ACTION DESIGN

sight base integral with the barrel. A blade sight was used on this base, and the rear sight was a special military pattern mounted on the barrel just ahead of the receiver ring. This model weighs about 8½ pounds. It was used in large quantities by the Government for training purposes during World War I, and it is still found in comparative abundance. During the first flurry of getting armed up when the .22 Hornet cartridge was introduced early in the 1930s, many of these rifles were chambered by gunsmiths for this cartridge.

The Winchester single-shot rifles have been made for practically all the cartridges in general use during its lifetime. A partial list of these is here appended:

*Subject to credit approval. $50 off Kenmore appliances $499 and over** excludes closeouts, everyday great price items, floorcare, home environment, air and water appliances. Applies to all Sears credit products excluding Sears Commercial One® and Sears Home Improvement Account℠ accounts. Not valid at HomeTown Stores, Home Appliance Showrooms, Hardware and Outlet stores, Parts & Repair Centers, catalog orders, Gift Cards, and protection agreements. One coupon per purchase. Cannot be combined with other Sears card offers. Void if copied, transferred or obtained via unapproved means and where prohibited. Any other use constitutes fraud. Cash value 1/20 cent. On return, coupon savings deducted from refund. Sears Holdings reserves the right to terminate or modify this offer at any time for failure to comply with its terms and/or due to any operational malfunction of the software, hardware or equipment required to process this offer or if due to any other error. Sears cards issued by Citibank, N.A. © 2014 Sears Brands, LLC.

**Purchase requirement calculated before taxes and after other discounts have been applied.

MasterCard® and the MasterCard Brand Mark are registered trademarks of MasterCard International, Inc.

Sales Associate: Please collect this coupon. This is a single use coupon. If unable to scan, manually enter the coupon number. Not to be used with any other coupon, pass, associate discount or during Family & Friends or Member events. Valid 8/1/14 to 9/30/14 in U.S.A. only.

To redeem online, enter 16-digit code into "promo code" field at checkout. Code limited to one time use only and applies to merchandise marked sold by Sears only. Savings shown in cart. To redeem in-store, please present coupon to store associate.

9 8 1 4 1 1 0 0 6 3 2 2 0 5 2 4

LTHAAPP82014

---

*Subject to credit approval. Savings off regular, sale and clearance prices apply to merchandise card (excluding Sears Commercial One® accounts). Sears Home Improvement Account℠ applies to installed merchandise only. Purchase requirement calculated before taxes and after other discounts have been applied and must be made in a single transaction. Not valid on footwear, Special Purchases, Everyday Great Price Items, Insane Deals, Introductory Offers, Levi's®, Lands' End® merchandise, Carhartt® baby gear and furniture, Two Hearts™ maternity and Scrubology, cosmetics, fragrance, fine jewelry, watches, clearance merchandise on Sears.com, Outlet store purchases, Catalog orders, Gift Cards, Protection Agreements and Sears Licensed businesses: One coupon per purchase. Void if copied, transferred or obtained through channels not approved by Sears Holdings. Void where prohibited by law. Any other use constitutes fraud. Cash value 1/20 cent. In the event of a return, coupon savings may be deducted from your refund. Sears Holdings reserves the right to terminate or modify this offer at any time for failure to comply with its terms and/or due to any operational malfunction of the software, hardware or equipment required to process this offer or if due to any other error. Sears cards issued by Citibank, N.A. © 2014 Sears Brands, LLC.

MasterCard® and the MasterCard Brand Mark are registered trademarks of MasterCard International, Inc.

Sales Associate: Please collect this coupon. This is a single use coupon. If unable to scan, manually enter the coupon number. Not to be used with any other coupon, pass, associate discount or during Family & Friends or Member events. Valid 8/1/14 to 9/30/14 in U.S.A. and Puerto Rico only.

To redeem online at searsstyle.com or Sears.com, type in **CODE5010** at checkout. Code limited to one time use only and applies to items marked sold by Sears. Savings shown in cart. To redeem in-store, please present coupon to store associate.

R 5 8 0 0 0 4 5 0 0 2 $ 1 0 0 0

Sears®

OFFER VALID: 8/1/14 – 9/30/14

VALID AT SEARS STORE OR SEARS.COM

SAVE $10 OFF*

a purchase of $50 or more of Clothing, Accessories and Lingerie when you use your Sears card at Sears.

*Exclusions apply. See reverse for details.
Shop online with promo code: **CODE5010**

Sears®

OFFER VALID: 8/1/14 – 9/30/14

VALID AT SEARS STORE OR SEARS.COM

GET AN ADDITIONAL $50 OFF*

a Kenmore® appliance purchase of $499 or more when you use your Sears card at Sears or Sears.com.

*Exclusions apply. See reverse for details.

Kenmore.

.22 Short rim-fire
.22 Long rim-fire
.22 Long Rifle rim-fire
.22 Extra Long rim-fire
.22 WRF
.22 Extra Long center-fire
.22 WCF
.25 Stevens rim-fire
.25/20 Single Shot
.25/20 WCF
.25/35 WCF
.28/30/120 Stevens
.30/30 WCF
.30 Army (30/40)
.303 British
.32 Winchester Special
.32/20 WCF
.32 Short rim-fire
.32 Long rim-fire
.32 Extra Long rim-fire
.32 Short Colt
.32 S & W Long
.32 Long center-fire
.32 Extra Long center-fire
.32 Ideal
.32/40 Ballard & Marlin
.33 WCF
.35 WCF
.38 WCF
.38/55 Ballard & Marlin
.38/56 WCF
.38 Short rim-fire
.38 Long rim-fire
.38 Extra Long rim-fire
.38/90/217 Winchester Express
.40/50 Sharps Straight
.40/70 Sharps Straight
.40/90 Sharps Straight
.40/70 Ballard
.40/60 WCF
.40/65 WCF
.40/82 WCF
.40/90 Ballard
.40/90 Sharps bottlenecked
.40/110/260 Winchester Express
.405 WCF
.44/40 WCF
.44 rim-fire
.45/60 WCF
.45/75 WCF
.45/70 Gov't.
.45/90 WCF
.45 Sharps
.45/125/300 Winchester Express
.50/100/300 Winchester Express
.50/70 Gov't.
.50/95 Winchester Express
.50 Eley
20-gauge shot shell

Some claim that these rifles were also made for rimless cartridges such as the .30-'06 and 7mm. Mauser, but I have never seen these, and the Winchester factory writes that this action was never barreled up for rimless cartridges at their plant. It is possible, of course, that they were so made, as many rifles were made by Winchester, as well as by other companies, of which there is no record today. This is a debatable question and I will reserve my decision until such time as I see one that I believe to be an original factory job.

The earlier Winchester catalogs carry the statement that "the .38/90/217, .40/110/260, and .45/125/300 Winchester Express cartridges will be available in the single-shot rifle made to order after October, 1886."

There is also another special Winchester caliber that was used in a special order single-shot rifle. This is the Winchester .70 Express cartridge. It was a special cartridge made up for an African expedition that went from the United States years ago. The quantity of cartridges produced in this size is unknown to me. Some of the old Winchester specimen cartridge boards show a specimen of this .70 caliber Express cartridge, and the catalog issued by a Western dealer a few years ago carries a picture of this rare one on the cover.

The single-shot rifles made to order in the .38/90, .40/110, and .45/125 Winchester Express calibers using the 3¼-inch bottlenecked

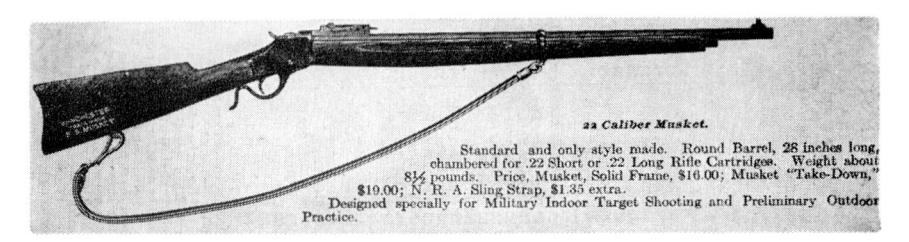

22 Caliber Musket.

Standard and only style made. Round Barrel, 28 inches long, chambered for .22 Short or .22 Long Rifle Cartridges. Weight about 8½ pounds. Price, Musket, Solid Frame, $16.00; Musket "Take-Down," $19.00; N. R. A. Sling Strap, $1.35 extra.
Designed specially for Military Indoor Target Shooting and Preliminary Outdoor Practice.

WINCHESTER SINGLE-SHOT MUSKET

cases usually had full-round barrels and the plain straight-grip shotgun buttstock with plain, uncheckered Winchester steel butt plates. These models were available upon order with the Special Express long bead front sight and Winchester 3-leaf or 4-leaf Express rear sights. These Express leaf rear sights were similar to those on certain foreign rifles and were available with or without a tangent.

My specimen of the .38/90/217 Winchester Express rifle has a full-octagonal 30-inch #3 barrel marked "38/90 Ex." The sights are the standard plain sporting bead front and sporting rear. The stock also has the regular steel rifle butt plate as seen on the common sporting rifle. My rifle has the casehardened, single-set trigger action.

The sights used on the various Winchester single-shot target rifles are similar in every way to Ballard and Remington sights of the same type. Some of these sights—with a Morocco leather case—for the midrange target variety are shown on page 29.

The October, 1900, Winchester catalog, offered the following single-shot models:

WINCHESTER SINGLE-SHOT RIFLES

Octagon or half-octagon barrel	$15.00
Round barrel	14.50
Musket	16.00
Carbine	14.50
Plain Sporting Rifle for the .30 U. S. Army (smokeless powder) [.30-40] cartridge, with special 30-inch round barrel. "Only one style barrel furnished in this caliber."	20.00

EXTRAS

Single- or double-set triggers	$2.00
Double Schuetzen triggers	6.00
Jointed rod in butt, .32 cal. or larger	.50
For leaving off rear slot	1.00

"Barrels available in weights #1 to #5."

Light-weight Carbine. Low-wall action, 15-inch round barrel, plain trigger, straight-grip stock and forearm of plain walnut. Sling ring on frame. Caliber .44 WCF. Weight, 4¼ lbs.   14.50

Plain Sporting Rifle. Octagon barrel, plain trigger, plain walnut stock, rifle or shotgun butt plate, blued frame.   15.00

Special Sporting Rifle. Octagon barrel, plain trigger, fancy walnut checkered pistol-grip stock, rifle or shotgun butt plate. ("Shotgun butt stock with either metal or hard rubber butt plate same price as rifle butt stock.")   30.00

SPECIAL TARGET MODELS

Special Single-shot Rifle. Half-octagon barrel, fancy walnut checkered pistol-grip stock with Swiss cheekpiece and nickel-plated Swiss butt plate. Blued frame. Plain trigger. Midrange vernier rear peep and wind-gauge front sights. Without slot cut in barrel for rear sight.   45.00

Winchester Schuetzen Rifle. Octagon barrel 30 inches long, #3 weight. Fancy walnut checkered pistol-grip stock, Schuetzen pattern, with cheekpiece. Schuetzen butt plate (Helm pattern). Blued frame, Schuetzen double-set triggers, spur finger lever, palm rest.[1] Midrange vernier rear peep and wind-gauge front sights. Without slot cut in barrel for rear sight. Weight, 12 lbs.   63.00
With #4 barrel; weight, 13 lbs.   65.00

[1] Catalog plate shows this rifle with earlier spur type lever and the split type palm rest. Also flat mainspring type action.

The single-shot frame shown on the "component parts" page in this 1900 catalog is the thick side-wall type, unmilled, and with octagonal top receiver ring.

This catalog still listed practically all the old Sharps cartridges, including the .45-3¼" new primed shells at $42 per M; 550-grain P.P. bullets at $20 per M.

The extras for the single-shot rifles were quoted as follows:

Regular set triggers on S.S. rifles	$2.00
Schuetzen double-set trigger rifles	6.00
Spur finger lever on S.S. rifles	4.00
Schuetzen butt plate on S.S. rifles	4.00
Swiss butt plate on S.S. rifles	2.00
Palm rest on S.S. rifles	6.00
Engraving from $5 to $250 additional	
.22 calibers are made only up to 28-inch barrel lengths. Other calibers are 36 inches long.	
Extra charge for #4 barrels	2.00
Extra charge for #5 barrels	10.00

The calibers available in 1900 were as follows:

.22 Short	.32 Ideal	.40/60 WCF
.22 Long	.32/40 WCF	.40/65 WCF
.22 Long Rifle	.38 WCF	.40/82 WCF
.22 WRF	.38 Express	.44 WCF
.22 WCF	.38/55	.45 Express
.25 Stevens rim-fire	.38/56	.45/60 WCF
.25/20 Single-shot	.40 Express	.45/70
.30 U. S. Army	.40/70 Straight	.45/75 WCF
.32 Short	.40/70 Ballard	.45/90 WCF
.32 Long	.40/90 Ballard	.50/95 Express
.32 WCF	.40/90 Sharps	.50/110 Express

In the Winchester catalog for 1916 the following models were still available.

PRICE LIST OF SINGLE-SHOT RIFLES

	Solid Frame	Take Down
Musket	$16.00	$19.00
Round barrel	14.50	17.50
Octagon barrel	16.00	19.00
Sporting rifle for .25/35 WCF, .30 WCF, .30 Army, .303 British, .32 Win. Spl., and .33 WCF cartridges require a nickel steel barrel	20.00	23.00
Sporting rifle in .35 WCF and .405 WCF cartridges require a nickel steel barrel	22.00	25.00

EXTRAS

Single- or double-set triggers	$ 2.00
Schuetzen double-set triggers	6.00
Interchangeable barrels for take-down single-shot rifles	
Round	9.00
Octagon	10.50
Round interchangeable barrels of nickel steel for take-down rifles (except .35 and .405 Winchester calibers)	12.00
Round interchangeable nickel steel barrels for take-down single-shot rifles cal. .35 and .405 Winchester [2]	14.00

Winchester Single-Shot Sporting Rifle. Octagon barrel, plain trigger, plain walnut rifle buttstock and forearm. Blued frame.   16.00

Special Sporting Rifle. Octagon barrel. Plain trigger, fancy walnut, checked pistol-grip, rifle buttstock and forearm.   34.00

    Both the above can be furnished with shotgun buttstock with either metal or rubber butt plate at same price.

.22 Caliber Musket. Standard and only style made. Round barrel 28 inches long, chambered for .22 Short or .22 Long Rifle cartridges. Weight about 8½ pounds.
  Musket solid frame   16.00
  Musket take-down   19.00

N.R.A. Sling strap, extra, $2.25. Designed especially for mili-

[2] These special nickel steel barrels for the .35 WCF and .405 WCF cartridges were made in a special #3½ size.

tary indoor target shooting and preliminary outdoor matches. [Has musket rear sight on barrel and long fore end with one band and steel tip. Illustrations show these three sporting models on solid frame high side-wall actions.]

Take-down Single Shot Rifle.   *Take Down* $19.00

Made in same calibers as the solid frame rifle. Sporting rifle with take-down octagon barrel, plain walnut stock, rifle or shotgun buttstock. [Illustration shows low-wall take-down action.]

Take-down Schuetzen Rifle.   62.00

Take-down octagon barrel, 30-inch, #3 weight. No rear sight slot. Fancy walnut checkered pistol-grip stock, new Schuetzen pattern, with cheekpiece, and new style Schuetzen butt plate. Checkered forearm, Schuetzen double-set triggers, spur finger lever, and new style palm rest, which can be adjusted in length and angle without tools. Weight about 12 pounds.

   List price of telescope $29.00
   List price of solid frame   59.00

[Plate 63 shows this rifle with high-wall take-down frame and full-octagonal barrel. It also has the later style spur finger level. The new palm rest is patterned after the "Stevens-Pope" type. This replaced the earlier Winchester split type palm rest. This Schuetzen model is shown with the Winchester A-5 telescopic sight and no iron sights. The new style stock has higher, sharper pointed comb and late heavy Schuetzen butt plate instead of the former "Helm" pattern.

Winchester Single-Shot Shotgun.

Same action as the single-shot rifle.[3] It has a 26-inch, 20-gauge full-choked nickel steel barrel, chambered for 3-inch shells or under. Length over all is 41¾ inches. Length of stock is 13$7/_{16}$ inches. Drop at comb, 1⅞ inches; drop at heel, 2$11/_{16}$ inches. Solid frame weighs about 5½ pounds. Take-down weight is given as 5¾ pounds. It has a straight-grip stock and forearm of plain walnut, and is fitted with hard rubber shotgun butt plate. The receiver is matted on top along the line of sight. Cylinder bore or modified choke barrels will be furnished instead of full choked barrels at no extra charge; and interchangeable barrels, full choke, modified choke, or cylinder bore will be furnished for take-down guns.

          Price: solid frame, $16.00; take-down, $21.00

[3] High side-wall take-down action is shown on this model in the accompanying illustration.

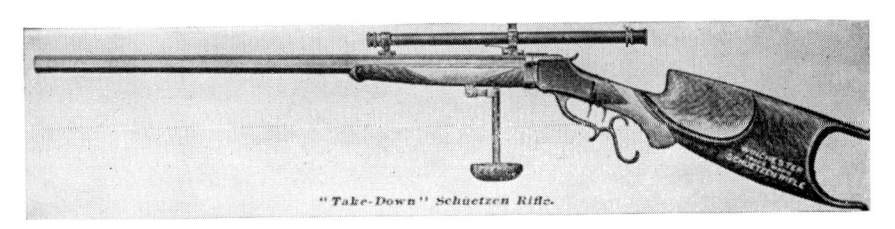

WINCHESTER TAKEDOWN SCHUETZEN RIFLE

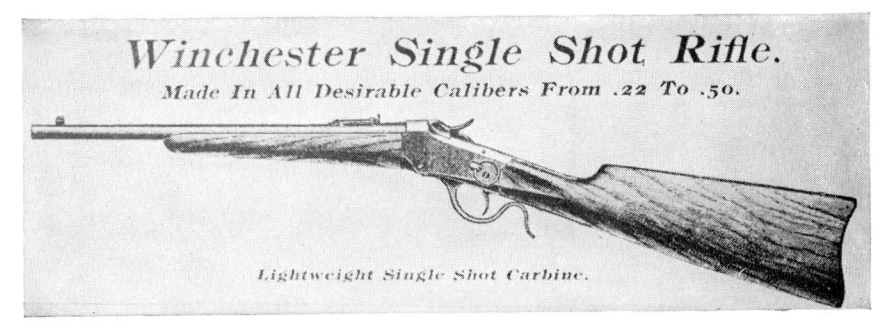

LIGHTWEIGHT SINGLE-SHOT CARBINE

WINCHESTER SINGLE-SHOT TAKEDOWN SHOTGUN

EXTRAS

Pistol-grip stock of plain walnut	$3.00
Interchangeable nickel steel barrel, 26 inches, complete with forearm	12.00
Matted rib, or matting barrel	5.00

On the page following the preceding description in the 1916 catalog is an illustration of the solid frame, nickel steel barrel. [The forearm has a snobble on the end that is slightly different from the rifle fore end.]

The "parts list" for the single-shot rifles as shown in this catalog includes parts for the "Takedown." Those shown are for the coil mainspring type of action, which was standard at this time; but the parts for the old flat mainspring under-barrel type were still available.

This 1916 catalog still listed practically all the Sharps and Winchester Express cartridges and primed cases which are shown in the earlier catalogs.

To quote further from the catalog:

The solid frame and "takedown" single-shot rifles are made for the following cartridges and with barrels of the styles and lengths given. The standard lengths and sizes of barrels as given will be sent on order, unless otherwise specified:

.22 Short	.30 WCF	.32/40
.22 Long	.30 Army	.38 WCF
.22 Long Rifle	.303 British	.38/55
.22 WRF	.32 Win. Special	.44 WCF
.25 Stevens	.33 WCF	.45/70 Gov't.
.32 Short center-fire	.35 WCF	.45/90 WCF
.22 WCF	.405 WCF	.50/110 Express
.25/20 Single-shot	.32 Ideal	.50 Eley
.25/35 Win.	.32 WCF	

Barrels as regularly supplied for the rim-fire cartridges were in #1 size, round or octagonal; and the musket barrel was round, 28 inches long, and musket type. Barrels as furnished in center-fire calibers were #1 round or octagonal, #2 and #3 round, and round or octagonal in the larger sizes.

The special #3½ round, nickel steel barrel was furnished in .35 WCF and .405 WCF calibers only.

The regular optional sizes for #1 barrels were usually #3 or #4 weights.

Barrels were furnished up to 30 inches in length in the #2, #3, #3½, and #4 weights ordinarily, but they would be made up to 34 inches in length at an extra charge of $1.00 per 2 inches of barrel over standard lengths.

There was an extra charge of $2.00 for #3½ and #4 barrels.

This catalog lists only a few calibers available in the single-shot compared with the variety which had been formerly offered. However, there may have been other sizes available upon special order. The following is quoted from the 1916 catalog:

For all desirable calibers from .22 to .50 caliber. Made in sporting, musket and Schuetzen and take-down styles.

The Winchester single-shot rifle has the old Sharps breechblock and lever. The firing pin is automatically withdrawn at the first opening movement of the gun and held back until the gun is closed.

The hammer is centrally hung but drops down with the breechblock when the gun is opened, allowing the barrel to be wiped and examined from the breech, and is fitted with a special form of fly whereby the hammer is left at half-cock instead of full-cock when the action is closed. This special fly can be fitted to the earlier style of rifle, when already equipped with a set trigger, at a cost of $1.00 list; or to one with plain trigger for $2.00 list.

Single-shot rifles can be furnished with or without set triggers, and with barrels of all ordinary lengths up to 30 inches, and in the calibers and weights enumerated on the following pages; also with rifle or shotgun butt, plain or fancy wood, or with pistol grip. All .22 caliber rimfire rifles are fitted with a kicking extractor which throws the shell clear of the gun.

The Take-down Single-Shot rifle, made for the same cartridge as regular styles of this rifle.

The two-part "take-down" system used on this rifle is simplicity itself. To take the gun apart it is only necessary to push forward the take-down lock on the under side of the receiver extension, open the action to clear the extractor from the barrel, and give the barrel a quarter turn to the left. A simple but positive device for taking up wear is embodied in the receiver extension, which permits keeping a perfectly tight joint at the junction of the receiver and receiver extension. [See page 204.]

This rifle has a special fly which leaves the hammer at half cock instead of full cock when the action is opened and closed.

It has a quick, spiral mainspring which is entirely housed within the receiver. It can be furnished with set triggers and with barrels of different lengths, chambered for the cartridges in the list given.

WINCHESTER SINGLE-SHOT RIFLE SYSTEM

To dismount the gun: Take off the forearm. Take out the ejector spring. Loosen the stop screw and take out the finger lever pin. Draw out the breechblock by the finger lever with the hammer attached. The extractor will drop out.

If it is desired to remove the trigger or sear, take off the stock, remove the side tang screws and tang. The pieces attached to the tang can then be removed by pushing out the pins which hold them. Remove the sear spring screw and spring.

To assemble the gun: Replace the sear spring and screw. Mount the trigger and other parts on the tang, and slide it into place. Replace the side tang screws. Assemble together the hammer spring, hammer, breechblock, and finger lever, and hold them in the same relation to each other as shown in the cut; that is, the firing pin protruding, and the hammer against the breechblock. In this position push them back into the underside of the gun, partly into position. Put back the extractor, and push the whole into place, holding back the trigger so that the sear may not catch on the hammer. Open the action, replace ejector spring, taking care to see that its inner end rests in its seat on the extractor. Replace stock and forearm.

THE WINCHESTER CARTRIDGES

The famous Winchester line of cartridges is long and varied. They run from the .22 Winchester rim-fire to the .45/125/300 Winchester Express and the .50/110 Express, with many sizes between.

This company seems to have made many of the cases and cartridges for the Sharps .45-3¼" and .50-3¼" rifles taking these long special cases. The Union Metallic Cartridge Company also made many cases and loaded cartridges in these sizes.

During the life span of the Winchester single-shot, these rifles were chambered for practically all the calibers in common use, and for many of the old Sharps and Ballard sizes.

This is one of the many things we have to be thankful for, because when Winchester offered their rifles chambered for these sizes, they also made the cartridge in good solid-head type cases. Were it not for this, the few cases left today as made in Berdan primed type by

Sharps would certainly not satisfy the great demand that exists for these sizes, and many men would be denied the pleasure of shooting some of these old rifles.

All the many Winchester calibers as offered in the Winchester rifles are comparatively easy to obtain today. Offhand I can think of no size that was reasonably popular—and all of them seem to have been popular—years ago that cannot be found today.

The only exception to this may be the Express series of cartridges in the 3¼-inch cases, the .38/90/217, .40/110/260, .45/125/300, which of course enjoyed only limited popularity. These sizes are not too easy to find, though one finds many more boxes of cartridges in all three sizes than he does the single-shot rifles to handle them.

They cannot be made of any other American-made cartridge cases that I know of. However, there are several cartridges as made in England in the older calibers that used 3¼-inch cases, and I am sure that I could make all these Winchester Express sizes from some of these if the need arose.

I have never owned a Winchester single-shot chambered for the .45/125/300 Express cartridge; however, the .40/110/260 and .38/90/217 Express rifles both came my way a few years ago. The .40 Express rifle had a #3, 30-inch full-round barrel and steel shotgun buttstock. A perfectly plain rifle it was, and as the barrel was not too good, it soon went the way of all such, to be replaced by a full-octagonal #4 barrel job. The .38/90 Express rifle I still have also, and this has a 30-inch full-octagonal #3 barrel, a rifle buttstock and single-set trigger. I have the Winchester loading tool with adjustable bullet-seating chamber, and the Winchester mold casting the 217-grain bullet, as well as a few cases. so my .38 is shot quite often.

I prefer the .38/90 cartridge to either the .40/110 or the .45/125 Express sizes, as it is a more attractive cartridge, and in my case it proved to be much more accurate than the .40/110.[4] As to the accuracy of the .45/125 I couldn't say, never having fired this size. I believe Ned H. Roberts has used all these sizes in the past, and

[4] A. C. Gould summed up the 40/110/260 cartridge thus: "The 40/110/260 is an Express cartridge. It will not shoot with the accuracy of the 40/82 W.C.F. It is not very reliable beyond 150 yards, but a killing cartridge at short range."

the *American Rifleman* for May, 1935, contains an article by Mr. Roberts mentioning these cartridges.

In shooting my .38/90 Winchester single-shot, I use Winchester cases, of course, primed with the large rifle primers in smokeless powder—non-mercuric, non-corrosive type—and about 4 to 6 grains of Dupont's shotgun bulk smokeless powder as a primary charge. The main charge of 80 to 85 grains of FG or FFG black powder is then loaded, and the 217-grain .38 Express solid ball cast 1 to 20 or 1 to 25 seated with the Winchester loading tool without crimping. This mold casts the bullets .378, and I size them to .3755, which is the exact bore diameter of my barrel. The accuracy is good practical hunting accuracy, which is to be expected from a cartridge of this powder capacity; but it would never win any turkey matches.[5] However, this cartridge is a thrill to shoot, providing, of course, you get a thrill out of shooting a large capacity black powder load.

To date I have not used a smokeless load in this rifle, but I intend someday to attempt to work up such a load. This action would, of course, stand a smokeless powder charge, such as Sharpshooter powder and a harder cast bullet. What the results will be on the target is anyone's guess.

All the other Winchester cartridges are too common and familiar to everyone to go into detail on here. The Ideal handbooks published even a few years back contain information on practically all these sizes, and the catalogs issued by the Winchester factory prior to 1915 or 1916 contain much loading data also. The older the catalog, the more information contained therein, is the usual rule.

There is one other cartridge with which I have experimented, which, while it is not, strictly speaking, a Winchester cartridge, is one that I happen to have a high-side single-shot chambered for. This is the .32 Long center-fire, the center-fire version of the common .32 Long rim-fire.

This caliber is usually found in Ballard or Remington rolling-block rifles, though it was made available in many others, such as the Wesson, Wurfflein, Stevens 44 and 44½, the Remington Hepburn, and others.

[5] A. C. Gould in *Modern American Rifles* said: "This 38/90/217 Express is strictly a hunting cartridge, the result of much experimenting, and it combines accuracy, low trajectory, and excellent killing power. It will shoot into an 8- or 10-inch circle at 200 yards when handled by an expert."

These—except possibly the Hepburn and the Stevens 44½ rifles—come along quite frequently, and possibly a few remarks on this size will not be out of order.

My high-side Winchester taking this .32 Long center-fire cartridge is a casehardened action with the #2 full-octagonal barrel, 26 inches long. This barrel has the small shank, of course, and the action is one of the few seen today accepting this size shank. The stock is straight-grip plain walnut type, with the Winchester smooth steel shotgun butt plate. The barrel is excellent inside, and should shoot extremely well. In any other caliber it probably would, but this .32 Long center-fire cartridge is an extremely exasperating one to load. The reason for this is best explained by quoting from one of the early Ideal handbooks:

Originally all ammunition was lubricated on the outside. All bullets were seated in the shell, on the powder, or up to a shoulder, without lubrication, and that part of the bullet that projected beyond the muzzle of the shell was dipped into hot lubrication and, when cold, packed into boxes ready for use. Such was the only ammunition made for years.

Another peculiarity of almost all these old cartridges is that the bullets were not straight on the outside. They had two distinct diameters, and were known as the "Heel Bullets." The heel, or base part of the bullet, is of the proper size to fit the shell into which the bullet is inserted up to the shoulder, where it is enlarged to the proper diameter for the bore of the barrel. Many arms were made for this type of ammunition. The rim-fire cartridges are mostly of this kind.

The first center-fire cartridges were made exactly the same length and size, and to take the same bullet as the rim-fire; the change being simply from rim to central fire; presumably to prevent the change in the bore, rifling, and chambering of the arms; for it is a serious thing to make such a change. So in some cases the ammunition has been changed, on account of the outside lubrication being exposed to dirt and grit as well as the probability of its removal by heat in warm weather.

To overcome these troubles, the shells have in some cases been lengthened to inclose more of the bullet, which now has grooves to hold the lubrication. The length of the cartridge over all remains the same as before, so they will chamber in all arms made for the original cartridge.

The peculiar feature about this ammunition is that the bullets are now straight, without heel, and they fit the shell the whole length, *but will drop through the barrel without touching.*

These new bullets have a deep cavity at the base, and are made of pure, soft lead, so that they will expand or upset when fired, in order to take the rifling. They rely wholly upon the upsettage or expansion of the hollow base to fit the barrel.

Therefore, lighter bullets, round or otherwise, that fit these shells cannot be used, for they drop through the barrel without taking the rifling, and the powder charges cannot be relied upon to expand them. Accuracy depends wholly upon the uniformity of expansion. We write this for the information of those who are continually asking us about bullets and light charges for arms made for heel bullets with outside lubrication such as the following: .32 Short, .32 Long, .32 Extra Long, .38 Short, .38 Long, .38 Extra Long, .41 Colt's Short, .41 Colt's Long, .44 Colt's Old Model Sharp Pointed Ball, etc., etc.

Another peculiarity of this ammunition is that in reloading with heel bullets, the shell cannot be crimped or the bullet sized on account of the two diameter bullets.

The foregoing quotation from the Ideal *Handbook* gives the reader who is unfamiliar with these cartridges some idea of the headaches to be encountered when attempting the reloading of any of them.

The .32 Long center-fire cartridges as loaded by the different loading companies are *usually crimped tightly*, and I have not been able to obtain any but the most mediocre accuracy with these factory loads.

If the unfired cases or cartridges are unloaded and the crimp carefully removed with a knife or reamer so that it will not shave the bullet when being seated, the accuracy will be greatly improved.

The mouths of the cases are resized if necessary to hold properly the bullets without crimping.

Another thing that adds greatly to the picnic of reloading these .32 Long cartridges is that the different factories made the cases of slightly different lengths—and ain't we got fun!

With this .32 Long center-fire rifle came an Ideal #1 combination tool and mold for this cartridge, casting a bullet of 80 grains. The base portion of the bullet measured .299, and the forward or grooved portion measured .313. This is the regular bullet for the .32 Short center-fire cartridge, and it gave fairly good accuracy, at short ranges, with black or with smokeless powder.

Later I obtained two other Ideal mold and tool combinations. One was the #1 Ideal for the 90-grain, .32 Long bullet #.299153, which when loaded into the cases with 4½ grains of #80 gave better accuracy up to about 75 yards. This bullet is the same diameter as the 80-grain.

The other tool and mold combination I tried was an Ideal #8 for the .32 Long Rifle cartridge as adapted to the Marlin 1892 rifle in rim- or center-fire interchangeable version. This bullet mold and tool came with a Ballard .32 rim- and center-fire #2 rifle in which this combination worked much better than in the Winchester. This bullet is the hollow base, full-grooved type which is seated into the longer case for use in the Marlin repeating rifle. The bullet diameter is .299 for the full length, and the Ideal number is .299155; weight, 101 grains.

This bullet requires 10 to 11 grains of FFFG black or semismokeless powder to upset, of course, and as I detest black powder, especially in these small cases, I usually use the 90-grains regular outside lubricated bullets from the Ideal #1 tool, bullet number .299153, and prime the broken-down factory loads with #6½ Remington non-mercuric, non-corrosive primer and 4½ to sometimes 5 grains of #80. Five grains of Dupont #4227 seem to squirt this little bullet out with more velocity, but with inferior accuracy.

I eventually came to the conclusion, however—as so many have before me—that this little cartridge just isn't accurate; at least, not accurate the way I prefer a cartridge to be.

Some day, perhaps, I shall have this barrel rechambered for the .32 Extra Long center-fire cartridge, a large supply of which size I have on hand; or it can be chambered for the .32/20 cartridge, as the barrel measures .313. And though the barrel is cut with a 26-inch twist, it should shoot well lighter bullets than the standard 115-grain .32/20.

This rifle will simply not deliver the accuracy at 50 and 75 yards that my #2 Ballard chambered for the .32 Long rim- or center-fire cartridge will. This Ballard has a 22-inch twist and a .313 bore diameter. Surprisingly enough, it shoots old, long-loaded, black powder .32 rim-fire cartridges even better than the center-fire version.

Another Winchester cartridge that is met with quite often is the .22 center-fire. This was a very popular small-game cartridge, and it is still with us in the fine .22 Hornet.

Very few Winchester single-shot rifles in the .22 WCF caliber are seen today with fine barrels. Most of them have been ruined years ago by black powder residue, poison primers, and other barrel enemies. The smaller bores are harder to keep clean, and possibly that accounts for the few specimens of these seen today that are bright and unpitted. A friend of mine, however, has a high side-wall Winchester with a #3 barrel that has a perfect bore. The high wall is unusual in this caliber, as the smaller cartridges were usually furnished on the low-wall action.

This .22 WCF rifle delivers fine accuracy at 100 yards with the 45-grain .22 WCF bullet cast 1-16 and unsized. The cases are primed

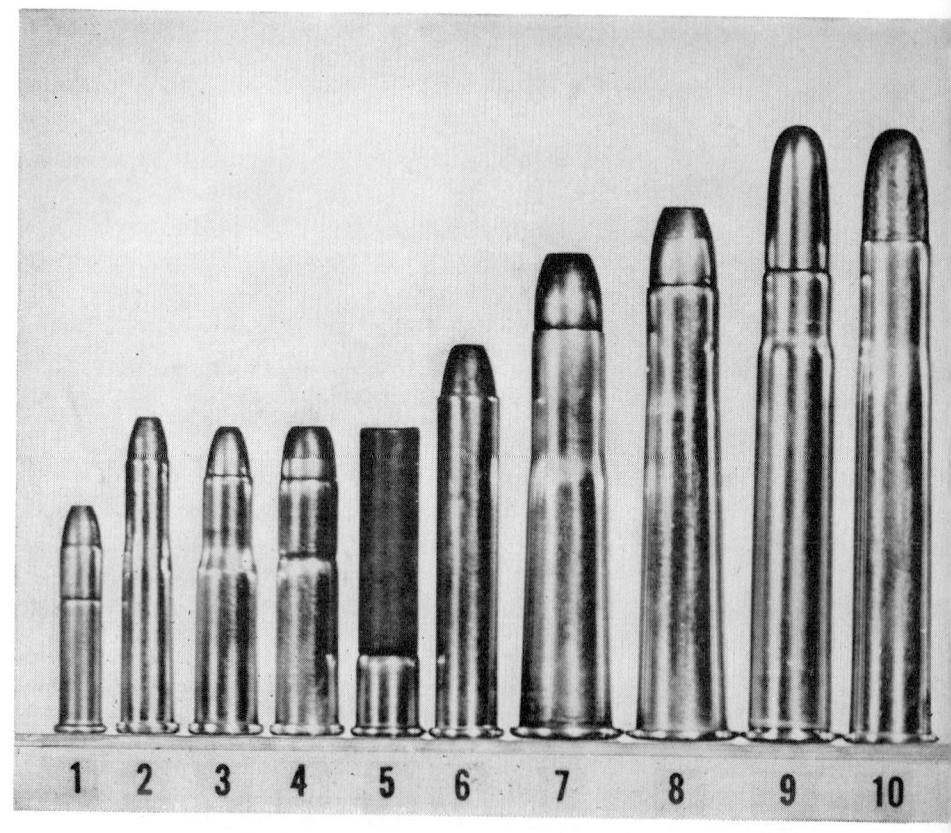

WINCHESTER AND MISCELLANEOUS CARTRIDGES

1. .22 Winchester rim-fire
2. .22 Winchester center-fire
3. .25/20 Winchester center-fire
4. .32/20 Winchester center-fire
5. 9mm. Winchester rim-fire shot shell
6. .32 Ideal
7. .38/56 Winchester center-fire
8. .38/70 Winchester center-fire
9. .35 Winchester center-fire
10. .38/72 Winchester center-fire

with #6½ Remington or #116 Winchester primer, and the best load is 6½ grains of #4759. The bullets are seated with the Winchester tool, and the cases are uncrimped. Heavier loads of #80, #4759, and #4227 powders have been tried, but this particular barrel prefers the above load. This is an easy cartridge to load and a fine small-game or plinking cartridge. It is very economical to shoot, of course, but in my experience the accuracy of the .22 WCF is not equal to that of the .22/15/60 Stevens Straight case.

Many other old Winchester cartridges come to mind as I write

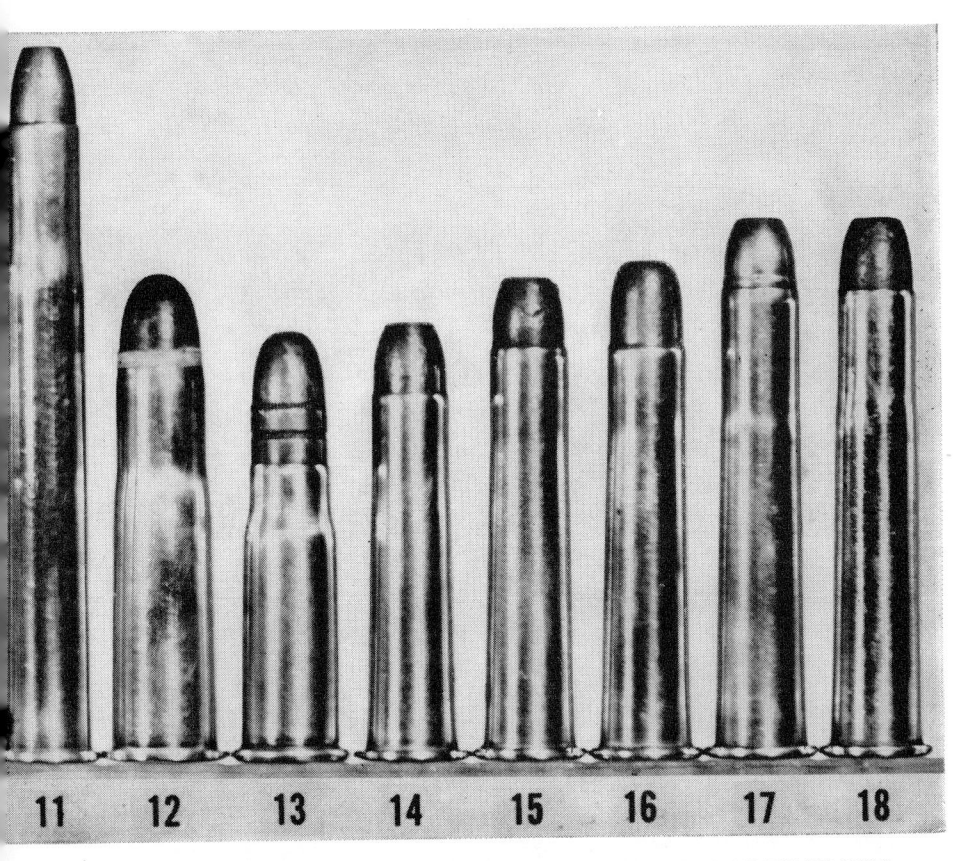

WINCHESTER AND MISCELLANEOUS CARTRIDGES

11 .38/90/217 Winchester single-shot express, 3¼-inch case
12 .43 Beaumont
13 .41 Swiss rim-fire
14 .40/60 Winchester center-fire
15 .40/65 Winchester center-fire
16 .40/60 Marlin
17 .40/70 Winchester center-fire
18 .40/82 Winchester center-fire

this; some of them have been a great deal of fun to load and shoot, and also instructive; however, it is well to end here discussion of the old Winchester series.

The Winchester company furnished loading tools of their own make for all the center-fire cartridges loaded by them which were adaptable to Winchester arms. These tools are of several styles and types, and were made over a long period of time. The earlier Winchester bullet molds were furnished with iron handles. Later the brass ferruled, walnut handles were added. These are all well-made

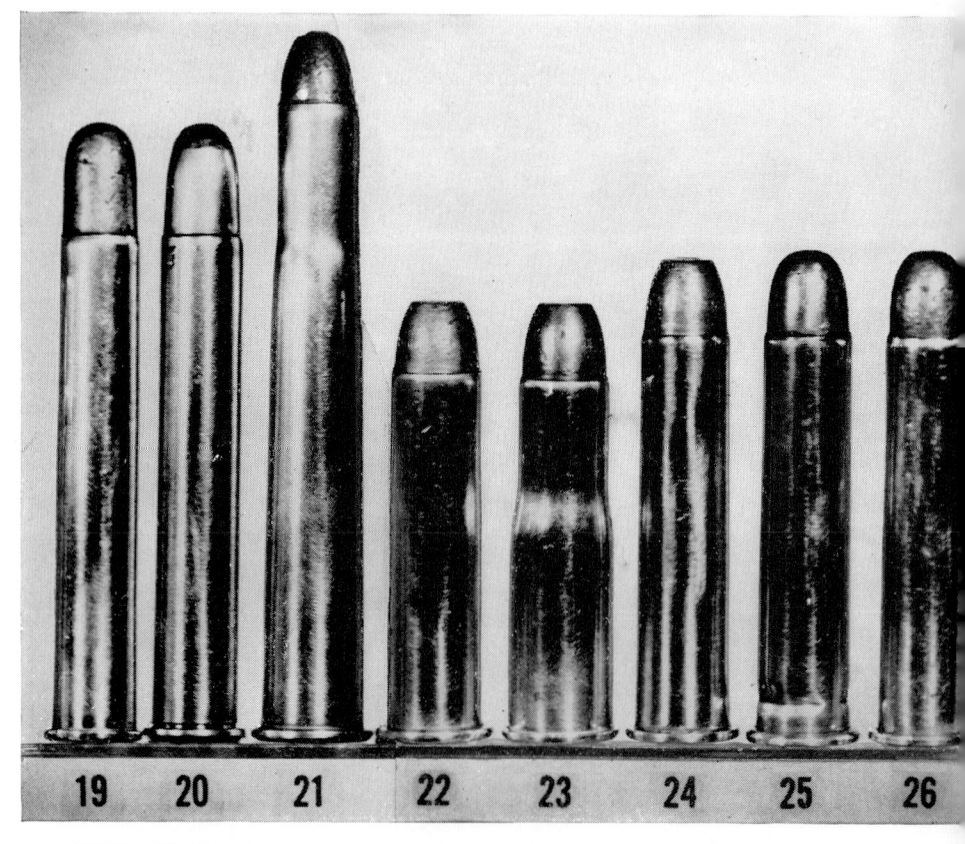

WINCHESTER AND MISCELLANEOUS CARTRIDGES
19 .40/72 Winchester center-fire
20 .405 Winchester center-fire
21 .40/110/260 Winchester single-shot express, 3¼-inch case
22 .45/60 Winchester center-fire
23 .45/75 Winchester center-fire
24 .45/85 Marlin
25 .45/55 Government carbine, inside primed
26 .45/70/405 Government

molds of heavier construction than most of the Ideal molds, and most men find the handles more comfortable.

Some of the Winchester loading tools and molds are shown on page 152. Also shown on that page are Ideal molds in regular early solid types as well as the later detachable mold block types. The Ideal Perfection and Cylindrical bullet molds for variable weights of grooved and paper-patched bullets respectively are also illustrated.

The Ideal #1 and Ideal #2 recappers and decappers, the Ideal

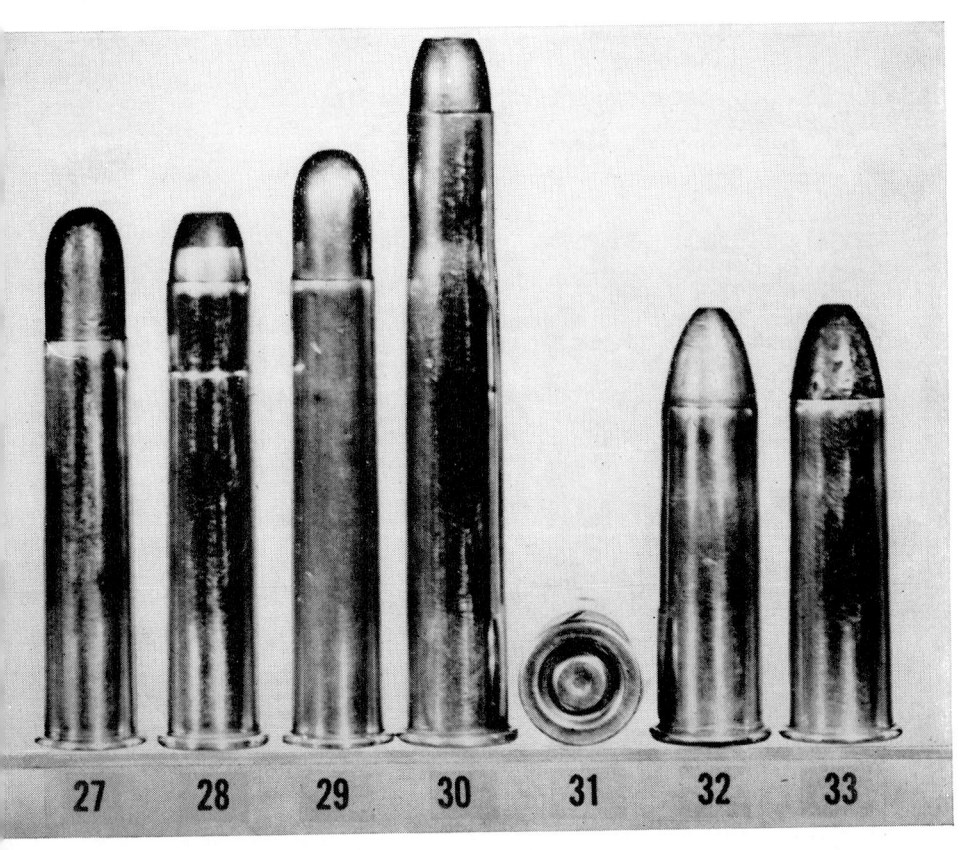

WINCHESTER AND MISCELLANEOUS CARTRIDGES

27 .45/70/500 Government
28 .45/90 Winchester center-fire
29 .45/80/500 Government Sharpshooter, 2⁴⁄₁₀-inch copper base
30 .45/125/300 Winchester single-shot express, 3¼-inch case
31 .50/45 Government carbine, case head showing Martin primer
32 .50/70 rim-fire, copper case
33 .50/70/450 Government center-fire

bullet seaters #1 and #2, shown also on this plate, were in extensive use with single-shot Schuetzen rifles.

One of the best methods of sizing cast bullets is by use of the Ideal bullet hand sizer shown with the tools, molds, and other utensils, for interchangeable dies of all sizes are easily inserted and cost very little. Lyman will also make the special sizes to order. The Ideal bullet lubricator and sizer machine can be used, of course; but a variety of dies and plungers will necessitate more of an outlay of cash.

Several powder measures which are extremely useful in reloading many of the cartridges discussed in the preceding chapters are also illustrated here, and these are as follows: the Geo. C. Schoyen measure; Schoyen and Peterson 2-powder measure; Ideal powder measure; Belding and Mull measure; Ideal flask powder measure.

Many of the Winchester molds in .40 and .45 calibers are suitable for use in Sharps and Ballard rifles. The Winchester mold for the

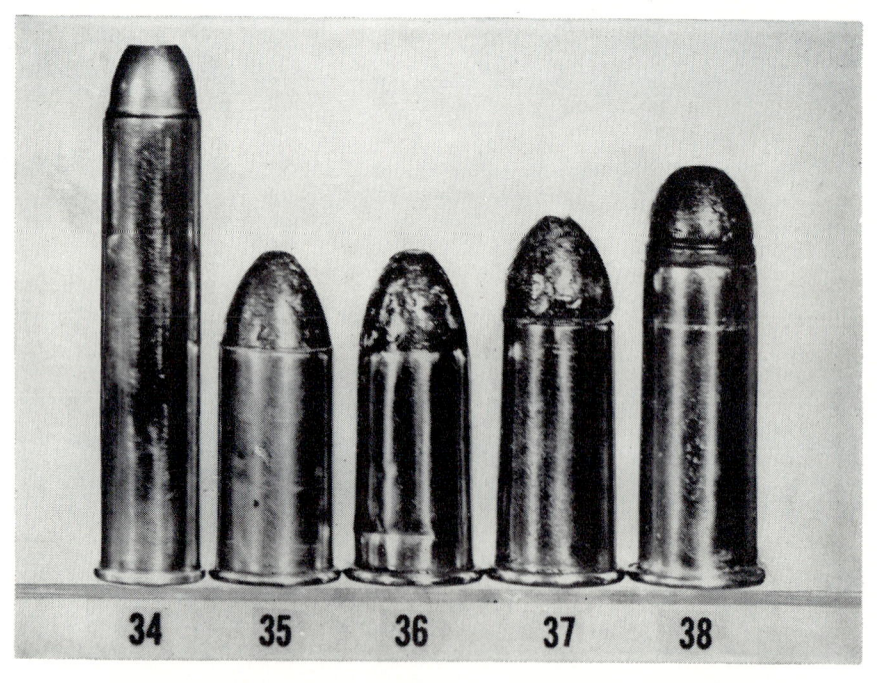

WINCHESTER AND MISCELLANEOUS CARTRIDGES
34 .50/110 Winchester Express
35 .58 Roberts rim-fire, copper case
36 .58 Musket center-fire, inside primed copper case
37 .58 Roberts center-fire
38 .58 Berdan center-fire

round-nosed .406 diameter bullet of the .40/72/330 WCF cartridge is .003 larger than most Winchester and Ideal .40 caliber bullets, and will fit many oversize barrels, which are common in these old single-shots. The .412 diameter of the .405 WCF bullet will also fit many barrels to better advantage than the standard smaller .40 caliber bullets.

In any of these old black-powder rifles, however, be they Sharps, Ballard, Stevens, Remington, Winchester, or what have you, the barrel will usually give good accuracy if the bullets are cast of soft mixture and black powder is used. They can be several thousandths of an inch smaller and still shoot satisfactorily in most cases. If larger than your barrel diameter, it is usually good policy to size them down to barrel groove diameter or to one-thousandth of an inch over groove diameter.

If the bullet when sized to fit your barrel is too small to fit the case mouth, seat it ahead of the case in the breech and put a card wad dipped in the bullet lubricant and then dried till hard over the *case full* of black or semi-smokeless powder. This case full of powder will upset the soft bullet to fit the barrel properly. Naturally, when using smokeless powder the case must not be filled level full, as with black powder, or you will be minus a rifle and very likely portions of your anatomy.

When smokeless powders are used, the bullets must fit the barrel tightly, as the smokeless loads will not give the quick hammer blow of the exploding black powder.

The bullets can be loaded ahead of the case with smokeless as with black powder, and the balance of the case may be filled with dry cream of wheat (use the cereal as it comes from the box, uncooked, and without sugar and cream).

The bullets, naturally, as used ahead of the smokeless powder loads, will be cast harder—say, 1 to 12, 1 to 15, 1 to 16, etc. Experimentation will determine this. The wads used over the case mouth in smokeless loads can be plain thin card wads about the thickness of the Government one-cent postal card stock, or it can be blotting paper dipped in melted bullet lubricant. The blotting paper is dried till the grease is cold and set, then wads cut therefrom.

Cheap and effective wad cutters may be made from leather harness punches, which are to be found at most hardware stores. These punches are reamed to the correct size inside, sharpened outside on a bevel edge, and then hardened.

Ready-made wad cutters may be purchased at very reasonable prices from the Lyman Gun Sight Corporation and from Belding and Mull.

Greased card wads or plain disks of lubricant, as sometimes used behind paper-patched bullets, should not be loaded into ammunition unless it is intended to be shot very soon, as the grease will sometimes affect the powder charge and, as a consequence, your accuracy will suffer.

Bullet lubricants may be mixed at home or bought in stick form from a loading tool manufacturer. There are many formulas by which to make these lubricants, and some rifles and calibers will prefer one and others an entirely different mixture. Also temperature will influence the choice of a lubricant. In warm weather a grease of a higher melting point is needed than one for a colder day.

Following is a list of bullet lubricants used by various firms:

Winchester Repeating Arms Co. advise use of Japan wax or beef tallow.

Marlin Fire Arms Co. says: "Make the lubricant of clear tallow 4 parts, beeswax 1 part."

Massachusetts Arms. Co.: 1 part beeswax to 3 parts tallow.

Ideal Mfg. Co.: 3 parts beeswax and 1 part common cylinder oil. Also, beef tallow with enough vaseline with it to soften it as desired.

J. Stevens Arms and Tool Co.: Make lubricant of clear tallow 4 parts, beeswax 1 part.

Sharps Rifle Co.: 1 part beeswax to 2 parts of sperm oil by weight.

Smith and Wesson: Melted tallow.

Bullard Repeating Arms Co.: Fill grooves with beef tallow or Japan wax.

The following formula was used for many years at Walnut Hill range, and was considered as good as anything tried. It was used by shooters still using grooved bullets, before the adoption of paper-patched bullets for target shooting.

Three parts mutton tallow to one part wax. Add about a teaspoonful of plumbago to a pint of the melted compound. Cool a little of it, and if it proves too hard, thin with a little sperm oil.

Another recipe advises Vaseline and paraffin, putting in just enough paraffin to make the mixture work well on the bullet. About a pound of Vaseline to a piece of paraffin the size of a duck egg. This mixture may be varied very easily to suit any barrel or climate. Since it is composed of mineral oils, it is less affected by heat and cold.

Another recipe in wide use recommends the use of plain tallow with the addition of a small amount of beeswax, also a small amount of Vaseline.

F. J. Rabbeth recommended beeswax and cylinder or other heavy oil. One part oil to four parts of beeswax.

All recipe enthusiasts agree that the fresher the ingredients, the better. Also, the mixture should not be allowed to get too hot or to burn while heating. Scorching destroys the lubrication qualities of the various tallows.

Graphite may be added to any of the given mixtures if desired—and it is sometimes desirable. However, graphite is hard to mix into the mass, and it makes a very dirty mixture to apply, so it is seldom made use of.

Lubricants have sometimes been manufactured by secret formula and sold in packages, but the formulas herein given are among the best ever tried, and anyone can make them; there are no deep, dark secrets concerning their ingredients. Beef or mutton tallow is the best lubricant, and most good formulas make use of these for the main part, or base, of the mixture.

Lubricants deteriorate with age; therefore, freshly lubricated bullets are superior to those which have been lubricated for a long time.

Mr. Charles J. Beise, in an article in the *Western Sportsman* magazine for January, 1940, entitled "Rifleman Extraordinary," stated that Charles W. Rowland of Boulder, Colorado, the famous rest shooter and experimenter, preferred horse tallow for a lubricant, and purchased it in thin sheets. When it became unobtainable in the sheet form, he designed a grease pump, which was made by George Schoyen of Denver, Colorado, in which the tallow, purchased in bulk, was squeezed out in the form of a thin ribbon. The wads were then cut from this thin strip of olio lubricant.

Beise stated that the famous Leopold's Banana Lubricant was Rowland's invention. That he gave the formula to Leopold, who in turn had the product placed upon the market by the Ideal Manufacturing Company. Dr. Mann, as well as many other famous riflemen, used this lubricant. This is the only original formula in existence today that shows the proper components called for in the famous "Leopold Olio Wads," and it is in the possession of H. A. Donaldson of New York State.

Throughout this book I have attempted to give at least one substitute case size that may be altered to fit the less-common chamber sizes. It is not always possible to find the original cartridges or cases in the sizes needed, and these substitute cases will in most instances serve quite well.

The use of forming dies is called for in many cases of alterations of this type, and of course they are not always at hand. Many gunsmiths will make these upon order, or a machinist friend can be called upon to make the dies up for you.

One of the surest means of obtaining odd size cartridge cases is to advertise for them in the *American Rifleman* magazine.

Some cartridge dealers who make a specialty of supplying specimen cartridges for collectors will furnish the shooter with limited quantities of special sizes at prices that are lower than the single specimen list.

In some instances, when it is impossible to find cases to fit or it is not practical to remodel cases, the barrel can be cut off and rechambered for some easier-to-get cartridge, such as one of the Winchester numbers. Do not, however, mutilate the original chamber until you have exhausted all the potential sources of supply. I know whereof I speak as I've been in the same boat and regretted my "can do" later.

If it becomes necessary to rechamber the rifle in order to shoot it, the following may contain some helpful suggestions.

The .45 Sharps 2$\frac{9}{10}$" and 2$\frac{7}{8}$" chambers may be shortened to use .45/70-2$\frac{1}{10}$" cases or the .45/90 WCF with 2$\frac{4}{10}$" case.

Various .44 caliber rifle chambers may also be shortened and rechambered for these same two .45 caliber cases, as the bore diameters of many of the old .44 calibers are close to a true .45. The bullets used may be .45/70 bullets sized to fit the barrel in most cases.

In the .40 calibers the chamber may be shortened, then recut for the .38/40 WCF cartridge, which is always available.

The .38/40 and .38/50 Remington chambers may be cut off and new chambers recut with a .38/55 Ballard & Marlin reamer. They usually shoot quite well, as the bore diameter is practically the same.

Many other possibilities along these lines will suggest themselves.

But when rechambering, be sure to select the case that will come the closest to the old neck diameter, as you will then avoid many of the neck-sizing troubles that plague us. The extractor changes for the new case are usually very minor, and they are easily made by any gunsmith, or by the shooter himself.

Most Schuetzen rifles are very temperamental brutes, and some will drive you to distraction or even further before you find just the right bullet temper and lubricant for that bullet. The only way out —unless you get the loading data with the rifle from the former owner—is exhaustive experimentation. But then, it is assumed that you like to shoot or you wouldn't have invested your hard-earned coin of the realm in such a contraption as a single-shot rifle.

The Winchester single-shot rifles from my collection are shown on the following pages.

FIGURE A. This is the low side-wall plain sporting rifle, 26-inch full-octagonal #1 barrel, .22 WCF caliber.

FIGURE B. Shows a low side-wall rifle, caliber .25/20 Single-shot, with 28-inch full-octagonal #2 barrel, pistol-grip, rifle butt plate stock, checkered grip and forearm. Single-set trigger. Target sights.

FIGURE C. Represents the commoner variety of high side-wall rifle. The plain sporting rifle with 30-inch #3 full-octagonal barrel, caliber .40/82 WCF.

FIGURE D. This is the .38/90/217 Express rifle taking the 3¼" case. This rifle has the 30-inch #3 full-octagonal barrel, single-set trigger, high side-wall action. (The Express calibers were usually made in full-round barrels and shotgun buttstock.) The sights on this rifle are the common blade front and Rocky Mountain sporting rear, while the Express type front and folding leaf Express rear sights were extra.

FIGURE E. Shows the .40/110/260 Express rifle with #4 full-octagonal barrel.

FIGURE F. This is the little .32 Long center-fire rifle on the high side-wall action, with 26-inch #1 full-octagonal barrel. This model shows the Winchester steel shotgun butt style of stock, which was available on all single-shots, with either rubber or steel plates upon order.

FIGURE G. The Special sporting rifle. This model has the pistol-grip stock, with Swiss butt plate, checkered grip and fore end. Walnut used is fancy crotch figure, and is varnished. This rifle has Win-

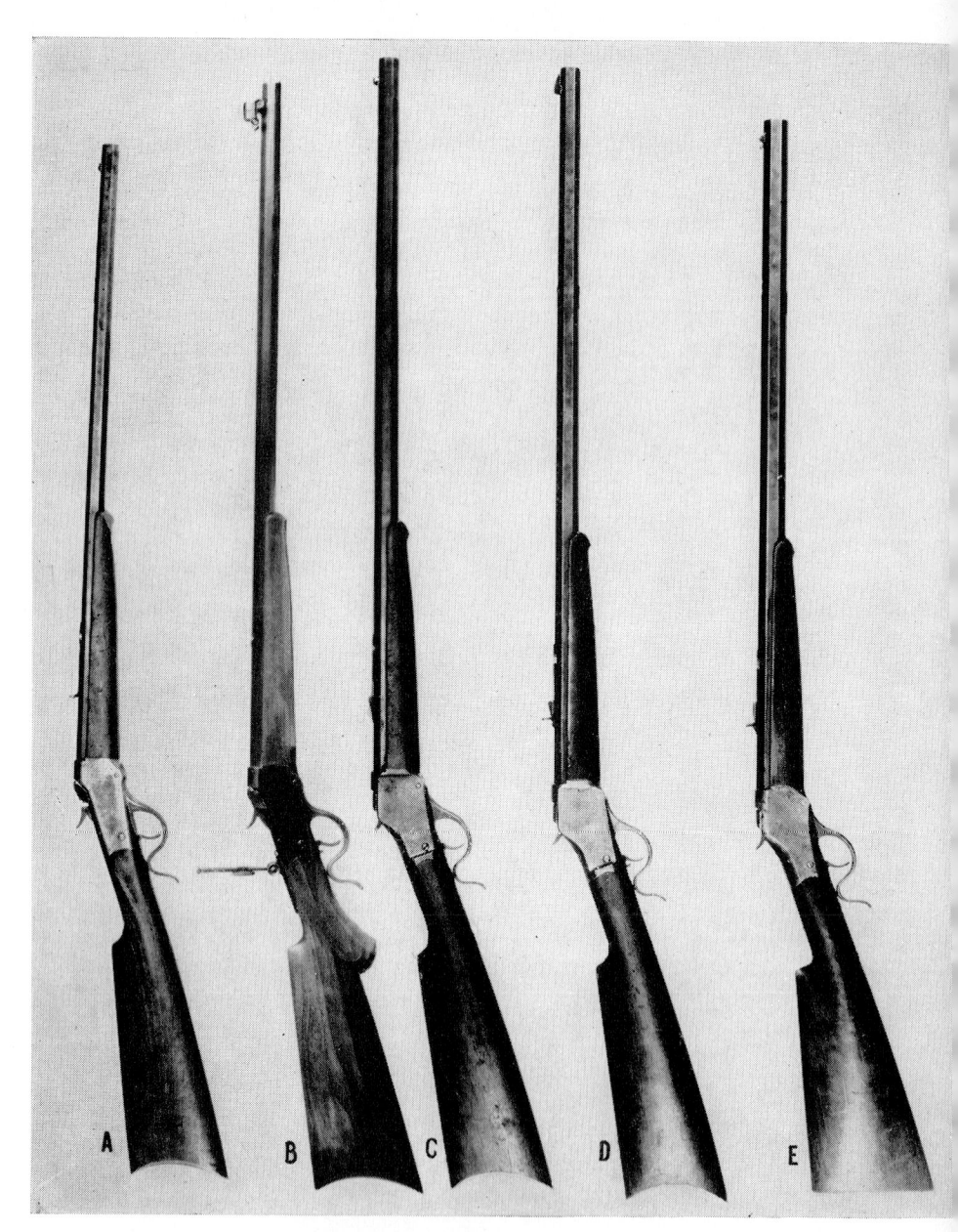

WINCHESTER RIFLES

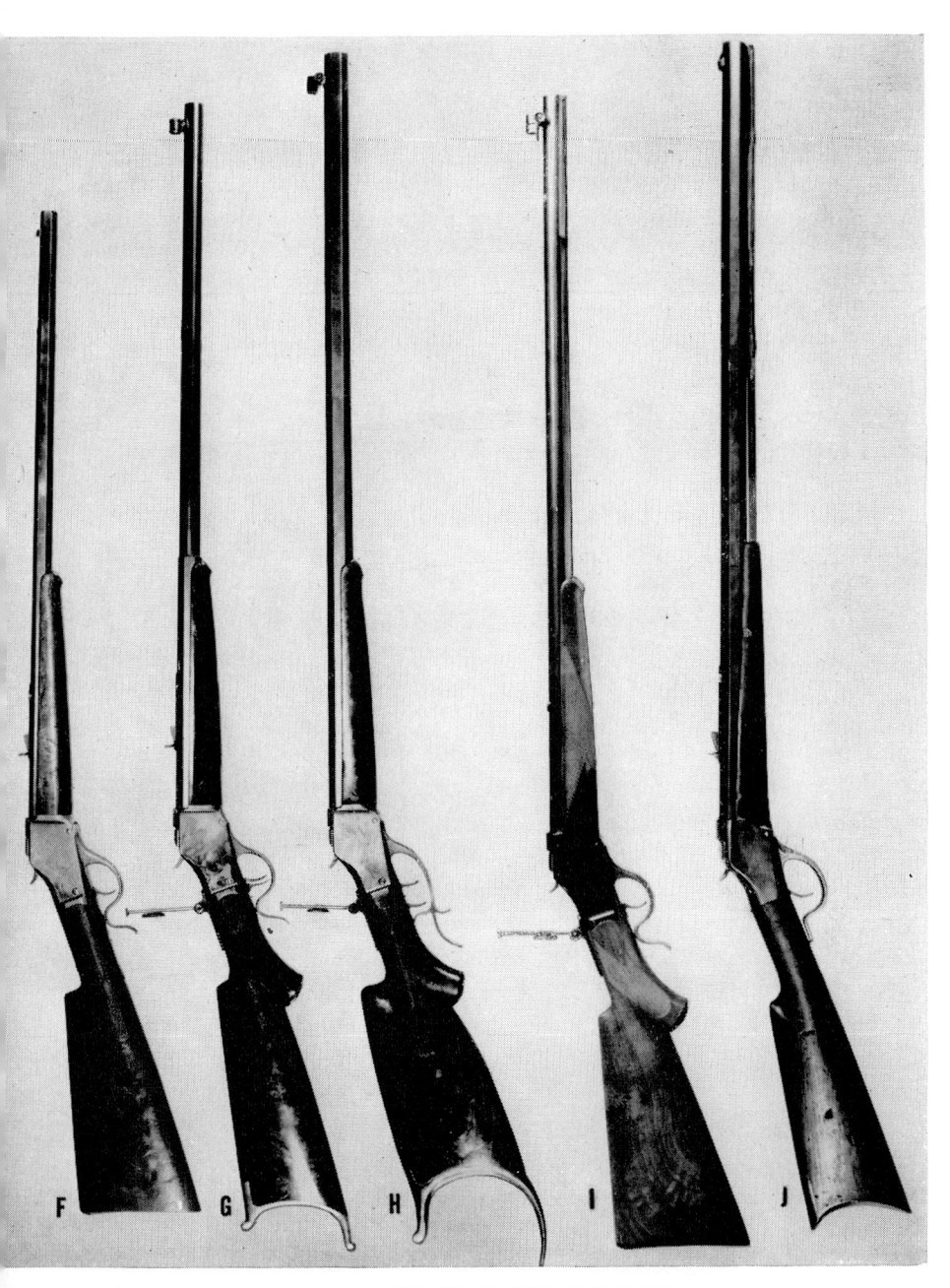

WINCHESTER RIFLES

chester double-set, close-coupled triggers, and is .32/40 caliber. It was a deluxe hunting or target arm.

FIGURE H. Shows the Winchester single-shot Schuetzen rifle. This has the Schuetzen double-set triggers and Schuetzen spur lever, pistol-grip, cheekpiece stock with Helm pattern butt plate. The walnut used in this stock is deluxe crotch figure. Barrel is 32-inch #4 full-octagonal. Caliber is .32/40 Ballard & Marlin. Sights on this model were usually vernier midrange rear and wind-gauge front. (The later Schuetzen rifle has a scroll finger lever and slightly different stock with newer design heavy Schuetzen butt plate.) This rifle has a blued receiver and is the flat mainspring type. (Late versions also had the blued receiver, of course, but they had spiral mainspring actions.)

FIGURE I. Winchester Sporting rifle with the factory-made pistol-grip stock with shotgun butt plate of hard rubber. Barrel is 30-inch proof steel #3 round. Caliber is .30/40.

FIGURE J. This is the J. M. Browning rifle made at Ogden, Utah, the granddaddy of all Winchester single-shot rifles of falling-block type. It is in .45/70 caliber, and has thimbles for ramrod underneath the barrel.

VI

F. Wesson Rifles

F. WESSON TIP-UP RIFLE. This rifle was patented in October, 1859, and November 11, 1862—Patent #36925—so it is a fairly early single-shot breechloader. It was made in deluxe grade as well as in the plainer grades that are usually seen.

The tip-up type is fairly common, and it is found most often in rim-fire calibers—.44, .38, .32, and .22; this last not so common. Very seldom is one of these tip-up, two-trigger type (front trigger to release the barrel at rear) found in fine condition. However, they do turn up occasionally. My .44 rim- or center-fire, with interchangeable firing pin, is an exception. It is fine inside and outside.

These tip-up models usually had receivers that were cast of malleable iron, and the barrels were cast steel. The higher grades, or falling-block type Wessons, were drop-forged and casehardened in colors. (See page 66.)

Occasionally one sees a tip-up sporting rifle that is rather completely scroll engraved, but I have never as yet seen one with animal or hunting scene engraving.

F. WESSON FALLING-BLOCK RIFLE. These rifles, being quite rare, are seldom found today. I have seen only four of them, and all were in fine shape. There were not many of this type made. Some collectors seem to think that the side-hammer, under-lever Wessons were made on Alexander Henry actions imported from Great Britain. This may be so; I have no way of verifying the fact today. If it is so, we don't need to feel too bad over it, as the Henry was copied from the Sharps side-hammer rifle. The only two Alexander Henry actions it has been my privilege to examine were both made with the hammer on the left side of the action. Whether they were all made in this way is another point I am in the dark upon. (See pages 238 and 239.) The under lever and manner of fastening to the trigger guard are, however, almost identical with the Henry; but of course this could have easily been copied.

These F. Wessons made up on the falling-block action are fine rifles. All I have seen were in the Creedmoor grades, and they were truly deluxe target rifles. There were three distinct variations of this falling-block type Wesson, so this leads me to believe that Wesson made the complete rifles. They are usually marked on the barrel, "F. Wesson's Long Range Rifle" or "F. Wesson's Mid Range Rifle," as the case might be. The patent date, July 10, 1877, was also stamped on some of these models.

F. Wesson Long Range Creedmoor Rifle. This rifle was chambered for a special .44 caliber cartridge. One specimen I examined accepted the Sharps .45-2$\frac{4}{10}$" case perfectly, and evidently some were chambered for this case. The actual difference between some of these old .44 and .45 caliber barrels is slight.

These models usually had small scroll and line engraving, though possibly some were more ornately engraved upon special order. The woods used were of fine figure, and they were well and finely checkered.

F. Wesson Mid Range Rifle. This model was chambered for the .42 Russian Berdan case. Like the Long Range model, these rifles usually had small scroll and line engraving and the woods used were similar to those of the Long Range.

F. Wesson Pocket Rifle. The first of these models was a tip-up barrel model similar to the rifle. Barrels ranged in length from 12 to 20 inches, and were chambered for .22 or .32 caliber, both rimfire. This pocket rifle had a detachable skeleton nickel-plated shoulder stock similar to the later side-swinging barrel type of pocket rifle.

Through the kindness of the late Mr. Fred Wainwright of Grayling, Michigan, I am able to quote from an F. Wesson circular dated 1886, which shows the various models offered at that time in both tip-up and falling-block types. This circular was mailed from Worcester, Mass., on August 20, 1886, to Mr. Arthur C. Dryk, Bridgewater, Mass.

F. WESSON'S CELEBRATED BREECH LOADING RIFLE

The new model Rifles are all made to fire both rim and central fire cartridges (free of extra charge) and both pin fire by the use of my Patent Adjustable hammer; Patented April 9, 1872. Their great superiority consists in their Simplicity, Rapidity, Accuracy, Penetration, Convenience, Recent Improvement, Durability.

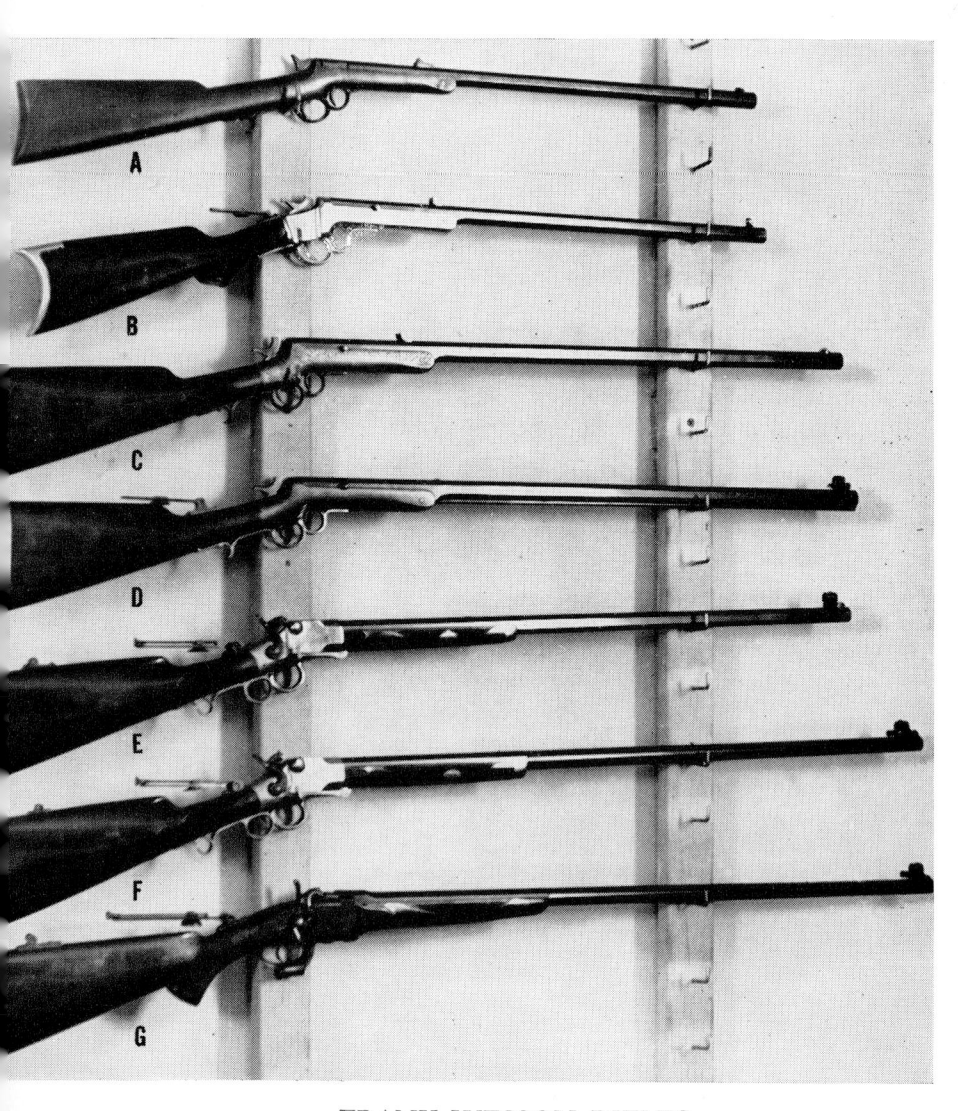

FRANK WESSON RIFLES
From the Frank Sargent collection

A Frank Wesson Tip-up rifle, caliber .44 rim-fire.
B Frank Wesson Tip-up rifle, caliber .22 rim-fire.
C Frank Wesson Tip-up target rifle, scroll engraved receiver, .425 Groove diameter, 2¾-inch straight shell.
D Frank Wesson Tip-up target rifle, .437 Groove diameter, 2⁷⁄₁₆-inch straight shell.
E Frank Wesson falling block Mid Range rifle, caliber .42 Russian Berdan.
F Frank Wesson falling block Long Range No. 2 rifle, caliber .44/90 bottleneck, 2⁷⁄₁₆-inch shell.
G Frank Wesson falling block Long Range No. 1 rifle, caliber .44/90 bottleneck, 2⁷⁄₁₆-inch shell.

Simplicity—It is impossible to load this Rifle wrong. Half cock, pull the forward trigger, and the barrel will rise at the breech; insert the cartridge, press the barrel back to its place, and it is already to cock and fire.

Rapidity—Twenty shots per minute.

Accuracy—It shoots where it is aimed.

Penetration—Remarkable, all that is desired.

Convenience—It is light, well balanced, handles pleasantly, requires no cleaning until you have done your day's work, and then one patch will clean it. By the removal of one screw, the barrel can be detached from the stock, and the rifle packed in a small space.

Recent Improvement—Patented April 9, 1872, which consists of an adjustable hammer or cock, so arranged as to fire both rim and central fire cartridges. This improvement has long been sought for, and by the use of the central fire cartridge which is reloadable, many hundred times, the very best of Rifle shooting is obtained.

Durability—The barrels are made of the finest steel, and the whole workmanship is without fault. There's no complicated machinery to get out of order. While the rifle is light, everything is compact, firm and strong. In a word it is justly pronounced, "The Best Breechloading Rifle Yet Constructed For Hunting or Sporting Purposes." I also make a Rifle barrel to insert in double guns, thus converting at pleasure one barrel into a Rifle and the other for shot, both breechloading. Price, $20.00.

FOUR CALIBERS—CARTRIDGES WATER PROOF

These cuts represent the exact size of the cartridge.

22-100   32-100   38-100   44-100   (All rim fire.)

(.22, .38 and .44 calibers have 2 grease grooves exposed)

Length of barrel is 24, 26, 28 or 30 inches.

Price—24-inch barrel, open sights, $25.00. Each additional inch in length of barrel, 50 cts. Globe sight, $5.00 extra. Swivels and straps, $2.50. Full set reloading tools complete with 50 shells, central fire, and box of primers, $5.00.

[This page shows the plain sporting rifle, two trigger style, straight grip no wood fore end, frame extends to take care of fore end in this model, rifle butt, called "F. Wesson's New Model."]

.   .   .   .

F. Wesson's Breech Loading Pocket Rifle, New Model patented May 31, 1870.

"Sportman's Jewel"

22-100   32-100

(Rim Fire)   (Rim Fire)

Embraces many advantages over the old style of tip-up barrel, which is liable to become loose with wear, shoot astray, and even cause accident; objections which are entirely overcome in the new model. The barrel is firmly attached to the frame, thus insuring the greatest possible accuracy in firing, and being simple in construction, it is less liable to get out of order. It operates easily. By pressing a stop under the frame, the barrel is readily turned aside to receive the cartridge and eject the empty shell. The Pistol is symmetrical in appearance, and can do better shooting than any on the tip-up principle besides being safer and more serviceable. Gallery and Dueling pistols furnished to order without extension breech. All are now made to explode the cartridges by a firing pin either central or rim fire cartridges as desired.

Prices 10 in. Oct. barrel .22 or .32 cal. rosewood stock plated frame rest $12.00
12 in. Oct. barrel .22 or .32 cal. rosewood stock plated frame rest 13.00
15 in. Oct. barrel .22 or .32 cal. rosewood stock plated frame rest 14.50
18 in. Oct. barrel .22 or .32 cal. rosewood stock plated frame rest 16.00
20 in. Oct. barrel .22 or .32 cal. rosewood stock plated frame rest 17.00

[The .44 cartridge shown in actual size with new model regular rifle described preceding this pocket rifle has a case $15/16''$ long. The .38 rim-fire has a case a scant $7/8''$ long. Evidently center-fire cartridges were the same length when used in this rifle.]

F. Wesson's Long Range Rifle, Breech Loading, The Champion Rifle of the World

No. 1—Long Range Rifle, National Regulation.

Calibers .44 and .45-100 Weight 10 lbs. and under hammer outside of lock plate, rebounding lock, full vernier peep sight, with spirit level on Wind-gauge muzzle sight, Rifle complete with full outfit $125.00

[This model has pistol-grip shotgun butt fore end wedged on, and full checkering. Henry lever action. Hammer or right-side lever locks on trigger guard with thumb push release, back action lock plate. Extra base on heel for tang rear. Full octagonal barrel.]

No. 2 Long and Midrange and Hunting Rifle. Full vernier peep sight, Windgauge Muzzle sight, with spirit level; with 100 solid head shells, and full set of reloading tools, $85.00.

[This model has a smaller modified right-side hammer action, a light-

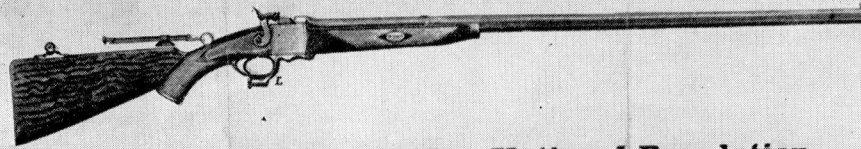

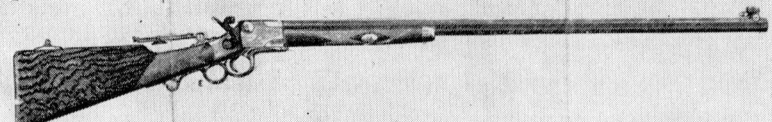

FRANK WESSON CIRCULAR

F. WESSON'S
CELEBRATED
BREECH-LOADING RIFLE.

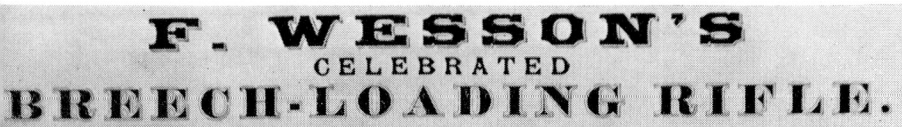

THE NEW MODEL RIFLES

are all made to fire both Rim and Central Fire Cartridges, (*free of extra charge*,) and both pin fire by the use of my Patent Adjustable Hammer; Patented April 9, 1872.
Their great superiority consists in their

SIMPLICITY, RAPIDITY, ACCURACY, PENETRATION, CONVENIENCE, DURABILITY.

Simplicity. — It is impossible to load this Rifle wrong. Half cock, pull the forward trigger, and the barrel will rise the breech; insert the cartridge, press the barrel back to its place, and it is ready to cock and fire.
Rapidity. — Twenty shots per minute.
Accuracy. — It shoots where it is aimed. *Penetration.* — Remarkable — all that is desired.
Convenience. — It is light, well balanced, handles pleasantly, requires no cleaning until you have done your day's work, and then one patch will clean it. By the removal of one screw, the barrel can be detached from the stock, and the Rifle packed in a small space.
Recent Improvement. — Patented April 9, 1872, which consists of an adjustable hammer or cock, so arranged as to fire both rim and central fire cartridges. This improvement has long been sought for, and by the use of the central cartridge, which is reloadable many hundred times, the very best of Rifle shooting is obtained.
Durability. — The barrels are made of the finest steel, and the whole workmanship is without fault. There is no complicated machinery to get out of order. While the Rifle is light, everything is compact, firm and strong. In a word, it is justly pronounced "THE BEST BREECH-LOADING RIFLE YET CONSTRUCTED FOR HUNTING OR SPORTING PURPOSES." I also make Rifle Barrel to insert in double guns, thus converting at pleasure one barrel into a Rifle and the other for Shot, both Breech loading. Price, $20.00.

FOUR CALIBRES. — CARTRIDGES WATER-PROOF.
These Cuts Represent the Exact Size of the Cartridge.

22-100   32-100   38-100   44-100

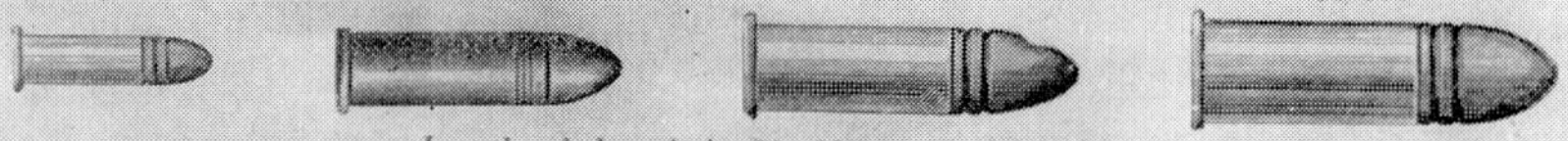

Length of barrel is 24, 26, 28 or 30 inches.
PRICE. — 24 inch barrel, open sight, $25.00. Each additional inch in length of barrel, 50 cts. Globe sight, $5.00 extra. Swivels and straps, $2.50. Full set Reloading tools complete, with 50 Shells, central fire, and box of primers, $5.00.

F. WESSON'S BREECH-LOADING POCKET RIFLE.
NEW MODEL, PATENTED MAY 31, 1870.

"Sportsman's Jewel."

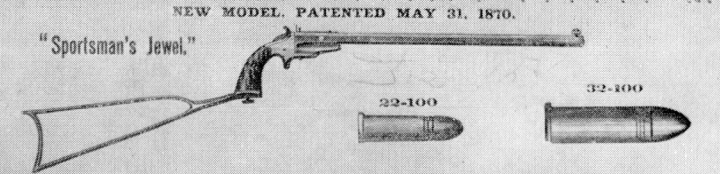

22-100   32-100

embraces many advantages over the old style of tip-up barrel, which is liable to become loose with wear, shoot astray, and can cause accident; objections which are entirely overcome in the New Model. The barrel is firmly attached to the frame, thus insuring the greatest possible accuracy in firing; and, being simple in construction, it is less liable to get out of order, operates easily. By pressing a stop under the frame, the barrel is readily turned aside to receive the cartridge and eject the empty shell. The Pistol is symmetrical in appearance, and can do better shooting than any on the tip-up principle, besides being safer and more serviceable. Gallery and Dueling Pistols furnished to order, without Extension Breech.
All are now made to explode the cartridges by a Firing Pin, either central or rim firing cartridges, as desired.

PRICES.— 10 inch octagon barrel, 22 or 32 calibre, Rosewood Stock, Plated Rest and Frame, - - $12.00
12   "   "   "   "   "   "   "   "   "   - - 13.00
15   "   "   "   "   "   "   "   "   "   - - 14.50
18   "   "   "   "   "   "   "   "   "   - - 16.00
20   "   "   "   "   "   "   "   "   "   - - 17.00

SEE OTHER SIDE.

REVERSE OF FRANK WESSON CIRCULAR

ened, somewhat straight-grip stock, wedged on fore end, full checkering, shotgun butt, lever forms trigger guard, full octagonal barrel. Action has firing pin put in on right side, and has the appearance of an M/L drum, etc. It also has an extra base on heel of stock.]

No. 1 Mid Range and Sporting Rifle.

Hammer in line of barrel, caliber .38, .40 and .45/100. Full pistol grip, checkered grip and forestock. Vernier peep and muzzle sight with spirit level. Full set of reloading tools, with 100 solid head shells, central fire. $65.00.

[This model has still another modified falling-block action with centrally hung hammer under lever with ring which forms trigger guard, shotgun butt, finely checkered stock, and fore end. Action looks somewhat like Ballard, also like Winchester single-shot half-octagonal barrel. Base on heel of stock for long tang rear sight. All three of the preceding models have tipped fore ends, but, I believe, no grip caps.]

No. 2 Mid Range Sporting and Gallery Rifle, with tilting barrel, half pistol grip, calibers .22, .32, .38, and .40/100. Barrel 28 to 30 inch.

This arm combines all the good qualities of first class rifles, with adjustable hammer to fire both center and rim fire cartridges. Full globe and open sighted. Price $55.00

[This is a deluxe tip-up two-trigger model, pistol-grip rifle butt stock; no fore end; scroll engraving on receiver tang; open barrel sights; checkered grip. Action extends forward to form the fore end, the same as plain models described previously.]

VII

Wurfflein Rifles

THE Wurfflein single-shot breech-loading rifle is comparatively rare today. It was never popular in comparison with contemporary target rifles, although well made of good materials. The action is one of the simplest of all breech mechanisms, and all the specimens I have owned or examined were well fitted and easily operated. (See page 242.)

The illustrations shown here have been taken from the 1889 catalog of "Wm. Wurfflein, 208 N. Second Street, Philadelphia, Pa., U.S.A." They represent the various models as made in that year. The detailed descriptions of these models are quoted from this catalog.

One peculiarity of Wurfflein rifles that will be noticed in reading the descriptions is that they had no special Wurfflein calibers but utilized Stevens, Ballard, and Winchester cartridges. Also the target sights as offered in this catalog are identical with those offered by Marlin for the Ballard rifle, so it is possible that the sights were purchased from Marlin.

THE WURFFLEIN BREECH LOADING RIFLE

This rifle is constructed on the tip-up barrel system, the quickest and handiest system in use. It possesses the following points of merit over others:

First—Automatic rebounding hammer, whereby the trouble of half cocking, the risk of breaking the firing pin, defacing the breech of barrel, or accidentally discharging the rifle is avoided as the hammer is never resting on the firing pin or at full cock, but always at safety.

Second—New Improved, patented, simple, strong, convenient and easy manipulated top-action, which is drawn back like a hammer to open the rifle, it can also be worked with the same motion of cocking the rifle, thereby making one motion; i.e., cocking and opening the rifle at the same time; it will be seen at a glance that this is the most complete, quickest and handiest action in the market.

Third—Improved hinge joint, with or without wood, fore end stock which is so constructed that it is impossible to pinch the hand in opening the rifle, as is the case with other tip-up barrel rifles. The full wood fore end stock gives a more natural feeling in handling and finer finished appearance.

Fourth—Patented, automatic, positive, strong, simple shell extractor, which returns to its place, giving a flat breech to more conveniently insert the cartridge.

Fifth—Pistol grip stock, which is a great improvement, as it gives a better and firmer hold and conforms more natural to the hand.

This rifle is unsurpassed for simplicity of construction, strength and durability, every part being of the best material, the barrel is of fine steel, carefully bored and rifled, with the most improved machinery, tested and warranted.

For safety and speed in loading and cleaning effectiveness and accuracy, it has no superior. It stands foremost as to symmetrical model, style and beauty of workmanship.

It has no equal!

Ask to see the Wurfflein rifle and do not be satisfied until you have seen it, and be convinced of the above facts.

The opposite page of the catalog (page 3) shows a sectional cut of the Wurfflein action.

The paragraphs following are from page 8 of the catalog.

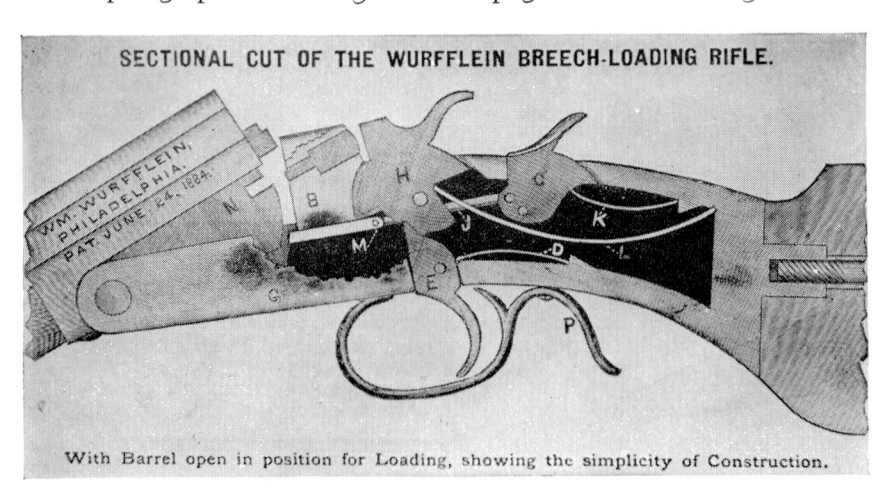

SECTIONAL CUT OF THE WURFFLEIN BREECH-LOADING RIFLE.

With Barrel open in position for Loading, showing the simplicity of Construction.

WURFFLEIN ACTION DESIGN

WURFFLEIN RIFLES

The Wurfflein breech loading shot gun. For taxidermists, specimen hunters and general sporting purposes. Pistol grip and fore end stock, nickel or blued finish made in the following calibers, viz: .32-100, .38-100, .40-100 and .45-100. Reloadable brass shells, 12, 16 and 20 gauge brass, or paper shells, 28 to 30 inch barrel price $15.00.

For extra finish refer to page 11.

[Gun shown is plain gun with fore end and shotgun butt stock.]

Brass shells used in the Wurfflein shot gun.
.32 Ex. long Ballard, .40-70-330 Sharps st.
.38 Ex. long .45-90-300 Winchester model 1886.

[These shells are shown without bullets used in above shotgun.]

The following paragraphs are from pages 9 to 19 of the catalog.

The Wurfflein stock and frame with barrel detached showing convenience in carrying.

We can furnish shot guns with extra rifle barrels, or rim or center fire rifles with extra shot gun or different caliber of rifle barrels, without changing any part, all that is necessary is to unscrew the barrel screw, which can be done in a few seconds and another barrel put in its place, you can have one stock and frame and a number of different size barrels to fit.

No. 1½. SPORTING AND GALLERY RIFLE.
Straight Hand Stock, without Wood Fore-end, Plain Trigger, Octagon Barrel, Open Sights, Nickel Pated Mountings.
24-inch barrel, 22 or 32 Cal. Rim Fire, 32, 38, and 44 centre fire.
Weight, 5¾ to 8¾ lbs.   Price, $15.00.
Made also in Ladies' size, 4½ lbs. The lightest Rifle in the World. Price, $15.00.

No. 1. SPORTING AND GALLERY RIFLE.
Straight Hand and Wood Fore end Stock, Plain Trigger, Octagon Barrel, Open Sight, Nickel Plated Mountings.
24-inch barrel, 22 or 32 Cal. Rim Fire, 32, 38, and 44 Cal. Centre Fire. Weight, 5¾ to 8¾ lbs.   Price, $16.00.
Made also in Ladies' size, 4½ lbs. Price, $16.00.
Barrels over 24 inch, for every two inches additional, $1.00.

WURFFLEIN RIFLES, MODELS NO. 1 AND NO. 1½

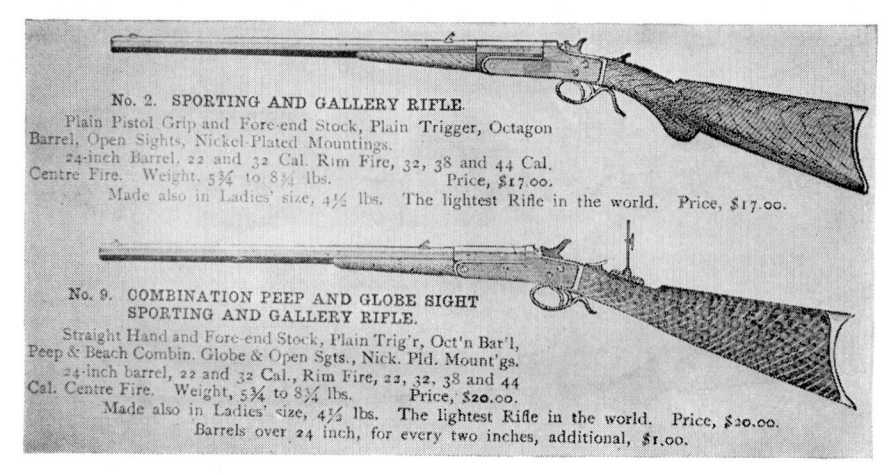

No. 2. SPORTING AND GALLERY RIFLE.
Plain Pistol Grip and Fore-end Stock, Plain Trigger, Octagon Barrel, Open Sights, Nickel-Plated Mountings. 24-inch Barrel, 22 and 32 Cal. Rim Fire, 32, 38 and 44 Cal. Centre Fire. Weight, 5¾ to 8¾ lbs. Price, $17.00.
Made also in Ladies' size, 4½ lbs. The lightest Rifle in the world. Price, $17.00.

No. 9. COMBINATION PEEP AND GLOBE SIGHT SPORTING AND GALLERY RIFLE.
Straight Hand and Fore-end Stock, Plain Trig'r, Oct'n Bar'l, Peep & Beach Combin. Globe & Open Sgts., Nick. Pld. Mount'gs. 24-inch barrel, 22 and 32 Cal., Rim Fire, 22, 32, 38 and 44 Cal. Centre Fire. Weight, 5¾ to 8¾ lbs. Price, $20.00.
Made also in Ladies' size, 4½ lbs. The lightest Rifle in the world. Price, $20.00.
Barrels over 24 inch, for every two inches, additional, $1.00.

WURFFLEIN RIFLES, MODELS NO. 2 AND NO. 9

Shot gun barrels, $6.00. Rifle barrels 1½ to 10, $8.00. Rifle barrels, 20 to 25, $15.00.

. . . .

The Wurfflein single shot gallery and target pistol.

This pistol is constructed the same as the rifle. It is without exception the most symmetrical model and finest balanced, the quickest loaded and handiest pistol in the market. It is the only pistol where 22 caliber rim fire and different center fire, either ball or shot cartridges can be used on the same frame and butt; which are changed in a few seconds, being far superior to any revolver of same caliber for accuracy and penetration, making the finest target pistol for practice.

No. 1 Half Oct., 10″ bbl. nickel plated mountings, open sights, grip and fore end plain	$16.00
No. 2 Half Oct., 10″ bbl. nickel plated mountings, wind gauge and elevating rear sights, grip and fore end plain	20.00
Made in .22 cal., short and long rim fire, .32 S. & W. .38 S. & W. and .44 S. & W. center fire cartridges, wt. 2¾ to 3½ lbs.	
No. 3. Shot pistol, same as No. 1 smooth bore, .32, .38, .40 and .45 calibers as shown on page 8	15.00
Extra shot barrel, $6.00. Extra rifle barrel open sights, $8.00	
Checkering grip and fore end, extra	2.00

. . . .

EXTRAS

Silver plating frame and mountings	$3.00
Fancy curl, walnut stock, extra	$3.00 to 10.00
Checkering pistol grip and fore end	3.00 to 6.00
Engraving from	2.00 to 15.00
Cheek piece	4.00
Shot gun, rubber butt plate	2.00
Shot gun, metal butt plate	1.50
Swiss metal butt plate	2.00
Set or double trigger	5.00
Swivels and sling straps	1.50
Sling strap	.75
Over the given lengths add for every 2 inches	1.00

[This page also lists component parts.]

. . . .

Everlasting center fire shells used in the Wurfflein Rifle.
.32/35, 5¢ ea., .32/40, 5¢ ea., .38/55, 6¢ ea.
.40/63, 7¢ ea., .40/85, 8¢ each. [Last four are all Ballard cartridges.]

Everlasting shells of all sizes take the No. 2½ primer. The advantage of the everlasting shell are numerous. There is less recoil than with a bottle neck shell; it is no trouble to clean them; they are exactly the same size as the bore so that the ball lies in the grooves as in a muzzle loader. They are made of heavy metal, specially prepared, and a fine quality of powder can be used, which would burst an ordinary shell and endanger the life of the shooter. There is no bother about reducing after discharging. They are cheaper in the long run than ordinary shells as each one will last for years.

Directions for Loading Shells

Care should be taken in loading shells that the charge is always the same, never crush the powder. Never crimp or crease the shell where fine shooting is required. Bullets should be seated in the shell with a ball seater, or seated in the barrel of rifle, with a seater for fine shooting. When grooved bullets are used, dip them in melted lubricant base end down, until the grooves are filled, have lubricant quite hot, make lubricant 8 parts pure tallow, and one part bee's wax, not letting it get too hot to burn. F. G. Powder has been found to be the best for rifles, the high grades are too quick and dry.

Reloading Shells

Care should be taken to clean shells after firing. First remove old primers, then boil in strong soapsuds or soda water, removing all burnt

SINGLE-SHOT RIFLES

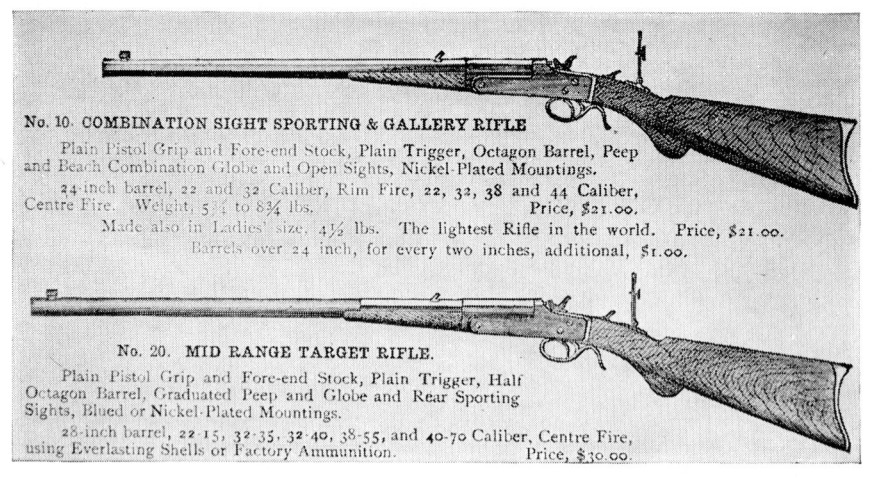

No. 10. COMBINATION SIGHT SPORTING & GALLERY RIFLE
Plain Pistol Grip and Fore-end Stock, Plain Trigger, Octagon Barrel, Peep and Beach Combination Globe and Open Sights, Nickel-Plated Mountings. 24-inch barrel, 22 and 32 Caliber, Rim Fire, 22, 32, 38 and 44 Caliber, Centre Fire. Weight, 5¼ to 8¾ lbs. Price, $21.00. Made also in Ladies' size, 4½ lbs. The lightest Rifle in the world. Price, $21.00. Barrels over 24 inch, for every two inches, additional, $1.00.

No. 20. MID RANGE TARGET RIFLE.
Plain Pistol Grip and Fore-end Stock, Plain Trigger, Half Octagon Barrel, Graduated Peep and Globe and Rear Sporting Sights, Blued or Nickel-Plated Mountings. 28-inch barrel, 22-15, 32-35, 32-40, 38-55, and 40-70 Caliber, Centre Fire, using Everlasting Shells or Factory Ammunition. Price, $30.00.

WURFFLEIN RIFLES, MODELS NO. 10 AND NO. 20

No. 22. MID RANGE TARGET RIFLE.
Checkered Pistol Grip and Fore-end, Fancy Curl, Walnut Stock, Plain Trigger, Half Octagon Barrel, Graduated Peep and Globe and Rear Sporting Sights, Blued Mountings, Swiss or Off-hand or Shot Gun Butt Plate. 28-inch barrel, 22-15, 32-35, 32-40, 38-55, 40-70 Caliber, Centre Fire, using Everlasting Shells or Factory Ammunition. Price, $40.00.

No. 25. THE WURFFLEIN "SPECIAL" MID RANGE TARGET RIFLE.
Checkered Pistol Grip and Fore-end, Fancy Curl, Walnut Stock, Plain Trig'r, Half Octagon Bar'l, Vernier Peep and Wind Gauge Sights, Shot Gun, Swiss or Off-hand Butt Plate, Blued Mountings. 28-inch barrel, 22-15, 32-35, 32-40, 38-55, 40-70, Caliber, Centre Fire, using Everlasting Shells or Factory Ammunition. Price, $45.00.

WURFFLEIN RIFLES, MODELS NO. 22 AND NO. 25

powder, and dry thoroughly to prevent shell from being destroyed by corrosion, replace new primer always before putting in powder, and have it well seated below the surface of the head to prevent premature explosion.

. . . . . .

Center Fire Cartridges Used in the Wurfflein Rifle

.32/40, Powder 40 grs. bullet 165 grs. per 1000 loaded	$27.00
.38/55, Powder 48 grs. bullet 255 grs. per 1000 loaded	33.00
.40/70 Bal. #5 Powder 65 grs. bullet 330 grs. per 1000 loaded	40.00
.45/90/300 Powder 90 grs. bullet 300 grs. per 1000 loaded	36.00

RIM FIRES

B.B.C. .22	$ 4.00 per M.	.32 Long	$11.50 per M.
C.B.C.	4.50 per M.	.32 Ex. Long	16.50 per M.
.22 Short	5.00 per M.	.38 Short	16.00 per M.
.22 L.R.	6.00 per M.	.38 Long	18.00 per M.
.22 Ex. L.	9.00 per M.	.38 Ex. Long	25.00 per M.
.32 Short	10.00 per M.		

CENTER FIRES

.22 Ex. Long	$13.00 per M.	.32 S. & W.	$11.00 per M.
.32 Short Colt	11.00 per M.	.38 Short Colts	13.50 per M.
.32 Long Colt	12.00 per M.	.38 Long Colts	14.50 per M.
.32 Ex. Long Ballard	18.00 per M.	.38 Ex. Long	23.00 per M.

Pages 16 and 17 of the catalog show the different sights used on Wurfflein rifles. The tang sights look exactly like Ballard, so they may be their sights. Prices are as follows.

Globe front, $1.00. Gallery peep sight, $2.50. Improved graduated peep sight, $3.00. Improved vernier Mid-Range peep sight, $4.00. Improved vernier long range peep sight, $7.50. Improved wind gauge sight, $3.00. Improved wind gauge sight with spirit level, $4.00. Spirit lever, $1.00. Interchangeable discs for wind gauge sights, 50¢. Beach combination front sight, $1.00. Front sight knife edge, 50¢. Lyman peep sight, $3.00. Lyman Ivory bead front sight, $1.00. Lyman plain ivory front sight, 50¢. Front sight .22 cal. rifles, 40¢. Rear sight .22 cal. rifles, 50¢ Sporting rear sight, 80¢. Blank piece for filling rear sight slot, 25¢.

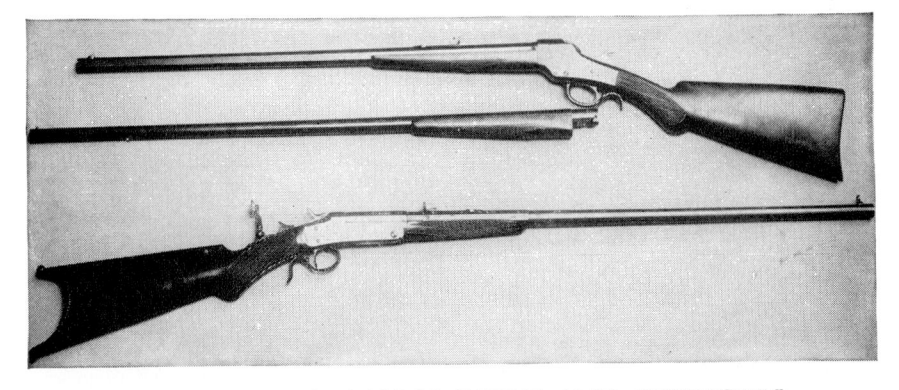

HOPKINS AND ALLEN RIFLE AND SHOTGUN
COMBINATION (TOP)
ENGRAVED WURFFLEIN RIFLE (LOWER)

Page 19 of catalog shows loading tools, etc., and these are the same as those shown in Ballard catalogs; the same type of bullet seater, recapper and decapper, powder scoop, wad cutter, bullet mold, etc. Five pieces make up the complete set.

They can be furnished in .32/40, .38/55, .40/63, .40/85 and .45/100, which are the present sizes in use also in .38/50, .40/65 and .40/90 which were formerly made. [Ballard catalog phrasing!]

The bullet seater simply seats the ball in the shell not crimping the latter. This is preferable in target shooting and the only feasible plan when patched bullets are used.

Detailed price list:

Grooved bullet mold, .32-165, .32-185, .38-255, .38-330, .40-260, .40-285, .40-330, .40-370, .45-285, .45-405	$1.10
Grooved bullet mold for Express bullets .40-260, .45-405	$2.25
Patched bullet mold with cut off, .45-420	2.00
Patched bullet mold same size as grooved	1.10
Swage for patched bullets	4.00
Ball seater, nickel plated	1.35
De and re capper, nickel plated	1.10
Wad cutter	.40
Powder scoop	.12
Wood mallet	.25
Reducing die	3.00
Loading tube	1.50
Wilkinson loader	3.00

The bullet molds furnished have a wooden handle which makes them much better to hold when hot than if the handles were of iron.

Page 20 of catalog shows Ideal No. 1 combination tool and mold in the following sizes: .32 Short, Long and Extra Long; .38 Short, Long, and Extra Long, at $2.25. No. 6 in sporting cartridges were as follows: .32/40, .38/55, .40/70, .45/70 at $3.00. There is also a plain plier type recapper listed on the same page in .32, .38, .32/35, .32/40, .38/55, .45/90 at 50 cents. Ball seater for breech-seating bullets in barrel, all sizes (different from regular Ideal later type) was priced at $2.00.

A fine engraved specimen of the Wurfflein Rifle from the author's collection is shown on page 247.

VIII

Peabody and Peabody-Martini Rifles

THE PEABODY RIFLE

THE Peabody rifle was patented on July 22, 1862, by Henry O. Peabody of Boston, Mass., under patent #35947. It was the outside hammer, hinged breechblock model that was first made in military models and was adopted by the Government and also by the Connecticut State Militia.

The first models were made evidently for the Peabody .50 caliber rim-fire cartridge (page 256), and later models were made in .433 caliber and in .45 sporting caliber.

The Peabody patent for transformed muskets was issued on December 10, 1867 (#72076), and some Springfield muskets were converted, using this breech system in caliber .58 Berdan.

The models as made by the Providence Tool Co., Providence, R. I., on the Peabody outside hammer action are as follows.

PEABODY SPORTING RIFLE. This was available in 26- and 28-inch barrel lengths, caliber .45 Peabody rim-fire, with sporting style stock and sights.

PEABODY CARBINE. This had a 20-inch barrel, and it also was chambered for the special .45 Peabody rim-fire as well as for the special .50/50 Peabody rim-fire cartridge. These rifles are marked "Peabody's Patent, July 22, 1862. Manfg. by Providence Tool Co., Providence, R. I." The over-all length was 39 inches, and the weight was 6½ pounds.

A few years later—in 1871—this same model was also chambered for the .50/70 Government cartridge.

PEABODY MILITARY RIFLE. This rifle had a full-length stock, and was chambered for the Peabody .50 caliber rim-fire musket cartridge. As far as can be learned, it was made in some quantity for the

Canadian Government. Philip B. Sharpe's *The Rifle in America* (page 76) also lists this rifle as having been made for the Swiss Government in .41 Swiss rim-fire, and for the Rumanian Government in .45 Rumanian center-fire. This same model rifle was also made in calibers .43 Spanish, .45/70 Gov't., and .50/70 Gov't. But these calibers were made in limited quantities, it is believed.

THE PEABODY-MARTINI RIFLE

THIS is a rifle that is practically unknown even among otherwise well-informed gun-minded men. Its very foreign appearance as compared with most of our common American single-shots probably accounted for its not being too popular during the days it was made. The few specimens seen in the higher grades are found mostly in the Eastern part of the country, very few of this type being seen in Western states.

This action was the Peabody patent #35947, and, as already stated, it was made first in an outside-hammer, tipping-block, under-lever type (see page 258). Not many sporting rifles with the outside hammer are extant today, although the military rifle and carbine models seem quite plentiful. The earlier models used a .50 caliber rim-fire cartridge. Later they were made in .43, .45, and .50 center-fire calibers.[1]

This action was improved by Martini, a Swiss inventor, who substituted a concealed, spiral spring striker for the clumsy outside hammer, thus making a very fine action with fast ignition.

A great number of these improved Peabody-Martini rifles were made by the Providence Tool Co., at Providence, R. I., in military pattern for several European Governments.

Two articles which will be of great value to anyone desiring further information on the Peabody-Martini action are "Expatriated by Force of Circumstances," by Captain Wotkyns, in the October, 1927, *American Rifleman*, and "Martini Equipping the International Rifle Team," by Colonel Hatcher in the June, 1928, *American Rifleman*.

The Peabody-Martini actions were well made and well hardened, so that today one sees them in fine working order when he sees

[1] See Satterlee on this.

them at all. I have been fortunate in obtaining several fine specimens of this rifle in the higher grades. Three models—the Creedmoor Mid Range, Creedmoor Long Range, and the Kill Deer—are shown on page 253. This comprises all the models as offered in 1881, according to my catalog. The catalog of George K. Tryon, of Pittsburgh, dated 1880, shows one other model, the Rough and Ready, caliber .45/70; but to date I have not run across this one. It was a plain-sighted, cheaper version of the Kill Deer model.

The Kill Deer model is in .45/70 Gov't. caliber with 28-inch part-octagonal barrel, straight-grip stock, and some fine combination peep, open, and globe and pinhead sights, which are somewhat similar to the combination sights used on later Stevens pocket rifles, but of course they were made by the Providence Tool Co.

This rifle is marked on right side of the frame, "Peabody and Martini Patents," and on left side, "Kill Deer." (See page 253.) The barrel measures about the same as a #3 Winchester, and the rifling is the same as all other Peabody-Martini rifling, consisting of convexly curved grooves with the center of the grooves as high as the lands, and a narrow triangular land between each pair of grooves. This barrel is stamped ".45 Gov't." at the breech, on the top barrel flat, and "Providence Tool Co., Providence, R. I." is engraved—not stamped—in a single line also on the top flat.

A SPECIALLY ENGRAVED PEABODY-MARTINI ACTION

This Kill Deer model has a very comfortable shotgun buttstock, uncheckered and of ample enough proportions so that the considerable shooting I have done with it has been accomplished with a minimum amount of suffering from recoil, even when using 70 grains of FG powder and a 405- or 500-grain bullet. This is one of the most superbly accurate .45/70 rifles I have ever owned.

The next higher grade is the Creedmoor Mid Range rifle shown in the center of the next page. This has a rifle butt and checkered pistol-grip stock and fore end. The barrel is part-octagonal in 28-inch length. Stamped on the muzzle is "40 caliber, 70 grains." The caliber is .40/70 "What Cheer" Peabody-Martini. The sights are Peabody-Martini vernier tang rear and wind-gauge front, of an unusual and fine design. The barrel is engraved—not stamped—"Providence Tool Co., Providence, R. I."

The second grade Mid Range Peabody-Martini is the same as the Creedmoor model except that it has a straight-grip stock, checkered, and it is marked on the side of the frame, "What Cheer—Mid Range." The caliber and barrel length are the same as the Creedmoor Mid Range.

These Mid Range rifles are very fine models, and they were evidently more popular than the Long Range Creedmoor Martinis, in .40/90 and .44/100 calibers, as more of them are to be found today. The .40/90 Peabody-Martini cartridge is $2\frac{1}{16}$ inches long, and uses a 500-grain bullet, paper patched, of course, as are all the other "What Cheer" cartridges.

The third model shown on the page is the Creedmoor Long Range model, with 32-inch, part-octagonal barrel stamped "44/100" at the breech and engraved, "Providence Tool Co., Providence, R. I." on the top barrel flat. This is a shotgun butt, pistol-grip model, with vernier tang rear and windage adjustment front sights. It was evidently the Creedmoor rifle, as far as the Providence company was concerned, and it is a mighty fine one at that, though I doubt if many of these rifles were ever used on the old Creedmoor Range on Long Island.

The second grade Long Range model also had a straight-grip stock, and was marked, "What Cheer," as was the second grade of the Mid Range models. There is no doubt that these What Cheer rifles were much more popular on the What Cheer Target Range, which lay a few miles from Providence, R. I., than on any other range. The

THREE PEABODY-MARTINI ACTIONS

.40/70, .40/90, and .44/100 What Cheer cartridges were named for this range. In Satterlee's *A Catalogue of Firearms for the Collector* (page 101) the opening date of the What Cheer Range is given as October 25, 1875.

The 1881 Peabody-Martini catalog shows one of the Creedmoor Martini rifles engraved quite fancily, with a scene showing a frog shooting prone at a bull's-eye painted on the underside of a turtle, the legs of which are held by two more frogs. Upon turning the rifle over, what happened when the rifle discharged is apparent, for the frog doing the shooting has been slid along several feet to the rear by the recoil, he has missed the turtle, which is making its escape as rapidly as possible, and instead has cut the leg on one of his target holders cleanly in two! The catalog page is shown on page 261.

Frogs evidently were quite a popular subject with the engraver who worked on these fine old Peabodys. Several years ago a fine Creedmoor Peabody-Martini turned up at Charles Johnson's shop for relining to .22 rim-fire caliber, that had scenes on both sides showing frogs engaged in quaffing beer, smoking huge cigars, and quite generally disporting themselves. It was very amusing to examine this engraving job, which was well executed.

Peabody-Martini rifles have been one of my favorites for a long time. With their odd rifling, odd actions, odder sights, and, oddest of all, their calibers, they have been almost odd enough to suit anyone!

The .40/70 What Cheer cartridge (page 256) is a squat bottleneck of 1^{11}⁄$_{16}$ inches length, although the earlier Winchester catalogs list it as 1¾ inches long. It has a Berdan primer and a paper-patch bullet weighing 380 grains. These cartridges were loaded only by UMC, I believe, though possibly by Winchester also. They are very rare today, and are found only once in a great while on specimen cartridge dealers' lists. The Peabody-Martini loading tools are shown on page 265.

Since I was determined to shoot my fine Mid Range Peabody-Martini, I eventually solved the problem of brass by having Johnson make me a die to reform .43 Egyptian cases to fit this chamber. After they are forced into the die with a little powdered graphite, then shortened slightly to proper length, they are loaded with 65 grains of FG powder. Sometimes I use a 330-grain grooved bullet, seating it right down on the powder; the accuracy of this load leaves nothing to be desired. I have quite a large supply of 370-grain paper-patch bullets, which were made by UMC for Sharps and Remington rifles, which shoot phenomenally accurately when seated with the fingers upon a thin grease wad, which in turn rests upon a card wad on the powder.

Tools for this .40/70 caliber never materialized, so since the .43 Egyptian cases that I have are all Berdan primed, it is a simple matter to pry out the exploded primer with an awl, clean out the debris in the pocket, and reprime, using a .45/75 WCF tool to seat the primer. Bullets are seated with the fingers after sizing to .403, which is the groove diameter of my barrel, and they are not crimped in the case. This is a superbly accurate .40 caliber rifle, with this load as described. To date I have not worked up a smokeless powder load, but I intend to do so sometime in the future.

The .50/70 Gov't. cases can also be used to make brass for the .40/70 What Cheer chamber. And since they are available in solid-head type, they would no doubt be very suitable for a smokeless powder case. However, it might be necessary to have two dies in order to draw the .50/70 case to this bottleneck shape. The .43 Egyptian, being already slightly bottlenecked, is easily formed and it is also easy to cut off the slight bit necessary for accurate fitting and shooting.

There is another .40 caliber What Cheer cartridge, the .40/90 What Cheer Peabody-Martini, $2\frac{1}{16}$-inch case, but this is even more rare than the .40/70, and I have yet to see a rifle chambered for it. Specimens of this .40/90-$2\frac{1}{16}$" What Cheer cartridge are illustrated with the other Peabody-Martini sizes on page 257. All the boxes of .40/90 What Cheer I have or have seen, are marked "40 caliber, seventy grains, Special." These are the regular .40/90 What Cheer case, and they have a paper-patched bullet of about 490 grains. The ball is $1\frac{5}{8}$ inches long. Whether they were special heavy ball loads for long-range shooting, or whether all the so-called .40/90 What Cheer were really loaded with only 70 grains, is still unknown to me at this writing.

Also rare today are the .44/100 What Cheer Peabody-Martini cartridges. I have two specimens of this size that came with my rifle. I have always thought it darned inconsiderate of the first owner that he shot up all the rest of the cartridges for it, leaving me with but a measly two.

The .50/95 Sharps-2½" cases may be reformed to fit the .44/100 What Cheer chambers, though it is rather heavy work. With a few of these and .45 caliber 420- and 500-grain bullets, I have shot this rifle quite a lot. My barrel measures .456 in the grooves, which is like so many of the early .44s—really a .45 caliber. In fact, the only box of this size cartridge I have seen is the one which came with my rifle and it is marked .45/100, while the barrel is stamped .44/100! I have also used quite a lot of E. Remington and Sons' 550-grain

CARTRIDGES USED IN THE PEABODY AND PEABODY-MARTINI RIFLES

1   .50 caliber Peabody rim-fire
2   .40/70/380 Peabody-Martini What Cheer
3   .45/50/290 Peabody-Martini Sporting
4   .45/55/405 Peabody-Martini Carbine

paper-patched .44 caliber bullets in this barrel with accurate results. I have really used more of these than of any other bullet, as I had quite a lot of them on hand.

The .45/75 WCF cases can also be used in the .44/100 chambers, although they are shorter than the .44/100 cartridge and must be loaded Schuetzen style; that is, with the bullet seated ahead into the rifling. A bullet seater is easily made from a .45/75 case that has been expanded to fit the chamber, by firing with black powder and a wad in the mouth of the case, then fitted with a rod handle which

CARTRIDGES USED IN THE PEABODY AND PEABODY-MARTINI RIFLES

5 .40/90/500 Peabody-Martini What Cheer
6 .45/85/480 Peabody-Martini Turkish
7 .44/95/550 Peabody-Martini What Cheer

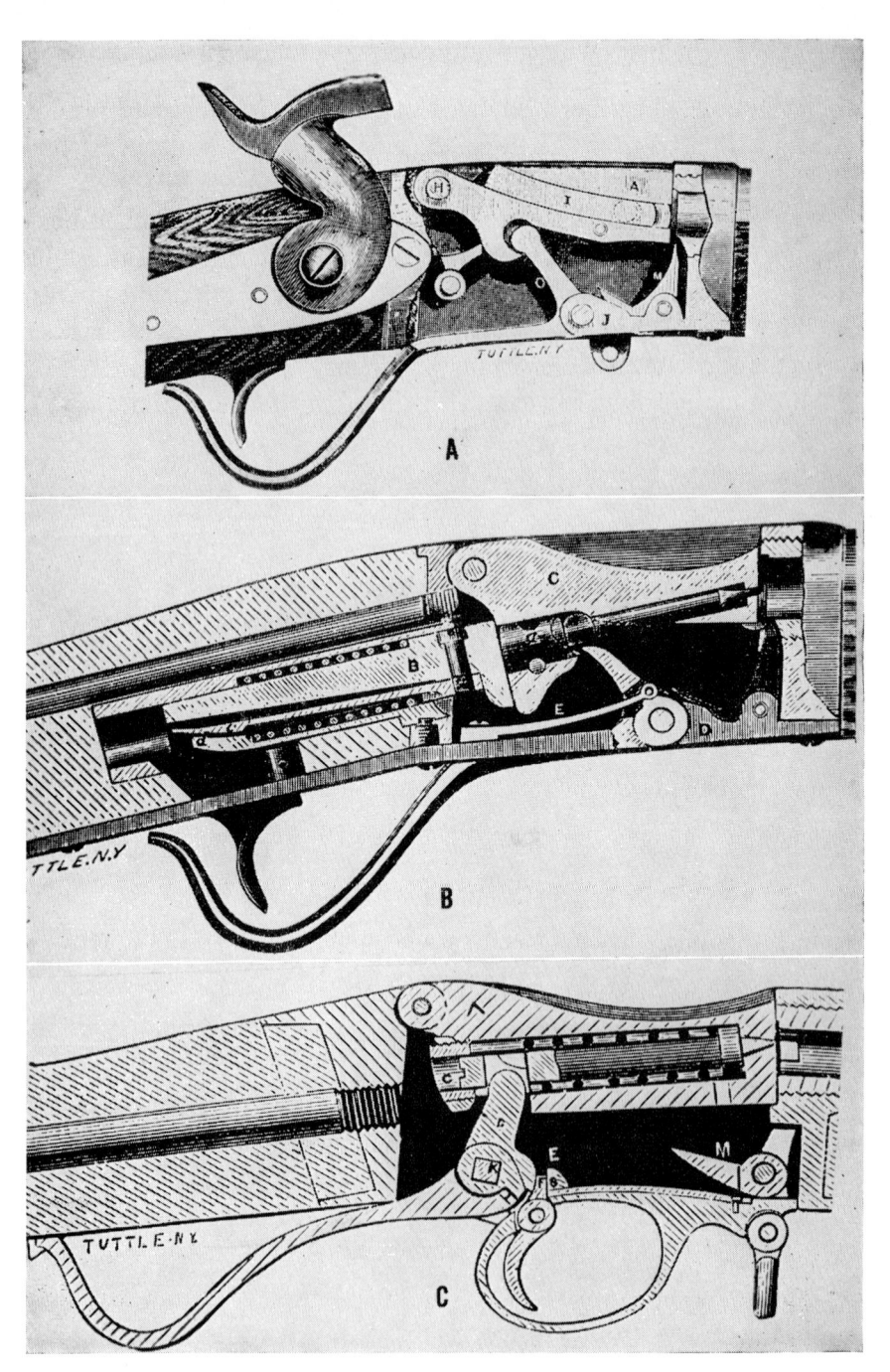

A. ORIGINAL OUTSIDE HAMMER PEABODY ACTION. B. ANOTHER ORIGINAL PEABODY AS OFFERED BY PROVIDENCE TOOL CO. UNDER PEABODY PATENTS. (Due to the fact that this was a Hammerless design, it was not well received by ordnance men who preferred the action shown under A.) C. MARTINI "IMPROVEMENT" OF THE PEABODY.

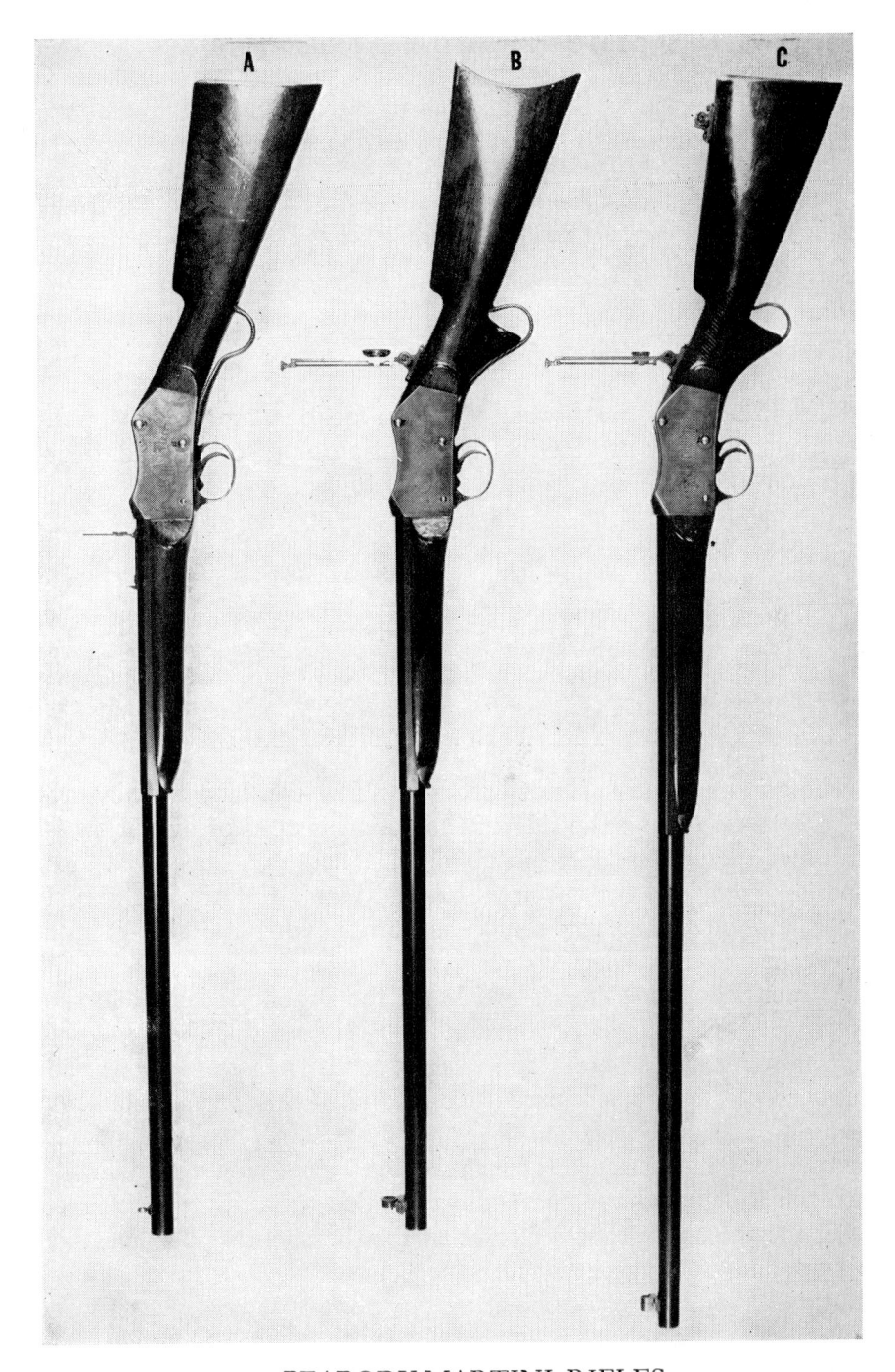

PEABODY-MARTINI RIFLES
A. Kill Deer Rifle .45-70 Government. B. Creedmoor Mid-range .40-70 What Cheer.
C. Creedmoor Long Range .44-95 What Cheer.

extends the necessary distance ahead of the .45/75 case, to seat the bullet into the rifling. There will be a certain amount of mortality among these cases, due to the degree to which the .45/75 WCF brass must expand in order to fit these larger and longer chambers; but not too many will be sacrificed. In fact, out of a batch of sixty old folded-head .45/75s I fired in this way only four were unusable. Of course, solid-head cases in .45/75 WCF size are easily obtained in large quantities if wanted, so there is no excuse for using the early ones at all.

The firing pins in Peabody-Martini actions are usually well-rounded, and they project just the right amount for these old cartridges and will fire any primer you care to use.

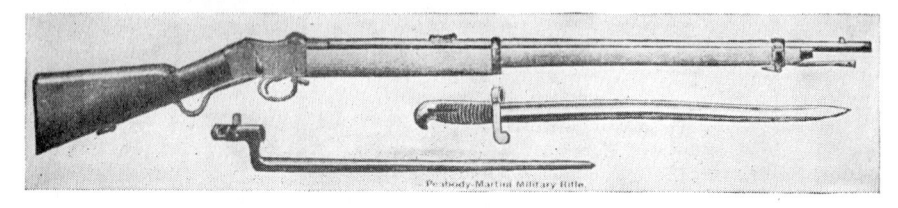

Peabody-Martini Military Rifle

PEABODY-MARTINI MILITARY RIFLE

The grip of this rifle is not exactly comfortable. However, by laying the thumb along the side of the action instead of over it, as is customary, a good squeeze is obtained. There is a checkered area especially provided for the right-handed man's thumb; but alas, I shoot left-handed, so my thumb must rest along the side or else dangle in mid-air.

As mentioned in Wagar's article on the Peabody-Martini in the *American Rifleman* for September, 1940, the grip of the Peabody-Martini can cause severe blood blisters on the fingers while seating stubborn cases. I have endured martyrdom in this way with all my Peabody-Martini rifles at one time or another. The pistol-grip models are the worst in this respect, of course, but I even pinched my finger with the Kill Deer lever once! However, this was unwarranted.

So, for the single-shot collector or for the shooter who likes his calibers odd and practically unknown, I recommend the Peabody-Martini as being a very fascinating type, one that will give you an endless amount of pleasure getting rigged up to shoot. You will find them to be well and beautifully made inside, and nicely finished throughout.

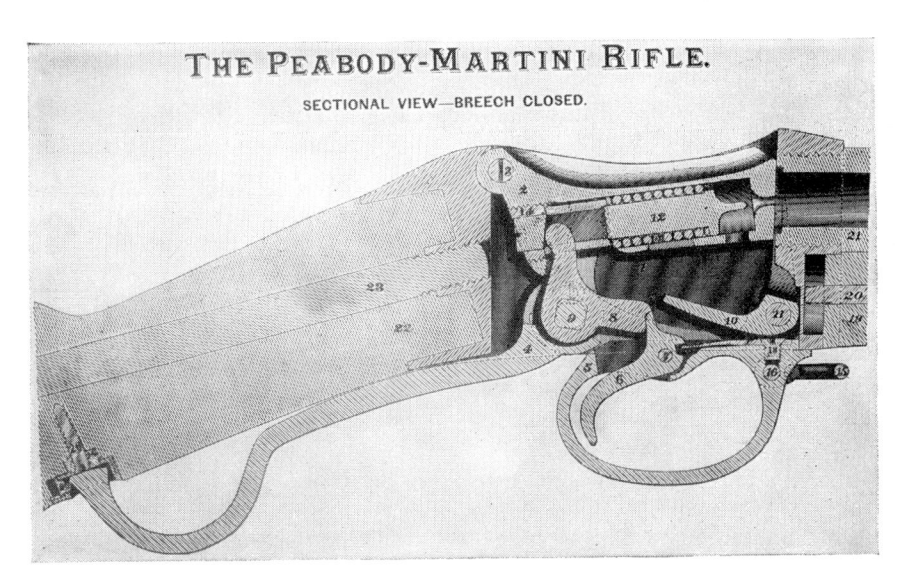

THE PEABODY-MARTINI RIFLE.
SECTIONAL VIEW—BREECH CLOSED.

PEABODY-MARTINI ACTION DESIGN

PEABODY-MARTINI MATCH RIFLE.
LONG RANGE "CREEDMOOR" PATTERN.

Half Octagon Steel Barrel, 32 inches long. Calibre, $\frac{44}{100}$.
Weight, just under 10 pounds. Pull of trigger, 3 pounds. Stock, hand made, from extra choice black walnut, with pistol grip, highly polished; grip and fore end checked; sides of breech frame handsomely engraved. Peep rear sight, with vernier scale, interchangeable from wrist to heel, giving elevation for 1500 yards on wrist, or 1100 yards on heel. Interchangeable globe and *open bead* front sight, with wind gauge and spirit level.

CARTRIDGE USED IN THE LONG RANGE "CREEDMOOR" RIFLE.

.44 CALIBRE, LONG RANGE.
Shell, 2⅛ inches long, holding 100 to 115 grains powder. Bullet, long, smooth, patched. Weight, 550 grains.

PAGE FROM PEABODY-MARTINI 1881 CATALOG

The Peabody-Martini was altered by Francotte to the quick demountable or take-down type and used by the Birmingham Small Arms Company in their Martini Match Rifle of .22 caliber. The really fine Martini as made in England was the little Rook rifle as made by Greener.[2] It reached its highest development in England in this model. This was a strictly fine sporting arm, and not to be confused with the Birmingham Small Arms target models, which are very clumsy by comparison.

The Martini action reached the very highest development of all in the fine German Schuetzen rifle which will be discussed in another chapter.

The following paragraphs are quoted from the 1881 Providence Tool Co. catalog.

THE PEABODY-MARTINI RIFLE

This rifle is a combination of the Peabody and Martini patent systems, the former covering the mechanism for closing the breech and extracting the cartridge shell, after the rifle has been fired, and the latter covering the device for igniting the cartridge. It is the adopted arm of the English and Turkish Governments after long and exhaustive trials in competition with all the prominent breech-loading rifles of the world. It has endured the test of actual experience in war during the contest between Russia and Turkey, and has obtained the highest reputation for solidity, accuracy, long range and other desirable qualities of a military weapon. The official reports from the armies in the field and the letters of army correspondence, write in praise of the efficiency of the Turkish rifles, manufactured by the Providence Tool Co.

The parts composing the breech mechanism combine the greatest possible strength with simplicity of construction and the system in its present perfection, is the result of long and careful study to produce a rifle meeting all the requirements of military service.

Its form is compact and graceful, and the symmetry of its lines is nowhere infringed upon by unseemly projections which besides being offensive to the eye are often prejudicial to the comfort of the soldier on the march or in the performance of its necessary manipulations. No movement of the barrel, or of any other parts except those immediately connected with the block, is required in the performance of any of its operation. These are performed in the simplest possible manner, and

---

[2] See Greener's *The Gun and Its Development*, edition of 1907.

without in the least infringing upon the strength and durability of the rifle, which is equal in these respects to the best muzzle-loader.

In the operation of loading, the whole movement of the block is made within the breech frame or receiver, the end of the block lever falling but a short distance from the stock. The block itself is a strong, substantial piece, and when in position for firing, is so firmly secured as to ensure its perfect safety, as has been repeatedly shown in the severe tests to which it has been subjected.

The position of the block when it is drawn down for loading is such as to form an inclined plane sloping toward the breech of the barrel, and the groove in its upper surface, corresponding with the bore of the barrel, facilitates the entrance of the cartridge so that it slides easily into the chamber without the necessity even of looking to see that it is properly inserted.

The adoption of the coil mainspring in place of the common gun lock mainspring is considered a great improvement, and this opinion is confirmed by the experience of the English and Turkish troops who have been supplied with the Peabody Martini Rifles. It has been found that in several instances where the coil mainsprings were broken, the defects were not noticed and the springs compressed in the blocks worked as usual. Had such mishaps occurred to the old gun lock mainsprings, the arm would have been rendered useless.

The accuracy and range of this rifle are very remarkable. The system of rifling used is that known in England as the Henry. There are seven grooves of peculiar shape, with a sharp twist (one turn in twenty inches). After a long series of experiments with different kinds of rifling, the English Arms Commission finally decided upon this system as giving the most satisfactory results both with regard to accuracy and range.

The manipulations for loading and firing are of the simplest kind. The movements are these:

First—throw down the block lever with considerable force, pressing with the thumb of the right hand.

Second—insert the cartridge.

Third—return the lever to place, which raises the block to its proper position, when the rifle is ready for firing. After firing, throw down the block lever with considerable force, and the empty cartridge shell is thrown out clear from the rifle, leaving the chamber ready for the insertion of another cartridge. This extraction of the cartridge shell is affected by the action of an elbow lever which throws it out with unerring certainty, the instant the block lever is lowered. This elbow lever derives its power simply from the action of the block itself, and cannot become deranged, as its action is not dependent upon any spring and is of such strength as to prevent the possibility of breakage or derangement by any service to which it can be subjected. If it is desired to preserve the cartridge shell for reloading, throw down the block lever with a gentle movement, and it is drawn out into the groove of the block from whence it can readily be taken by the person firing.

For rapidity of firing, the Peabody Martini Rifle is believed to be equal if not superior to any other single loader, and in continuous firing to any repeater. It cannot be fired until the block is in its proper position, so that it is impossible for accidents from premature explosion to occur. The objection to the excessive recoil of this rifle, which has been raised in some quarters, has been obviated in the arms manufactured by the Providence Tool Company by the adoption of a different form of ammunition.

After the decision of the English Arms Commission in favor of the Peabody Martini Rifle, and its subsequent adoption as the standard national arm, the Imperial Ottoman Government contracted with the Providence Tool Company to manufacture 600,000. The productive capacity of this company's factories is 1000 rifles per day.

In conclusion it may be said that wherever the Peabody Martini Rifle has been introduced, its superior qualities of safety, strength, simplicity, easy manipulation accuracy and long range, have been fully conceded.

PLATE NO. 4 SHOWS

Peabody Martini Military Rifle, with quadrangular and saber bayonets.

3,300,000 shots fired from 550,000 of these rifles by United States Government Inspectors at the Providence Tool Company's Works without accident. 200,000 service charges have been fired from a regular military rifle, Turkish model, without injury to the breech mechanism and without impairing the efficiency or accuracy of the rifle. The service charge of powder is 85 grains.

Length 49″. Length of barrel, 32½″. Wt. without bayonet, 8½ lbs. Length of quad bayonet, 23¼″. Length of saber bayonet, 28 7/16″. Wt. of saber bayonet, 2 lbs.

Caliber, .45/100 inch [.45/85?].

PLATE NO. 5 SHOWS

Peabody Martini Carbine.

Entire length, 38½ inches. Lt. of bbl., 22″. Wt., 6¾ lbs. Caliber, .45/100 inch.

Cartridges used in the P.M. Rifles and Carbines Musket ctge. Turkish model, cal. .45, powder 85 grs. bullet smooth patched, wt. 480 grs. lub. discs in shell musket ctge. English model, cal. .45, powder 85 grs., bullet

Re-Loading Tools.

DIRECTIONS FOR RE-LOADING CENTRAL FIRE CARTRIDGE SHELLS, ANY CALIBRE, SPORTING AND MILITARY.

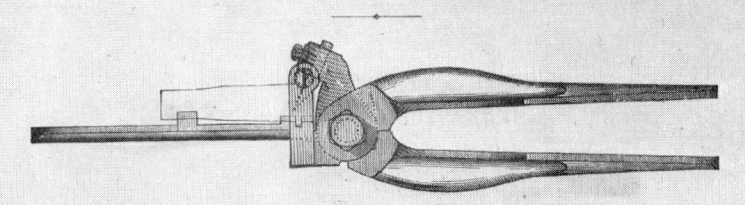

PRIMER EXTRACTOR.

After inserting the shell, close the handles just enough to cause the chisel to penetrate the primer;—then elevate the tongue sufficiently to throw it out.

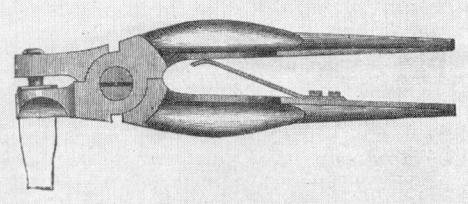

RE-PRIMER.

After putting the primer into the shell, put the shell into the receiver and close the handles with some force.

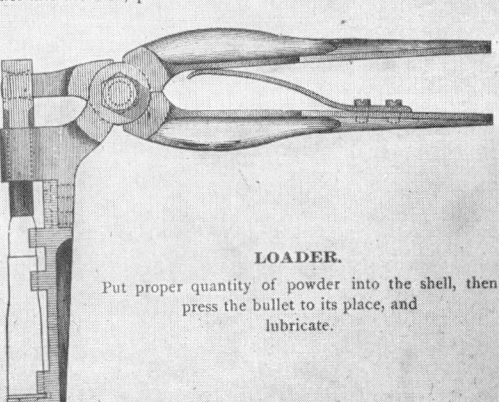

LOADER.

Put proper quantity of powder into the shell, then press the bullet to its place, and lubricate.

PAGE FROM PEABODY-MARTINI 1881 CATALOG

smooth patched, wt. 480 grs., lub. disk in shell. (English ctge. Martini Henry is a slightly shorter and fatter ctge. than Turkish model.)

Musket ctge., United States Government model, cal. .45, Powder 70 grs., bullet 3 cannelures, wt. 405 grs., also used with 55 grs. powder in .45 cal. carbine.

Carbine ctge., Providence Tool Co. Model, cal. .45, powder 60 grains, bullet smooth patched, wt. 400 grs., lub. disk in shell.

Lengths as measured on full scale illustrations in catalogue:

.45/85	2 5/16″	Turkish Model
.45/85	2 1/4″	English Model
.45/70	2.1	English Model
.45/60	carbine 1 9/16	

PLATE NO. 6 SHOWS

Peabody Martini—Match Rifle.
Long Range "Creedmoor" pattern.

Half oct. steel barrel, 32″ long caliber .44/100 (44/100 What Cheer) Wt. just under 10 lbs. Pull of trigger 3 lbs., stock handmade from extra choice black walnut with pistol grip, highly polished, grip and fore end checkered, sides of breech frame handsomely engraved. Peep rear sight, with vernier scale, interchangeable from wrist to heel, giving elevation for 1500 yards on wrist or 1100 yds. on heel. Interchangeable glove and open bead front sight, with windgauge and spirit level.

Cartridge used in the long range Creedmoor Rifle, .44 caliber, long range shell 2 5/16″ long, holding 100 to 115 grains powder, bullet, long

PLATE NO. 7 SHOWS

Peabody Martini Hunting and Sporting Rifle—"Kill Deer Pattern."

Designed for use on the Plains, for hunting large game or for offhand practice at 100 to 600 yds.

Half octagon steel barrel, 28 inches long. Caliber .45/100, Wt. of rifle 8 to 9 lbs. Pull of trigger, 3 pounds. Stock, handmade, from first-class black walnut. Broad, flat butt plate. Interchangeable globe and peep and open sights.

Sights can be changed while the game is in view.
(Caliber .45/70 Gov't.)
Directions for dismounting and assembling breech action.
Numbers refer to Plate No. 1 on Page 6.

TO DISMOUNT BODY NO. 1

1. Push out Block Axis-pin No. 3.

2. Open the Breech, and with the thumb press with force on front end of Block, No. 2, and at the same time raise Lever No. 4.
3. Turn Keeper-screw so as to allow Indicator No. 9 to be pushed out.
4. Take out Extractor Axis-screw No. 11. The parts now are all disengaged.

TO ASSEMBLE BODY NO. 1

1. Put Lever No. 4 back to its place in assembled Guard No. 5, and insert both in Body No. 1; Drop in Extractor No. 10, and turn in Extractor Axis Screw No. 11.
2. Put Tumbler No. 8 in place, and put in Indicator No. 9, point upright, and secure Keeper-screw.
3. With the right hand raise the Lever No. 4 so as to touch the Lever Catch No. 24, then with the first finger pull the Trigger No. 6 back, and with the thumb push the Indicator No. 9 forward, and drop in the assembled Block No. 2, the front end entering first; Apply a little force to back end of Block with the left hand, moving the Lever a little at the same time with the right hand, and the Block will drop into place.
4. Insert Block Axis-pin No. 3.

TO DISMOUNT GUARD NO. 5

1. Take out Trigger Spring Screw No. 18, relieving Trigger Spring No. 17.
2. Take out Trigger Axis-screw No. 7, relieving Trigger No. 6.

TO ASSEMBLE GUARD NO. 5

1. Hold Trigger No. 6 in place, and turn in Trigger Axis-screw No. 7.
2. Restore Trigger Spring No. 17, and turn in Trigger Spring Screw No. 18. (The parts are now ready to be attached to the Body No. 1.)

TO DISMOUNT BLOCK NO. 2

Turn Keeper-screw on end of Block No. 2, and take out Stop-nut No. 14. The striker No. 12 and Coil Spring No. 13, will then drop out.

TO ASSEMBLE BLOCK NO. 2

Restore Striker No. 12 and Coil Spring No. 13 to place, turn in Stop-nut No. 14 and turn Keeper-screw to secure it.

Note.—The Striker No. 12 has a rectangular slot near one end. This slot is longer on one side than on the other. The long side should be so placed as to admit end of Tumbler No. 8 freely.

After a little practice the Breech-Action can be assembled in detail in three minutes.

IX

Whitney Rolling-block and Phoenix Rifles

WHITNEY ROLLING-BLOCK RIFLES

THE Whitney rolling-block action was patented March 21, 1871, by Eli Whitney under the number 112997, and it was manufactured by Whitney at New Haven, Connecticut.

Claude E. Fuller in *The Breech Loader in the Service* states that this action—or one similar to it—was first patented in 1866. The patent number 54743 was issued May 15, 1866, to Laidley and Emery. The Laidley of this partnership was Col. T. S. S. Laidley of the United States Ordnance Bureau. It is possible that this was the original action, and that it was later adopted and manufactured by Whitney.

The action is practically identical with the Remington rolling-block action. A comparison of the component parts of the two mechanisms is shown on page 272.

Of my two specimens of this breech action, one is the lighter frame sporting rifle, caliber .32 rim-fire, with octagonal barrel, as illustrated and described on the reproduced 1886 Whitney circular shown on pages 270 and 271. This is a plain rifle, but it has a fancy grade of walnut in the stock, and the fore end is tipped with hard rubber. This .32 rim-fire specimen is stamped on the top tang with the patent date only and no name.

The second specimen is a heavier frame, round-barreled model, with 30-inch barrel and plain walnut stock. The caliber is Sharps .45-2 $4/10''$ case. This rifle has no name or patent number stamped upon it at any point.

To the average eye this rifle looks the same as the plain Remington grades made up on the rolling-block action; however, the Whitney action corners are rounded off more on all points than the Remingtons, and the actions appear somewhat neater and smaller, as a result.

The 1886 Whitney circular as reproduced show the details of the rifles as offered at that time. The following models and calibers are listed in L. D. Satterlee's *A Catalogue of Firearms for the Collector*.

WHITNEY SPORTING AND TARGET RIFLE. Caliber .38 Long centerfire. This model was also offered in the following calibers: .38/40 WCF, .44/60 and .44/77 Sharps bottleneck, .40/50 and .40/70 Sharps Straight, .40/90 Sharps Straight, .44/40 WCF, .45/70 Gov't., .50/70 Gov't., .32 rim-fire, .32/20 WCF, .38 Long rim-fire, .44 Long rim-fire.

WHITNEY GALLERY RIFLE. Caliber .22 Long or Short rim-fire.

WHITNEY LONG RANGE CREEDMOOR No. 1 RIFLE. Caliber .44/90 to 105 necked.

WHITNEY MID RANGE CREEDMOOR No. 2 RIFLE. Caliber .40.

WHITNEY MILITARY RIFLE. Calibers .45/70 Gov't. and .50/70 Gov't.

WHITNEY MILITARY CARBINE. Calibers .45/70 Gov't. and .50/70 Gov't.

The .50/70 caliber had a rim- or center-fire breechblock, so either style of cartridge could be used.

WHITNEY LIGHT CARBINE. Caliber .46 Long rim-fire, .44 Henry rim-fire, .44/40 WCF, .44 S & W American, .44 Short rim-fire.

PHOENIX RIFLES

VERY few modern riflemen have ever heard of the Phoenix rifle. It was most popular in the decade of 1874 to 1884, but sometimes I am led to wonder if it was quite as popular as some writers would have us believe. I base this upon the fact that it is extremely hard—in fact, it is almost impossible—to find a good clean specimen of this type.

I hunted and advertised for years to get good specimens of the Phoenix and returned some of the most woebegone collections of scrap iron and wood that I ever paid express charges on. If this system had been as popular as some claim it to have been, without a doubt there would be many more specimens available now.

The Whitney Improved Breech-Loading Rifle.

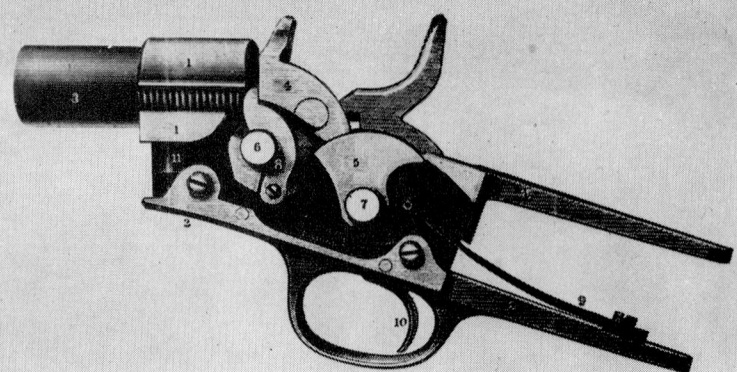

1. Receiver. 2. Guard. 3. Barrel. 4. Breech Block. 5. Hammer. 6. Breech Block Pin. 7. Hammer Pin. 8. Extractor. 9. Main Sp[ring]. 10. Trigger. 11. Ram-Rod Stud.

DIRECTIONS FOR TAKING APART AND ASSEMBLING.

TO TAKE APART.

1st. Turn the screw in the side of the receiver that holds in place the two large pins (hammer and breech-block pins) [suffi]ciently to release the heads or flanges, then turn them away from the screw.

2d. Bring the hammer to full cock, take out the extractor screw (found on the side of the receiver below the breech-b[lock pin), take out the breech-block pin and remove the breech-block and extractor together.

3d. Let the hammer down so as to relieve it from the pressure of the main-spring, take out the hammer-pin and the hamm[er].

TO ASSEMBLE.

1st. Put the hammer in position in the receiver, pressing it forward so as to avoid the pressure of the main-spring, pu[t in] the hammer-pin and cock the hammer.

2d. Put the breech-block and extractor into the receiver together, as when taken out, and after replacing the breech-block and extractor screw, bring the flanges of the two side pins together and tighten the screw that holds them.

SPECIAL ORDERS.

As any departure from our regular list involves a large outlay for hand labor, all orders which require deviations from [re]gular calibres, lengths, weights and finish, will be subject to extra charges proportioned to the amount of labor required, [ad]ditional time will be required to fill them.

The above applies to all our arms.

For Price List of Military Arms, apply to

WHITNEY ARMS CO.,
NEW HAVEN, CON[N.]

October 1886

WHITNEY RIFLE CIRCULAR 1886

The Whitney Improved Breech-Loading Rifle.

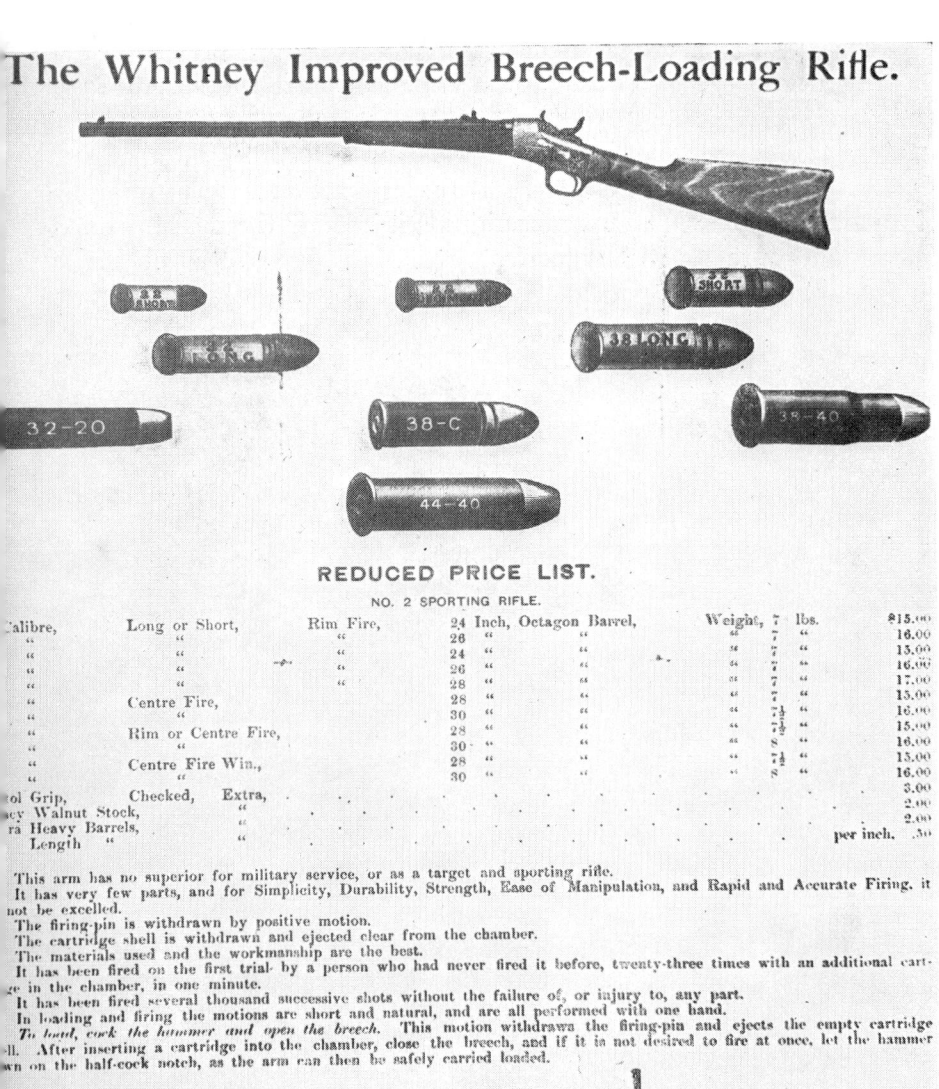

REDUCED PRICE LIST.
NO. 2 SPORTING RIFLE.

Calibre,	Long or Short,	Rim Fire,	24 Inch, Octagon Barrel,	Weight, 7 lbs.	$15.00
"	"	"	26 " "	" 7 "	16.00
"	"	"	24 " "	" 7 "	15.00
"	"	"	26 " "	" 7 "	16.00
"	"	"	28 " "	" 7 "	17.00
"	Centre Fire,	"	28 " "	" 7 "	15.00
"	"	"	30 " "	" 7½ "	16.00
"	Rim or Centre Fire,	"	28 " "	" 7½ "	15.00
"	"	"	30 " "	" 8 "	16.00
"	Centre Fire Win.,	"	28 " "	" 7½ "	15.00
"	"	"	30 " "	" 8 "	16.00
ol Grip,	Checked,	Extra,			3.00
cy Walnut Stock,	"				2.00
ra Heavy Barrels,	"				2.00
Length "	"			per inch,	.50

This arm has no superior for military service, or as a target and sporting rifle.
It has very few parts, and for Simplicity, Durability, Strength, Ease of Manipulation, and Rapid and Accurate Firing, it not be excelled.
The firing-pin is withdrawn by positive motion.
The cartridge shell is withdrawn and ejected clear from the chamber.
The materials used and the workmanship are the best.
It has been fired on the first trial by a person who had never fired it before, twenty-three times with an additional cart- e in the chamber, in one minute.
It has been fired several thousand successive shots without the failure of, or injury to, any part.
In loading and firing the motions are short and natural, and are all performed with one hand.
To load, cock the hammer and open the breech. This motion withdraws the firing-pin and ejects the empty cartridge ll. After inserting a cartridge into the chamber, close the breech, and if it is not desired to fire at once, let the hammer wn on the half-cock notch, as the arm can then be safely carried loaded.

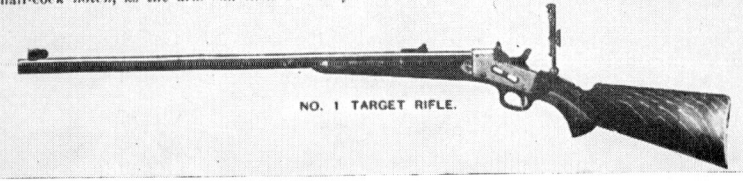

NO. 1 TARGET RIFLE.

WHITNEY RIFLE CIRCULAR 1886

Eventually, after I had given up hope of finding a Phoenix in fine shooting condition, a list came to me which included one in .40/50 bottlenecked caliber and one in 14-gauge shot-shell caliber. The shotgun caliber, it transpired, had been sold before my order was received, but in a few days the .40/50 rifle, together with a supply of cartridges, arrived, and upon examining it I found the metal parts throughout were practically perfect, retaining about 99% of the blue; and the bore was spotless. The wood had been heavily varnished at the factory, but the varnish was greatly discolored, almost black, and badly checked.

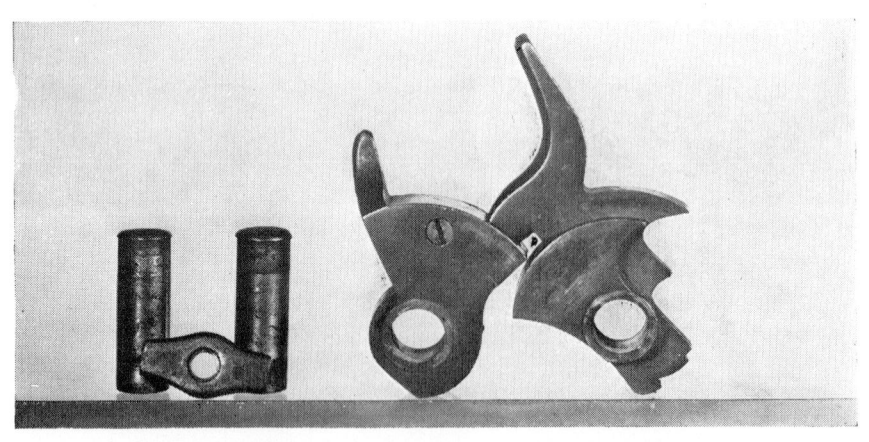

A COMPARISON BETWEEN THE BLOCK AND HAMMER OF THE WHITNEY ROLLING BLOCK (UPPER) AND REMINGTON ROLLING BLOCK (LOWER) RIFLES
In these specimens parts are almost identical.

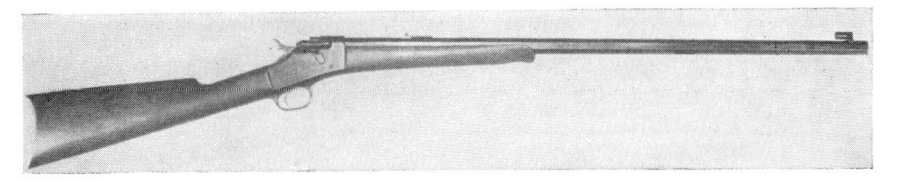

PHOENIX SPORTING RIFLE

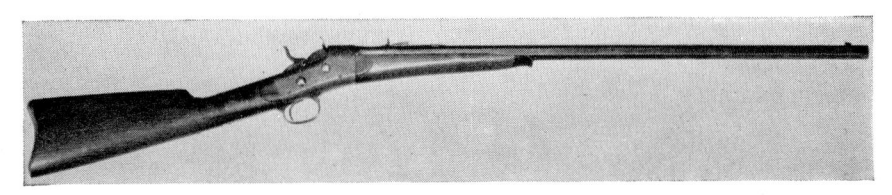

WHITNEY ROLLING-BLOCK SPORTING RIFLE

The old varnish finish was removed with paint and varnish remover, and the wood beneath it was found to be of a nice color and well filled; so with the addition of a little boiled linseed oil, the rifle was ready for action. This is the plain, straight-grip stock type of sporting rifle with 30-inch full-octagonal barrel of about #3 weight. A perfectly plain model, but of clean, symmetrical lines.

The rifle proved to be adequately accurate after the old cartridges were unloaded and fresh primers, powder, and lead were installed. I happened to have a Winchester mold for the .40 caliber, 285-grain patched ball, and found it to be just the right bullet for this case. By cleaning between shots to get around the caking of the black powder fouling, I was able, with the open sights as illustrated, to obtain a group of about 2½ inches at 100 yards, muzzle and elbow rest. I feel sure that with a proper smokeless load, grooved bullets, and possibly a scope sight, it would do even better.

A short time later another Phoenix in the same grade, and in .45/70 Gov't. caliber, appeared from out a clear sky, and later still another one. This last specimen was fine outside, but the .38 rim-fire barrel was ruined, as most barrels of this caliber seem to be.

The Phoenix rifle system has the fewest parts and the simplest mechanism of any breechloader to my knowledge. The moving parts consist of a breechblock, firing pin, extractor, hammer and trigger, and that is all; there are no more.

Two of the four different types of extractors used are shown here in the illustrations representing the three specimens in my collection.

None of the three Phoenix rifles that I own—nor any of the others I have seen, mostly in parts—show the manufacturer's name at any place. Two of my three have the patent date stamped on the upper tangs; the third is absolutely blank.

These rifles were, of course, made at the New Haven, Conn., plant of the Whitney Arms Co., and they were invented by Eli Whitney III in 1871. Successive patents on improvements—no doubt extractors—were received up to 1874.

The Phoenix system was never adopted by the Government as a military arm, though it was offered to several War Department arms boards at various times. However, this is to the rifle's credit, and testifies to the excellence and simplicity of the mechanism. It was just too simple and practical for the military mind to fathom.

It is not only hard to find Phoenix rifles in good condition, it is impossible to find any literature of the Whitney Arms Co. describing this system. I have a circular of Whitney's showing the Whitney rolling-block and Kennedy repeating rifles dated 1886, but no mention whatsoever is made of the Whitney Phoenix rifle.

Due to the lack of data available on this old rifle, several authors have made errors in discussing it. For instance, in Mr. C. W. Sawyer's *Our Rifles* (page 240), in discussing the 1872-1874 Phoenix .44 caliber rim-fire carbine, the author states that the hinged breechblock, after opening, was "then drawn rearward to extract." Evidently Mr. Sawyer was confusing the American-English Snider and the Tabatière, the French imitation of it, made in 1869-1870. The carbine illustrated by Mr. Sawyer with the above description does not in any way appear to differ from Phoenix rifles I have examined.

To Dr. Paul Jenkins, in his article, "The Remarkable Old Phoenix Rifles" in the *American Rifleman* for July, 1934, we are indebted for a list of Phoenix calibers available at one time or another. According to Dr. Jenkins the rifles were made in the following:

.22 Short and Long rim-fire	.44/90 center-fire
.32 Long rim-fire	.44/100 center-fire
.32 Extra Long rim-fire	.44/105/520 Sharps necked
.38 Long rim-fire	.45/70 Gov't.
.38 Extra Long rim-fire	.50/70 Gov't.
.44 rim-fire	.38 Schuetzen
.44 Long rim-fire	.40 Schuetzen

.44 Extra Long rim-fire
.40/50 and .40/70 Sharps
.44/40 center-fire
.44/60/300 center-fire
.44/77 center-fire
.40/70 Sharps necked

.58 Gov't. carbine
.22 caliber smooth bore
16-gauge shotgun
14-gauge shotgun
12-gauge shotgun
10-gauge shotgun

What cartridges the .38 Schuetzen and the .40 Schuetzen in Dr. Jenkins' list might be, I have no way of knowing; there is no mention of these cartridges in any other literature I have seen.

Dr. Jenkins states:

The third feature mentioned is, of course, the unique one indicated above, not found in the Sharps or Winchester single-shot records of the shotguns factory made on the system. It is true, as perhaps everyone knows, that a good many old Sharps were eventually rebored smooth, both the percussion and later cartridge models, for use as shotguns, but none were originally so produced at the factory.

This is an error, of course, as the Sharps catalogs as reproduced in L. D. Satterlee's *Fourteen Old Gun Catalogues* settle the Sharps factory-made shotgun question, as not only did they make shotguns, they also made double-barrel shotguns. (See page 10 of the 1878 catalog of Sharps Rifle Co.)

The Winchester single-shot shotgun made on the same action as the rifle *at the factory* is described in the Winchester chapter in this volume. According to Dr. Jenkins' article, the Phoenix rifle was available in sporting, target, Schuetzen, military musket, or carbine models, or as a shotgun; but I have never seen any literature describing these particular models.

L. D. Satterlee lists the following Phoenix models as being available.

PHOENIX SPORTING AND TARGET RIFLE. This had either a round or an octagonal barrel, in 26- and 30-inch lengths. Weight was from 7 to 10 pounds. Calibers were: .38 Long or Extra Long rim-fire; .44 Long or Extra Long rim-fire; .40/50, .40/70, .44/60, .44/77, .44/90, .44/100 and .44/105 Sharps necked; .45/70 and .50/70 Gov't.

PHOENIX GALLERY RIFLE. Made with 24-inch barrel and in .22 rim-fire only. Barrel was full- or part-octagonal, and rifle weighed from 7 to 8½ pounds. This gallery model was made in several grades, from the plain standard model to fancy target grades.

PHOENIX SCHUETZEN TARGET RIFLE. This was the fancy Schuetzen model with selected polished stock, checkered grip and forearm, and nickel-plated Schuetzen butt plate. Barrels were supplied in lengths of 30 or 32 inches, and were full- or half-octagonal. Calibers were .38 Extra Long center-fire and .40/50 Sharps Straight, 1⅞-inch case. The sights were similar to those in use at the time—vernier tang rear and wind-gauge front with a spirit level. Weight of the rifle was from 10 to 12 pounds.

PHOENIX MILITARY RIFLE. There was a Phoenix military model made in .43 Spanish, .45/70 Gov't., and .50/70 Gov't. calibers. This had a 35-inch barrel and full musket type forearm. Weight was about 9 pounds.

PHOENIX MILITARY CARBINE. This was the carbine version of the military rifle. It had a 20½-inch barrel, and was made in the same calibers. The fore end was about half the barrel length, and this model had the customary carbine butt plate and ring on the side of the receiver. Weight was about 7 pounds.

X

The Maynard Rifle

THE Maynard embodies the tip-up barrel type of action in a manner somewhat similar to the Stevens and Frank Wesson tip-up models, with the important difference of having an under lever and link arrangement.

This action was patented May 27, 1851, under the number 8126. A second patent, #26364, was taken out December 6, 1859, and the first rifles made under this new patent utilized the famous Maynard tape primer as used extensively on other rifles such as Harpers Ferry muskets, Sharps carbines, and other models of the day.

The 1865 Maynard used a percussion nipple and a brass case in .35, .40, or .50 caliber, with a wide, flat base riveted or soldered to the case, to facilitate extracting the case. Like the Burnside cartridge and certain others of that period, the flash from the percussion cap entered a small central flash hole in the Maynard case.

The .50 caliber carbine is the most numerous in this 1865 type, many specimens of this caliber being found in quite good condition; and there are still plenty of cases available. The .35 and .40 caliber 1865 Maynards are a different story, and the cartridge cases, especially the .35 caliber, are becoming increasingly rare. There was also a .55 and a .64 caliber shot cartridge available.

On February 18, 1873, Maynard was granted patent #135928, covering the altering of this 1865 percussion model to a center-fire primed cartridge. The patent also covered a tumbler connection between the lever and hammer.

The 1873 Maynard rifles were a simple conversion from the percussion models, having a central-fire firing pin instead of the percussion tube, or nipple, of the 1865 model. These '73 rifles used a wide-rimmed case with Berdan primer and a central flash hole instead of the common Berdan type of two or three small flash holes. These cases were of a sufficient diameter to be grasped and removed after the small and sometimes ineffectual extractor started them from the chamber.

The 1873 rifle was made in the following calibers: .35/30, .40/40, .40/60 and .44, with 70 to 100 grains of powder; also .50 caliber in two lengths of case, .55 caliber shot, and .64 caliber shot.

In 1882 the Maynard cartridge was improved to the point where it was comparable to contemporary ammunition used in Sharps, Remington, and other rifles. It was a regular type, narrow-rim case, using Berdan primers, at first; later becoming available with Winchester type primers, using the self-contained anvil. These 1882 cartridges were available in some of the old '73 sizes and some new ones. The list in '82 type is as follows:

.22 Extra Long center-	.40/40	.50/50
fire	.40/60	.50/70
.32/35	.40/70	.50/100
.35/30	.44/60	.55/100
.35/40	.44/70	.55 shot
.38/50	.44/100	.64 shot

These were furnished for either the #1 Berdan or #2 Winchester primers. The .22 Extra Long center-fire cases were first primed with the tiny #0 primer. For details on the origin of this cartridge, see *The American Rifleman* for February, 1936. This .22 center-fire cartridge was available with either a grooved or a paper-patched bullet of 45 grains weight.

In addition to the calibers just given, barrels for fixed ammunition in .40/70 caliber and .45/70 Gov't. were available.

The 1882 model Maynard was, like the 1873 model, not breeched up tight; that is, there was considerable space between the breech end of the barrel and the face of the standing breech, which was filled only when the cartridge case was inserted. All calibers in '73 and '82 models were made this way except the .22 rim-fire, and in this case the barrel was counterbored at the breech, with a wide counterbore in the '82 rifle. Hadley's patent device for using rim-fire cartridges in the Maynard 1873 rifle, is illustrated on page 291.

Sectional View of the MAYNARD RIFLE.

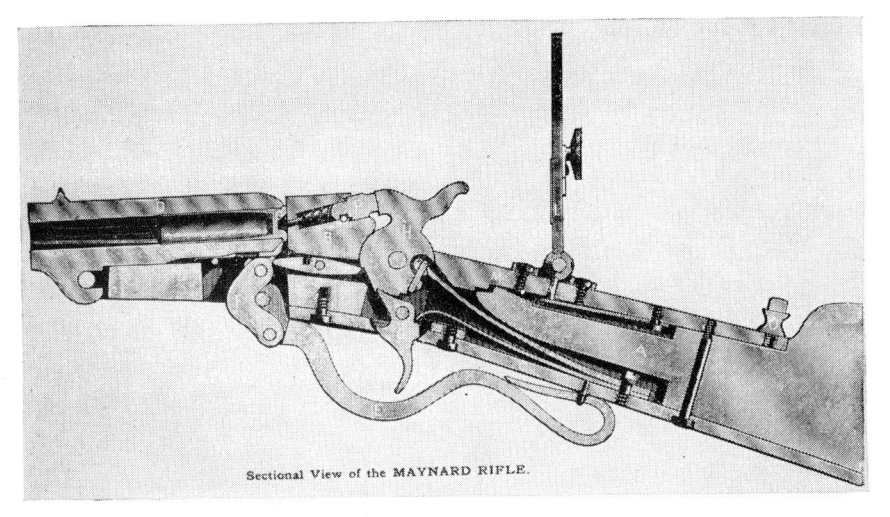

MAYNARD RIFLE DESIGN

The .32/35 cartridges as used in the 1882 model are the .32/35 Stevens taper cartridges as introduced and used in the Stevens tip-up rifle.

The Maynard Special cartridges I have been able to find are shown on pages 280 to 283. The 1885 Maynard catalog lists a .55/100 ball cartridge, but I have never seen a specimen of this one. Usually, the .55 caliber was a shot cartridge, as was the .64 caliber.

Maynard rifles were extremely well made, embodying a lot of handwork in their manufacture, which accounts for their being priced higher than other contemporary types. All I have examined in the higher grades have a beautifully smooth hammer and trigger action, smoother by far than any other type made at that time, unless it would be the Ballard. The hammer fall is light and short.

Maynards were unique in many respects, and among the more exceptional features were the odd rack-and-pinion tang rear sights. One of my No. 16 Maynards lacked this sight and had instead a Ballard midrange vernier rear mounted on it. I remember looking for a considerable length of time before locating one of these original Maynard rack-and-pinion sights to install on the rifle.

Hadley's device for recapping and decapping Maynard cartridge cases, and the Maynard one-piece bullet seater are certainly unique, and are shown in pages 284 and 285.

Multibarrel Maynard outfits are often seen, as a barrel was easily and quickly changed for one of another caliber, or for a shot barrel. Sometimes these Maynard outfits are found cased in leather or fine wood, and are quite complete. But the old Maynard cartridge cases in all calibers are very hard to find, especially the model '73, and so these outfits, unless they include a .22 rim-fire or shot barrel in 20-gauge, are hardly worth an investment. The only outfit of this type that I have retained is one in .22 rim-fire, .35/30, .40/60, and 20-gauge shot barrel. The .22 happened to be in fine condition, as were

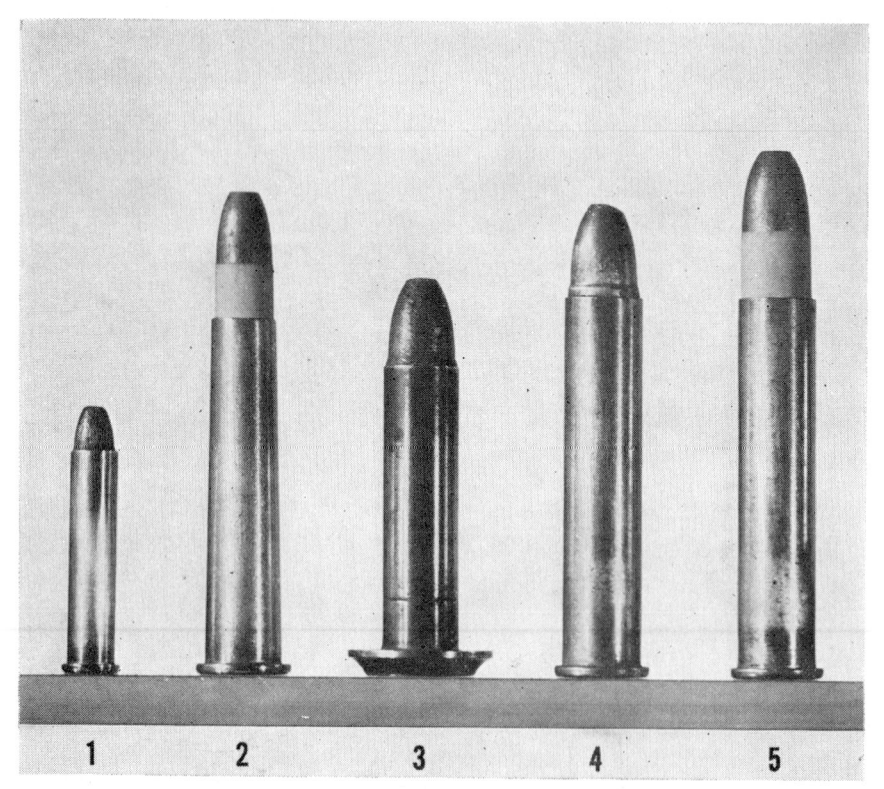

CARTRIDGES USED IN MAYNARD RIFLES AND SHOT GUNS
1 .22 Extra Long center-fire
2 .32/35 Maynard Everlasting, 1882 case
3 .35/30 Maynard, 1873 case
4 .38/50 Maynard Everlasting, grooved bullet, 1882 case
5 .38/50 Maynard Everlasting, paper patch bullet, 1882 case

THE MAYNARD RIFLE

all the other barrels. For the .35/30 and the .40/60, I had a machinist friend make for me cases to fit, of solid brass stock in the '73 pattern and pocketed for modern #8½ primers. So without much trouble I am able to shoot these two rifle barrels to my heart's content. The 20-gauge shot barrel will accept regular modern paper 20-gauge cartridges, so that takes care of that. I located for this shot barrel 20-gauge shells loaded with black powder, and for the small amount of hunting done with this barrel, they have proved adequate. I would hesitate to use smokeless powder loaded shot shells in this one.

CARTRIDGES USED IN MAYNARD RIFLES AND SHOT GUNS
    6 .40 Maynard 1873 case showing primer pocket
    7 .40/40 Maynard 1873 case
    8 .40/60 Maynard 1882 case
    9 .40/70 Maynard 1873 case
  10 .44/100 Maynard 1873 case

My No. 16 Maynard in .32/35 Stevens taper caliber (page 287) takes a cartridge that is still available in limited quantities, and an inherently accurate one, too. A very pleasant cartridge this is, to shoot, and though I have used a lot of black-powder loaded cartridges in this barrel, lately I have used mild loads of #80 and #4759 in it, and as the barrel is perfect inside, the accuracy is extremely fine.

The No. 16 Maynards were the highest grades made and listed in the old catalogs. These models had fine crotch walnut buttstocks and checkered forearm to match. The stock was pistol-grip type, with the lower tang let in straight back through the grip, and the slot through the grip was filled with a carefully fitted insert held in place by a single screw. The workmanship on this No. 16 is of the very finest throughout. This was the only model that carried the pistol-grip stock and a forearm without extra charge.

The various models as listed in the Maynard catalog for 1885 are as follows.

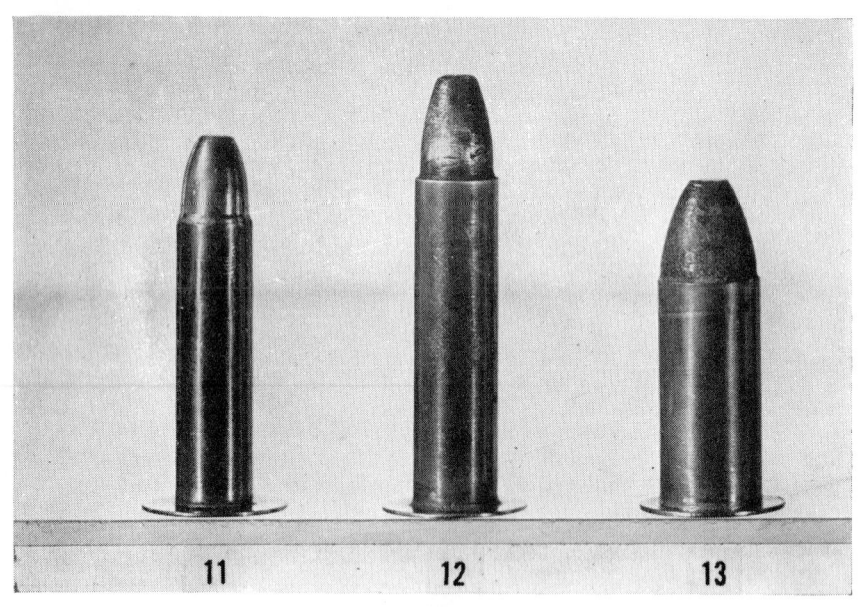

CARTRIDGES USED IN MAYNARD RIFLES AND SHOT GUNS
11 .35 Maynard Percussion
12 .40 Maynard Percussion
13 .50 Maynard Percussion

MAYNARD IMPROVED GALLERY RIFLE NUMBER 1. In "Model 1873" with rim-fire attachment or "Model 1882" without the attachment; .22 caliber rim-fire; open hunting sights; plain oil finish stock.

          20-inch barrel $20.00
          24-inch barrel   22.00

This rifle uses the standard fixed ammunition and is adapted for hunting small game. The new patent attachment enabling the "model 1873" rifle to use standard fixed ammunition can easily be removed by taking out two small screws; and barrels constructed to use the Maynard central fire reloading cartridges, "model 1873," can be used with the same breech piece.

MAYNARD GALLERY OR SMALL GAME HUNTING RIFLE NUMBER 2. In "Model 1873" with rim-fire attachment, or "Model 1882" without the attachment; .22 caliber, rim fire, elevating graduated peep sight, open hunting sights, plain oil finish stock.

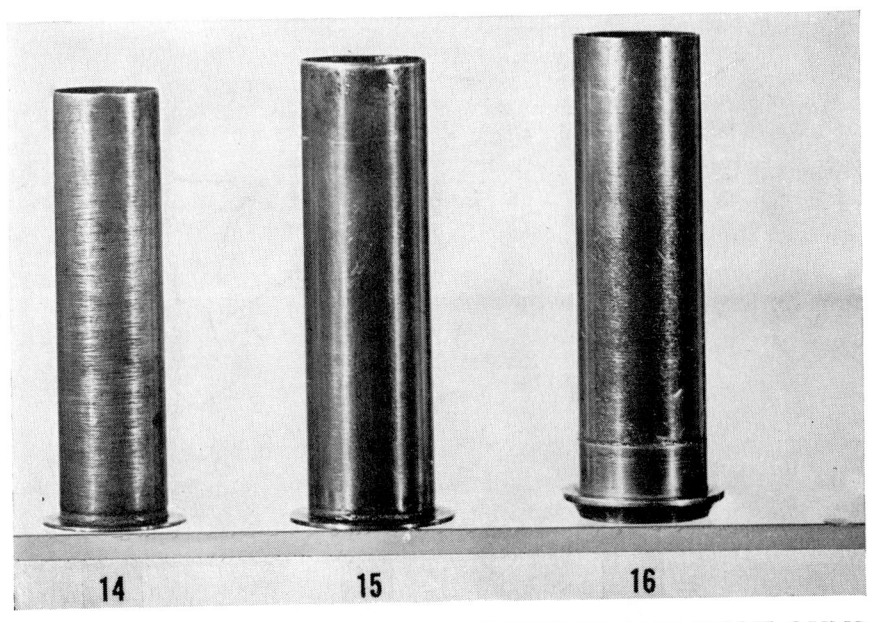

CARTRIDGES USED IN MAYNARD RIFLES AND SHOT GUNS
          14 .55 Maynard Percussion shot shell
          15 .64 Maynard Percussion shot shell
          16 .64 Maynard 1873 case shot shell

HADLEY'S

NEW DEVICE FOR

Capping and De-Capping Rifle and Shot Shells

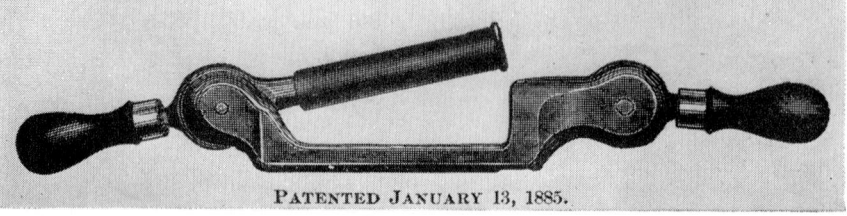

PATENTED JANUARY 13, 1885.

HADLEY'S RE- AND DECAPPING DEVICE FOR MAYNARD CARTRIDGES

20-inch barrel	$23.00
24-inch barrel	25.00

The .22 caliber fixed ammunition barrels will be chambered for short or long cartridges, as may be ordered; we recommend the "short" as giving the best results. For target practice with the gallery rifle, we would recommend the elevating peep and Beach combination sights.

MAYNARD IMPROVED HUNTING OR TARGET RIFLE NUMBER 3. In "Model 1873" with attachment for rim fire, or "Model 1882" for central fire fixed ammunition; .32 caliber, open hunting sights, plain oil finish stock.

24-inch barrel	$20.00
26-inch barrel	22.00

MAYNARD IMPROVED HUNTING OR TARGET RIFLE NUMBER 4. "Model 1873," with attachment for rim fire, or "Model 1882" for central fire fixed ammunition; .32 caliber, elevating graduated peep sight and open hunting sights. Plain oil finish stock.

24-inch barrel	$23.00
26-inch barrel	25.00

The above barrels of No.'s 3 and 4 will be chambered for Short, Long or Extra Long cartridges. The Long shoot the best. Also chambered for the Winchester rifle cartridge, 20 grains of powder and 115-grain bullet.

MAYNARD IMPROVED HUNTER'S RIFLE, NUMBER 5. "Model 1873" with attachment for rim-fire, or "Model 1882" for central fire fixed ammunition; .38 caliber, open hunting sights, plain oil finish stock.

    26-inch barrel $22.00
    28- or 30-inch barrel 24.00

MAYNARD IMPROVED SPORTING RIFLE, NUMBER 6. "Model 1873" with attachment for rim-fire or "1882" for central fire fixed ammunition; .38 caliber, elevating graduated peep sight, open hunting sights, plain oil finish stock.

    26-inch barrel $25.00
    28- or 30-inch barrel 27.00

An interchangeable central fire attachment can be furnished for "Model 1873" to use .32 caliber central fire cartridges in No.'s 3 and 4, and .38 caliber central fire cartridges in No.'s 5 and 6 if desired.

MAYNARD IMPROVED HUNTER'S RIFLE, NUMBER 7. "Model 1873" or "Model 1882"; .35 caliber, 30 grains, open hunting sights, plain oil finish stock; weighs about 6½ lbs.

    20-inch barrel $20.00

Appendages, less shells: single bullet mould, loader, loading block, capper, cap picker, rod, brush, rag holder and screw driver, $3.50.

    Shells for "Model 1873," 15¢ each
    Shells for "Model 1882," 7¢ each

For a game hunter, this rifle cannot be surpassed. In procuring a Maynard rifle, the purchaser may provide himself with an armory of weapons suitable for all possible wants, or he may select such an arm as he has

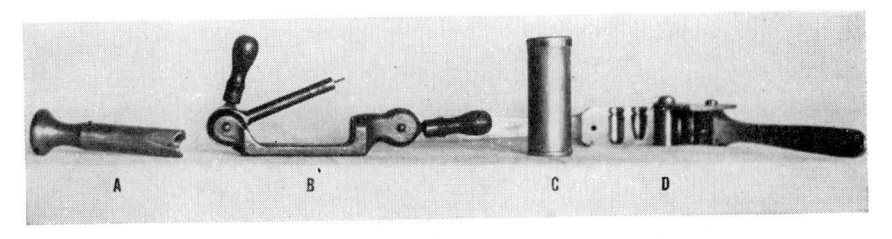

MAYNARD RELOADING ACCESSORIES
 A Bullet seater
 B Re and decapper, Hadley's Patent
 C Metal container for Maynard tape primer rolls
 D Mold, casting one conical and one cylindrical bullet

occasion for, and at any subsequent time may order from the manufactory either of the patterns of barrels, and thus, at comparatively trifling cost, provide himself with another arm adapted to a different use, and of such size that stock and barrel may be packed in a valise or rolled in a shawl and carried when travelling without exciting observation.

NUMBER EIGHT. "Model 1873" or "Model 1882"; .35 caliber, 30 grains, elevating graduated peep sight and open hunting sights, plain oil finish stock.

20-inch barrel $23.00
Appendages, same as Number 7, $3.50

MAYNARD IMPROVED HUNTING OR TARGET RIFLE, NUMBER 9. "Model 1873" or "Model 1882"; .35 caliber, 30 grains; or .40 caliber, 40 grains; elevating graduated peep sight and open hunting sights, plain oil finish stock. Weight, about 7½ pounds.

26-inch barrel · $27.00
Appendages, same as Number 7, $3.50
Shells for "Model 1873," 15¢ each
Shells for "Model 1882," 7¢ each

This is a splendid hanging and close shooting rifle. A valuable and special feature of the Maynard arm is that which admits of an interchange of barrels of any length or caliber—between the Creedmoor, midrange, or sporting models.

MAYNARD IMPROVED MID RANGE TARGET AND HUNTING RIFLE, NUMBER 10. "Model 1873" or "Model 1882"; .35 caliber, 30 or 40 grains; .40 caliber, 40, 60, or 70 grains; elevating graduated peep sight; plain oil finish stock; barrel is octagon, 9 inches at breech. Weight 8 to 9 pounds.

28-, 30- or 32-inch barrel $30.00

Appendages, less shells: single bullet mould, loader, loading block, capper, cap picker, rod, brush, rag holder and screw driver. $3.50.

Shells for "Model 1873," 15 and 18¢ each
Shells for "Model 1882," 7 and 8¢ each

In above number, "Model 1882" we can furnish .40 caliber barrels chambered for fixed ammunition using a central fire cartridge, containing 70 grains of powder, and a grooved bullet weighing 270 grains which is particularly adapted to the barrel, and which we recommend as giving the best possible results. The shells can be reloaded a limited number of times if desired. The new Ballard cartridge, .40 caliber, 70 grains, can be used in this barrel.

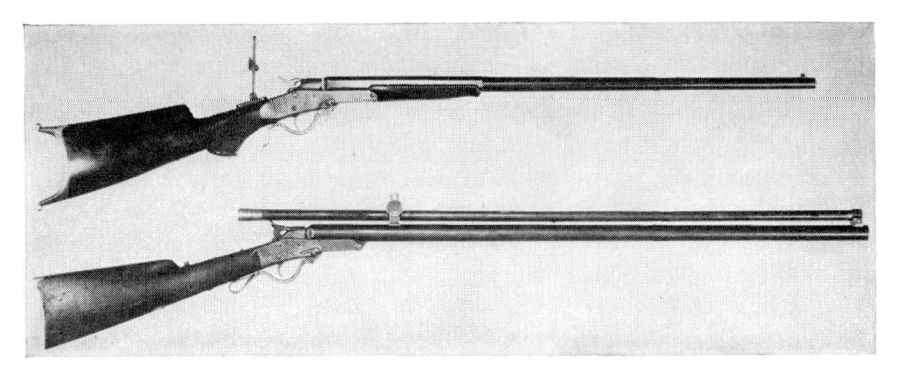

MAYNARD RIFLES

(TOP): Maynard No. 16 Target Rifle, caliber .32-35, 1882
(BOTTOM): Maynard No. 11 Sporting Rifle, caliber .44-100, Maynard 1873, with full length Malcolm telescope

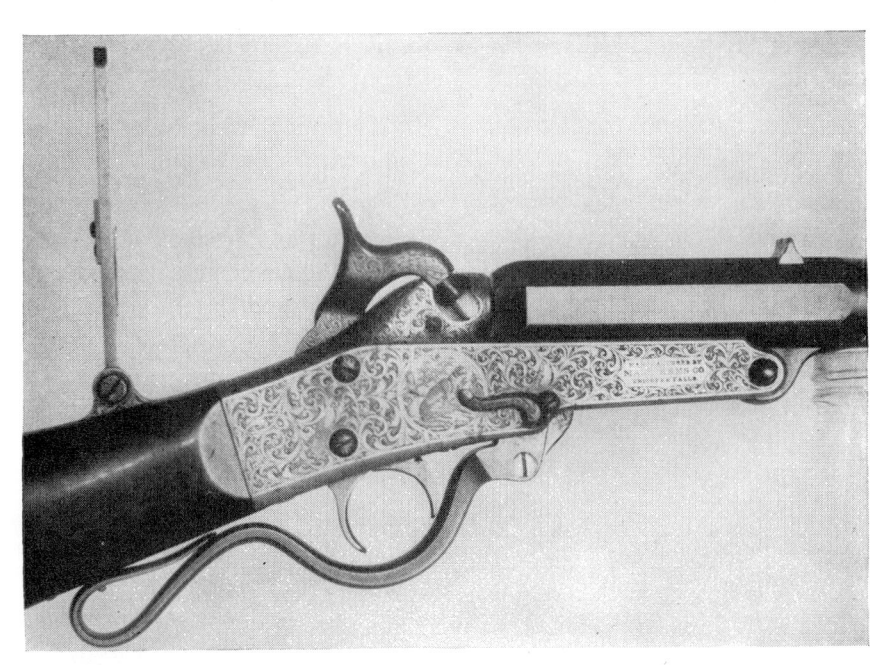

ENGRAVED SET TRIGGER MAYNARD PERCUSSION SPORTING RIFLE
From the Frank Sargent collection

Central fire .40 caliber, 70 grains, per hundred $4.00
Central fire primed shells .40 caliber, 70 grains, per hundred   2.50

Extra fancy wood in stock, checkered stock or change in sights will be furnished at prices shown in general price list of parts.

The Beach combination and rear sporting sights are recommended when better than the common open sights are desired.

These celebrated target and sporting arms with interchangeable rifle and shot barrels, for convenience, accuracy and penetration, have secured a reputation beyond that of any other breech loading arms.

MAYNARD IMPROVED HUNTER'S RIFLE, NUMBER 11. For large and dangerous game: "Model 1873" or "Model 1882"; .44 caliber, 60, 70, or 100 grains; .45 caliber, 70 grains; for U. S. Gov't. ammunition, .50 caliber, 50, 70, or 100 grains; or .55 caliber, 100 grains; elevating graduated peep sight, open hunting sights, plain oil finish stock.

26-, 28-, 30, or 32-inch barrel $32.00

Appendages, less shells: bullet mould, loader, loading block, capper, cap picker, rod, brush, rag holder and screw driver, $3.50.

Shells for "Model 1873," 15 and 18¢ each
Shells for "Model 1882," 8 and 10¢ each
Mould for express bullet, extra $3.50

MAYNARD IMPROVED MID RANGE TARGET RIFLE, NUMBER 12. "Model 1873" or "Model 1882"; .40 caliber, 60 or 70 grains; elevating graduated peep sight with circular eye piece. Rear sporting and Beach combination sights; checkered oil finish stock; barrel is octagon, 9 inches at breech; weight about 9 lbs.

28-, 30-, or 32-inch barrel $36.00

Appendages, less shells: single bullet mould, loader, loading block, capper, cap picker, rod, brush, rag holder, and screw driver, $3.50

MAYNARD IMPROVED MID RANGE TARGET RIFLE, NUMBER 13. "Model 1873" or "Model 1882"; barrel is octagon, 9 inches at breech; .40 caliber, 60 or 70 grains; checkered oil finish stock; sights, patent vernier and wind-gauge with spirit level; weight, about 9 pounds.

28-, 30- or 32-inch barrel $45.00

Appendages, less shells: same as with No. 12, $3.50.

Shells for "Model 1873," 18¢ each
Shells for "Model 1882," 8¢ each

For hunting and target practice at all ranges, the Maynard more completely supplies the wants of hunters and sportsmen generally than any other rifle in the world, as many barrels can be used on one stock; and for accuracy, conveniency and durability is not excelled.

MAYNARD LONG RANGE CREEDMOOR RIFLE No. 14. "Model 1873" or "Model 1882"; .44 caliber; 32-inch barrel, round full length, with checkered pistol grip stock of fancy branch walnut. It has the patent vernier and windgauge sights with spirit level; weight just under 10 pounds.

The appendages are 25 cartridge cases of 100 grains, cartridge capper, cap picker, charger, loader, loading block, cartridge cleaner, 3 rods and brush, 2 rag holders, screw driver, and 100 patched and swaged bullets, 520 or 550 grains.

Price of rifle and appendages $65.00

BEVELED EDGE METAL PATCH GUIDE
Make guide exact size and shape of patch to be cut. Run knife around edge of guide to cut paper patch.

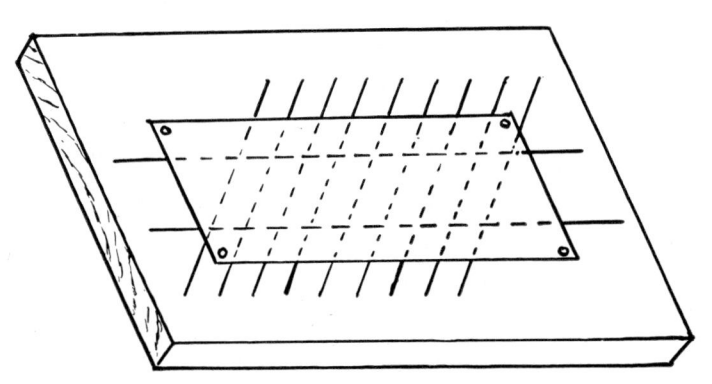

GUIDE FOR CUTTING SEVERAL PATCHES AT ONE TIME
To a wood base 10 x 18 inches in size several sheets of patch paper are held with thumbtacks through corners. Patches are cut by running knife along steel rule laid over guide lines which extend out beyond margins of the paper.

MAYNARD IMPROVED TARGET RIFLE, NUMBER 15. "Model 1873" or "Model 1882"; .38 caliber, 50 grains; or .40 caliber, 60 or 70 grains, for patched bullets; checkered stock, nickeled Swiss pattern butt plate, with hunting butt plate to interchange; elevating graduated peep sight with circular eye piece and windgauge sight.

26-, 28-, 30- or 32-inch barrel	$42.00
Forearm or tip stock, checkered	2.00
Forearm or tip stock, plain	1.50

Appendages for patched bullets, less shells, capper, cap picker, loader, loading block, 2 rods, brush, rag holder and screw driver, $3.00.

Shells for "Model 1873," 18¢ each
Shells for "Model 1882," 8¢ each

MAYNARD IMPROVED TARGET RIFLE, NUMBER 16. Particularly adapted for offhand target shooting. "Model 1873" or "Model 1882"; .38 caliber, 50 grains; or .40 caliber, 60 or 70 grains for patched bullets. Checkered Pistol grip Stock, of extra Fancy Branch Walnut, varnished and polished, nickeled Swiss Pattern butt plate with hunting butt plate to interchange; Checkered Forearm or Tip stock; Mid Range Patent Vernier and Windgauge sights.

26-, 28-, 30- or 32-inch barrel $56.00
Appendages same as with No. 15, $3.00
Shells for "Model 1873," 18¢ each
Shells for "Model 1882," 8¢ each

The extra fancy branch [1] in the pistol grip stock is a very great improvement to the appearance of the arm.

We have a special .32, .35, .38, and .40 caliber naked bullet which may be used in these caliber barrels intended for patched bullets, which gives very satisfactory results for hunting purposes. The .32 caliber weighs 153 grains; the .35 caliber, 240 grains; .38 caliber, 245 grains; and the .40 caliber, 270 grains.

.22, .32 and .35 caliber barrels can be fitted up in models No. 15 and 16 when ordered.

MAYNARD BREECH LOADING SHOT GUN, NUMBER 1. "Model 1873" or "Model 1882"; .55 caliber, plain oiled stock.

26-inch barrel $20.00

Appendages, less shells: capper, cap picker, rod, brush, rag holder, shot loader, wad cutter and loading block, $2.50.

[1] Crotch walnut grain is meant here.

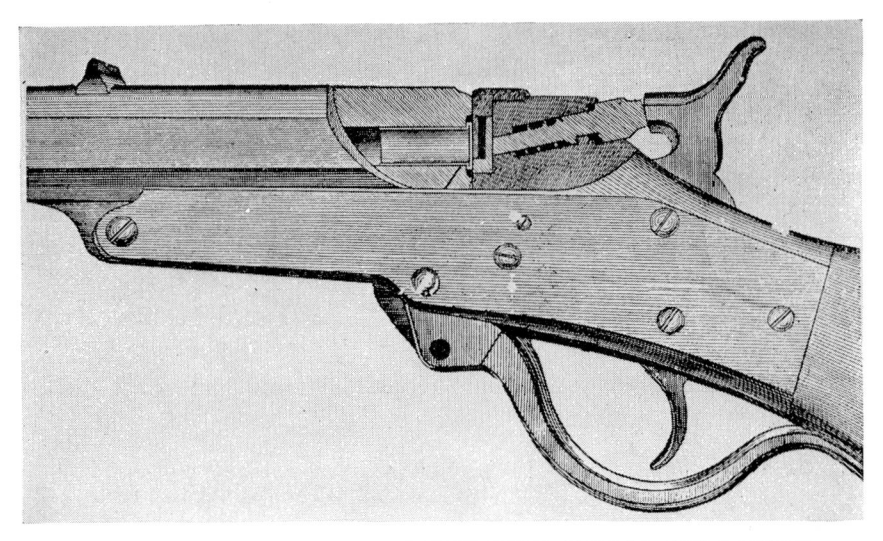

HADLEY'S PATENT DEVICE FOR USING RIM FIRE CARTRIDGES IN THE 1873 MODEL RIFLE

Shells for "Model 1873," 18¢ each
Shells for "Model 1882," 10¢ each

MAYNARD IMPROVED BREECH LOADING SHOT GUN, NUMBER 2. "Model 1873" or "Model 1882"; .64 caliber, plain oiled stock.

26-inch barrel $22.00
Shells for "Model 1873," 18¢ each
Shells for "Model 1882," 10¢ each

MAYNARD IMPROVED BREECH LOADING SHOT GUN, NUMBER 3. "The Sportsman's Favorite." "Model 1873" or "Model 1882"; .64 caliber, plain oiled stock.

28-, 30- or 32-inch barrel $24.00
Appendages, same as for No. 1, $2.50
Shells for "Model 1873," 18¢ each
Shells for "Model 1882," 10¢ each

Shotgun barrels in "Model 1882" may be chambered to use the 20-gauge paper shell if desired.

Extra rifle barrels for Maynard rifles were offered in all calibers from .22 to .55 at prices varying from $8.00 to $12.00.

The shot barrels for either 1873 or 1882 models ran from $6.00 for the 20-inch, 55 caliber, to $12.00 for the 32-inch, 64 caliber.

The common bullet for the Maynard rifle seems to have been the conical, whether loaded in 1865, 1873, or 1882 type. However, regular cylindrical bullets and the molds for them were available, if wanted. The more common Maynard mold seems to be the two-cavity type—one conical and one cylindrical, especially in .35 and .40 calibers. There were .40, .44 and .50 caliber molds for an "explosive" bullet offered at $6.00 and $6.50. These evidently were hollow point molds casting a bullet with a cavity to accept a .22 rim-fire blank, as was common in those days for "Express" rifles. The .22 caliber double-cavity molds, or .32 caliber single molds were offered at $1.50.

In shooting the Maynard rifles today one can hardly count on finding enough brass to use for that purpose. Occasionally a few .50 caliber percussion cartridges for the Maynard 1865 model are located, but these are becoming increasingly hard to find. The thick head, large rim cases for the 1873 models are collectors' items today in single specimens, and so it is difficult to find even a specimen. These cases were made to take Berdan primers, of course, and not many of these primers are to be had at the corner hardware store. The best and most practical way out of this lack-of-case predicament is to have turned up out of brass stock—or even steel—cases that will fit your chamber. These can be made with thin enough case walls so that they will expand enough to seal the breech, and to dimensions obtained from a sulphur or other cast of chamber it is desired to fit. Have them pocketed to hold properly a large modern rifle primer, and with the correct size of flash hole.

The 1873 cases usually have a head about ⅛-inch thick, and large enough to be easily grasped by the fingers after the extractor has started them from the chamber. One of these cases is all that is needed, reloading it at the range between shots, and this will enable a rifle of very odd caliber to be enjoyed.

The cases for the .35, .40 or .50 caliber 1865 Maynard, using the percussion cap on the nipple, may be made the same way as the 1873, and with a flash hole in the center of the base, percussion caps will supply the ignition. The case may be removed after each shot, recharged, and a bullet seated in the case mouth; or the case may be left in the chamber and powder and lead inserted via the muzzle, as

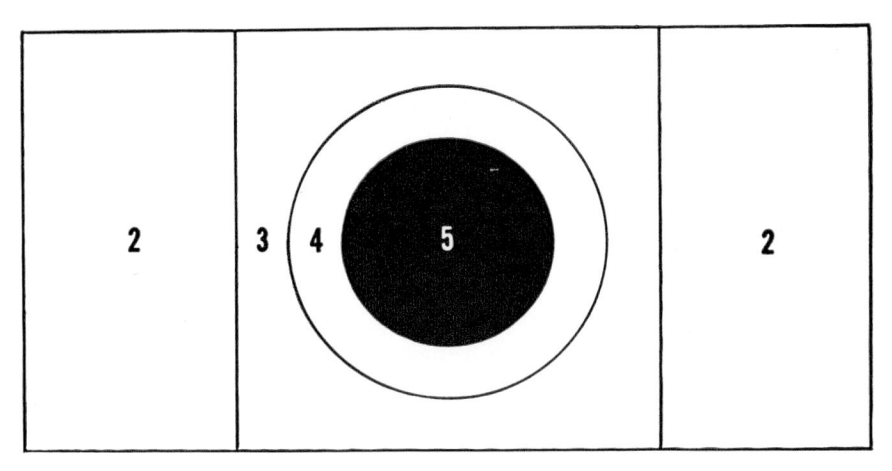

First Class Target 6 x 12 feet. Bullseye, 36 inches diameter counts 5. Center, 54 inches diameter counts 4. Inner square, 6 x 6 feet counts 3. Outer, remainder of target counts 2.

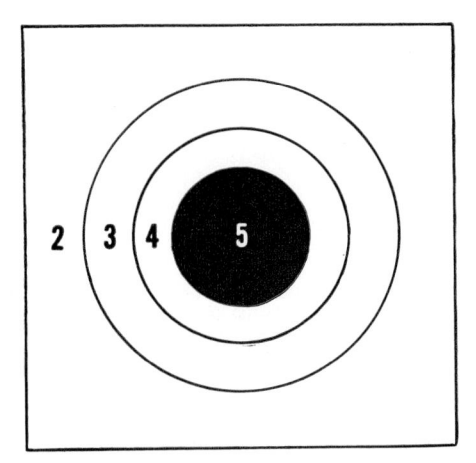

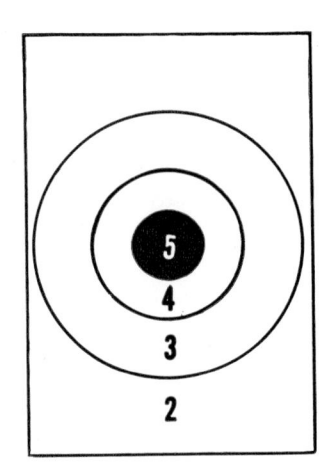

LEFT: Second Class 6 x 6 feet. Bullseye, 22 inches diameter counts 5. Center, 38 inches diameter counts 4. Inner, 54 inches diameter counts 3. Outer, remainder of target counts 2.
RIGHT: Third Class 4 x 6 feet. Bullseye, 8 inches diameter counts 5. Center, 26 inches diameter counts 4. Inner, 46 inches diameter counts 3. Outer, remainder of target counts 2.

CREEDMOOR TARGETS
In use about 1892. Scale: ⅜ inch equals 1 foot.

in a true muzzle loader. A new cap on the nipple for each shot, and *voilà!* There you are!

I have shot an 1873 Maynard Hunter's model in .44/100 Maynard a great deal with just one case I had made. This case is 2⅞ inches long, as were the original factory-made cases; and I use the large rifle primers #8½, which fit the pocket turned in the solid brass base.

The lubricated 430-grain bullet cast about 1 to 40 is seated with the fingers on the powder charge, and it is a simple matter to punch the old primer out, seat a fresh one, and recharge the case between shots. All the old Schuetzen shooters used just one case, and after it had been fired a few times, all sag and wobble of the case was gone. They will lay central and concentric, as they should, thus ensuring the best possible accuracy.

The 1882 Maynard series of rifles use cartridges that look like cartridges instead of the peculiar items of the 1865 and 1873 series. There are some of these sizes that cannot be located today, but most of them are easily made up from other common cartridge cases.

The 1873 barrels lack about ⅛-inch of breeching up tight, as the case heads fill this up; while in the 1882 rifles the space between the rear end of the barrel and the standing breech is just the thickness of the case rim of the 1882 cartridge. In most cases this rim is about the same thickness as the common cartridge rims such as the .30/40.

In making cases for the 1882 rifles in .35/30 and .35/40 Maynard calibers, I have used .38/72 and .40/72 Winchester cases, which I have found to be entirely satisfactory. Trim the cases to the proper length, which in the .35/30 is 1 9/16 inches and in the .35/40 is 2 1/16 inches.

There are other common sized cases which may be utilized also. Dig out your cartridge collection and "mike" a few; you will be agreeably surprised.

In the .38/50 Maynard 1882, which is about 2 1/16 inches long in most cases (though I have seen them just an even 2 inches long), the .38/55 Ballard and Marlin brass may be used by shortening it slightly. I have also expanded good .32/40 cases with black powder to fit a .38/50 Maynard chamber. There are many possibilities for finding something to utilize in this .38/50 size, and most .38/50 Ballard 1 15/16" cases, if you happen to have them, will usually fit.

The .40/40 1882 Maynard case is about 1¾ inches long, and the .40/60 1882 case is 2 3/16 inches long, so it is also a simple job to find something to shorten to fit this caliber. The cartridge collection box will yield a plentiful supply of cartridges with the proper head sizes, then you will know what to look for.

The .40/70 1882 Maynard case is about 2⅜ inches long, so .40/70 Ballard cases will fit most of these chambers, and .40/70 Ballard or Maynard cases may be made of several common Winchester sizes, such as the .40/82 or .40/70 WCF.

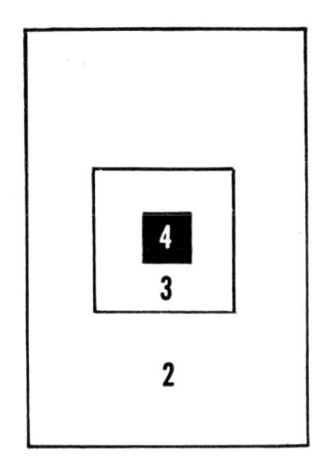

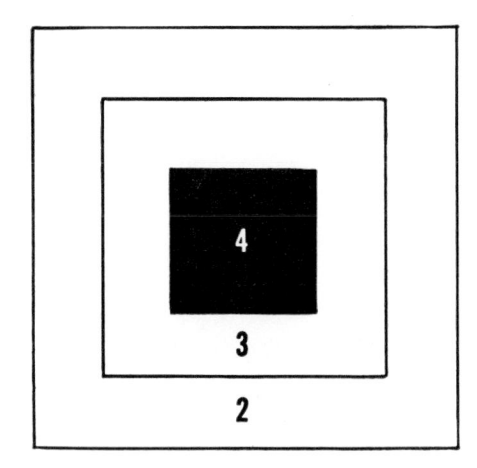

A   Target; bullseye 8 inches square.   B   Target; bullseye 2 feet square.

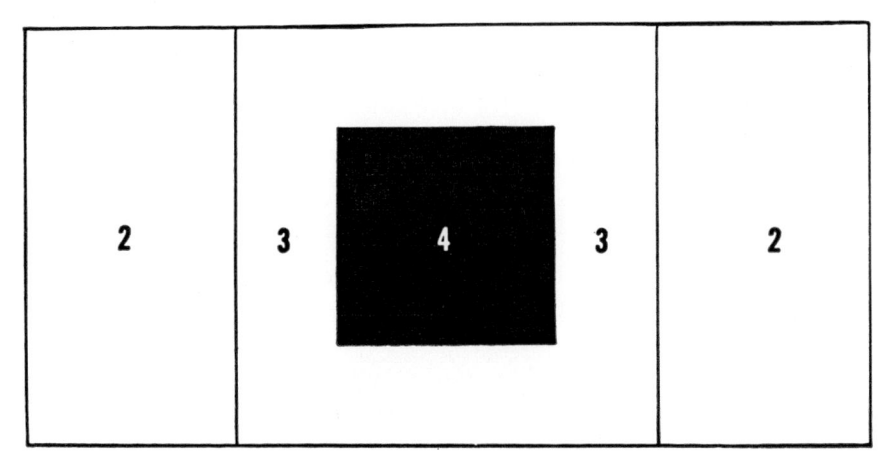

C   Target; bullseye 3 feet square.
EARLY CREEDMOOR TARGETS
Scale: ⅜ inch equals 1 foot

There is a .44/70 Maynard 1882, but I have never run across a rifle for this cartridge. It should not be hard to fit with some readily obtainable size, and after slugging the barrel to learn the groove diameter, you may find the proper sized bullet at hand in one which is used for an entirely different caliber.

Maynard rifles were chambered for .45/70 Gov't. and .50/70 Gov't. sizes also, and while these are not too common, they are found occasionally.

In all these Maynard cartridges, as well as in all other old cartridges, case lengths will vary. Sometimes two cartridges as made by UMC and other companies will vary as much as 1/16 of an inch in length. The proper thing to do is first slug the barrel to obtain the groove diameters and then make a cast of the chamber. Working from the dimensions thus known, it is almost impossible to go wrong in fitting the rifle to shoot fodder you can make from what materials you have at hand.

The Maynard rifle is most commonly seen in one of the plain, straight-grip stock, no forearm models; usually with no checkering on the grip, and with plain elevating rear tang sight. More rare is the finer Number 16, as illustrated, with crotch walnut pistol-grip stock, nickeled Swiss butt plate, and Maynard patent vernier elevating rear sight. The catalogs list a Creedmoor model and give some scores made with one of this grade in 1877 at 800 and 1000 yards. However, I am inclined to be of the opinion that the Maynard rifle was used largely for short and midrange shooting.

The only long-range Creedmoor Maynard I ever ran across was a 32-inch round-barreled model in .44 caliber with straight grip, shotgun butt stock of the plainest variety of walnut, no forearm or tip stock, and with Maynard midrange height of vernier rear sight mounted on the heel of the stock. It was such a perfectly plain and nondescript rifle it hardly seemed worth-while keeping.

The Maynard company failed sometime during the 1890s, and many men attribute that failure to their attempt to produce a rifle which entailed a lot of handwork in an era when mass production was really getting underway in the repeating firearms field.

The J. Stevens Arms and Tool Company acquired the rights to the Maynard rifle, together with the tools, fixtures, and gauges, and the good will, but never made use of them, at least, to the point of sharing them with the shooting public in the form of continuing the fine old Maynard line. However, they finally put on the market the Stevens Maynard Junior rifle, which was a tip-up model utilizing an under lever like the Maynard, but it was very cheaply made and of inferior materials. This is a light, small boy's rifle.

One, cannot, however, conscientiously censure the old Stevens company for not continuing the Maynard, as they naturally thought that the Stevens 44 rifles, then being made by them, were superior, and having recently abandoned the manufacture of their own tip-up models, except in pistols, it is small wonder that the days of the fine old Maynard were over.

So passed another single-shot rifle which had its origin in Civil War time.

XI

Bullard Single-shot, Hopkins & Allen, and Farrow Rifles

THE BULLARD
SINGLE-SHOT RIFLE

The Bullard single-shot rifle was made by the Bullard Repeating Arms Company of Springfield, Mass. As far as can be ascertained, the Bullard single-shot was first made somewhere around 1883, although the repeater was not patented until sometime in 1886. Some authorities claim that the first catalog was issued and the first rifles placed on the market in the year 1887. Regardless of the exact date, the fact remains that the Bullard single-shot, and the repeater, too, for that matter, were certainly unique arms.

The repeating rifle made use of a rack-and-pinion device for opening and closing the breech bolt, and an extremely simple and powerful system it was, too.

The single-shot mechanism made use of certain parts contained in the repeater design; in fact, the single-shot action is essentially the repeater action without the rack and pinion. The breechblock is propped shut and will remain closed in spite of some of the powerful cartridges used in this rifle.

This Bullard single-shot is an extremely thin action, probably the thinnest of all the better single-shots. The action opens and closes with the greatest of ease. There is no tugging and straining necessary on the lever to operate the breechblock. It works the smoothest and quickest of all the falling- or rolling-block mechanisms.

One model of the Bullard utilized a rather ingenious device for interchangeable barrels. In this model the barrels were threaded into sleeves which dovetailed into the top of the action, being held in place by a large screw. This device was perfectly safe and contributed greatly to the convenience of changing calibers when wanted. The forearm on this model being attached to the barrel in the usual manner, it was of course removed with the barrel when it was desired to remove that.

The various models of single-shots offered in the 1887 Bullard catalog were as follows:

BULLARD SINGLE-SHOT TARGET GALLERY AND HUNTING RIFLE. This was a light Bullard model made with pistol-grip stock and rifle butt plate. Barrels were made in .32, .38 and .45 calibers up to 28-inch lengths. Weights ran from 8 to 10 pounds, and the price of this plain model was only $25.

At the same price a special, lighter-barreled .22 rim-fire model with open sights was also offered.

BULLARD TARGET RIFLE. This was a fancy model made with fancy checkered pistol-grip stock and Swiss butt plate. The forearm was checkered to match the stock. Barrels were round, part-octagonal or full-octagonal, and any length up to 28 inches. Barrels of longer lengths were supplied at a charge of $1.00 extra per additional inch. This rifle was made in a wide variety of calibers in .32, .38, .45 and .50. Sights were vernier tang rear and wind-gauge front types. This model was priced at $44. The regular rifle butt plate could be supplied instead of the Swiss type at the same price if desired.

BULLARD SCHUETZEN RIFLE. This rifle was a slightly heavier model than the two preceding models. It had a pistol-grip stock and lever and set triggers. The butt plate used was the Swiss type, nickeled. The barrels were all half-octagonal, and of several weights. Sights were the usual vernier tang rear and wind-gauge front. Weights were around 12 pounds, depending on barrel length, of which there were several choices. This model was also offered in a detachable barrel version. The rifle listed at $42.50, and extra interchangeable barrels with forearm were priced at $14.

BULLARD SPECIAL DETACHABLE BARREL MODEL. This was a special, lighter model, weight 7 pounds, in .22 rim-fire caliber, with 26-inch barrel, priced at $25. Extra interchangeable barrels for this model were priced at $12. These barrels were offered in .32 and .38 calibers.

BULLARD SINGLE-SHOT MILITARY RIFLE. This was a .45/70 caliber rifle with a slightly different locking system from other Bullards. The

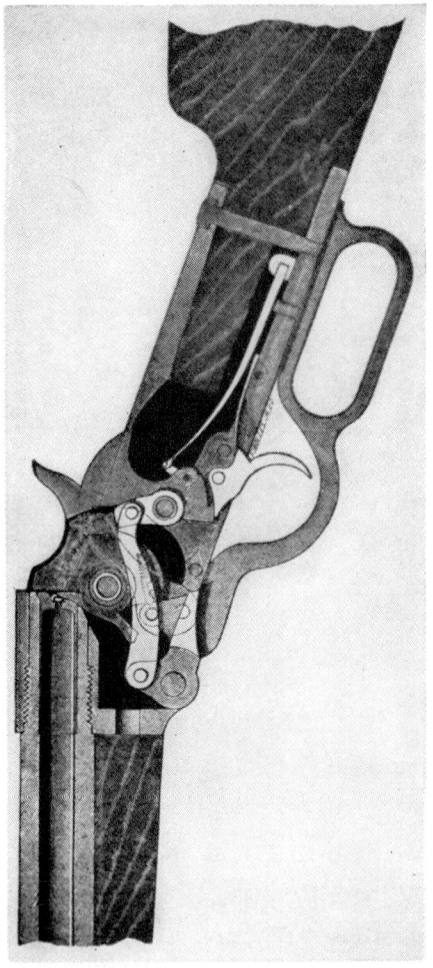

BULLARD SINGLE-SHOT RIFLE ACTION

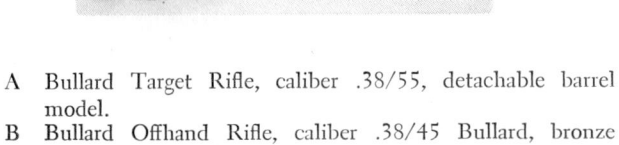

A Bullard Target Rifle, caliber .38/55, detachable barrel model.
B Bullard Offhand Rifle, caliber .38/45 Bullard, bronze frame, solid barrel model.
C Bullard Sporting Rifle, caliber .38/90 Bullard, solid barrel model with scroll lever.
D Bullard Sporting Rifle, caliber .32/40 Ballard, detachable barrel model.
E Bullard Offhand Target Rifle, caliber .32/40 Bullard, detachable barrel model.

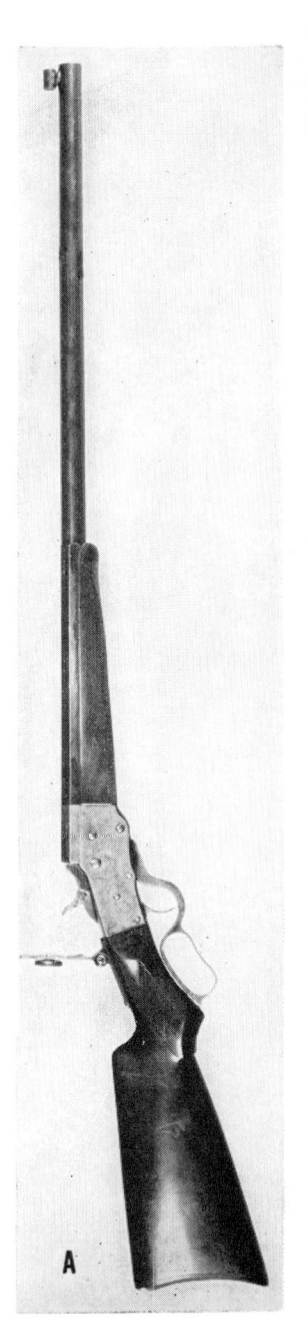

BULLARD SINGLE-SHOT RIFLES
Rifles B, C, D and E are from the Frank Sargent collection.

.32 rim-fire calibers were chambered for the .32 Short, .32 Long, and .32 Extra Long. The .38 rim-fire calibers were for the .38 Short, .38 Long, and .38 Extra Long. The .32 center-fire calibers were chambered for the .32 Short, .32 Long, and .32 Extra Long Ballard cartridges. In .38 center-fire caliber they were chambered for the .38 Short Colt, .38 Long Colt and .38 Extra Long Ballard sizes. A .22 center-fire model using the .22 Extra Long center-fire Maynard caliber was also available. Upon order, rifles were also chambered and bored for the .32/20 WCF, the .32/40 Ballard & Marlin, and the .38/55 Ballard & Marlin cartridges.

There were several "Special" Bullard calibers which were peculiar to the Bullards, no other rifles using them. These were the following:

.32/40/150 Bullard   .40/75/259 Bullard   .40/90/400 Bullard
.38/45/190 Bullard   .40/85/290 Bullard   .50/115/300 Bullard

In this series of cartridges the .32/40/150 was, of course, different from both the common .32/40/165 Ballard & Marlin and the Rem-

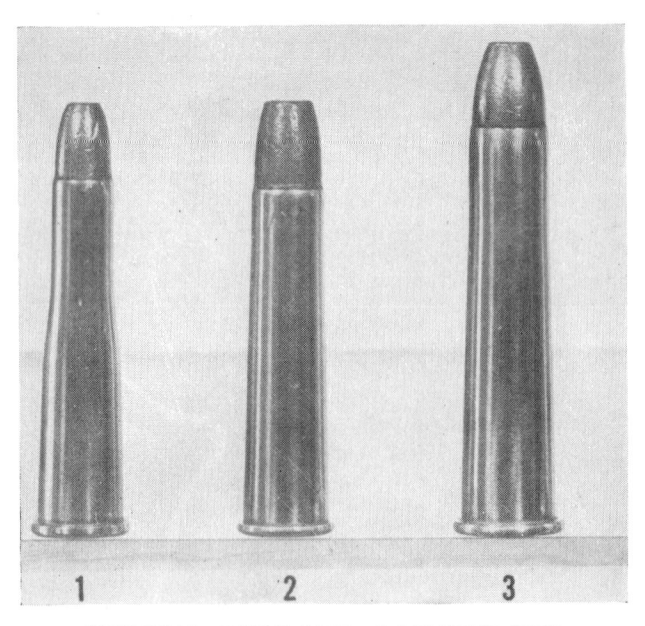

SPECIAL BULLARD CARTRIDGES
1 .32/40/150 Bullard   2 .38/45/190 Bullard
3 .40/70/232 Bullard

ington .32/40/150 cartridge. This Special .32/40/150 Bullard is a slightly bottleneck cartridge with bullet of .311 diameter.

These rifles were offered subject to many extras such as special stocks and checkering, and they were engraved to order.

Bullard Special loading tools for the Special Bullard cartridges were offered complete with mold at $5.00. Double-cavity molds, casting one solid- and one hollow-point bullet were offered at $3.50.

The Bullard single-shot rifle was well made, and of the best materials. It is to be regretted that they are not more plentiful. Possibly their being chambered for some special Bullard calibers prevented their more widespread use; but whatever the reason, we could use more of them than are now to be found.

Of the several Bullard single-shot rifles I have owned, only one was a Special Bullard caliber, a .40/75, and by the time I acquired it the barrel was practically ruined.

I then accumulated a supply of .32/40/150 Bullard cartridges and a loading tool and attempted to find a rifle in that caliber, but to no avail. Of three .32/40s I bought not one turned out to be chambered

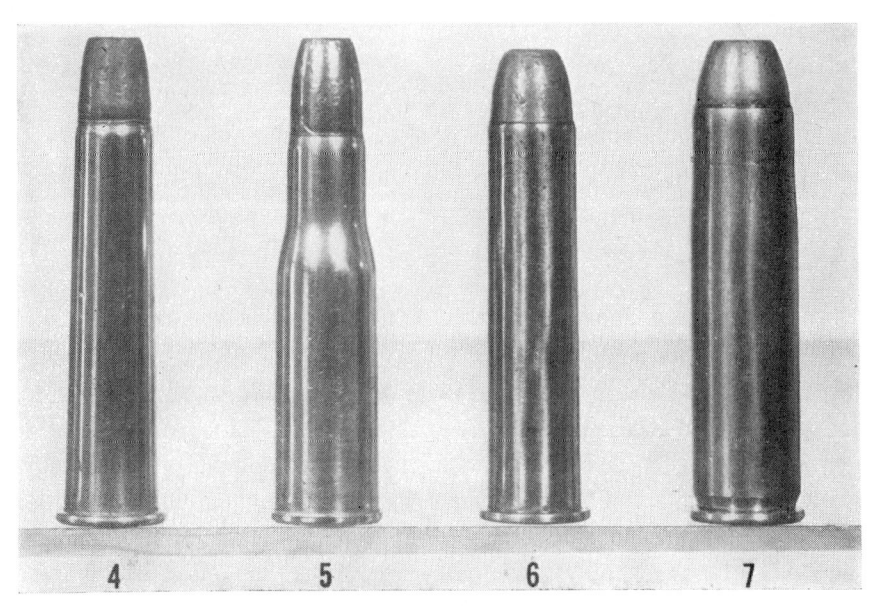

SPECIAL BULLARD CARTRIDGES

4 .40/75/259 Bullard
5 .40/90/400 Bullard
6 .45/85/295 Bullard
7 .50/115/300 Bullard

for this Special Bullard .32/40 but for the Ballard .32/40. The next Bullard I acquired happened to be a .32 Ideal caliber with perfect 30-inch #4 barrel, Swiss butt straight-grip stock; and a fine shooting rifle it was, too.

I have never seen the single-shot barreled for the large Bullard .50/115/300 cartridge, and do not know definitely that it was even so made, but I have seen a couple of Bullard repeaters for this powerful cartridge. This is a semi-rimless case and possibly the first so made.

The *Special Bullard Target Rifle* is shown on page 300. This is a deluxe, checkered, pistol-grip stock model, with shotgun butt, 28-inch part-octagonal barrel, in .38/55 Ballard & Marlin caliber, and with vernier sights. The butt plate has the wild turkey design seen on many repeating Bullard stocks. The pistol-grip tip on this rifle is of an odd design: instead of being capped or scrolled, it is leveled off from center to both sides and is rather attractive and different from any used on other single-shot stocks. The accuracy of this Bullard is equal to any .38/55 rifle I have ever fired. With 12 grains of #80 Dupont powder and the standard 255-grain .38/55 bullet, and using muzzle and elbow rest, the groups averaged right along with much heavier-barreled Ballards and Remingtons.

The Special Bullard cartridges have been shown. Many of these cartridge cases can be made from other cases. For instance, the .32/40/150 Bullard and the .38/45 Bullard can be made from .30/40 Krag cases with a full length die. The .38/45 Bullard chambers may also be fitted by using the .38/40 Remington case.

HOPKINS & ALLEN RIFLES

THIS firm was established in 1868 in Norwich, Conn., and remained in business until the end of World War I. During most of these years it produced chiefly revolvers in the lower price brackets. However, after 1888 it offered several different single-shot lever-action rifles. Among these rifles there were only about two models that interest serious riflemen, and they were evidently not too terribly interesting to most, for today the actual specimens are not plentiful.

Between 1888 and 1892 the Hopkins & Allen single-shot lever-action rifle was offered in .22 Long rim-fire caliber in 24-, 26-, and

Hopkins & Allen New Model Rifle, Number 722

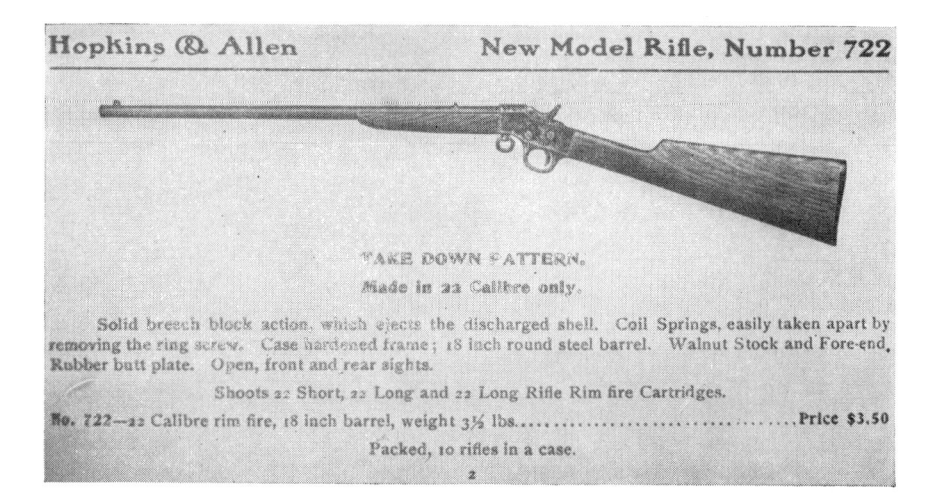

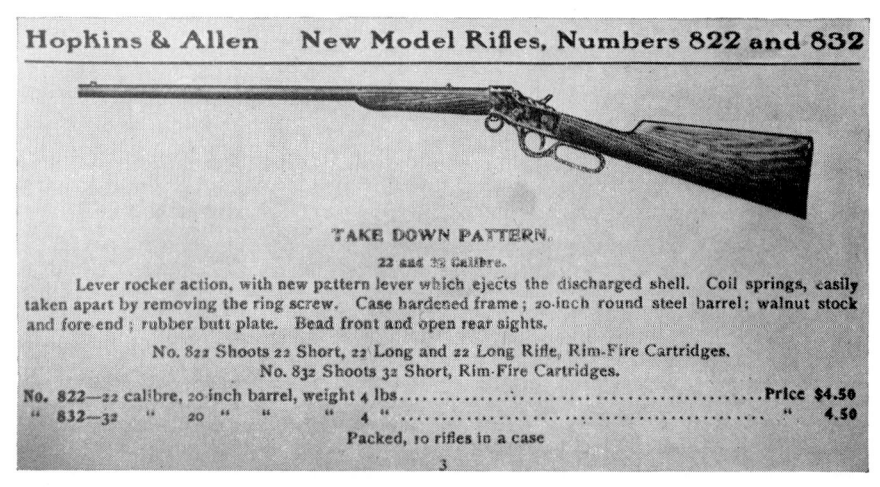

TAKE DOWN PATTERN.

Made in 22 Calibre only.

Solid breech block action, which ejects the discharged shell. Coil Springs, easily taken apart by removing the ring screw. Case hardened frame; 18 inch round steel barrel. Walnut Stock and Fore-end. Rubber butt plate. Open, front and rear sights.

Shoots 22 Short, 22 Long and 22 Long Rifle Rim fire Cartridges.

No. 722—22 Calibre rim fire, 18 inch barrel, weight 3½ lbs.................................Price $3.50

Packed, 10 rifles in a case.

Hopkins & Allen New Model Rifles, Numbers 822 and 832

TAKE DOWN PATTERN.

22 and 32 Calibre.

Lever rocker action, with new pattern lever which ejects the discharged shell. Coil springs, easily taken apart by removing the ring screw. Case hardened frame; 20-inch round steel barrel; walnut stock and fore end; rubber butt plate. Bead front and open rear sights.

No. 822 Shoots 22 Short, 22 Long and 22 Long Rifle, Rim-Fire Cartridges.
No. 832 Shoots 32 Short, Rim-Fire Cartridges.

No. 822—22 calibre, 20 inch barrel, weight 4 lbs................................Price $4.50
" 832—32 " 20 " " 4 "................................." 4.50

Packed, 10 rifles in a case

PAGES FROM HOPKINS AND ALLEN CATALOG

28-inch barrels. The same rifle was next offered in .32 Long rim-fire and in the same barrel lengths. The .32/20 WCF was also offered, but only in 26-inch barrel. A heavier frame model was next introduced in .32/40 and .38/55 Ballard & Marlin calibers, in 28-inch barrels. These heavier rifles proved to be more popular than the preceding models. They were followed by a 26-inch barrel model in .38/40 Winchester caliber.

Next on the market were the Hopkins & Allen Junior single-shot rifles. These were a light-weight, cheaper job, weighing about 5

Hopkins & Allen — New Model "Junior" Rifle

TAKE-DOWN PATTERN.

22, 25 and 32 Calibre, Rim Fire, and 38 S. & W. Center Fire.

Lever action, drop breech block. Automatic ejector, rebounding hammer. Walnut military stock with steel butt plate walnut fore-end. Rocky Mountain front and adjustable step rear sights. Case-hardened frame; 24-inch round steel barrel.

No. 922—22 calibre, 24-inch barrel, weight 5½ lbs. Shoots 22 short, long and long rifle rim fire cartridges.	Price $6.00
" 925—25 calibre, 24-inch barrel, weight 5½ lbs. Shoots 25 calibre rim fire cartridges.	" 6.00
" 932—32 calibre, 24-inch barrel, weight 5½ lbs. Shoots 32 short and long rim fire cartridges.	" 6.00
" 938—38 calibre, 24-inch barrel, weight 5½ lbs. Shoots 38 center fire S. & W. cartridges.	" 6.00

Packed, 10 rifles in a case.

We also supply **Numbers 1922, 1925, 1932** and **1938**, same description as above, excepting that these Rifles have **FULL Octagon Barrels. Price $6.50.**

4

Hopkins & Allen — New Model "Junior" Rifle

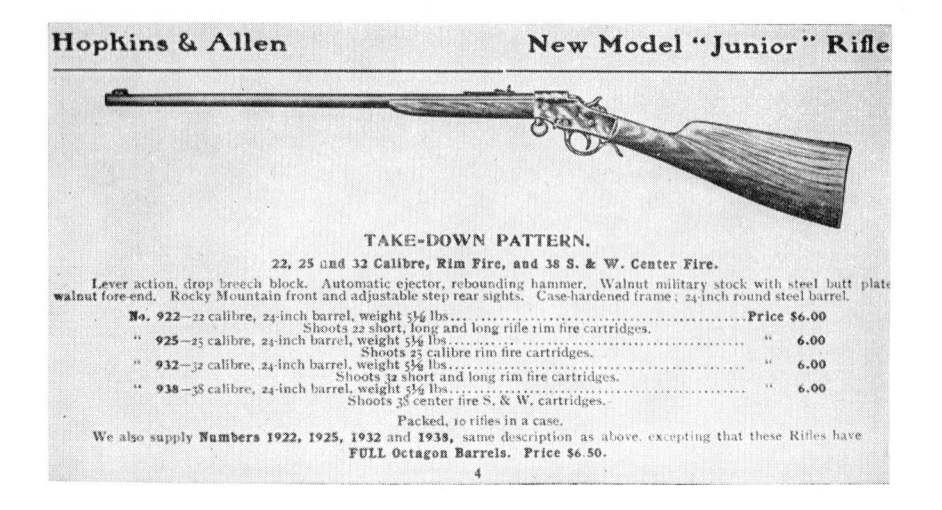

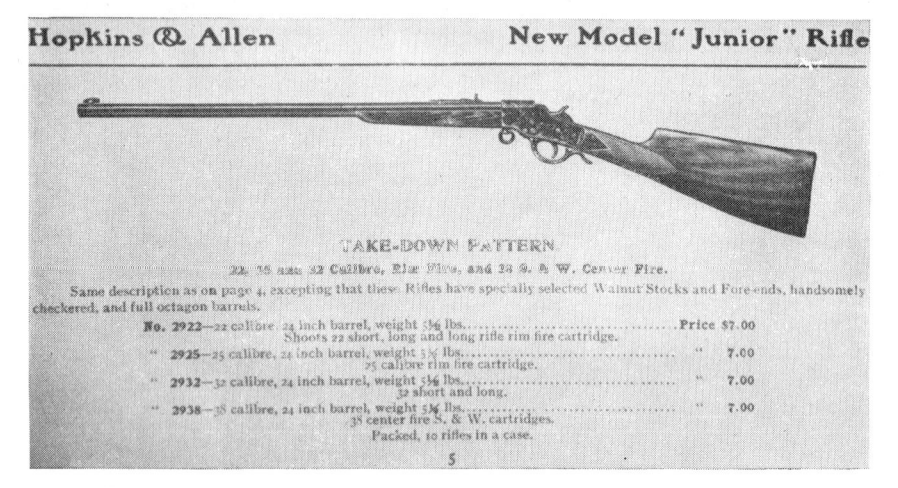

TAKE-DOWN PATTERN

22, 25 and 32 Calibre, Rim Fire, and 38 S. & W. Center Fire.

Same description as on page 4, excepting that these Rifles have specially selected Walnut Stocks and Fore-ends, handsomely checkered, and full octagon barrels.

No. 2922—22 calibre, 24 inch barrel, weight 5½ lbs. Shoots 22 short, long and long rifle rim fire cartridges.	Price $7.00
" 2925—25 calibre, 24 inch barrel, weight 5½ lbs. 25 calibre rim fire cartridge.	" 7.00
" 2932—32 calibre, 24 inch barrel, weight 5½ lbs. 32 short and long.	" 7.00
" 2938—38 calibre, 24 inch barrel, weight 5½ lbs. 38 center fire S. & W. cartridges.	" 7.00

Packed, 10 rifles in a case.

5

PAGES FROM HOPKINS AND ALLEN CATALOG

pounds, and made for the .22 Long rim-fire case. A 6-pound, 26-inch barrel rifle in .32 Long rim-fire was also offered in this style.

The firm next introduced a long series of rifles for various rim-fire cartridges, including the .22 rim-fire, .25 Stevens rim-fire, .32 Long rim-fire, .38 Long rim-fire, and the Smith & Wesson .38 center-fire cartridge. These model numbers ran from #722 to #2938.

The Hopkins & Allen Schuetzen rifle #3925 had a 26-inch barrel, octagonal in shape, caliber .25/20 Single-shot. It also had a Schuetzen

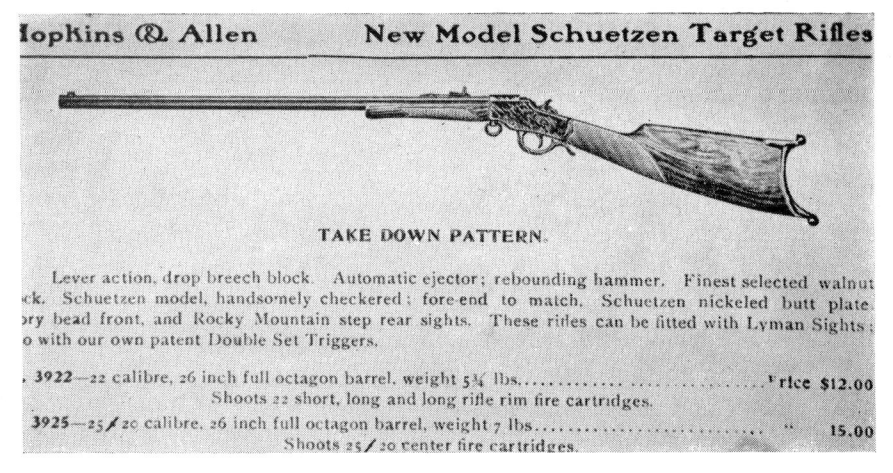

PAGE FROM HOPKINS AND ALLEN CATALOG

butt plate and, in addition, set triggers. This was a light Schuetzen rifle, more on the order of a "Ladies" model.

These rifles were usually stamped "Made by the Hopkins & Allen Manfg. Co., Norwich, Conn., U.S.A." and also "The Merwin Hulbert & Co., Junior, Pat. June 23, '85, Oct. 2, '88."

A .32/20 Hopkins & Allen rifle with an extra shot barrel in 20-gauge on page 247. This barrel interchanges with the rifle barrel after unscrewing the barrel-holding screw. The barrels slip into place and have no threads on them. The .32/20 rifle barrel carries its own extractor with it, and the 20-gauge shot shell extractor remains in the frame on the left side.

THE FARROW RIFLE

The Farrow single-shot rifle was the product of the Farrow Arms Company, which was headed by W. Milton Farrow. For many years Mr. Farrow was associated with Marlin at the time the Ballard rifles were being manufactured, and it was he who was responsible for many of the improvements on the Ballard rifle and for many of the fine target models in the Ballard line. The famous #6½ Ballard Offhand Butt Plate was of his devising, and the catalogs for many years designated this as the "Farrow Offhand Plate." His famous bullet lubricant offered with the Ballard rifles also carried his name.

The Smithsonian Institution in Washington, D. C., displays a fine midrange Ballard rifle with which W. Milton Farrow set several records.

In view of his association with fine rifles, and of the fact that he himself was a target rifleman of ability, it is not surprising to find that the rifle he eventually developed and marketed is a fine one.

This action is a close-coupled, falling-block, hammer type, in which the wood of the stock covers much of the actual length of the frame. The centrally hung hammer has a very short and fast fall, and the hammer spur is quite long and curved.

The lever is a four-finger loop lever, similar to the Ballard lever, except that the Farrow lever is slotted to fit over the trigger instead of having an open space for the trigger, as is the case with the Ballard.

The Farrow rifles were all pistol-grip type; at least, I am inclined to believe this to be true inasmuch as I never saw a straight-grip type.

There were two grades of Farrow rifles, No. 1 being the best grade, having a stock and fore end of fine imported walnut and fine checkering. Schuetzen butt plates were standard on this rifle, but other types were available upon order. Barrels round, part-octagonal or full-octagonal, in a great variety of calibers, were to be had. Farrow had no special odd calibers of his own; his rifles were chambered for almost all standard calibers available.

The No. 2 grade was stocked with American walnut in plain quality, and it was not checkered. Blued frames on these rifles were usual, but nickel-plated frames could be had.

Men who really know the Farrow rifles say that while the design was most excellent, the materials used in the actions left a great deal to be desired.

The Farrow rifle was evidently largely a custom proposition, as no two are exactly alike. Testifying to the fact that the company was open to suggestions and would listen to almost any idea, is one barrel that was made by Farrow Arms Co. and so marked. This is a .38/55 30-inch #4 full-octagonal barrel that came on one of my engraved Ballards. This barrel has 14 grooves—count 'em—14!—and what it was originally made for, I have no idea, of course. Of all the bullets I have put through it, it handles the 330-grain .38 caliber

A BOX OF THE FARROW LUBRICANT AS OFFERED IN THE
1882 BALLARD CATALOG

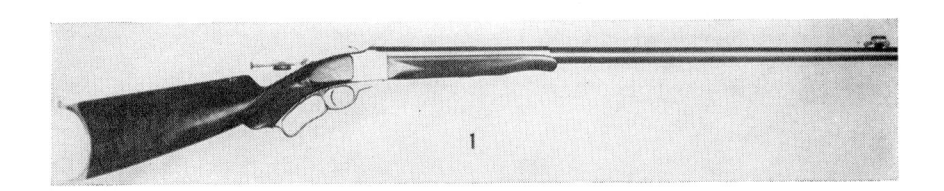

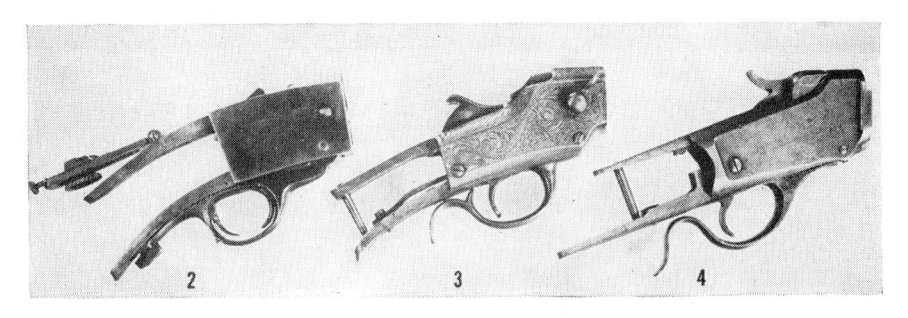

FARROW TARGET RIFLE
1. Farrow Target Rifle .32/40 caliber.
2. A later Farrow action showing the Vernier windage and elevation rear sight integral with top tang. Also the odd set triggers. This action number is 116.
3. Engraved Hopkins and Allen action.
4. The earlier type Winchester single-shot low side-wall action showing the unmilled breechblock which looks similar to the high wall breechblock but is not interchangeable with the latter.

paper-patch bullets best, and will really shoot these with superb accuracy. This barrel, as stated, is marked "Farrow Arms Co." No number or caliber markings are to be seen. It was evidently made from fine-grained soft steel or iron, as the bore has a beautiful finish and is still perfect, with sharp lands and deep grooves.

Farrow rifles were never made in quantity—they appeared on the single-shot scene too late for that—so today they are found only in the hands of collectors.

A very illuminating article on the Farrow, by N. H. Roberts, appeared in the *American Rifleman* for May, 1937.

XII

Foreign Single-shot Rifles

SWISS AND GERMAN SCHUETZENS

The single-shot falling-block rifle was an American invention; rather, it was the result of several different patents which were first made in the United States. It is slightly ironical, however, that this type of action reached its greatest development in Continental Europe. It evidently answered a need over there, and the great variety of actions which were made in Germany, Switzerland, and, to a limited extent, in the British Isles, is amazing.

There were so many conversions and perversions on the Peabody-Martini action made in Germany, Austria, and Switzerland, that it is impossible to show them all. This action was made and used in these countries long after it was abandoned in the United States; in fact, only World War II put a stop to the manufacture of this type.

The original Peabody-Martini as made by the Providence Tool Company, Providence, R. I., was—and is—a fine action; but it is only when a fine specimen of German or Swiss manufacture is examined that we see the possibilities of this system.

In the United States the companies who made only single-shot rifles such as the Peabody-Martini and Sharps found the competition offered by the various repeating rifles too keen to buck. The trend was to more fire power, whether the buyer was able to utilize it or not. The fine target rifles made in single-shot style were naturally doomed. The same trend, though in a modern tempo, may be noticed in the vast amount of interest which prevails in the autoloading mechanisms. The American buying public is very quick to adopt the newer ideas in any line and to discard the old, regardless of the merits of the discarded article.

In Europe the whole firearms field is on a much different basis

V. Chr. Schilling · Suhl, Prussia.

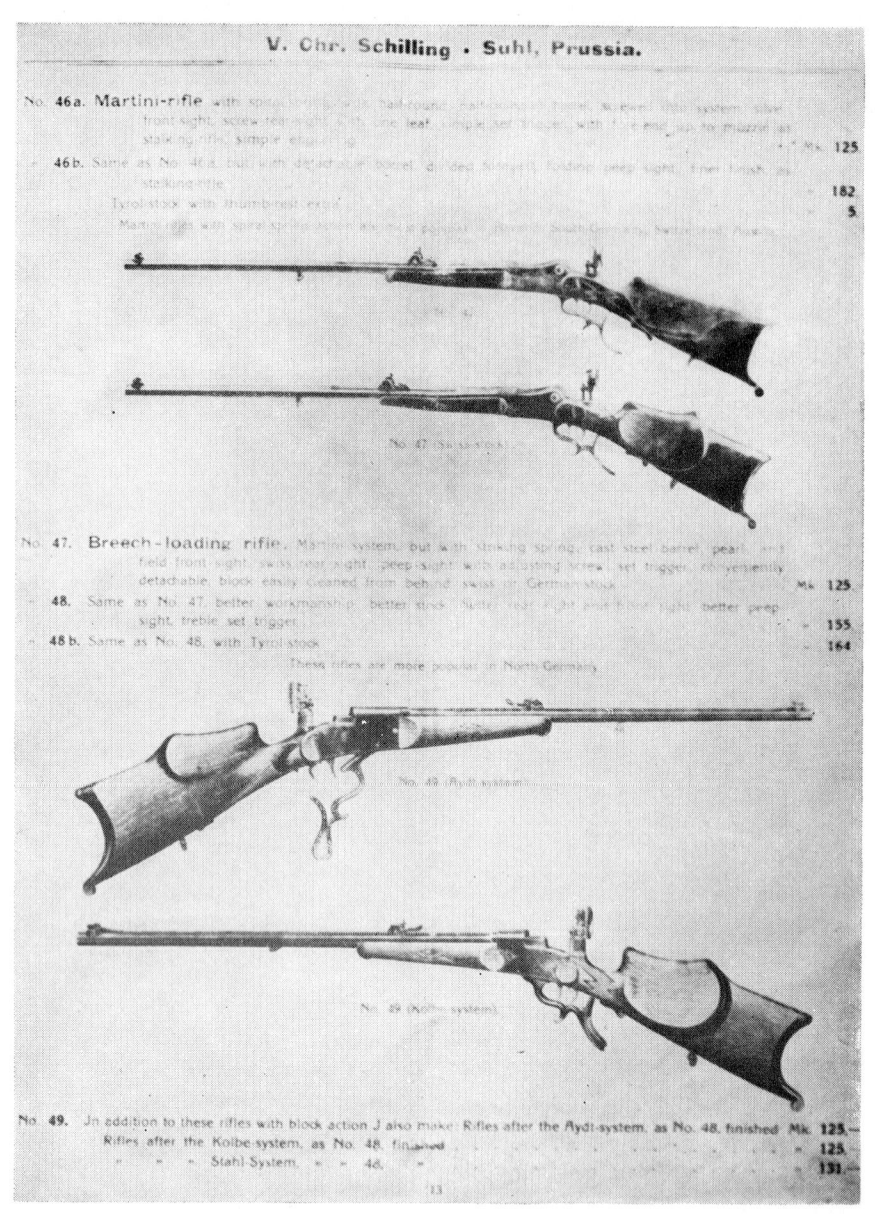

No. 46a. Martini-rifle with .... Mk. 125
  46b. Same as No. 46a, but with detachable barrel 182
       Tyrol stock with thumbrest 5

No. 47. Breech-loading rifle. Martini system, but with striking spring, cast steel barrel, pearl ... field front sight, swiss rear sight, peep sight with adjusting screw, set trigger, conveniently detachable block, easily cleaned from behind, swiss or German stock .... Mk. 125
  48. Same as No. 47, better workmanship, better stock 155
  48b. Same as No. 48, with Tyrol stock 164

These rifles are more popular in North Germany.

No. 49. In addition to these rifles with block action J also make: Rifles after the Aydt-system, as No. 48, finished Mk. 125.—
       Rifles after the Kolbe-system, as No. 48, finished .... 125.—
       "   "   " Stahl-System, " " 46,   "   .... 131.—

PAGE FROM THE CATALOG OF V. CHR. SCHILLING, SUHL,
PRUSSIA

V. Chr. Schilling · Suhl, Prussia.

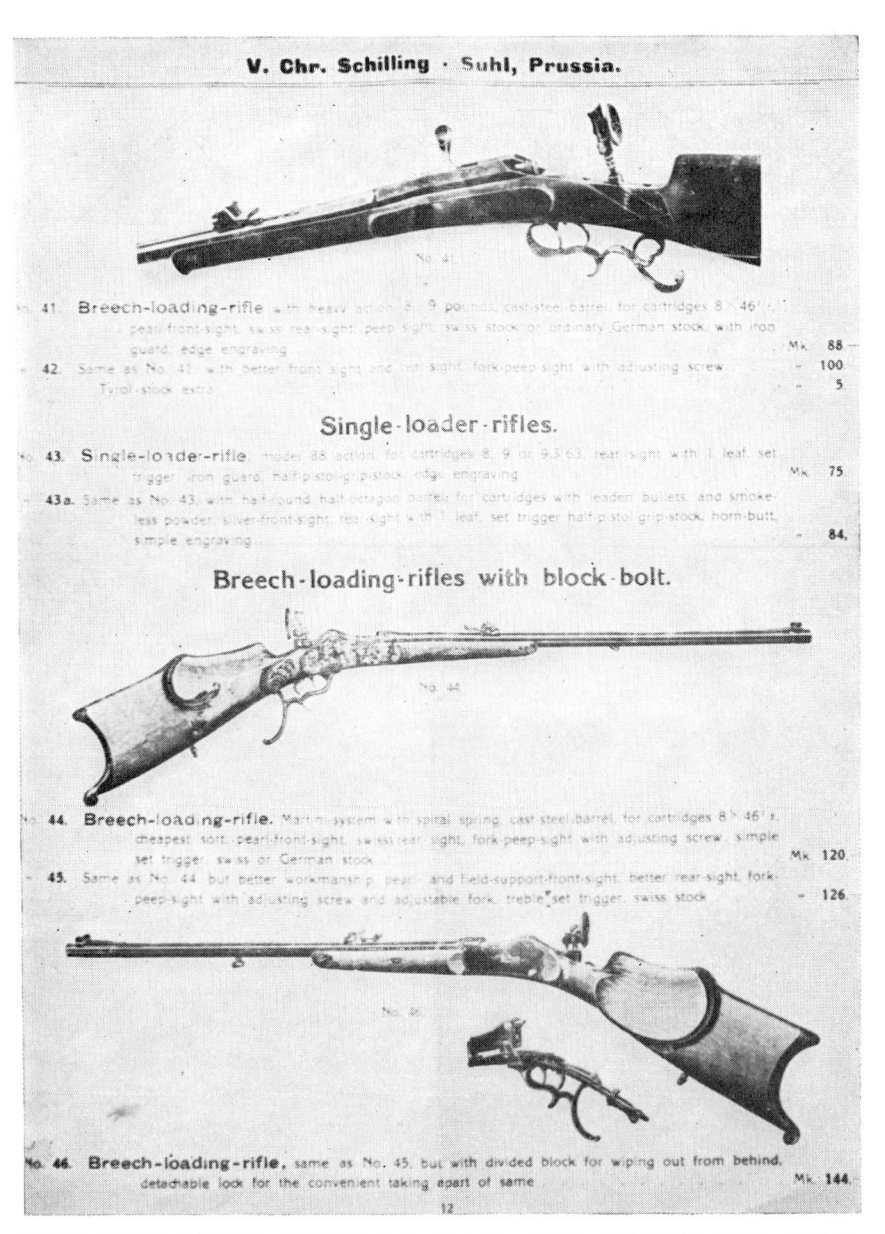

No. 41.

No. 41. **Breech-loading-rifle** with heavy action, 8—9 pounds, cast-steel-barrel, for cartridges 8×46½, pearl-front-sight, swiss rear-sight, peep-sight, swiss stock or ordinary German stock, with iron guard, edge engraving .... Mk 88.—
No. 42. Same as No. 41, with better front sight and rear sight, fork-peep-sight with adjusting screw. — 100.—
Tyrol-stock extra .... — 5.—

Single-loader-rifles.

No. 43. **Single-loader-rifle**, model 88 action, for cartridges 8, 9 or 9.3/63, rear sight with 1 leaf, set trigger, iron guard, half-pistol-grip-stock, edge engraving .... Mk 75.—
No. 43a. Same as No. 43, with half-round half-octagon barrel for cartridges with leaden bullets, and smokeless powder, silver-front-sight, rear-sight with 1 leaf, set trigger, half-pistol-grip-stock, horn-butt, simple engraving .... — 84.—

Breech-loading-rifles with block-bolt.

No. 44.

No. 44. **Breech-loading-rifle**, Martini-system with spiral spring, cast-steel-barrel, for cartridges 8×46½, cheapest sort, pearl-front-sight, swiss rear-sight, fork-peep-sight with adjusting screw, simple set trigger, swiss or German stock .... Mk 120.—
No. 45. Same as No. 44 but better workmanship, pearl- and field-support-front-sight, better rear-sight, fork-peep-sight with adjusting screw and adjustable fork, treble set trigger, swiss stock .... — 126.—

No. 46.

No. 46. **Breech-loading-rifle**, same as No. 45, but with divided block for wiping out from behind, detachable lock for the convenient taking apart of same .... Mk 144.—

PAGE FROM THE CATALOG OF V. CHR. SCHILLING, SUHL, PRUSSIA

from that of the United States. Hunting is available to but a select few, and so the great freedom of owning a gun or many guns as Americans know it is unknown over there. For the most part, the only firearm the ordinary man could possess in those countries would be a target rifle. Due to the usually highly specialized style of these rifles they naturally were not used a great deal in the pursuit of game, therefore the temptations and opportunities to poach upon the rich landed gentry were minimized. Since all the game supply was controlled by this so-called landed gentry, the need for a hunting rifle or shotgun was very small.

In certain sections of Germany—notably South Germany—and Switzerland, the single-shot target rifle was very popular. It offered the only means of satisfying the urge and fascination of the rifled tube that is common to outdoors men the world over. Target shooting in these sections became a national pastime, and consequently the highly specialized Schuetzen was a natural result. If the decline in this sport in America had been ten or fifteen years later, it might possibly have resulted in the evolution of our own rifles to a point comparable with some of the fine foreign specimens.

In conversing with men who lived in Germany, Austria, Switzerland, and other European countries before the war broke out, in 1939, I found them to be in agreement on one thing: that the rifles seen on the target ranges of Europe were fancy models. These men did not seem to be interested in the plain models. As a consequence, when one of these rifles falls into American hands today it is usually a highly decorated masterpiece.

The craftsmanship shown in some of these rifles is in a class by itself and almost unbelievable to the man who is prone to judge fine rifle-making by our own somewhat plain, though excellent, modern rifles. There are some specimens that are inferior, of course, and many are cheaply made, and of not too good materials; but the great majority as made by the large arms manufacturers and the specimens as hand-fabricated by the smaller gunmakers are truly beautiful weapons. The handwork is, of course, what makes them so desirable, and naturally the great difference in the wage scale between European and American workmen is an item not to be overlooked.

Many of these European expert gunmakers took a pride in their craftsmanship that is hard for some modern workmen—especially Americans—to understand. It was a family tradition in the old countries to hand down from father to son the vocation that had been in the family for years. Also the creed of these artisans—to judge by some of their work—was evidently, "Do the job, no matter how much time is involved."

Quantity production as Americans know it was unknown to these master craftsmen of Europe. This, no doubt, accounts for the great variety of different systems used in constructing Continental target rifles. The most popular system seems to have been the Martini, and different sections of the country favored different variations on this pattern. For instance, in southern Germany, Bavaria, and other nearby areas, the Martini as made with a coil mainspring was the most popular; while in the northern parts of the same countries the same action made with a flat mainspring was more popular.

The Stahl system Martini is perhaps the best-known of these various systems. It featured a demountable lower tang and quickly removable breechblock, and usually was not cleanable from the breech; however, some variations are cleaned from this end.

The Swiss Martinis were made in several styles also, though the great variety as shown in the German versions is lacking in the Swiss rifles. These Swiss and German Martinis were almost invariably made with double-set triggers; something never seen in the Peabody-Martini and the Martini-Henry.

The set triggers as used on these Martini actions of German and Swiss make are the finest set triggers I have ever used. They show more thought and engineering, plus careful workmanship, than were ever put upon American set triggers. These, like many of the actions, barrels, etc., were largely handmade, and so are beautifully finished on all parts, and show a great variety of systems used.

The lower tang containing the triggers is usually quickly removable, and sometimes it also has the lever or sear attached, as well.

As an example of the confusing and varied actions used on some of these rifles, the following is quoted from the 1912-1914 catalog issued by Ernst Friedrich Büchel in Thüringen:

BÜCHEL'S ORIGINAL "MEISTER" BÜCHSEN. This is a falling-block, hammerless Schuetzen action and lever. The front trigger of the set triggers is reversed, so it must be pushed instead of pulled to set the rear or pull trigger. The stock is the Swiss, or "Tirolerschaft," pattern.

The same action is also offered with a demountable barrel and auto-

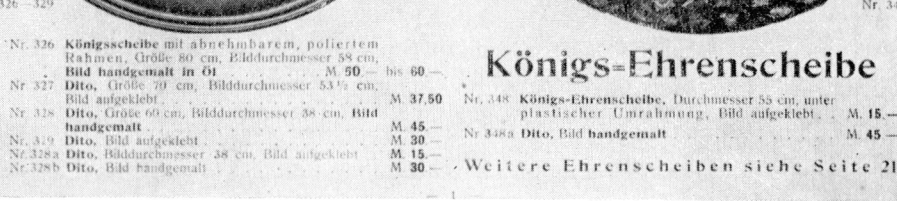

PAGE FROM THE CATALOG OF G. C. HAENEL, SUHL, PRUSSIA

Haenel-Original-Aydt-Scheibenbüchsen

Viele erste Preise und Meisterschaften sind damit errungen.

Die Haenel-Original-Aydtbüchsen sind als **anerkannt allerbestes Fabrikat** überall zur Genüge bekannt, so daß sich weitere Empfehlung, sowie die besondere Hervorhebung der Vorzüge erübrigt. Mit Haenel-Original-Aydtbüchsen wurden u. a. folgende Preise errungen:

Beim deutschen Bundesschießen in Hamburg:
Erster, zweiter u. vierter Preis d. Hansameisterschaft.
Erster Preis der Feldmeisterschaft
Erster Preis für die meisten Blättchen an einem Tage
Erster Preis auf Feldfestscheibe „Deutschland"

Beim Mitteldeutschen Bundesschießen in Berlin:
I. Preis Feldfestscheibe „Deutschland"
II. Preis Standfestscheibe „Heimat"
I. Preis Standfestscheibe „Gera"
II. Preis Standmeisterscheibe
II. Preis Feldmeisterschaft
II. Preis Standmeisterschaft

Bei den deutschen Kampfspielen im Juli 1922 in Berlin: Beide Meisterschaften v. Deutschland auf Stand u. Feld, sowie weitere Preise. 1924 und 1925 viele erste Preise und Meisterschaften. 1926: 48. Bundesschießen in Hamburg:
Goldene Senatsmedaille und **I Preis** mit dem seltenen Resultat: **20 — 19 — 20 — 20.**

Haenel-Original-Aydt mit Schweizerschaft

Nr. 1300	Scheibenbüchse Haenel-Original-Aydt, für Normalpatrone (8,15×46 Norm.), bestes Fabrikat mit ff. Patent-Stecher, Supportvisier, auswechselbarem Perl- und Feldkorn (leicht ohne Werkzeug auswechselbar), Visierschiene, ff dreifaches Stechschloß, bester Stahllauf mit besonders feinen Zügen, Schweizer Schäftung, ca. 11 Pfd. schwer, mit Aufschrift Haenel-Original-Aydt, ohne Gravierung, einschl. Reservefeder	M. 210.—
Nr. 1301	Haenel-Original-Aydtbüchse, wie Nr. 1300, aber mit **Daumenauflage**	„ 215.—
Nr. 1303	Haenel-Original-Aydtbüchse, wie Nr. 1300, aber mit hochfeiner altdeutscher Wetzgravur	„ 240.—
Nr. 1304	Haenel-Original-Aydtbüchse, wie Nr. 1303, mit hochfeiner altdeutscher Wetzgravur, mit gefalztem Lauf und Laufabnahme-Vorrichtung	„ 270 —

Haenel-Original-Aydt mit Tirolerschaft und Daumenkanzel

Nr. 1305	Haenel-Original-Aydtbüchse, Kal. 8,15×46, Normal-Ausführung wie Nr. 1300 aber mit Tirolerschaft und Daumenkanzel	M 225
Nr. 1308	Haenel-Original-Aydtbüchse, wie vorstehende Nr. 1305, jedoch mit hochfeiner altdeutscher Wetzgravur	„ 250.—
Nr. 1309	Haenel-Original-Aydtbüchse, wie Nr. 1308, aber noch mit gefalztem Lauf und Laufabnahme-Vorrichtung	„ 280.—

Wehrmannsbüchse **Original-Haenel-Lorenz** Nr. 1314
Kal. 8,15×46 — Einzellader

Von Grund aus aus vollkommen neuen Teilen gefertigt. Sorgfältigste Präzisionsarbeit mit der bekannten hervorragenden Schußleistung aller Haenel-Läufe M. 115.—

Korntreiber für Wehrmannsbüchsen M. 3.—

Nr. 1315 Einzellader
Wehrmannsbüchse
Modell 98

Nr. 1315 Wehrmannsbüchse, in bester Qualität, mit neuem Lauf, Kal. 8,15×40 für die Schützenpatrone M. 95.—

— 4 —

PAGE FROM THE CATALOG OF G. C. HAENEL, SUHL, PRUSSIA

matic thumb safety which has a rod extending up through the grip of the stock, and is terminated in a button let into the thumb rest part of the stock.

System Müller Büchel. This is another variation made in hammerless style and with the same reversed front trigger. This action is available in plain and engraved models.

System Büchel Stecherspanner. This is another hammerless action, different of course from the two preceding models. The model is beautifully designed, with a flat, almost square breechblock containing all the essential parts, including a spiral mainspring around the firing pin. The set triggers are contained on a small plate which fastens to the bottom of the block. A Ballard-inspired design, of course, but incredibly compact and efficient. [Shades of C. H. Ballard and J. M. Marlin!] This model has a fine finger-roost Schuetzen lever. It is shown in this catalog engraved in the Altdeutsche Gravierung manner, which is a form of relief engraving, and very elaborate and striking.

System Büchel Stecherspanner with Quickly Removable Barrel. This is the same as the preceding model except that the barrel is removed by turning back a lever which lies along the forearm and holds or releases the barrel on the same principle as the little #4 Remington rolling-block take-down model. Of course in this Stecherspanner model the barrel unscrews with an easy thread instead of the plain, unthreaded shank of the #4 Remington.

System Büchel Brilliant. This is another variation on the regular Büchel Original action. The block is of slightly different design, and set triggers are mounted on the usual demountable lower tang.

System Büchel Original. This is a streamlined falling-block action with regular pattern set triggers and Schuetzen lever. This is shown with Tyrol or Swiss stock and Renaissance Gravierung, a form of relief engraving of the highest grade.

This model is also available with an extra fancy Tyrol pattern stock with finger grooves and thumb rest on right-hand side of stock. There is an extra charge for this stock.

Büchel's Perfect Büchsen. This action appears to be the same as the Original, except that the block is square at the back instead of sloping down to meet the frame. It is shown with the German pattern stock with shotgun butt. It is available also with the Tyrol or regular Schuetzen stock.

Konkurrenz Büchse System Büchel. This is an extra heavy action with still another type of block, containing all the hammer and set-trigger mechanisms. It is shown with an ornate Swiss pattern stock with the regular high Swiss style cheekpiece rolled well over the top of the

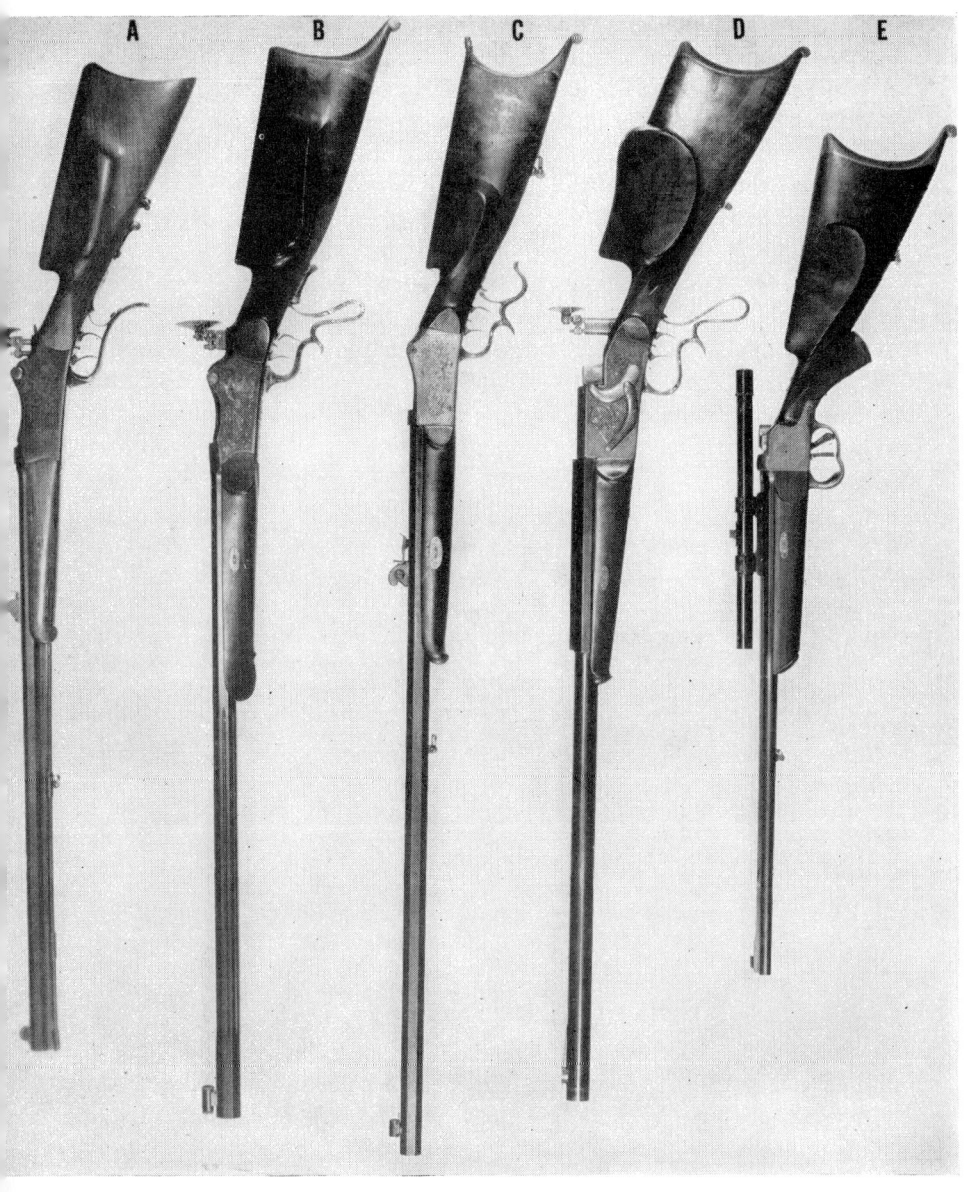

FOREIGN SINGLE-SHOT RIFLES
(See page 324 for explanation)

comb. The stock has an extreme castoff. The action is shown with the English type of small scroll engraving. Available at extra cost with German types of engraving.

SYSTEM AYDT. This is a plain version of the Aydt.[1] It is also offered with Altdeutscher Figuren Gravierung, and either the Tirolerschaft (Swiss) or Schweizerschaft (German) pattern stocks.

AYDT SCHEIBEN-BÜCHSEN. This is another variation on the Aydt system shown without the extractor and take-down pieces on the outside of the frame. This is a fancy model, with fancy checkered stock and Figuren Gravierung.[2]

SYSTEM KOLBE. Another hammerless action with locking finger lever and finger rest Tirolerschaft, etc. Available in plain and engraved types.

SYSTEM KESSLER. A plain specimen of this usually ornate rifle, as made by Büchel, it has a shotgun butt plate on the one-piece stock. [Evidently a plain target or sporting rifle.]

SYSTEM MARTINI. A Martini Schuetzen model with Swiss pattern stock is available with English type or Renaissance engraving. [This action seems to be a shorter action than the Stahl Martini, and evidently is cleaned from the breech.]

SYSTEM MARTINI WITH SPIRAL SPRING. This shows a plain Martini action with take-down feature for block and lower tang. Schuetzen lever and stock.

SYSTEM STAHL. This is a fine, demountable block and lower tang model. It has a Schuetzen lever and the regular long Stahl-Martini frame. Shown with beautiful Renaissance type engraving and German pattern stock and Schuetzen butt plate.

Shown on the same page with the Stahl described is another Martini version, with removable cheekpiece for stock. This model is unnamed.

All these Schuetzen rifles on the actions described have nicely tapered, full-octagonal barrels, plain or fluted in a variety of designs. They have a barrel rib for middle or open barrel sight, and elaborate front and rear target sights.

Most of these models were available with one of three styles of engraving: English style, German style, and the Renaissance style, which, as has been said, was the highest grade of engraving and a deep relief pattern.

[1] The Aydt is described on p. 326.
[2] This page of the catalog states that the Aydt system is an original system of C. G. Haenel, Suhl.

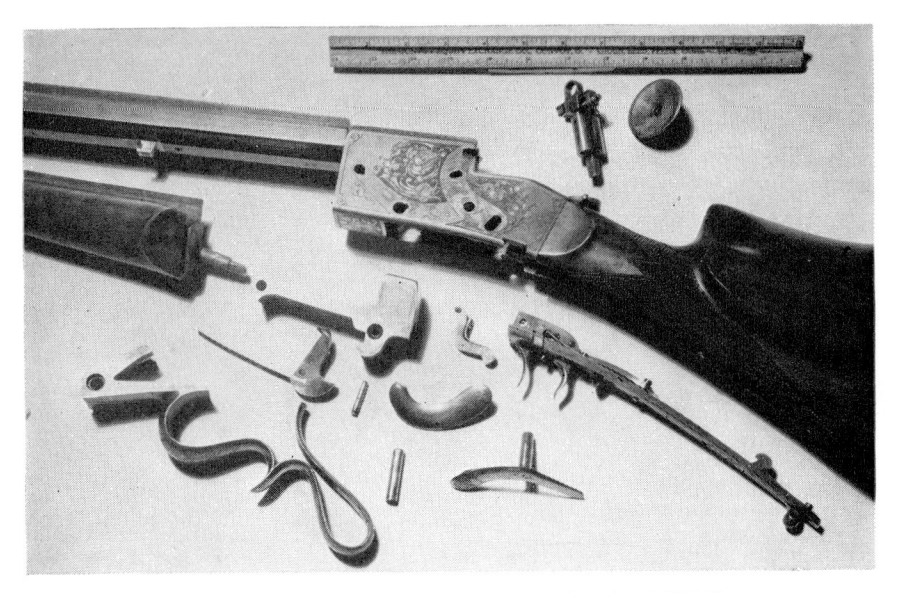

HAENEL AYDT ACTION DISMOUNTED

There are several other actions shown in this catalog, but they are for the most part minor variations on those quoted.

Plain hunting or sporting rifles were also available made up on these various actions. These models had either round or octagonal barrels, and plain levers. Stocks were usually pistol-grip style, with shotgun butt plate and small sporting pattern cheekpieces. The *Patrone Magazin*, or receptacle for three or four cartridges, was usually let into the stock at the heel or toe in these models.

Various plainer little rifles on several types of single-shot actions are also shown in this catalog, at prices greatly below the Schuetzen models. These were apparently boys' rifles. The fine Büchel and Tell target pistols are listed in this catalog in almost as great an assortment as the rifles.

On pages 312 and 313 will be seen the reproduction of a page from the catalog of V. Chr. Schilling, of Suhl, illustrating some of the various actions as manufactured by this firm. Kolbe, Aydt, and various Martini actions are shown here also.

Reproductions of pages from the catalog of C. G. Haenel, also located in Suhl, are shown on pages 316 and 317. These pages show several rifles made up on the Aydt system.

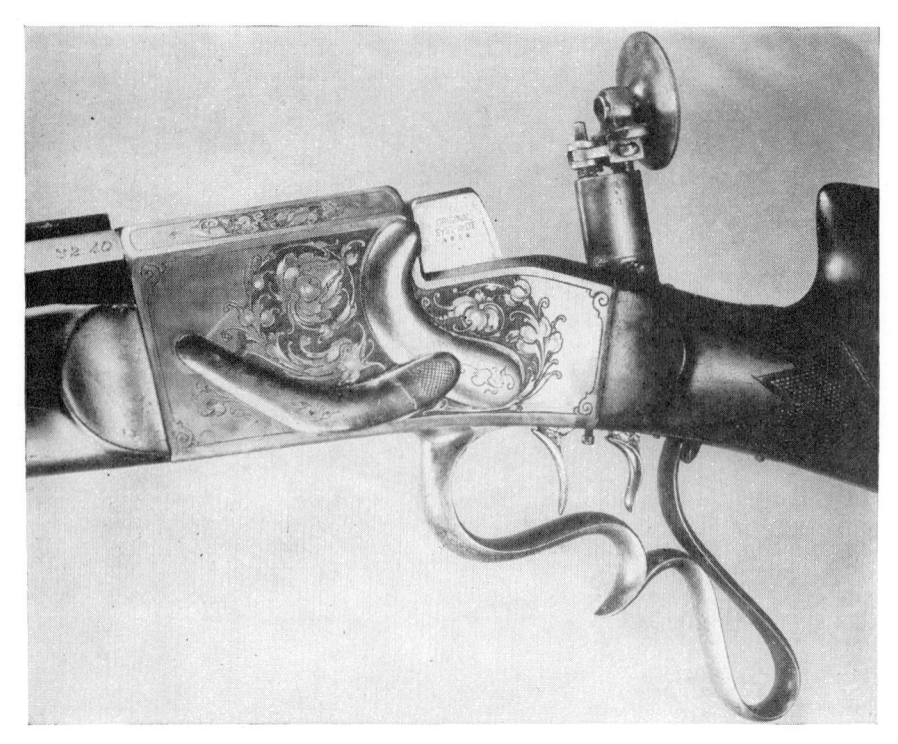

THE LEFT SIDE OF HAENEL AYDT ACTION

These foreign catalogs show many models that were made by the larger manufacturers of Europe, but of course there were many small gunshops which made up rifles on actions that were obtained from these or other makers. These custom models are naturally in a great variety, and one seldom sees two that are identical in all respects.

One of the most painstaking of these smaller custom makers was Kessler. The Kessler rifles were, for the most part, made on the Martini action after Kessler's own variation. One detail which is peculiar to the Kessler-made rifle is that the stock and fore end are made in one piece. The wood extends along the action frame on both sides, and the barrel and action are readily demountable.

Kessler usually used a ramrod under the barrel, held in thimbles on his Schuetzen and stalking models. One of his custom jobs that I once almost acquired was made in that manner. It had a full-octagonal, sharply tapered, 32-inch barrel, and a beautifully carved and checkered Schuetzen stock of fine Italian walnut. The action, lever, butt plate, and swivels were beautifully engraved in relief. The sights were the usual precision-made, hooded front and open barrel sliding on the matted rib, and several varieties of rear sights. It had a complete reloading outfit, mold, and other accessories, and many new cases. The caliber was for one of the many bottlenecked cartridges seen in these rifles, and was about 10.5mm. bore.

I looked at this rifle long, and debated pro-and-con with myself during the time it was offered for sale at one of the meetings of the Ohio Gun Collectors Association, several years ago. The price was

THE RIGHT SIDE OF THE HAENEL AYDT ACTION

UNDER SIDE OF THE HAENEL AYDT ACTION

high, as is too often the case with these superb rifles. But what halted me and caused me eventually to pass it up was the stock. It had a high Swiss or Tyrol pattern stock with the rolled-over cheekpiece, and of course it was made for a right-handed man. Since I shoot from the left shoulder, I could not even get the stock to my shoulder on that side, and as the stock was perfect in every way, I couldn't see cutting off the projection of the cheekpiece which hung over on the right side of the stock. To restock it in a manner due the balance of the rifle would have been prohibitive in expense, so very reluctantly I passed it up.

The Kessler name was inlaid in gold on the top flat of the barrel, and two gold bands encircled the barrel near the breech. It was truly a beautiful piece, and if any of these rifles were available today I know one gun crank who would pawn his family jewels to obtain one made to his specifications as regards stock.

Several fine foreign single-shot rifles from my collection are shown on page 319.

FIGURE A. The first is a German Martini made on a modified Stahl system by G. Benz, in Kiel, Germany. This is evidently a stalking or hunting rifle. It has a full-octagonal barrel, caliber 10.5mm., bottleneck.

The action is easily taken apart without tools, the lower tang carries the superb set trigger assembly and also the lever. The breechblock is removed by pushing out the pivot pin, and it comes out the top, of course. The barrel can be cleaned from the breech by turning out a large headless screw that fills in the cut at the rear between the side walls. This action is engraved in a floral scroll motif; it is not elaborate, but well-balanced. The breechblock and lever are also engraved lightly, as well as the steel shotgun butt plate. The front, middle, and rear sights all are adjustable by means of a key. This is the means of adjustment used on most of these rifles. The cartridge, recapper and decapper mold, and other tools are shown with the rifle.

The only markings on the rifle are the words "G. Benz in Kiel" on the top flat of the barrel. The wood is plain European walnut of some variety unknown to me, and is checkered only on the grip. The pattern is the Schweizerschaft, or German style stock.

FIGURE B. This is a deluxe German Martini, manufacturer unknown. The action is one version of the Stahl system, in which the

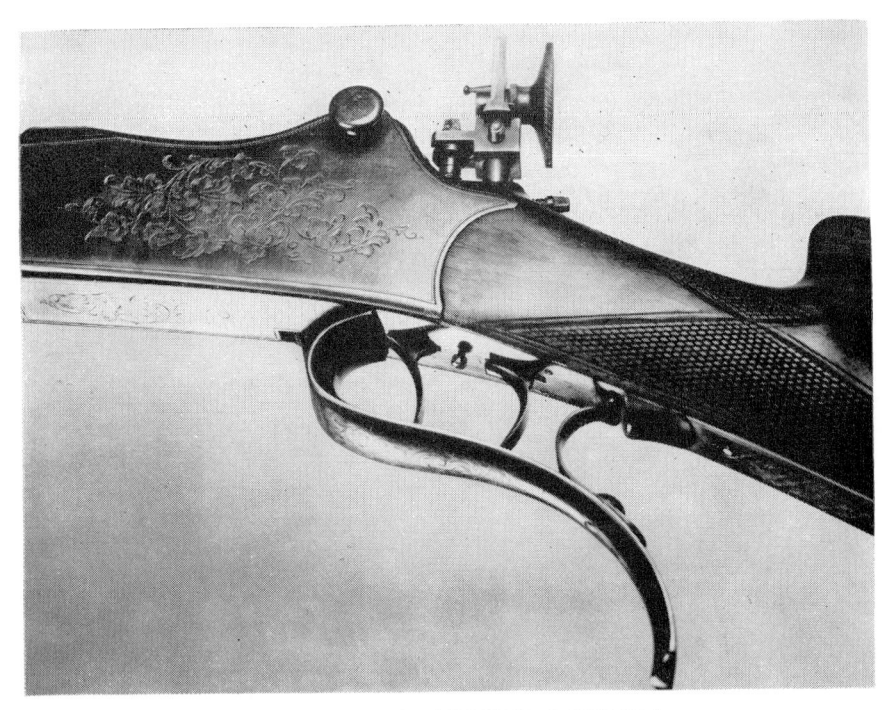

THE BENZ MARTINI ACTION

frame is split at the rear, facilitating cleaning from the breech. This split portion is filled by a lug on the breechblock which must, of course, be removed to clean from the breech. In this action the lower, quickly removable tang carries the triggers only. The breechblock comes out the top, of course, as in all Martini systems.

The action is engraved in a beautiful style of relief engraving, showing a Schuetzen rifleman in typical Tyrolean costume on the right side, and a barmaid rushing large foaming steins of beer to the thirsty shooters on the left side. The lever, butt plate, upper and lower tangs and rear of barrel are also engraved. This rifle has a 30-inch heavy (about #5) full-octagonal barrel. The octagonal flats are all fluted for most of the length, and the top flat is full length matted in a fine pattern. Sights are the usual type, adjusted by a key fitting the square heads of the screws. The stock is in the German pattern, of very dark Italian or French walnut, and it has a heavy butt plate which is adjustable for various degrees of pitch by pushing a small release on one side of the two-piece plate. The barrel is bored and chambered for the .30/30 Winchester center-fire case, and was made for use with lead bullets.

This rifle is one of a pair made for a Cincinnati, Ohio, rifleman a few years ago. The other was made to handle the .30-'06 case and lead bullets.

The results I have obtained with this rifle and the proper lead bullets, with mild loads of smokeless powder, would no doubt surprise many who believe that the .30/30 is a not too accurate hunting caliber.[3]

There are no markings on this rifle showing the manufacturer. It is the finest Martini I have ever owned or hope to own.

FIGURE C. This shows a beautiful Swiss Martini rifle, caliber .41 Swiss rim-fire. The action is made more nearly like the Peabody-Martini than any German or Swiss action examined by this author. The take-down is the same as the Peabody-Martini's, but it has fine set triggers. This action is not quickly demountable—as are many of the Swiss types—and of course it is not cleanable from the breech. Instead of the usual double-firing pin holes seen on the .41 rim-fire Swiss Martinis, this one has a single hole, and some day I plan to have an extra center-fire pin made and fitted so that center-fire reloadable cases may be used.

This fine Swiss Schuetzen has a German pattern stock with small cheekpiece of the most beautiful burl walnut imaginable. It has the lighter type butt plate, with a top prong that screws into the wood, thus serving also the purpose of a top butt plate screw. This rifle is #147, and the word Gusstahl (caststeel) is stamped on the top flat of the barrel at the breech.

Both sides of the action are engraved in a similar scroll design, but the right side has a ribbon worked into the scroll work with the words "Widmer Ettiswil Luzerne" inlaid in gold thereon. This was evidently the maker's name, and I wonder if it is the same "Widmer" who made many fine pistols in Lucerne, Switzerland?

This rifle has a full-octagonal plain barrel, 34 inches long.

FIGURE D. This is the Aydt system as made by Haenel in Suhl. It is little known in the United States. I have seen less than a dozen of these actions in this country.

This particular specimen has been rebarreled at some time in

---

[3] The cartridge is accurate, but its light repeaters are not.

A FINE GERMAN MARTINI SYSTEM RIFLE

the past with a #5 part-octagonal .32/40 Stevens barrel. The number on the barrel is 25, and action number is 4014.

The levers shown on the left side of the receiver are the extractor and take-down release to dismantle the action. Various parts of this action dismounted are shown on page 321. The lever is beautifully engraved in a mythical figure design somewhat similar to that on the left side of the action. The right side of the frame shows a winged cherub with bow and arrow. (Can this be that legendary cherub, Cupid?)

This rifle shows the "Tirolerschaft," or Swiss, pattern of stock in a beautifully made pattern. It has the high Schuetzen cheekpiece, and also the thumb rest carved on the right side of the stock.

The action has fine set triggers, and the rifle is the most finely accurate Schuetzen rifle I have ever shot (and I own some fine Pope and Schoyen muzzle-loading rifles also.) With 9 grains of #80 powder and the 200-grain Dr. Hudson .32/40 bullet seated in the breech with a breech bullet seater, it shoots with gilt-edged accuracy. The quick ignition of the action, the fine set triggers, and other excellent features no doubt have a great deal to do with this accuracy, but the fine old Stevens barrel (pre-Pope Stevens) will no doubt take the lion's share of the credit, as well it should. However, the amazing thing about this barrel is the way it handles a usually mediocre load of ordinary smokeless powder with none of the great pains taken in the loading that is customary with other Schuetzen rifles I use. This rifle weighs 14¾ pounds without the Stevens scope, which fits the dovetail rib on the barrel.

Figure E. This shows an odd rifle which, for lack of a better name, I call the "Nagel." The right side of the frame is marked "Nagel U. Menz Hofbüchsenm: in Baden"; and the left side, "Patent Arthur Heeren Y Massa."

This is a hammerless set trigger action of unusual and intriguing design. The trigger guard opens from the front instead of the rear, as is customary. The trigger is set by pushing forward the rear trigger, which is really a continuation of the inside striker, or hammer. A gold inlay line on the inside of the guard shows when the trigger hammer is on safety. It is cocked by simply pulling down the lever.

THE NAGEL ACTION OPEN TO RECEIVE CARTRIDGE

I have found very few men who are familiar with this largely handmade single-shot. To most machinists to whom I have shown the rifle, many of the milling cuts on the inside of this frame appear impossible to make.

Hervey Lovell, the Indianapolis, Indiana, gunmaker, showed me, on one of my visits with him, three of these rifles. One had a deluxe shotgun butt stock with a gold name plate. It was originally a 9mm. caliber, but it had been relined to .22/3000 Lovell caliber. Another one—the mate to the first—was relined to the same caliber, and both were imported by an Indiana shooter and converted by Mr. Lovell to the smaller caliber. These rifles were beautiful sporting models of the best possible finish, and were marked similar to my specimen shown here, though they were a later version and their serial numbers were higher than my number 82 action. Mr. Lovell had still another Nagel, this one having essentially the same action as the others except that it was made with a take-down barrel and was marked "Bland, London." Evidently the famous Bland had imported some—or at least one—of these actions and marked them with his name. This one was a very light, short-barreled model, originally

THE NAGEL ACTION, CLOSED, UNCOCKED

in .303 British caliber, and Mr. Lovell had made a K-Hornet of it. The stock work was much inferior to that on the German-made rifles of the same pattern action.

When I first obtained my Nagel it had an old full-octagonal .22 Winchester barrel fitted to it, and was chambered—evidently with a rattail file—for the .218 Bee cartridge. This action was no doubt barreled up in heavy barrel style as a Schuetzen rifle originally, but I wanted something else and finally found a fine little short Mauser action with ruined ribbed barrel 22 inches long.

This barrel was fitted to the Nagel by Charles Johnson and lined with a nickel steel liner for the .218 Bee cartridge. The breechblock was bushed properly and a new fore end of imported walnut was fitted to the smaller barrel. This barrel, being of part-octagonal, part-round pattern, with a full-length raised, matted rib, looks very well on the action, and the shooting qualities with scope leave nothing to be desired for a varment rifle. I made a scope mount that straddled the rib and is pinned on with $\frac{1}{16}$-inch drill rod pins. This did not mutilate the fine barrel, and it is easily removable.

The heavy stock of dense European walnut and the Schuetzen style butt plate of course unbalance the rifle with this light-weight barrel, and I have often thought of having the rifle restocked. Most gun stockers, however, take one look at the terrific curves on the frame and tangs of this action, shudder, and quickly change the subject; so my Nagel still sports the original stock.

I went into Niedner's at Dowagiac, Mich., once, dragging this rifle behind me, and even Thomas Shellhamer hadn't seen one like it. Needless to say, Mr. Shellhamer didn't enthuse too much over the stocking problem.

This action seems to be extremely strong in every way; the only weak feature is the extraction, which could be improved upon somewhat as the leverage upon the end of this extractor is rather short.

The Nagel is one foreign single-shot action that we cannot state was copied from an American type. It is unique and original in every respect.

This section on continental single-shot rifles could be expanded indefinitely, as there is a host of this type to fascinate the collector, but for lack of space—and paper—they must go unsung here.

BRITISH SINGLE-SHOT RIFLES

THERE are several single-shot rifles made in Great Britain at various times in the past which deserve mention, but unlike British shotguns, which are typically British and of the finest design, the single-shots have little to impress the true dyed-in-the-wool single-shot lover. Some long-range, prone-pattern rifles were made after various American rifle teams convinced the British at Creedmoor, Long Island, U. S. A., and at Dollymount, Ireland, that the American arms were superior to their own muzzle-loading, long-range target rifles.

I have yet, however, to see a British-made Schuetzen pattern of rifle; and as for set triggers, the only ones to be seen are the single-set type as used on some British percussion or flintlock arms. There may have been some single-shot breech-loading rifles made in Great Britain with double-set triggers, but I have never run across a single one. However, as has been said so often, "There is no new thing under the sun"; or as Shakespeare so aptly put it, "There are more things in heaven and earth, Horatio, than are dreamt of in your philosophy." So I may yet see a specimen of British arms manufacture so equipped.

The *Martini-Henry Rifle* as made in England on the Peabody-Martini action is common and familiar to almost everyone. The removable mechanism of the Martini action was first made by M. Francotte, of Liége, Belgium, and one sees many British Martini rifles stamped with "Francotte Patent." Certain Martini actions which were sent to Hervey Lovell a few years ago from South America also carry Francotte's patent.

The Martini action was adopted by Great Britain in 1871, and W. W. Greener, in *The Gun and Its Development* (Eighth Edition, 1907), states the following:

> Mr. Martini submitted his rifle in 1869 and the committee reported on it in the same year. The action was somewhat modified at the Enfield factory. The .450 barrel of Mr. Henry was used with the Boxer cartridge case holding 85 grains powder and a bullet of 480-grains weight. The Henry barrels consisted of seven grooves. The lands and the centers of the grooves are contained in the same circle.

In a later model the bore was reduced to .400 caliber, and some thousands were made. Shortly after this the Martini-Henry was given up for a magazine arm.

There were a few other Martini actions made at various times in England, and all I have seen were very plain actions. Some are seen in large sporting calibers as well as in the later .303 caliber.

The British-made Swinburn action closely resembles the Martini, but has the ordinary "V" mainspring instead of the spiral type.

The *Henry Breechloading Rifle* is described by Greener as follows:

> This rifle closely resembles the Sharps carbine, the only difference is that the latter has the lever and trigger guard in one piece, while the Henry has a separate lever fitting over the trigger guard.
>
> Mr. Henry improved his breechloader by making it hammerless and fitting an extractor similar to the Martini, retaining the same breechblock but dispensing with the side lock. This reduced the movements to the same number as the Martini.

This Henry is seen in several types, the earlier models having a large side hammer like the Sharps (from which the action was copied) and an under lever similar to those found on the Farquharson. Some of these Henry side-hammer actions have the hammer on the left side of the frame. This Henry was, of course, a step along to the later hammerless Farquharson.

Another early British action was the *Field*, which was made in two types. In one model the block was of the falling type, as in the Sharps and Henry, and the other model contained a hinged breechblock similar to the Martini. In both models the blocks were actuated by a side lever. The lever is pushed forward to depress the block; and this is not a hammerless action but has an outside central hammer.

The *Westley Richards Sliding Block Rifle* is another action noted by Greener:

> This action, the joint production of Messrs. Deeley and Edge, consists of a vertically sliding breechblock which contains the tumbler (or hammer), mainspring, and other lock work. The guard and lever are in one, and pivoted to action beneath the barrel.

Another variation of this model had a horizontal striker and hammer and fewer parts than the above.

FOREIGN SINGLE-SHOT RIFLES 333

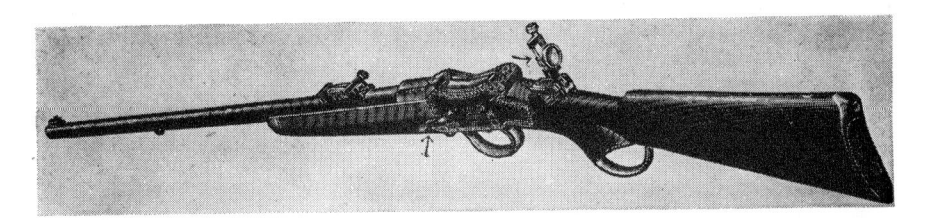

BRITISH MARTINI RIFLES AS MADE BY GREENER

The *Farquharson Match Rifle* is probably the best-known British single-shot, unless it would be the BSA [4] Martini Match rifle.

There is a great deal of misinformation concerning this action known as the Farquharson. Greener states that it was first known as the "Gibbs and Pitt breech action." Other authorities trace it down through the Sharps, Henry, and Westley Richards actions to its present form. It is present in many variations and marked with several manufacturers' names.

Thomas Shellhamer of the Niedner Rifle Corporation, at Dowagiac, Mich., states that he knows of at least seven different types of Farquharson actions, and on one trip up to Dowagiac he showed me four types of actions which were awaiting new barrels.

Another man who has visited England and brought back many fine specimens of this type states emphatically that this action was never made in England but was manufactured in Belgium for various British gunmaking firms who fitted it with their barrels, stocked it, and otherwise adapted it to their own equipment.

The Farquharson is a very strong action, the strongest we have in single-shot type, and was made for many powerful black powder and cordite cartridges. If in good condition or properly reconditioned, it is probably strong enough to hold almost any of our modern calibers. Its best use is, no doubt, when barreled up as a powerful rimmed caliber for large-game shooting. To use an action of this

[4] Birmingham Small Arms Company.

ENGRAVED SWISS MARTINI

size and bulk on a small-game or varment job is certainly wasting a lot of scrap iron. It is a bulky action and not adaptable to restocking with a modern close pistol-grip pattern stock.

Some of these actions seen are finely engraved with the small English type scroll engraving, and are very handsome. They are seen marked with Gibbs, Westley Richards, and other famous firm names, and with several types of safeties; some are even seen without a safety of any kind.

The side-lever actions as made by Westley Richards are the hammerless type and contain essentially the same parts and mechanism as the Farquharson, while being much neater in appearance.

A specimen of this action as shown on page 341, Figure I, has been rebarreled and restocked.

Page 745 in the 1907 Edition of Greener's *The Gun and Its Development* shows a *Farquharson Match Rifle* made up on the long-range prone pattern, with tall vernier rear and wind-gauge, spirit-

---

THE FRASER RIFLE—FARQUHARSON'S PATENT
A   The Fraser Side Lever Rifle, Caliber .303, British. Fraser's Patent, Daniel Fraser & Co., Edinburgh. This rifle has a shotgun type safety and leaf rear sight with 100, 200 and 300 yard leafs.
B   Farquharson's Patent, made by George Gibbs, Bristol. Caliber .255 Jeffrys.

A THE FRASER RIFLE. B FARQUHARSON'S PATENT
(See facing page for explanation)

level front sight. (A *Greener Match Rifle* of the same style is also shown here.)

The *Martini Match Rifle* as made by the Birmingham Small Arms Company, and also by Vickers, is too well known among modern riflemen to permit of detailed description here. These are well-made, accurate rifles, and are the standard small-bore match rifle used by the British Miniature Rifle clubs. The Vickers rifle uses a one-piece stock similar to the fine Schuetzen rifles made by Kessler of Germany on his variation of the Stahl-Martini.

THE ROOK RIFLE. Of all the British single-shot rifles I have examined, only two were outstanding and comparable, in my humble opinion, to other single loaders. One is the small neat action made by Fraser of Edinburgh. This is a side-lever action. The block is the hammerless, vertically sliding type, and the lever must be held down to keep the breech uncovered, as it is under spring tension. It closes automatically when the lever is released.

Fraser made larger actions on this same system, I believe, but I have reference to the very small action as used on the fine little Rook rifles. The barrel shank is very small, and possibly the largest modern cartridge that can be used in this frame is the .22 Hornet.

There have been two of these rifles sent into Charles C. Johnson's shop for relining to .22 Hornet caliber, and both were for the .310 bore Rook cartridge, one that was evidently very popular in Great Britain for rabbit and bird shooting. These two rifles were made up in deluxe style, with line engraving on the receiver, finely checkered pistol-grip and fore end of fine English walnut, horn tipped and capped. The barrels were round, about 26 inches long, and nicely tapered. They were fine, light-weight rifles, and are seldom seen in the United States.

The other British single-shot that made my mouth water was a *Greener Martini Rook Rifle*. This action was a small size, somewhat smaller and neater than the BSA Martini action, and was engraved in an unusual pattern. The finger lever was curved to follow the line of the graceful pistol grip, and was ringed at the end. The light-weight round barrel was in the same .310 Rook rifle caliber as the Fraser rifle herein described. The stock and fore end were beautifully checkered, and horn capped and tipped.

This rifle was converted to a K-Hornet by Mr. Johnson, and it made an arm weighing about 5½ pounds, as I recall.

Page 652 in the Eighth edition of Greener's *The Gun and Its Development* shows a cut of one of the Greener Martini Rook Rifles almost as I have described it. They were made in both straight- and pistol-grip stock models, and were deluxe arms throughout. They have a safety button on the side of frame. The calibers were listed as: .310 bore cartridge, bullet weight 125 grains; Eley's .300; .380 Long; .360 No. 5; Eley's .250; Eley's .287/230; Eley's .320. All are rook and rabbit cartridges and of low power and light recoil.

XIII

Remodeling the Single-shot Rifle

THIS volume could hardly be considered complete without some sort of cognizance being taken of the main function of these various fine actions in the modern rifleman's scheme of things. Possibly more than any other type of firearm, the single-shot rifle has been used as the basis of a specialized, modernized target or sporting arm.

The single-shot actions, from the time of their advent to the present, have been altered, converted, perverted, cut off, welded to, bent, straightened, ruined, improved, battered, hammered, drilled, filed, and had dozens of other operations performed upon them. They have suffered and prospered at the hands of gunsmiths good and bad, amateur gunsmiths, blacksmiths, and plain woodshed butchers. No doubt they will continue to be subject to major and minor operations so long as there are any of them lying around loose and professional and amateur gun doctors are extant.

The only other type of rifle that might compete for the honor(?) of being the most altered is the military bolt action. However, being one of those peculiar guys who abhors anything that smacks of military ordnance, I would say that to my knowledge none of the military arms have ever been ruined by alterations. Even the crudest remodeling job on one of these monstrosities appears beautiful to my eyes compared with the gun as issued.

If this book were likely to be purchased by the collector of military arms there would be many repercussions from the foregoing expression of opinion; however, I feel comparatively safe. Not that the many military collectors I know aren't a fine, intelligent bunch; far from it. I have a great amount of respect for all of them and appreciate the fact that their pieces mean just as much to them as mine do to me. It is every man to his own dish, and mine happens to be single-shot target rifles, and I have no quarrel with any other collecting field. Some men like stamps, some coins, and some collect paper match covers; and so when we attack the other man's hobby we only make ourselves ridiculous. It is just that I have seen too many beautiful and useful arms made from Mauser, Springfield, and Krag actions to find any appeal left for me in the unaltered Service rifle. However, when you speak of one particular Service rifle—the American Kentucky rifle—you are on a different level altogether. I do not believe there is a man who loves the rifled tube who doesn't thrill to a fine Kentucky; but then, this was really originally a sporting and target arm, so there we are again! It's a vicious circle, isn't it?

But back to the single-shot, as that is what this volume purports to be treating of.

The Ballard, Winchester, Sharps Borchardt, and other single-shot rifles were always popular with genuine dyed-in-the wool riflemen, so it is small wonder that Pope, Zischang, Peterson, and other able gunsmiths used these actions extensively. In most cases the resulting rifle was not only a fine shooting job but a fine appearing one as well, and we can hardly call these specimens ruined. Then, too, practically all these actions were being manufactured at about the same time, so there could not have been the feeling existing then that exists now about the collection value of the original rifles.

During the last few years—most particularly since the introduction of the .22 Hornet, the .22/3000 Lovell, the R-2, .218 Bee, and other like cartridges—these actions have been more and more in demand as foundations for rifles in these calibers. They are simple mechanically, easy to work on, and comparatively easy to find. They offer the only real solution to the man wanting a fine accurate target or hunting rifle in these calibers. The various military bolt actions are usually more difficult to rebarrel and restock, and using one of these strong, large bolt actions for the smaller series of cartridges is certainly overdoing it. Of course some prefer the bolt action, and so do I for the .30-'06, the .270 WCF, and cartridges of this size or larger; and I have even enjoyed owning and shooting the fine No. 54 and No. 70 Winchester models in .22 Hornet caliber. However, I incline toward fitting the action to the cartridge, if I make myself clear. The various single-shot actions lend themselves admirably to rifles of any weight wanted, and they are a source of much pride of ownership when properly remodeled.

I have never yet remodeled—or caused to be remodeled—any fine, rare, or odd-caliber single-shot rifle, as I prefer them in the original shape. But I do use many that are converted to modern calibers, as I enjoy crow, hawk, and woodchuck shooting more than any other kind, unless it is playing with an old odd-caliber single-shot.

There are too many plain, ordinary hunting rifles on single-shot actions with ruined barrels, shattered stocks, and other disorders to

CONVERTED SINGLE-SHOT RIFLES
(For explanation see: A—p. 352; B—p. 353; C—p. 356; D—p. 360; E—p. 361.)

REMODELING THE SINGLE-SHOT RIFLE 341

necessitate the dismantling of a fine specimen. Yet this has been done by some riflemen. In fact, it has always been done, it seems; and many finely engraved Ballard actions are seen today that have been drilled for large taper pins to hold the Schuetzen barrel in the frame. This was a common practice in the days when these rifles were in their heyday, and I for one deplore it. If the action is still

CONVERTED SINGLE-SHOT RIFLES
(For explanation see: F—p. 367; G—p. 357; H—p. 368; I—p. 357; J—p. 354.)

barreled with a fine barrel by a famous maker, nothing much can be done about it. However, on a few of these altered rifles I have filled these holes with threaded plugs and thus restored them to their original appearance. If the action is engraved, it is a little different, but with care it can be done and then a good engraver can continue the scroll work over the plugs, making in most cases a very neat job and one that will scarcely be noticed.

I have even seen a few Winchester high-side actions that have had part of the right wall cut away, presumably to facilitate loading. One of these I recall was a finely engraved high-side action, and of course the engraving made no impression on this "gunsmith." He not only ruined a model that is rare in engraved form, but he ruined the action itself for any use, as the block was practically unsupported on the one side, and naturally the barrelmaker in whose shop I saw the rifle refused to barrel it in R-2 caliber.

In remodeling the most popular of all, the Winchester high-side action, for a modern cartridge, there is very little information that I can add to what is already known. This is our strongest action, and it is the most abundant. Literally thousands upon thousands of these have been rebarreled and remodeled. To visit Charles Johnson's shop at Thackery, Ohio, or Charles Diller's at Dayton, Ohio, one would think there were an unending supply of these. During the past ten or twelve years these two fine workmen have relined or rebarreled hundreds and hundreds of this type. Every visit I have made to either of these shops has revealed a new lot awaiting modernization. It has seemed as though every gun bug in the country had at least one of the plain sporting rifles and was bent on having a Hornet, a .22/3000, an R-2, a Niedner Magnum, or a .219 Zipper made of it.

In these shops I have also seen many fine and perfect .40, .45, .50, or other hard-to-come-by caliber barrels drilled out and fitted with nickel steel liners, and naturally this made me very sad. I realized then that I could never be a gunsmith, as I am afraid I would attempt to separate barrels of that condition from their owners and naturally that would create quite a hardship when it came to the rent or the groceries.

The Winchester is the easiest of all single-shot actions to work on. This fact, coupled with the ample margin of safety they afford for most rimmed cartridges, is the main reason for their popularity with gunsmiths. The firing pin fits into the breechblock more in line with the cartridge and bore than the Stevens 44½ or Remington Hepburn; therefore it is easier to bush and install new pins. New center-fire or rim-fire breechblocks, as well as other parts, can—or could be—had from the Winchester factory, and this is the only action for which parts are thus obtainable. The hammers and breechblocks available are made for the later coil-spring type actions, but these parts can be installed in the older actions and the flat mainspring under the barrel used only as a means to hold the lever up in position.

Single-set as well as double-set triggers are also available from the factory, and thus a plain trigger action can be fitted with good set triggers which are, to my notion, very valuable on a varment rifle.

The hammer, if for plain triggers, must of course be fitted with a fly, unless a new hammer is obtained. This necessitates an annealing and milling job; however, many gunsmiths do this.

Like most pistol-grip tang single-shot rifles, the Winchester factory tang is curved very little, and is made for the older long grip.

In remodeling these actions, a close modern pistol-grip is always desirable. Fortunately, the Winchester tangs are easily bent to form a close, modern grip without interfering with any trigger parts, springs, or other gadget. The tangs can be cut off quite a bit, the lower one bent down to suit the intended grip, and a stock bolt installed to hold on the stock, similar to Ballard and Sharps Borchardt.

I have seen several rifles so altered, and in some the long screw from upper to lower tang is retained. The upper screw can be turned into a new seat welded up on the more sharply bent lower tang. It is wise policy to retain this screw, as it stiffens the lower tang, which I feel was never too solidly held by the frame mortises and side screws. If the screw is retained in the remodeled job, it may also be reversed, and go from the lower to the upper tang.

One fine job I saw on this action had the screw reversed in this manner, and it was threaded into a steel block screwed and brazed onto the under side of the shortened top tang. The bolt, which extended from the butt to hold the stock on, was threaded into the rear end of the same block. It was a very neat and rigid alteration job.

By shortening the top tang and also shortening the lower tang when bent, a modern close pistol grip of graceful lines and the proper high comb may be obtained without the extremely high appearance of comb and the corresponding too deep hand hold.

Whether the tangs are shortened or left full length, the rifle will be more accurate and hold its zero better if a stock bolt is installed. The stock will be almost as one piece with the frame, and the Winchester needs this.

Most Winchester high-side rifles of plain straight-grip sporting type, when they have had much use, have stocks that are cracked in one or more places at the tangs. The wood mortises into the action well enough, and the only reason I can think of for this splitting is that the stock and tang side screws were not kept tight. These screws must be very tight or the lower tang on this action has a tendency to wobble up and down, and this will in time crack any stock in the grip.

The reader is referred to the books on gunsmithing by Clyde Baker, James V. Howe, and W. F. Vickery for detailed instructions on the metal work necessary to convert these actions. Several back issues of the *American Rifleman* magazine have excellent articles on these actions, from the standpoint of altering the tangs, bushing firing pins, and other alterations. *The Modern Gunsmith,* by Howe, shows in detail the Pope type finger lever pin which enables the Winchester single-shot action to fire rim- or center-fire cartridges with the same block, or to convert one to the other. W. F. Vickery in *Advanced Gunsmithing* gives the simplest and most graphic comparison of the strength of the various single-shot actions. He also gives firing-pin sizes and complete instructions for bushing the blocks to hold these new smaller pins.

The Mann-Niedner firing pin as fitted to the Winchester action by Niedner is probably the best pin for use with modern cartridges such as the .22/3000, the R-2, the .22 Niedner Magnum, the .219 Zipper, and other small cartridges.

The modified Mann-Niedner two-piece firing pin as installed by Charles Johnson is also very good; it is my favorite for this action.

The firing pin must always be bushed when converting one of these rifles to the new hot cartridge; otherwise they will squirt gas, primers, and other debris into the shooter's face, and this is not conducive to good shooting; it might even in time cause you to flinch a little!

The Winchester levers are easily bent hot, and may be lengthened to follow the new close grip. This makes the rifle have a much more finished appearance than leaving the lever in the original curved

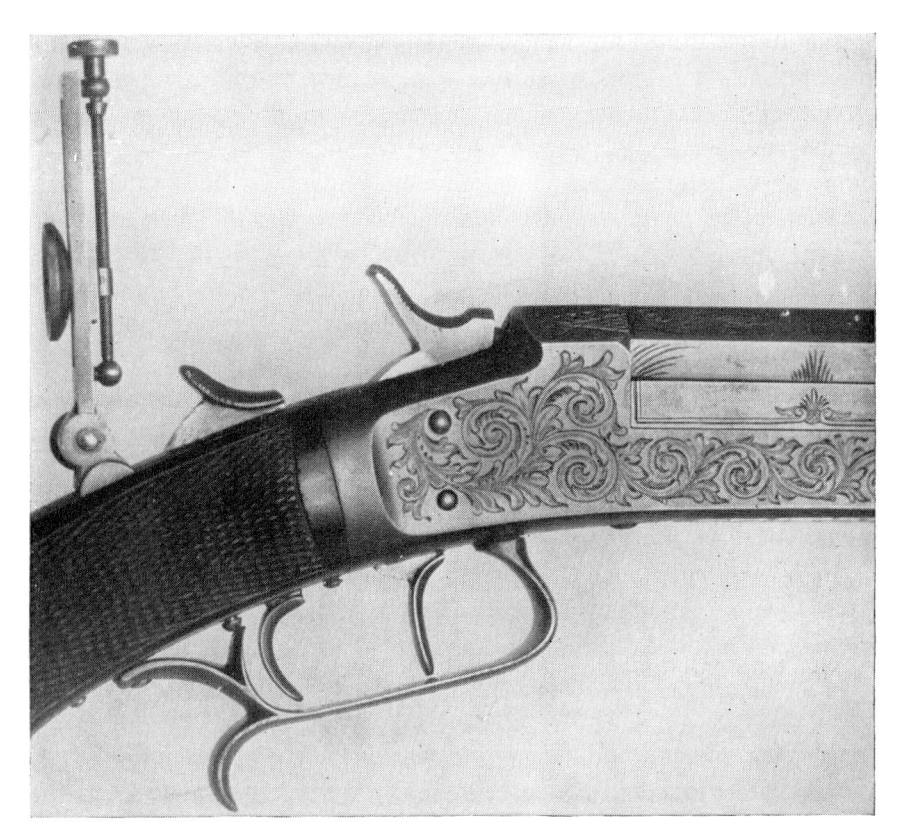

ENGRAVED SET TRIGGER WURFFLEIN RIFLE

shape. Even if left thus, it must be heated and bent down a little so that the block will close properly when the lever bears upon the more sharply curved tang.

The older actions may be altered so that they will come to half cock instead of full cock by installing a fly similar to the one used in the musket action. If the hammer is the old type, it must of course be annealed and a slot milled in to accept the fly.

The later, blued Winchester high-side actions are usually more in demand than the casehardened finish, but for cartridges no more powerful than the .22 Niedner Magnum made on the .25/35 case, with a powder capacity of around 26 grains, I have found the casehardened version amply strong enough. I also had a .30/40 with nickel steel barrel on the casehardened action, and fired many modern 180- and 220-grain loads in it. (Casehardening varies in depth and some examples are too brittle.) However, for cartridges of this and similar push it is more desirable to have the later heat-treated proof-marked action.

I have had several rifles built up on these good Winchester single-shot high-side actions but have gradually disposed of them as I do not particularly care for this action. My reasons for this are: first, it is hard to load under a low-mounted scope, due to the high receiver walls, and hard to get the fired brass out; second, I don't like the clicking and clacking noise the action emits when opened; third, on the earlier models the hammer stays at full-cock unless altered; fourth, the breechblock shows a tendency to slide down a little with wear. This last is the main reason why this action was not more popular with the old-time Schuetzen barrelmakers. This detail is explained very fully in J. V. K. Wagar's article in the *American Rifleman*.

A. W. Peterson once told me that due to this same block trouble he could never make a rifle made up on this action shoot as well as one based on the Ballard or Borchardt.

The low-wall Winchester action is a fine little foundation for cartridges no more powerful than the .22 Hornet, and many have been so made. They lend themselves admirably to the lighter type of rifle, and are much easier to get brass in and out of, due to the cut-away side walls.

The Winchester factory has never sanctioned using this action for the .22 Hornet, but neither has it condemned this practice. However, it is generally understood that the more powerful cartridges, such as the .218 Bee, .22/3000 Lovell and R-2 are a little too hot for maximum safety in this low-wall frame. Charles Johnson has refused time and again to build on this frame a rifle using the R-2 or the .22/3000 cartridge.

The low-wall frame may be altered in the same manner as the high-wall type, and will make a fine little rifle when so modernized.

THE STEVENS 44½ ACTION

This is my favorite action for a modern varment rifle, but then, I am a Stevens fan, and anything old man Stevens made is tops with me. The plain basic 44½ makes a very desirable foundation, as it is much easier to load under a scope than any of the other popular

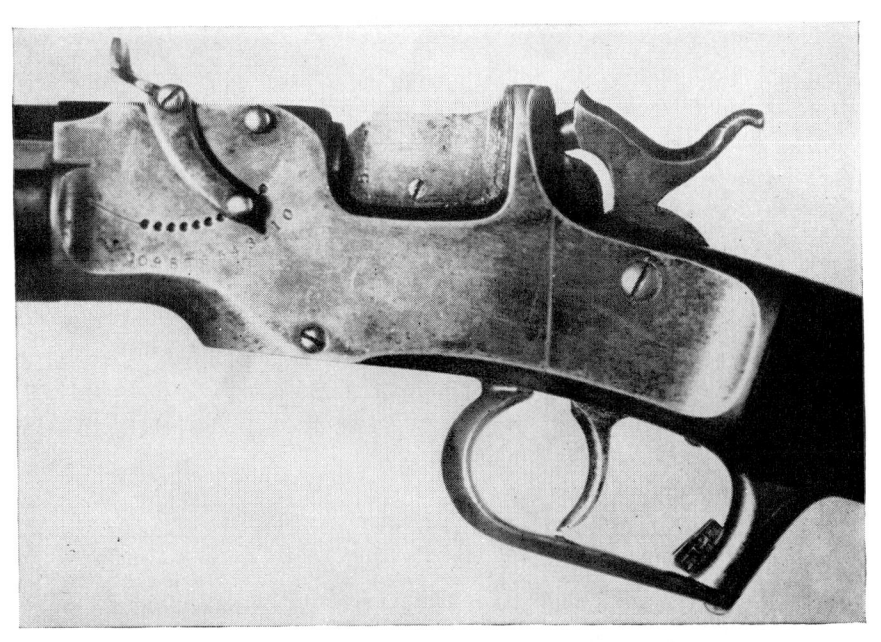

ALLEN AND WHEELOCK RIFLE, CALIBER .35 RIM FIRE, SHOWING PECULIAR REAR SIGHT

actions. Then, too, the rocking, sliding motion of the block when it ascends, more surely seats a hurriedly inserted cartridge.

This action is practically as strong as the Winchester, even though it is made only in casehardened type frame. The later ones are also proof-marked. I have used a fine Model 54-44½ with a heavy Savage barrel chambered for a .22 Wildcat on the .219 Zipper case. This case altered holds 32 grains of #3031 powder, and the action handles this cartridge very smoothly and with perfect safety.

I also have a plain 44½ with a .30/30 caliber barrel. This rifle has been fired many times with all factory loads and is perfectly satisfactory.

The strength of the Stevens 44½ action is greatly underrated by many men. For an interesting and informative article on the strength of this action see the one written by Mr. Allyn Tedman, the "godfather" of Stevens Rifles, in the *American Riflemen* for July 1930. When I visited Mr. Tedman, we had many enthusiasms in common, our fondness for the 44½ Stevens being particularly outstanding.

The Stevens has long tangs, like the Winchester, but it is not quite so easy to alter these tangs, as the lower tank supports the hammer spring near the rear end of the tang. This spring may be discarded, however, and a shorter one, made on the spiral spring and plunger from the modern Stevens 44 action, utilized. These parts are obtainable from the Stevens factory and are quite inexpensive.

The lower tang, when divested of the responsibility for holding the long hammer spring, may be bent when heated to the proper degree. In remodeling one plain 44½ action, I bent the lower tang in a curve just slightly more than the regular factory pistol-grip tang, and then bent the spring also at the rear end to fit the tang. The spring was, of course, rehardened and tempered after bending.

To get a modern, well-proportioned stock for scope use on this action, it is necessary to shorten the upper tang quite a bit, then screw fasten or braze a block to the under side of the tang to accept a long stock bolt. The lower tang can be shortened slightly and mortised straight back into the grip, covering the slot necessary to admit the tang with a steel plate curved to conform with the new shorter grip line. If well and carefully done, it makes a very neat job and obviates the necessity of installing a new spring system for the hammer. With the stock mortised into the action and the stock bolt drawn up tightly, you have a rigid assembly that will not work loose. If the top tang is not shortened, the stock will have a rather clumsy, high-combed appearance which is not pleasing.

When I rebarreled the 54-44½ Stevens to .22 Magnum caliber, this action was restocked, for not only was the original barrel ruined but the original stock as well. I couldn't bring myself to cut off the nicely engraved and colored tangs, so they were left as is, and the lower tang mortised straight back and the grip extended down to the desired dimensions. The mortise was covered with a curved steel plate secured at the grip, just above the grip cap, with a small wood screw countersunk flush with the plate. The other end of this plate was slotted to fit around the rear set trigger and held in place with a very small screw tapped into the tang. The resulting stock, though rather clumsy in appearance, is a well-fitting, comfortable scope-height specimen, and since the wood used was French walnut, the job looks not too bad.

The plain Stevens levers are of malleable iron, and they are very ticklish to bend or alter; however, if a good welder is at hand, he may get it to just the right degree of heat to bend it without any trouble. I have had some levers turn out real well, and some snapped right off when pressure was applied to make the bend. These levers are, of course, difficult to weld extensions on to, but if the old lever is cut off about where the tip of the trigger almost meets it, and a mortise and tenon joint are made with the steel which is used for the extension, and then this joint is pinned in two or three pieces with small steel dowels, the whole may be made rigid by careful welding over the outside. When filed and polished, if the mortise joint was carefully made and if not too many bubbles appear in the weld, it will defy detection. When reblued, it will take very careful inspection to detect the joint.

The pistol grip as made by the Stevens factory was designed for the beautiful flowing lines of the models 49, 52, 56, and others of this pattern. When this original stock is present in unaltered form there is no more pleasing stock on any single-shot rifle, to my knowledge, and it should be left in this state. However, this stock can be used in unaltered form by removing the Swiss or Schuetzen butt plate and fitting a hard rubber plate, first softening it in hot water so that it may be bent to fit the curve of the butt.

The combs on most of these stocks are full, and though not high, are sufficiently so to enable a low-mounted scope to be used comfortably.

The firing pin in the Stevens is on a sharper angle than the Winchester pin, and some men condemn the 44½ for this reason. If the pin is of the correct size to fit the breechblock properly and is bushed to the correct diameter, it is a very smooth action. It takes, however, a gunsmith who has a feeling for this action to install the proper pin, as it is much more difficult to fit than on the Winchester. Some of the Stevens blocks are seen with a firing pin retractor which operates from a lug on the link. Usually these retractors work very well, though being very small they are sometimes worn to the point where they no longer function. New ones of tool steel are easily filed out, and when of the proper size to function well, they should be well hardened. When the 44½ action is well fitted, it is one of the smoothest of all actions and is perfectly quiet in operation.

When the Stevens is rebarreled, most men prefer the barrel to be screwed in tightly, and for the larger cartridges I prefer it that way also. However, the easy-thread, take-down barrel detracts nothing

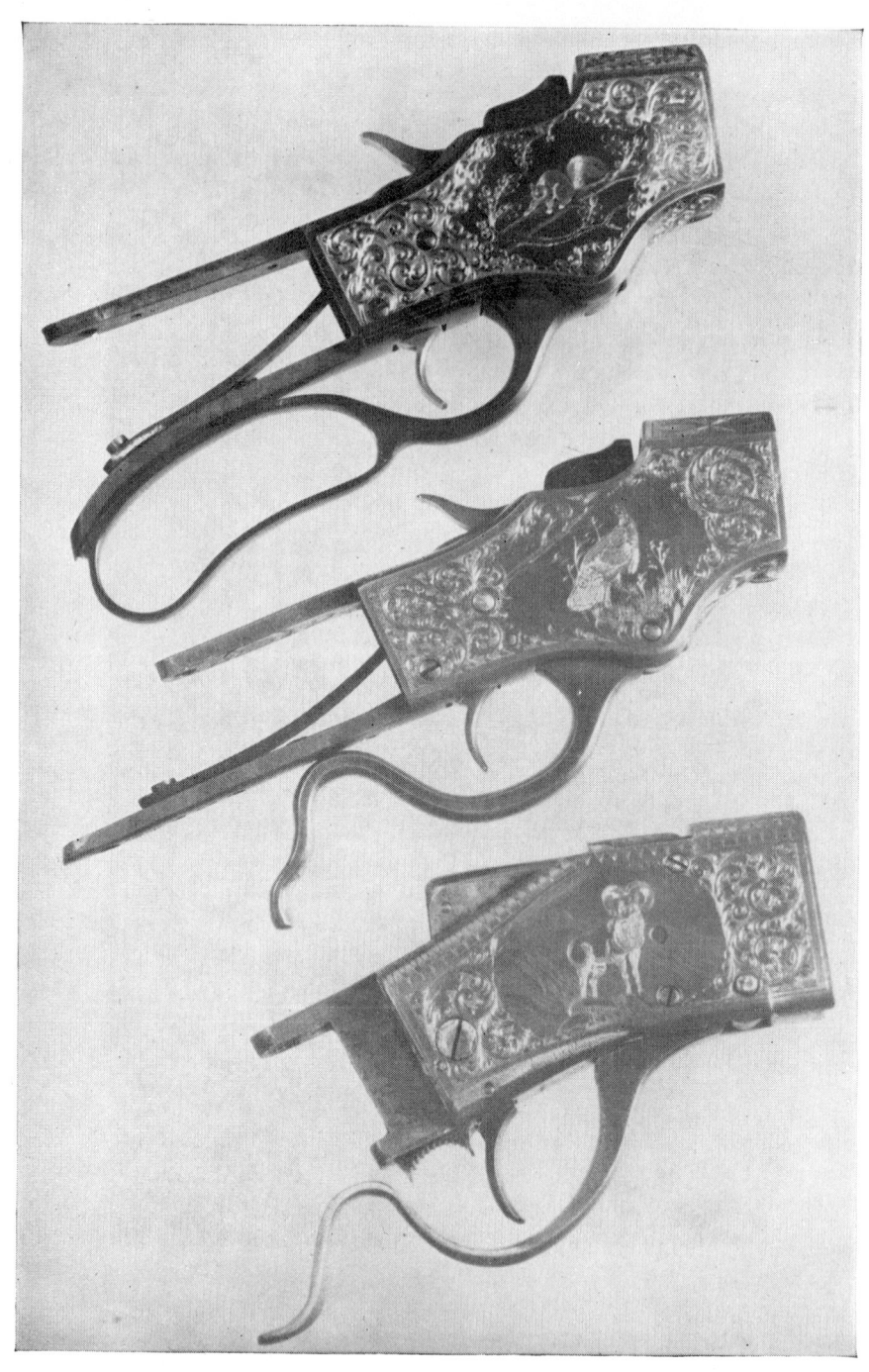

SPECIALLY ENGRAVED ACTIONS

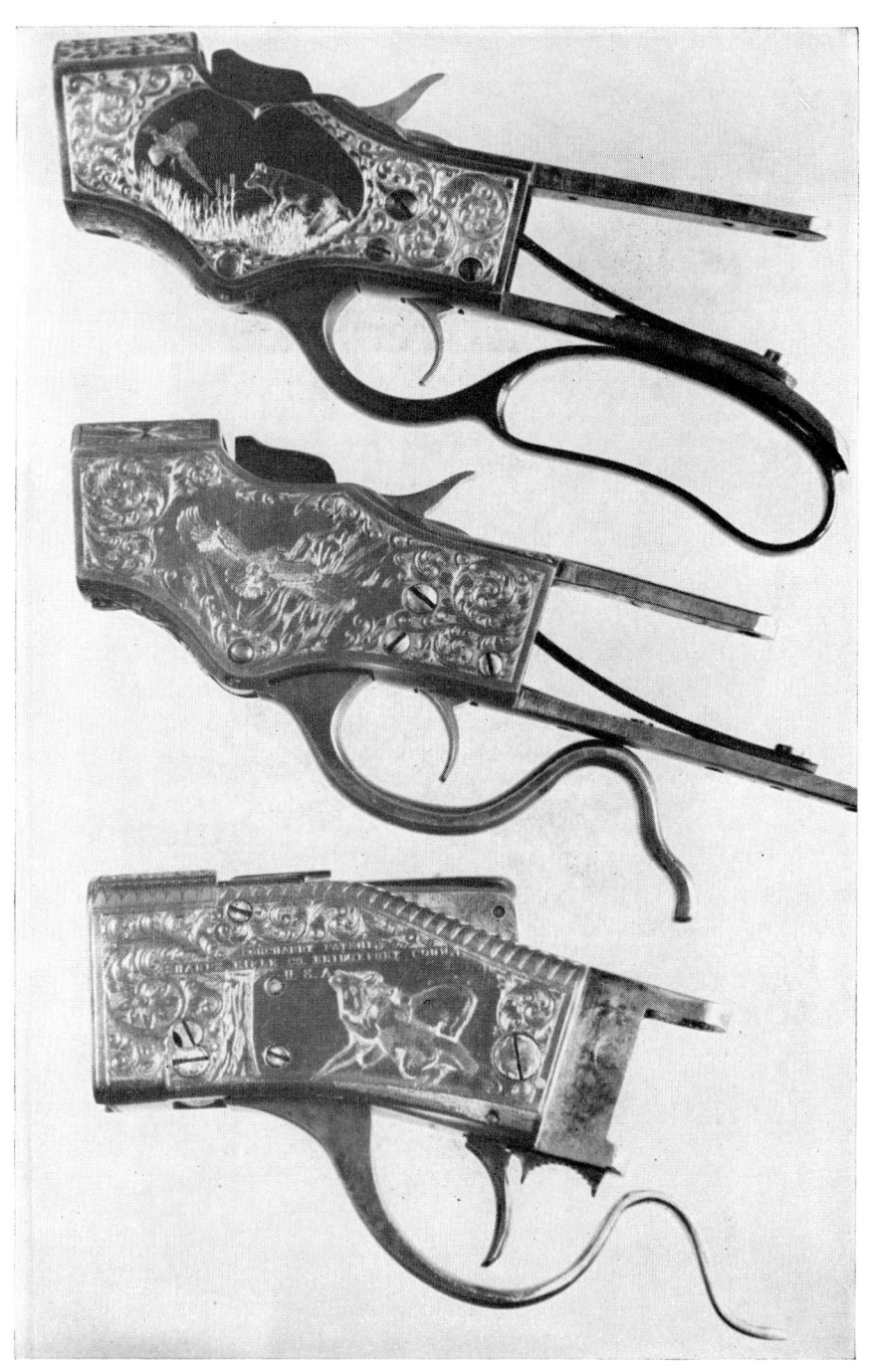

REVERSE SIDE OF SPECIALLY ENGRAVED ACTIONS

from the gun's accuracy. I have tried them both ways; but after all, there is no advantage in the take-down system unless you have several barrels.

I once had a 44½ rifle that had the take-down barrel holding screw replaced by one with a large knurled head fully 1 inch in diameter. Evidently the man who installed that screw didn't wish to be bothered to hunt a screw driver when he wanted to remove the barrel. I have often wondered if he had a holster made to carry the extra barrels with him in the field!

The set triggers found on Stevens 44½ rifles are usually very fine and sensitive. They are generally in working order, which is more than can be said for some Ballard and Winchester triggers. The single-set trigger on the Stevens is superior to the single-set found on Winchester actions, but it is, of course, not so trouble free as the double-set variety. New parts for these triggers are not available from the factory, and they have not been available for many years. Worn parts are easily replaced by filing out new ones from tool steel that is properly hardened. None of these parts are difficult to make, and this is not as arduous a job as it may sound.

Two remodeled Stevens 44½ rifles are shown on page 340. The first (A) was the little English Model 044½ on the thin action and with the 26-inch #1 barrel. As the barrel was worn out—and in fact it looked like a dug well inside—it was sent to Charles Johnson, who relined it with a nickel steel liner for the .22 Hornet cartridge. The breechblock was, of course, bushed to the correct small diameter and a new firing pin was fitted. When it was returned, I cut off the top tang just behind the rear tang sight screw hole and counterbored this hole to serve as the top stock screw hole. In this manner a slightly closer comb was secured.

The rifle was stocked in curly maple with a long pistol grip by mortising the lower tang straight in and then covering the mortise with a steel plate fastened to the tang behind the trigger and at the other end just above the grip cap. The lever was broken at the tip by attempting to bend it cold, and so the piece was merely turned over and welded on in that position. It is a comfortable lever and is a very satisfactory substitute for a close pistol grip.

A friend engraved this action, and as it looked very nice in the white, it has been left that way. On one side the engraving shows a wild turkey cock, and on the reverse side is an eagle in flight.

The barrel and block were reblued, using Clyde Baker's Basic Bluing Formula #1, and these Stevens barrels take this solution beautifully. The curly maple stock and forearm were finished in oil, and they took a very mellow tone. A Weaver 29 S scope in an Albree Monomount completes the job, and the rifle weighs about 6 pounds.

The blue of the barrel, the satin finish on the curly maple, and the fine engraving of the bright receiver all contribute to make a very beautiful little Hornet for my wife. The hammer and trigger on this rifle are gold plated.

Mr. Johnson was rather skeptical about the shooting qualities of this very light, relined barrel, but it will shoot consistently into 1½ inches at 100 yards with practically all factory loads, and this I consider very good for a barrel that is about the size of an Irishman's pipe stem.

The next rifle shown on page 340 (B) was originally an old model 45-44½ in. 25 rim-fire caliber. When I came into possession of it, the whole works were just a mass of rust, as it had sat for several years next to a brine tank.

After quite a lot of work with emery cloth, the action and barrel were worked down to the point where the small shallow rust pits no longer showed, and we then decided it might have possibilities. The lower tang was heated and bent to the exact shape of the factory pistol grip on the models 47, 49, and 52, and the end of the original spring was bent enough still to function when replaced with the original screw.

The original plain finger lever was cut off at the thick part below the trigger and a flat piece of cold rolled steel spliced on with steel dowel pins and welding. It was then heated and shaped into the form of loop lever shown on the completed rifle. Incidentally, this is somewhat of a chore, but interesting work at that. After a nice blue job, the action looked pretty well to our fond eyes, so it was sent to the engraver along with the O44½ action on the Hornet described before. On the left side the engraving shows a fox flushing a cock pheasant, and on the right side of the frame a fox squirrel is perched on an oak limb. Oak leaves, acorns, and scroll work adorn the three flats of the barrel housing, the upper and lower tangs, and the under side of the action.

The newly cut engraving contrasted nicely with the blued background, so it was left that way and has not yet been reblued.

The upper tang being left full length, the comb is somewhat sharper and higher than it should be for the best appearance, but the new stock and forearm of deluxe crotch walnut certainly make up for that defect.

This ruined .25 rim-fire barrel was relined to .22 Long Rifle by P. O. Ackley of Trinidad, Colorado, and it is very accurate. Mr. Ackley also changed the breechblock to fire the .22 rim-fire cartridge. The barrel was reblued with the same formula as that used on the O44½ Hornet described, and the trigger and hammer were also gold plated.

The .22 rim-fire and the Hornet make a pair of beautiful little rifles, and they have been the object of much admiration and several attractive cash offers. They prove that a good gun may never be too rusty or too obsolete to convert into something that will provide a vast amount of satisfaction at a reasonable cost.

Figure J, on page 341, shows a Stevens 44½ rebarreled with a round .30/30 caliber barrel and a new stock.

CONVERTING THE REMINGTON HEPBURN ACTION

This is a very suitable action for a varment rifle, and with very little labor it can be made into a fine alteration job. I have always felt that the action had possibilities, and I altered one in the following manner.

The upper tang was cut off just ahead of the rear tang sight hole and the end rounded up as it was before. The front tang sight screw hole was welded shut and an old Ballard stock bolt tang was cut off and welded on the under side of the top tang. The lower tang was shortened by cutting it off ahead of the serial numbers stamped thereon, and bent to form a good, close pistol-grip tang. The seat for the hammer spring was then built up to the level of the original seat by welding, and the hole drilled and tapped in this seat for the spring-holding screw.

It is advisable to make a careful drawing of the action before any cutting or bending is done, and to make another drawing to ascertain the wanted bend to the lower tang, also being careful to locate the new built-up seat for the spring.

The screw which formerly held the stock on is, of course, discarded, and the Ballard stock bolt utilized to hold the new stock in place. Any bolt can be used, and a block of steel drilled and tapped for the under side of the tang. I used the Ballard tang and screw as it was handy and, as usual, I was in a hurry.

The lever was altered by welding on an extension and bending it down to follow the trigger guard a short distance. This gives more leverage if needed, though it is seldom needed with the Hepburn extractor.

For a right-handed shooter the lever as originally made is extremely handy, but for a south paw it is just a little unhandy to reach the thumb under the scope.

When a case does stick, the original strong Hepburn lever may be opened as far as it will go, and usually a tap on top of a fence post or any convenient solid object will start the case.

The easiest way to alter the Hepburn lever to follow the guard is to take out the lever and turn it one quarter turn downward; thus when the block is up in firing position, the lever extends downward instead of extending along the side of the frame in its normal closed position. While in this position the torch may be applied until the metal is hot enough to bend easily under the frame, and the turn made to follow the guard. A short piece of steel is welded on to the end of the lever and extended back as far as desired.

In the case of the lever shown, only a short extension was welded on, and the tip was bent down slightly to enable the thumb to start the lever. All that is needed is that the lever be started. The wide lever spring will flip the lever down quickly and the case will come tumbling out.

When the altered lever is in place, a new seat for the holding screw which extends through the tumbler into the squared end of the lever is drilled with the proper size drill. This keeps the lever shank from working out.

This particular Hepburn action was fitted with a new barrel chambered for the K-Hornet cartridge, and it was stocked in curly maple, finished natural.

When it came to the bluing of the action, I had expected a great deal of trouble, as these actions are very hard surfaced. The bluing solution used was Clyde Baker's Basic Bluing Formula #1 as given in his *Modern Gunsmithing*. Much to my surprise this action took the bluing immediately without preliminary etching, and came into a beautiful blue. The contrast between the blued parts and the natural finish of the beautiful curly maple must be seen to be appreciated fully. The completed rifle is shown on page 340, C.

This well-dimensioned modern stock shows what can be accomplished upon the Hepburn action with very little work. The shortening of the tangs and the pistol grip enables a properly designed stock for scope use to be used without resorting to the ugly, extremely high combs seen on some so-called modern stocks.

There is no need for a comb to extend high up in the air all by its lonesome if the upper tangs are shortened and the depth of the hand-hole consequently lessened. In remodeling the Hepburn in this manner it is well to keep in mind that in destroying the serial numbers of the action by shortening the lower tang they must be replaced. This is easily done by taking the lower tang to someone who has the proper size of steel figure stamps and having the numbers replaced. When covering up the lower tang on the Stevens 44½ by extending the tang straight into the pistol grip with a plate covering the original numbers, these can be stamped on the plate or on the under side of the barrel just ahead of the forearm, as Stevens barrels have them.

This Hepburn breechblock was, of course, bushed, and the proper-sized firing pin for the cartridge was fitted to it. The retracting spring around the pin was retained as well as the rebounding feature of the hammer, as these are features that I particularly admire in the Hepburn. Some gunsmiths advise removing the rebounding hammer feature, and with cartridges of very heavy pressures this might be advisable.

Due to the slant of the firing pin through the breechblock, the opening on the face of the block is naturally more oblong or oval than it is round. For this reason the hole in the face and the tip of the pin must be made slightly smaller than those used in the Winchester or Stevens blocks, to prevent too large an opening.

I have seen but one Hepburn action wrecked by extreme high pressure. This rifle had a .30/40 caliber barrel, and the hand-loaded cartridges used in it were dangerously overloaded. The only damage done was the cracking of one side wall just behind the block. As it was on the left side of the receiver, the shooter escaped injury. This rifle was the #3 High Power model, with ordnance steel round barrel and the high pressure breechblock with small firing pin. It was made to handle the .30/40 cartridge, and it handled all factory loads perfectly and only gave up when pressures were reached that would no doubt have wrecked the Krag action.

These high power Hepburn rifles were made with exactly the same color-hardened frames as the regular rifles. The only differences were in the special round ordnance barrel and the high-pressure block. I have nothing but the greatest respect for the Hepburn; but then, I like 'em!

ALTERATIONS ON THE SHARPS BORCHARDT

The military Borchardt is found quite often and is easily made into a fine sporting rifle. These models have a beautifully tapered 32-inch round barrel which when cut to 26 or 28 inches and relined to any desired caliber is still a fine barrel. Of course there is nothing to prevent a new barrel being installed if it is desired.

The military action is rather boxlike and clumsy in appearance when compared to the fine sporting Borchardt actions, but it is easily improved. If you have a sporting action to copy, the square corners at top and bottom of the military frame are quickly ground, filed, and polished to the shape of the sporting type. The lug that holds the swivel is also removed at this time, and you then have an action that is symmetrical and the foundation of a real rifle.

The military breechblocks, as well as some of the sporting blocks, have firing pins that are about an eighth of an inch in diameter and project beyond the face of the block almost that distance. The block must, of course, be bushed properly, and the point of the firing pin must be turned down and the properly rounded profile on the end shaped. A new complete firing pin is easily made, or the old tip may be cut off and drilled to admit a new tip of tool steel.

I have seen several alterations on these blocks, but the best I have is one bushed by Charles Johnson. In this job he counterbored the face for a plate about $3/8$ of an inch in diameter, which is held in place, after screwing it into the recess turned into the block, by two small flush-headed screws.

The firing-pin tip and its aperture in the block must, of course, be greatly reduced from the original. These pins must also project less from the face of the block than most bushed pins, because there is no retractor in this action. Less trouble will be experienced with the firing pin hanging up in the fired primer if it is short.

The Borchardt has a very short, fast hammer fall, but ignition with this action can be speeded up even more. W. F. Vickery in *Advanced Gunsmithing* describes a method of speeding up the fall of the striker, if this is felt to be desirable, by making a new spiral striker spring of "V"-shaped spring wire.

The Borchardt is one of the hardest actions in existence to get a good trigger pull on if it doesn't happen to have one to begin with. This is due to the odd shape of the sear and the sear notch, and the complicated method of connecting the sear with the trigger. However, when the desired pull and let-off is obtained, and the parts are rehardened, they usually hold that adjustment.

The original Sharps set triggers are not too good, and regular set triggers may be made and installed by milling out the receiver to fit them in. But this is a job that requires a great amount of very careful, tedious work, and it is hardly worth the effort.

The Borchardt action is extremely simple to restock—even more so than the Ballard; and the very short tangs permit of any stock design that is wanted. The heavy stock bolt draws the stock and action very tightly together and makes a rigid stocking job.

The steel, well-checkered butt plate as furnished on the military rifle and carbine Borchardt stocks is a very good plate to use in restocking, though some prefer a slightly larger plate. The comparison between this well-designed plate and the one used on the trap-door Springfield military rifle is almost comical. The Springfield plate shows the reluctance of the military mind to abandon the old muzzle-loading traditions, while the butt plate used on the military Borchardt is as well designed and advanced as the other parts of this rifle.

The sporting Borchardt action requires much less work than the military to make a fine foundation, as it is an extremely trim and neat frame. The trigger pull on these models is usually better, and the Creedmoor triggers are finely checkered. Most of the sporting frames have removable top tangs which have the tang sight base made integral with the tang. If made into a modern varment rifle, these lugs for the sight screw are ungainly and may be removed by grinding them off and filling the spring plunger hole between the lugs by welding.

The sporting and target model Sharps Borchardt rifles have usually very fine pistol-grip, checkered stocks. These excellent and sometimes beautiful stocks may be used, if the scope is mounted very low on the barrel, in mounts such as the Weaver B or the Albree twin mounts.

I have modernized only one sporting Borchardt, as I consider these rifles to be among the most valuable of collection pieces. The military model makes just as fine a sporting piece when properly remodeled, and no loss to the collector is occasioned when just one more military rifle bites the dust.

I acquired a nice midrange Borchardt which was originally a very fine rifle in .40/70 Sharps Straight caliber. When the rifle came into my possession, the barrel looked like the inside of a chimney or a mine shaft, and the beautiful stock was splintered and shattered in the grip. This action was a paneled job, and the black hard-rubber panels had that discolored look that appears on the stem of a cheap pipe.

Charles Johnson cut the round .40/70 barrel to 28 inches, doing away with the front sight slot, and relined it with a nickel steel liner. It was rifled with a 14-inch twist and chambered for the R-2 Lovell cartridge.

This rifle had the removable upper tang, with the tang sight lugs, and as I needed this for another rifle, I removed it and filed up a new tang to fit, then secured it with the same screw that held the original one. This new tang was made ¾ of an inch shorter than the old one, to allow a shorter hand-hole.

The receiver at the point where the stock joins on was milled out slightly to cause the wood to have a tendency to compress inward when the stock bolt was tightened. This is advisable when a Borchardt is restocked. The many rifles with split and shattered grips are mute evidence that this is needed. Of course not many modern varment rifles are slammed down butt first, as were the military rifles, but it will pay to file or mill the Borchardt frames so that the stock cannot spread at the grip.

On this particular action, due to the very slight division between the rear of the rubber side panels and the wood of the stock, not much metal could be removed except clear up in the corner where the stock bolt lug extends rearward. However, on the plain sporting and military actions a groove ⅛ of an inch wide and almost that deep can be milled in the center on each side. This slot should, of course, be started inside the edge of the receiver and stopped short of the opposite edge, to prevent it showing on the top and bottom of the action. However, if it is desired, it can be run right straight across, and the resulting channel filled with the wood of the stock by tenoning it into these slots. The resulting stock grip will be much stronger, whichever method is used. The tenon necessary to prevent the grip from separating or spreading is very slight.

This paneled Sharps R-2 rifle was stocked with fancy Oregon myrtle, and new side panels of the same wood were fitted.

The pack-hardening colors being long gone from this action, the complete action was blued to match the barrel. Baker's Basic Formula was used, and it worked beautifully on the barrel. However, it would not take on the very hard receiver until this was etched very lightly with the etching solution, as described by Mr. Baker. When this was done, the action colored up as blue-black as the barrel. This rifle is a favorite varment gun of mine, and with the 50-grain Sisk bullet and #4198 or #4227 powder has made many a crow and woodchuck bite the dust. It is a rather heavy job, and with the scope weighs about 11 pounds, so it is used mostly when there isn't a great amount of walking ahead. This rifle is shown on page 340, Figure D.

The round military barrel will make up into a lighter rifle, depending, of course, on the wood used in the stock.

The Borchardt when remodeled is one of our finest actions, but the cartridge must be inserted well into the chamber, else the block will hang up on the case head. I usually grind and file a more gradual curve on the top front edge of the block when using a small-head cartridge. This will facilitate loading and may be carried to any degree desired, as the block is quite heavy at this point.

Some actions are found that have very sloppy fitting blocks. In these there is very noticeable end play in the block when the striker falls. Some of this may be taken out when the new barrel is fitted, by letting the barrel extend through the necessary amount to tighten up the slack. However, if you have one of those specimens in which the block is tight in the guides when opened and loose when at the top, that is a different matter, and some do turn up in this way. About the only thing that may be done in a case of this kind is to remove the cocking plates which are held into the block channel by two screws and make new ones to correct the end play. Sometimes these plates may be built up by welding on a hard steel welding rod and dressing them to fit.

I have had Borchardt actions in which these cocking plates were cracked or broken, and these were successfully repaired by welding. An experienced welder can sometimes accomplish the seemingly impossible. We must resort to all sorts of antics with some of these old actions as, after all, we can't write to Mr. Sharps and tell him to send in the new parts needed.

An example of the possibilities existing in the military Borchardt is shown on page 340, Figure E. This action was rounded up slightly, just enough to relieve the angularity of the frame, and it was engraved by the same engraver who executed the two Stevens 44½ special jobs shown in this chapter.

The barrel is a .25 Krag by Niedner, and the breechblock was bushed accordingly.

The plug at the rear of the breechblock was removed in this action and a new one made of tool steel was held in place with a new tool steel pin. This was purely an extra precaution and no doubt was unnecessary. But it is very comforting to know that the rear end of the block is securely plugged when your face is so close during that "terrific instant."

The stock and forearm are of deluxe crotch walnut, and the action and barrel were blued by a process similar to hot niter bluing. This bluing was done by a local plating works for me, as I personally hesitated to attempt the bluing of this action because of the engraving. We buffed the action to a high polish, and the resulting finish is a beautiful blue-black that closely approximates the deep lustrous finish seen on Smith & Wesson revolvers. This is a very handy deer rifle, if you are one of the men who believe, with me, that one shot is enough to kill a deer. I never could see the advantage of scaring the poor critters with a volley of shots when one shot will do the trick.

THE BALLARD AS A FOUNDATION

In remodeling one of the old Ballard actions into a modern rifle there is really not much that can be done to the frame. There are no tangs to shorten or to bend into a closer pistol grip. The frame as originally made definitely limits the extent to which the new stock may be made along the lines of individual preference.

The Ballard is at its best as a .22 rim-fire match rifle, as the block action is peculiarly adaptable to this caliber. The block drops completely out of the way when opened, and there are no side walls to interfere with the loading of the cartridge.

As a basis for a .22 match or hunting rifle, probably the best frame to use is the one that is the easiest to find, which happens to be the #2 and #3 action. These are the cast frame models that were made mostly in the rim-fires. Many of these were made in .22 rim-fire caliber, and if one of these is obtained, the changing of the firing pin is avoided.

The factory-made .22 rim-fire Ballards have two-piece extractors, the bottom piece of which works on the lever screw, as in the center-fire models. This piece merely serves to move the extractor proper, which is a round rod fitting a hole bored parallel to the chamber. The end of the rod, of course, has the proper shape to extract the fired case.

This type extractor was no doubt adopted because it avoids the tendency or chance of a cartridge being inserted into the chamber under the extractor. This occurs quite often when an extractor of the regular center-fire Ballard type is used, unless the throw of the extractor is shortened. When rebarreling a Ballard action to .22 rim-fire it is advisable, in my opinion, to specify that the gunsmith install this two-piece type of extractor. Some gunsmiths, however, do not care to fit this type because the hole to accept the rod part of the extractor must be drilled close to the chamber. It requires very careful workmanship here to avoid damaging the chamber, but it can be done if the workman is willing to spend the time.

The larger sizes of rim-fire and center-fire extractors may, of course, be welded and reshaped properly to extract .22 rim-fire brass, and will prove perfectly satisfactory if care is used when inserting the cartridge. I have seen these extractors which had been fitted with a small spring to snap them back into place when the case had been extracted and the lever and block raised slightly. This is very handy, especially for a prone match rifle when every unnecessary movement is to be avoided.

These cast frames of the Ballard models 2, 3, 3F, and 4 are perfectly satisfactory for .22 rim-fire or other mild cartridges. Some say otherwise, but they were made in fairly large black powder calibers up to the .40/63, .40/70 Ballard, and other like calibers, and if they were satisfactory for these, naturally they are also satisfactory for mild-mannered modern sizes. Practically all the thrust of the cartridge head when the charge explodes is borne by the link, and the link should always be replaced by a new one of tool steel, that has been properly hardened and tempered. The slackness which allows the lever to drop slightly after the block is closed is caused by the wearing of the link, and a new one with very slightly differently spaced holes will correct this annoying detail.

If a plain lever, cast action is used and a close pistol grip is desired, the lever may be made to carry the grip. The action is stocked in straight-grip style to the dimensions desired, and a wood pistol grip is added to the lever. Incidentally, the Ballard frame is probably the easiest of all the single-shots to restock. There are no annoying tangs to fit. The only difficult part is getting the hole for the stock bolt through in the correct place, and this is generally done on a lathe. A woodworking lathe is just as satisfactory in this respect as the metalworking type, and is actually to be preferred in my case as it is all I have. The chuck with proper size drill is fitted in the headstock and the drill centered on the correct spot. The tail stock with center—the regular wood-turning center is best—is run up and the center spotted on the mark at this end.

Hold the blank in the left hand, start the motor, and feed the blank into the drill with the tail-stock feed. Simple! And the hole will always be in the wanted location. I usually drill the action end of the blank first with a drill large enough to admit the large part of the bolt tang, then deepen it sufficiently with a smaller drill to accept the small part of the tang. The hole from there on to the butt is then drilled with a proper small bit to accept the stock bolt. If your bit isn't long enough to reach, take the blank out and fit a snugly fitting plug made of a maple dowel, or other hard wood, to the large hole in the front end of the blank. The center is carefully marked on this plug, and this end fitted on the dead center at tail stock, then the drill in the headstock is fed into the butt end till it meets the hole started from the tang end. When holes meet, remove the blank and insert a small rod into the butt end; a light tap will force out the maple plug. The mortising in to the action is very simple compared to some actions, particularly the Winchester single-shot.

The blank is then shaped to suit the individual, and the lever is altered if desired. The plain lever as supplied on the lower number model Ballards is heated and flattened to fit along the action and straight-grip stock. A close pistol grip is easily made of matching walnut and fastened to this flattened lever with two wood screws countersunk on the top side of the lever. The wood grip makes a better appearance if the lever is mortised into the grip and the wood of the grip rounded to fit around the under side of the stock and frame and extended up a short distance.

The lever when flattened out in this manner may be hollowed out slightly on the top side, to fit more closely the curve of the lower part of the action and stock.

When a new link and lever pivot screw are made and properly fitted, there will be no side play in a pistol grip made in this manner. It will give a very comfortable grip and is really the only practical way to obtain a close grip on the Ballard frame.

The Pacific frame is, of course, straight-grip style, and is a forged action. The block of the Pacific is fitted with set triggers, and it is a fine basis for a hunting or target rifle when used in matches in which set triggers are permitted.

The Ballard models numbered 4½, 6, 6½, 7, 8, 9, and 10 have the pistol-grip frames, in which the grip is slightly started by the swell at the lower rear of the frame. These models—except the No. 6—have the four-finger loop style of lever and are the handsomest of the Ballard line. These levers are for the most part fairly satisfactory substitutes for a close pistol grip. These loops may be filled in solid with walnut to match the stock. In this manner they will serve even better the purpose of a closer pistol grip.

If it is desired to fit a wood pistol-grip block to these models of actions, the loop lever should be removed and an entirely new lever made, as these loop pattern levers are too rare and in too much demand today to alter or otherwise disfigure them.

It is practically impossible to find a lever of this loop type today, and I hunted quite a while when I needed one to restore a fine old Ballard.

In Denver, Colorado, I once bought quite a few new unused Ballard parts—set triggers, hammer and trigger springs, links, several levers, including one four-finger loop type lever. These parts were part of the stock of the old J. P. Lower Sporting Goods Store, distributors of Ballard and Sharps rifles in the days when these rifles were made. Needless to say, it is very seldom that parts in new unused condition are found today, and when these parts are needed it is usually necessary to make them by hand. There are very few parts that cannot be filed out by hand, and these when properly fitted and hardened are just as satisfactory as the original parts. The mainspring or the hammer spring sometimes needs replacing, and it is possible to grind down certain flat shotgun springs and use these in the Ballard breechblocks.

The single-trigger Ballard blocks when obtained in unaltered form are usually very smooth in action, and these of course make the best blocks for use in a .22 match rifle. The trigger face may be annealed and checkered or stippled, to provide better control of the trigger. Some of the trigger shoes with deeply grooved or checkered faces will fit the Ballard triggers and are easily attached.

To control the trigger pull, a set screw may be installed. Probably the best of these adjustment devices for the Ballard is the one used by Charles Johnson. Mr. Johnson uses certain easily obtained parts from a current model shotgun to make this adjusting device, and the trigger pull adjusting screw is easily reached by opening the action and inserting the screwdriver between the lever and block at the front bottom corner. The double-set trigger blocks are easily converted to single-trigger type. There are several ways to accomplish this, and many gunsmiths have their own methods. They are all good. However, one way I have used, and prefer, is to make a new trigger plate with single trigger to replace the set trigger plate, using the same attaching screws. A trigger of this type may be made in any dimensions desired, and positioned to fit the trigger reach of the individual shooter. The trigger is made long enough to reach up and contact the sear which these blocks contain. A trigger tension spring is installed on the top side of the plate behind the trigger, and an adjusting screw to regulate the amount of pull in connection with this tension spring is easily installed.

Using this method, either a double-set or a single adjustable trigger may be had at will by merely taking out the screws and switching plates. The double-set triggers furnished on Ballard rifles are very good, and they are capable of fine adjustments. The earlier set triggers are made somewhat heavier and are the best. These triggers are not exactly interchangeable, as there is a slight difference in the plates, as one can see by looking on page 16. Also shown on that page is a special set of triggers which have a front trigger made of a spring wire. There is also a folding guard for this wire trigger. Needless to say, these triggers are very sensitive. They are not Ballard triggers, of course, but were made years ago by a famous gunsmith.

Several gunsmiths have altered the original Ballard breechblocks, or they have made new blocks which extend straight back from the position occupied by the top of the original blocks to form a housing which conceals the hammer. This gives the appearance of a hammerless action, and the hammer is, of course, brought to full cock by a projection on the special link when the action is opened. They are somewhat handier for a prone match rifle than the original type, but of the several I have examined none worked too well. There is too much machinery here to keep in the necessary fine working order essential for the fine match rifle.

The Ballard breechblock as originally made is almost impossible to improve upon for a match rifle. The hammer throw may be shortened somewhat if desired, but very little is gained by this, and the shooter usually regrets it.

The flat firing pin as used on the factory-made .22 rim-fire Ballards is also very hard to improve upon. With the nose of this pin properly shaped, the ignition will be better than with a round pin. At least this has been my experience with the various styles of firing pins used.

W. F. Vickery in *Advanced Gunsmithing* gives the most complete and detailed discussion I have seen on the proper firing-pin profile.

The Ballard extractor being on the left side, a firing pin for this action may be either at the top or at the bottom of the chamber. Some prefer one position, some another. I incline toward the latter contact point to avoid the chance of the pin being dragged across the head of the case.

The Ballard frames seen today very rarely show much of the pack-hardening color which they originally had. If much color remains, it may be preserved for a considerably longer time if given a thin coat of lacquer or varnish. These frames may be repack-hardened, and some gunsmiths have had good results with this process, others not so much success. Sometimes the frame will shrink slightly, and if this happens it really complicates matters, as then the breechblock usually must be refitted and rehardened.

I prefer to leave the frames strictly alone, and if the colors have vanished, reblue the frame. These frames being quite hard on the surface are rather difficult to blue. I have had excellent results by first lightly etching with the etching solution of Clyde Baker, mentioned earlier in this book. Nitric acid alone may also be used, but care must be exercised when using this, as a rather pitted surface may result if the acid is used in too great strength. After etching, the frame will usually blue nicely with either Baker's or Howe's basic #1 formulas, either of which give beautiful results.

The cold rusting process is also good for these frames, the only drawback being that they require several days to blue properly. If they are timed so that a new coat may be given every evening or some other time convenient to the operator, it will usually work out satisfactorily, but if one treatment is missed, it usually means that the whole job must be done over.

These cold rusting processes are about the best I have found for rebluing the Rigby barrels furnished on some of the higher grades of Ballards. These barrels are very hard to blue by the hot, quick solutions I have tried on them. When the Ballard frame is blued to match the new barrel and lever, a nice contrast is obtained by engine turning or damascening the breechblock. This finish on the block is easily done by following the instructions given in the various volumes on gunsmithing, and of course should only be done on a remodeled rifle, never on one which it is desired to recondition or refinish as a collection piece.

The engraved Ballard frames I prefer to leave unblued and in their original colored state. Even if the color is entirely gone and the action is almost white, they still appeal to most men more than when reblued. If the action is discolored or stained or rusted—which is sometimes the case—it is probably better to blue it.

Figure F on page 341 shows a restocked engraved #6½ Ballard that made up into a fine squirrel rifle. This action I acquired on a visit to Niedner Rifle Corporation at Dowagiac, Michigan. They had bent the lever somewhat to form a closer pistol grip, and had rehardened it in colors. The action had been barreled by A. W. Peterson at one time, and had the take-down pin through the frame, so I sent it back to Mr. Peterson and had him make a new .22 Long Rifle barrel in the same take-down style. The rifle was then restocked in dense American walnut, with pistol-grip cap and butt plate of horn. The fore end is a very slightly beavertail type, and is also tipped with horn. The swivels are the quick detachable type, and the front one is fastened to a band around the barrel through the forearm. With the 28-inch round barrel, this rifle weighs about 8¼ pounds without the scope, and is a very fine squirrel rifle. I have made a single-trigger plate to replace the double-set triggers shown when the rifle is used as a match rifle.

Figure H, page 341, shows a deluxe .22 rim-fire Schuetzen rifle made up in a #6½ Ballard action with special double-set triggers. The barrel is a .22 caliber Pope.

Marble-Goss—and possibly some of the other sight manufacturers—supplies very fine micrometer rear sights for the Ballard action, which fit on the barrel at breech, thus requiring no holes to be drilled into the frame. It is surprising—and disgusting, too—to see the great many fine engraved Ballard frames that have been drilled and tapped so that a scope block may be mounted on the top flat of the barrel housing. This is unnecessary, as a scope block mounted on the breech of the barrel serves just as well.

When converting any of these fine old rifles, consider carefully if the piece is a desirable collection piece before starting the job. The plain models are usually easy to find, and they make just as fine shooting match or varment jobs. Save the fine, original piece for your own pleasure, or dispose of it to a collector who will usually pay a handsome price to obtain it for his collection. There are too few of these really fine specimens to satisfy the demand, so think twice before you destroy one forever.

Figure I, on page 341, shows a British side-lever rifle, the Westley Richards side-lever Farquharson, restocked and rebarreled in .22/3000 improved Lovell caliber.

Figure G, on the same page, depicts a fine little R-2 rifle made of a Birmingham Small Arms Martini .22 rim-fire match rifle, and restocked with curly maple. This rifle is from the M. L. Kennedy collection.

This concludes the single-shot story as I am able to tell it. It has been a great pleasure to attempt, by spreading the gospel as it might be called, to repay in some small measure the vast number of interesting hours this type of rifle has given me. Possibly this little effort will help this sorely neglected style of rifle to attain the recognition it deserves. But neither this volume nor any other effort in the book field will make these rifles more desired or sought after than they now are among men who appreciate them.

As time goes on, it is only natural to expect that these guns will be even more desirable. It is not likely that there will ever be any more Ballards or Stevens 44½ rifles made, and possibly this is as it should be; for after all, fashions in shooting and in rifles change, as do all other things. This, I presume, we can dismiss under the heading of progress.

APPENDIX

TABLE I

Rifling Twists Used in Various Single-shot Rifles

Caliber	Powder load	Bullet weight	Twist	Remarks
.22 rf	3 grs.	30 grs.	20 to 25	Early abandoned by some for .16 or .18
.22 rf	5 grs.	40 grs.	16 to 18	Used by some for .22 Long rifle
.22 cf	7 or 8 grs.	45 grs.	16	Maynard .22 Ex. Long cf
.22 rf		45 grs.	14	WRF .22 Model 1890
.22 cf	13 grs.	45 grs.	16	WCF .22-13-45
.22 cf	15 grs.	60 grs.	12	Stevens .22-15-60
.25 rf	11 grs.	67 grs.	17	Stevens
.25 cf	19 and 20 grs.	77 and 86 grs.	12 to 15	Stevens and Maynard .25-20 single-shot
.25 cf	19, 21, and 25 grs.	86 grs.	13 and 14	Stevens .25-21 and .25-25
.28 cf	30 grs.	120 grs.	14	Stevens
.32 rf	9 and 13 grs.	82 and 90 grs.	20 and 22	.32 Long and Ex. Long rf
.32 cf	13 grs.	90 grs.	20	.32 Long cf
.32 cf	20 grs.	115 grs.	16 to 20	Winchester
.32 cf	20 grs.	100 grs.	24	Colt and Marlin
.32 cf	35 grs.	165 grs.	16	Stevens and Maynard
.32 cf	40 grs.	150 grs.	16	Remington .32-40-150
.32 cf	30 grs.	125 grs.	16	Remington .32-30-125
.32 cf	25 grs.	150 grs.	18	Ideal .32
.32 cf	40 grs.			Bullard .32-40
.32 cf	40 grs.	165 grs.	16	Ballard and Marlin .32-40
.35 cf	40 grs.	240 grs.	16 to 18	Maynard
.38 cf	40 grs.	180 grs.	18, 28, 36	Winchester, Marlin, Colt, etc.
.38 cf	45 grs.	190 grs.		Bullard
.38 cf	55 and 48 grs.	255 grs.	16 to 20	Ballard and Marlin
.38 cf	40 grs.	245 grs.	16	Remington .38-40-245
.38 cf	50 grs.	265 grs.	16	Remington .38-50
.38 cf	50 grs.	255 grs.	20	Ballard .38-50
.38 cf	56 grs.	255 grs.	20 to 25	Winchester .38-56
.38 cf	90 grs.	217 grs.	26	Winchester
.40 cf	40 grs.	265 grs.	18 to 20	Maynard
.40 cf	45 grs.	265 grs.	18 to 20	Sharps and Remington
.40 cf	50 grs.	265 and 285 grs.	18 to 20	Sharps and Remington
.40 cf	60 grs.	210 grs.	40	Winchester
.40 cf	60 grs.	260 grs.	20	Marlin
.40 cf	65 grs.	260 grs.	20 to 26	Winchester
.40 cf	65 grs.	330 grs.	18 to 20	Sharps and Remington
.40 cf	70 grs.	330 grs.	18 to 20	Ballard .40-70
.40 cf	82 grs.	260 grs.	28	Winchester

TABLE I (Continued)
Rifling Twists Used in Various Single-shot Rifles (Continued)

Caliber	Powder load	Bullet weight	Twist	Remarks
.40 cf	90 grs.	370 grs.	18 to 20	Sharps and Ballard
.40 cf	110 grs.	260 grs.	28	Winchester
.43 cf	77 grs.	395 grs.	20	Spanish .43
.44 cf	40 grs.	200 grs.	20 and 36	Winchester
.45 cf	60 grs.	300 grs.	20 and 25	Winchester
.45 cf	70 grs.	405 grs.	18	Sporting
.45 cf	70 grs.	405 grs.	20	Winchester, Marlin, and Remington
.45 cf	70 grs.	405 grs.	22	U. S. Government
.45 cf	70 grs.	500 grs.	22	U. S. Government
.45 cf	75 grs.	350 grs.	20	Winchester
.45 cf	85 grs.	295 grs.	25	Colt Magazine Rifle
.45 cf	90 grs.	300 grs.	32	Winchester
.45 cf	125 grs.	300 grs.	36	Winchester
.50 cf	70 grs.	450 grs.	42	U. S. Government .50-70
.50 cf	95 grs.	300 grs.	60	Winchester
.50 cf	95 grs.	300 grs.	54	Colt
.50 cf	110 grs.	300 grs.	60	Winchester
.50 cf	115 grs.	300 grs.	72	Bullard

TABLE II
Sight Slots Found on Single-shot and Repeating Rifles

REAR SLOTS

Rifle	Inches	Rifle	Inches
Colt .22	$21/64$	Hopkins & Allen (old)	$22/64$
Stevens	$21/64$	Hopkins & Allen (new)	$24/64$
Frank Wesson	$21/64$	Remington No. 4	$24/64$
Winchester	$24/64$	Maynard	$18/64$
Colt .32, .38, .44	$22/64$	Winchester M1890	$24/64$
Remington	$21/64$	Ballard and Marlin	$24/64$
Sharps	$30/64$	Bullard	$24/64$

FRONT SLOTS

Rifle	Inches	Rifle	Inches
Remington (old)	$30/64$	Colt Old Model	$20/64$
Remington No. 2 (new)	$25/64$	Bullard	$24/64$
Marlin and Ballard	$24/64$	Maynard	$30/64$
Winchester	$24/64$	Remington No. 4	$24/64$
Colt .32, .38, .44	$23/64$	Sharps	$27/64$
Colt .22	$20/64$	Hopkins & Allen (old)	$22/64$
Stevens .25 (regular)	$29/64$	Hopkins & Allen (new)	$24/64$
Stevens Special	$24/64$		

NOTE: The sight slots of different rifles of the same manufacture will be found to vary slightly. The measurements here given were taken with a Brown & Sharpe steel rule.

APPENDIX

TABLE III
Case Lengths and Factory Load Cartridge Data

Cartridge	Powder load	Bullet weight	Case length
.22 Ex. Long cf Maynard M1882	8 grs.	45 grs.	$1\tfrac{5}{32}$ ins.
.22 Winchester cf............	13 grs.	45 grs.	$1\tfrac{13}{32}$ ins.
.22-15-60 Stevens............	15 grs.	60 grs.	2 ins.
.25-20 Single-shot...........	19 grs.	86 grs.	$1\tfrac{5}{8}$ ins.
.25-21 Stevens...............	21 grs.	86 grs.	$2\tfrac{1}{16}$ ins.
.25-25 Stevens...............	25 grs.	86 grs.	$2\tfrac{3}{8}$ ins.
.28-30 Stevens...............	30 grs.	120 grs.	$2\tfrac{1}{2}$ ins.
.32 Long cf..................	13 grs.	90 grs.	$\tfrac{13}{16}$ in.
.32 Ex. Long cf..............	20 grs.	115 grs.	$1\tfrac{7}{32}$ ins.
.32-20 Winchester............	20 grs.	115 grs.	$1\tfrac{5}{16}$ ins.
.32-30 Remington.............	30 grs.	125 grs.	$1\tfrac{5}{8}$ ins.
.32-35 Stevens and Maynard Taper...................	35 grs.	165 grs. and 153 grs. PP	$1\tfrac{7}{8}$ ins.
.32-40 Bullard...............	40 grs.	150 grs.	$1\tfrac{27}{32}$ ins.
.32-40 Remington.............	40 grs.	150 grs.	$2\tfrac{1}{8}$ ins.
.32-40 Ballard and Marlin.....	40 grs.	165 grs.	$2\tfrac{1}{8}$ ins.
.35 Maynard M1873 and M1882	30 grs.	250 grs. PP	
.35 Maynard M1873 and M1882	40 grs.	240 grs. PP	
.38 Long cf..................	19 grs.	150 grs.	$1\tfrac{1}{32}$ ins.
.38 Ex. Long cf..............	38 grs.	160 grs.	$1\tfrac{5}{8}$ ins.
.38-35 Stevens Everlasting.....	35 grs.	Shot load(?)	$1\tfrac{5}{8}$ ins.
.38-40 Winchester............	40 grs.	180 grs.	$1\tfrac{5}{16}$ ins.
.38-40 Remington.............	40 grs.	245 grs.	$1\tfrac{3}{4}$ ins.
.38-45 Bullard...............	45 grs.	190 grs.	$1\tfrac{25}{32}$ ins.
.38-45 Stevens Everlasting.....	45 grs.	Shot load(?)	$2\tfrac{3}{16}$ ins.
.38-50 Ballard Everlasting.....	50 grs.	255 grs.	$1\tfrac{13}{16}$ ins.
.38-50 Remington.............	50 grs.	265 grs. and 330 grs. PP	$2\tfrac{1}{4}$ ins.
.38-55 Ballard and Marlin.....	48 grs.	255 grs.	$2\tfrac{1}{10}$ ins.
.38-56 Winchester............	56 grs.	255 grs.	$2\tfrac{1}{10}$ ins.
.38-70 Winchester............	68 grs.	255 grs.	$2\tfrac{5}{16}$ ins.
.38-72 Winchester............	72 grs.	275 grs.	$2\tfrac{6}{10}$ ins.
.38-90 Winchester Express.....	90 grs.	217 grs.	$3\tfrac{1}{4}$ ins.
.40-40 Maynard M1873 and M1882.................	40 grs.	270 grs.	$1\tfrac{55}{64}$ ins.
.40-45 Sharps and Remington Straight [1].............	45 grs.	265 grs.	$1\tfrac{7}{8}$ ins.
.40-50 Sharps and Remington Bottleneck..............	50 grs.	285 grs.	$1\tfrac{11}{16}$ ins.
.40-60 Winchester............	62 grs.	210 grs.	$1\tfrac{7}{8}$ ins.
.40-60 Marlin................	60 grs.	260 grs.	$2\tfrac{1}{10}$ ins.
.40-63 Ballard Everlasting.....	63 grs.	330 grs.	$2\tfrac{3}{8}$ ins.
.40-65 Winchester............	65 grs.	260 grs.	$2\tfrac{1}{10}$ ins.

[1] The .40-45 and .40-50 SS are the same cases.

TABLE III (*Continued*)

Case Lengths and Factory Load Cartridge Data

Cartridge	Powder load	Bullet weight	Case length
.40-65 Sharps and Remington Straight [2]	65 grs.	330 grs.	$2\frac{1}{2}$ ins.
.40-65 Ballard Everlasting	65 grs.	330 grs.	$2\frac{3}{8}$ ins.
.40-70 Ballard	70 grs.	330 grs.	$2\frac{3}{8}$ ins.
.40-70 Sharps and Remington Bottleneck	70 grs.	370 grs.	$2\frac{1}{4}$ ins.
.40-70 Peabody Martini What Cheer	70 grs.	380 grs.	$1\frac{11}{16}$ and $1\frac{3}{4}$ ins.
.40-70 Bullard	72 grs.	232 grs.	$2\frac{3}{8}$ ins.
.40-70 Winchester	70 grs.	330 grs.	$2\frac{4}{10}$ ins.
.40-70 Maynard M1873	70 grs.	270 grs. and 330 grs. PP	$2\frac{7}{16}$ ins.
.40-75 Winchester (Hollow Point ball)	75 grs.	260 grs.	$2\frac{4}{10}$ ins.
.40-75 Bullard	75 grs.	259 grs.	$2\frac{1}{10}$ ins.
.40-85 Ballard	85 grs.	370 grs.	$2\frac{15}{16}$ ins.
.40-90 Ballard	90 grs.	370 grs.	$2\frac{15}{16}$ ins.
.40-90 Peabody Martini What Cheer [3]	90 grs.	500 grs.	$2\frac{1}{16}$ ins.
.40-90 Sharps Straight	90 grs.	370 grs.	$3\frac{1}{4}$ ins.
.40-90 Sharps and Remington Bottleneck	90 grs.	370 grs.	$2\frac{5}{8}$ ins.
.40-90 Bullard	90 grs.	300 grs.	$2\frac{1}{32}$ ins.
.40-90 Ideal Everlasting	90 grs.	370 grs.	$3\frac{1}{16}$ ins.
.40-110 Winchester Express	110 grs.	260 grs.	$3\frac{1}{4}$ ins.
.40-82 Winchester	82 grs.	260 grs.	$2\frac{4}{10}$ ins.
.42 Russian	77 grs.	370 grs.	$2\frac{1}{4}$ ins.
.42 Russian Carbine	60 grs.	370 grs.	$1\frac{7}{8}$ ins.
.43 Spanish	77 grs.	395 grs.	$2\frac{1}{4}$ ins.
.43 Carbine	60 grs.	400 grs.	$1\frac{7}{8}$ ins.
.43 Egyptian	70 grs.	400 grs.	$1\frac{15}{16}$ ins.
.44-40 Winchester	40 grs.	200 grs.	$1\frac{5}{16}$ ins.
.44 Evans Old Model	28 grs.	215 grs.	$\frac{63}{64}$ in.
.44 Evans New Model	42 grs.	280 grs.	$1\frac{9}{16}$ ins.
.44 Long Center Fire			$\frac{7}{8}$ in. and $1\frac{1}{16}$ ins.
.44 Extra Long Center Fire	48 grs.	250 grs.	$1\frac{19}{32}$ ins.
.44-50 Stevens Everlasting	50 grs.	Shot load(?)	2 ins.
.44-60 Sharps and Regular Bottleneck	60 grs.	395 grs.	$1\frac{9}{10}$ ins.
.44-65 Stevens Everlasting	65 grs.	Shot load(?)	$2\frac{1}{2}$ ins.
.44-75 Ballard Everlasting	75 grs.	405 grs. and 420 grs. PP	$2\frac{1}{2}$ ins.
.44-77 Sharps and Regular Bottleneck	77 grs.	470 grs.	$2\frac{1}{4}$ ins.

[2] The .40-65 and .40-70 SS are the same cases.

[3] The .40-90 What Cheer case was also loaded with 70 grains of powder and a 500-grain ball.

APPENDIX

TABLE III (*Continued*)

Case Lengths and Factory Load Cartridge Data

Cartridge	Powder load	Bullet weight	Case length
.44-90 Sharps and Regular Bottleneck	90 grs.	470 grs.	$2\frac{1}{4}$ ins.
.44-90 Remington and Sharps Special	90 grs.	520 grs.	$2\frac{5}{8}$ and $2\frac{7}{16}$ ins.
.44-105 Remington and Sharps Special Bottleneck	105 grs.	520 grs.	$2\frac{5}{8}$ and $2\frac{7}{16}$ ins.
.44-95 Peabody Martini What Cheer	95 grs.	550 grs.	$2\frac{5}{16}$ ins.
.44-100 Remington Special Straight [4]	100 grs.	550 grs.	$2\frac{6}{10}$ ins.
.44-100 Ballard Everlasting	100 grs.	500 grs.	$2\frac{13}{16}$ ins.
.44-100 Maynard M1873	100 grs.	430 grs. and 520 grs. PP	$2\frac{7}{8}$ ins.
.45 Sporting	50 grs.	290 grs.	$1\frac{3}{24}$ ins.
.45 Government	70 grs.	500 grs.	$2\frac{1}{10}$ ins.
.45 Government Carbine	50 grs.	405 grs.	$2\frac{1}{10}$ ins.
.45 Gov't Sharpshooter Special	80 grs.	500 grs.	$2\frac{4}{10}$ ins.
.45-75 Sharps	75 grs.	420 grs. PP	$2\frac{1}{10}$ ins.
.45-70 Sharps patched	70 grs.	420 grs.	$2\frac{1}{10}$ ins.
.45 Wolcott	75 grs.	475 grs.	$2\frac{2}{10}$ ins.
.45 Peabody Martini Carbine	55 grs.	400 grs.	$1\frac{5}{8}$ ins.
.45 Peabody Martini	80 grs.	500 grs.	$2\frac{5}{16}$ ins.
.45 Martini-Henry	85 grs.	480 grs.	$2\frac{5}{16}$ ins.
.45 Danish	50 grs.	380 grs.	$1\frac{21}{32}$ ins.
.45 Roumanian	70 grs.	380 grs.	$1\frac{15}{16}$ ins.
.45 Van Choate	70 grs.	420 grs.	$2\frac{1}{4}$ ins.
.45-75 Winchester	75 grs.	350 grs.	$1\frac{7}{8}$ ins.
.45-60 Straight Single Shot Target	60 grs.		$1\frac{31}{32}$ ins.
.45-60 Winchester	62 grs.	300 grs.	$1\frac{7}{8}$ ins.
.45-70 Marlin	70 grs.	405 grs.	$2\frac{1}{10}$ ins.
.45-85 Marlin	85 grs.	285 grs.	$2\frac{1}{10}$ ins.
.45-85 Bullard	85 grs.	295 grs.	$2\frac{1}{10}$ ins.
.45-82 Winchester	82 grs.	405 grs.	$2\frac{4}{10}$ ins.
.45-85 Winchester	85 grs.	350 grs.	$2\frac{4}{10}$ ins.
.45-90 Winchester	90 grs.	300 grs.	$2\frac{4}{10}$ ins.
.45-100 Sharps Special	100 grs.	500 grs.	$2\frac{4}{10}$ ins.
.45-100 Sharps Special	100 grs.	500 grs.	$2\frac{6}{10}$ ins.
.45-100 Sharps Special [5]	100 grs.	550 grs.	$2\frac{7}{8}$ ins.
.45-120 Sharps Special	120 grs.	550 grs.	$3\frac{1}{4}$ ins.
.45-125 Winchester Express	125 grs.	300 grs.	$3\frac{1}{4}$ ins.
.45-100 Ballard Everlasting	100 grs.	550 grs. PP	$2\frac{13}{16}$ ins.
.50 Remington Pistol cf	25 grs.	300 grs.	$\frac{7}{8}$ in.
.50 Carbine	50 grs.	400 grs.	$1\frac{7}{20}$ ins.

[4] This is the Special straight cartridge for the Remington Military Creedmoor rifle.
[5] This Sharps $2\frac{7}{8}$-inch case was also loaded with 120 grains of powder.

TABLE III (Continued)
Case Lengths and Factory Load Cartridge Data

Cartridge	Powder load	Bullet weight	Case length
.50 Musket	70 grs.	450 grs.	1¾ ins.
.50 Sporting	70 grs.	425 grs.	1¾ ins.
.50-90 Sharps	90 grs.	473 grs.	2½ ins.
.50-95 Winchester Express	95 grs.	312 grs.	1¹⁵⁄₁₆ ins.
.50-95 Winchester Express	95 grs.	300 grs. HP	1¹⁵⁄₁₆ ins.
.50-100 Winchester	100 grs.	450 grs.	2⁴⁄₁₀ ins.
.50-110 Winchester Express	110 grs.	300 grs. MPHP	2⁴⁄₁₀ ins.
.50 Sharps Special	140 grs.(?)	700 grs. PP(?)	3¼ ins.
.58 Musket	85 grs.	530 grs.	1¾ ins.
.58 Carbine	40 grs.	530 grs.	1⅛ ins.
.58 Roberts	70 grs.	480 grs.	1⅜ ins.
.58 Snyder Turkish Model	85 grs.	480 grs.	1⁹⁄₁₆ ins.

TABLE IV
Case Lengths and Loads of Rim Fire Cartridges

Cartridge	Powder load	Bullet weight	Case length
.22 WRF Rim Fire	7 grs.	45 grs.	⁶³⁄₆₄ in.
.22 Extra Long rf	7 grs.	40 grs.	⁵⁰⁄₆₄ in.
.25 Stevens rf	11 grs.	65 grs.	1⅛ ins.
.32 Long rf	13 grs.	90 grs.	²⁵⁄₃₂ in.
.32 Extra Long rf	20 grs.	90 grs.	1⅛ ins.
.38 Long rf	21 grs.	148 grs.	⅞ in.
.38 Extra Long rf	38 grs.	148 grs.	1¹⁵⁄₃₂ ins.
.41 Swiss rf	55 grs.	310 grs.	1³⁰⁄₆₄ ins.
.44 Henry Flat Rim Fire	28 grs.	200 grs.	²⁹⁄₃₂ in.
.44 Long rf (Howard)	28 grs.	220 grs.	1¹⁄₁₆ ins.
.44 Extra Long rf	30 grs.	220 grs.	1³⁴⁄₆₄ ins.
.46 Long rf	40 grs.	300 grs.	1¹⁵⁄₆₄ ins.
.50 Remington Pistol rf	23 grs.	290 grs.	⁵⁵⁄₆₄ in.
.50 Peabody rf	45 grs.	320 grs.	1¹⁴⁄₃₂ ins.
.50-70 Gov't rf	70 grs.		1⁴⁷⁄₆₄ ins.
.52-70 Sharps rf	70 grs.		1¹⁵⁄₃₂ ins.
.52 Carbine rf	50 grs.		
.56-46 Spencer rf	45 grs.	330 grs.	1¹⁄₃₂ ins.
.56-50 Spencer rf	45 grs.	350 grs.	1¹⁄₃₂ ins.
.56-52 Spencer rf	45 grs.	386 grs.	¹⁵⁄₁₆ in.
.56-56 Spencer, Ballard, and Joslyn rf	45 grs.	350 grs.	⁵⁷⁄₆₄, 1⁵⁄₁₆, 1⁵⁄₃₂ ins.
.58 Miller rf			1⁷⁄₃₂ ins.

Index

Italics indicate illustrations

Ackley, P. O., 354
Allen and Wheelock rifle, 347
Aydt system, *317*, *320*, *321*, *322*, 326-328

Baker, Clyde, 344
Ballard single-shot rifles, 1-49, *3*, *5*, *7*, *9*, *216-217*, 219; finger levers, *11*; breechblocks and set triggers, *16*, *17*; ammunition, *21*, 23, *24*, 41-48; shotgun butt plates, *27*; sights, *29*, *31*; Everlasting cases, 32-33, *42*, 44-48; implements, 33, 48-49; engraving, *34*, *35*, *38*, *40*, *43*, *45*, *48*; shooting the, 41-49; action, 49; extractor, 49; firing pin, 49; Farrow association with, 307-308, 309; remodeling, 361-368.
Listing—
Creedmoor A-1 Long Range No. 7, 9
Far West No. 1¾, 12, 37
Gallery No. 3, (1876) 7-8; (1883) 15, 22, 37; (1888) 34
Gallery No. 3F, (1883) 15; (1888) 34-35, 37
Hunter's, (1875) 6
Hunter's No. 1, 6
Hunter's No. 1½, 12, 14, 20, 36
Long Range No. 7, 10
Long Range No. 7-A, 13, 24-25, 39
Long Range No. 7-A-1, (1876) 10, 12; (1878) 13, 25, 26, 39-40; (1883) 18
Long Range No. 7-A-1 Extra, 14, 40, 40-41
Mid Range No. 4½, 13, 37
Mid Range No. 4½-A-1, 13, 23-24, 34, 37
Montana No. 5½ (1880) 14; (1883) 18, 22, 37
Offhand No. 6½, 14, 38, 38-39

Ballard single-shot rifles (Cont.)
Listing (Cont.)—
Pacific No. 5 (1876) 8, 12 n., 13; (1882) 15, 18, 22, 26, 35, 37
Perfection No. 4, (1876) 8; (1884) 15, 22, 37, 41; (1888) 34
Pistol Grip Offhand No. 6½, 18, 23, 25, 26
Rigby Offhand Mid Range No. 6½, 13, 25, 26, 36, 39
Schuetzen Junior No. 10, 19, 35, 41
Schuetzen Offhand No. 6, (1876) 8, 18, 22; (1882) 25, 26, 35-36, 38
Sporting, Brown Manufacturing Co., 6, 36
Sporting No. 2, (1876) 6; (1879) 12; (1881) 15, 20, 22, 37; (1888) 33
Sporting No. 4½, 12
Target No. 3½, 12
Union Hill No. 8, 19, 35, 41
Union Hill No. 9, 19, 35, 41
Barnes, F. M., 172 n.
Beise, Charles J., 227
Belding and Mull, 224, 226
Benz, G., 324
Billings and Spencer Company, 49 n.
Birmingham Small Arms Company. See Martini BSA.
BSA Martini, 262, 333, 336, *341*; remodeling, 357. See also Rook rifle.
Breechblocks, Ballard, *16*, *17*, 18
Bridgeport Gun Implement Company, 159
British single-shot rifles, 331-337; Martini-Henry, 331-332; Swinburn action, 332; Henry Breechloading, 332; Field action, 332; Westley Richards Sliding Block action, *332*, *334*; Greener Martini, 333; Farquharson Match, 333-334, *335*, *336*; BSA Martini Match, 333; Fraser,

335; Martini Match, 336; Rook, 336; Greener Martini Rook, 336-337
Browning, John M., 201
Browning single-shot rifle (Winchester), 203, 231, 232
Brown Manufacturing Company, 6
Büchel, Ernst Friedrich, 315
Büchel system, 315, 318; target pistols, 321
Bullard Repeating Arms Company, 297
Bullard single-shot rifles, 297-304; cartridges, 302-304; loading tools, 303.
Listing—
Military, 299, 302
Offhand, 301
Offhand target, 301
Schuetzen, 299
Special Detachable Barrel, 299
Special Target, 300, 304
Sporting, 301
Target, 299
Target, Gallery, and Hunting, 299
Bullets, 217-218
Burnside cartridge, 277
Butt plates, shotgun, 26, 27

Carbines: Remington, 117, 131, 132, 133; Sharps Borchardt, 176, 196, 197, 198, 277; Winchester, 207, 211; Peabody, 249; Peabody-Martini, 264, 266; Whitney, 269; Phoenix, 276; Maynard, 277; Sharps, 277
Cartridges: Ballard, 21, 23, 24, 32-33, 41-49; Stevens, 55, 56, 57, 61, 85, 104-111; Remington, 127, 128, 134, 136, 146-159; Sharps, 178, 179, 180, 181, 182, 183-194; Winchester, 204-206, 208, 214-229, 220, 221, 222, 223, 224; Wurfflein, 245-247; Peabody and Peabody-Martini, 254-260, 256, 257; Whitney, 271; Maynard, 278, 279, 280, 281, 282, 283, 290, 292-296; Bullard, 302, 303
Chandler, M. G., 4
Creedmoor Rifle Range, 331
Creedmoor rifles: Ballard, 9, 18, 39-40; Remington, 117, 120, 121, 123, 131, 135-137, 140, 143, 145, 160; Sharps, 168-170, 176; Wesson, 234; Peabody-Martini, 251, 252, 253, 254, 259; Whitney, 269; Maynard, 289, 296
Creedmoor targets, 293, 295

Diller, Charles, 342
Dollymount Rifle Range, 331
Donaldson, H. A., 227
Dryk, Arthur C., 234

Egyptian .43 cases, 254, 255
Engraved actions, 350, 351
Everlasting shells, 32-33, 42, 44-48, 184-188, 245

Farquharson single-shot rifles, 332, 333-334, 335, 336, 341; remodeling, 368
Farrow, W. Milton, 307
Farrow Arms Company, 307
Farrow Offhand Plate, 307
Farrow single-shot rifles, 144, 307-310; lubricant, 309; target rifle, 309
Field action, 332
Foreign single-shot rifles, 311-337; Swiss and German, 311-330; British, 331-337
Francotte, M., 262, 331
Fraser, Daniel, and Company rifles, 334, 335, 336
Freund (F. W.) Rifle, 195
Fuller, Claude E., 268

German single-shot rifles, 311-330; Schilling, 312, 313; Stahl system Martini, 315, 320, 324, 325; Büchel system, 315, 318; Haenel, Aydt, and Haenel Aydt, 316, 317, 320, 321, 322, 323, 326-328; Kolbe action, 320; Kessler action, 320, 322-324; Martini system, 320, 324-326, 327; Nagel, 328-330
Gibbs and Pitt breech action, 333
Gould, A. C., 193, 215 n., 216 n.
Greener, W. W., 331-332; rifles made by, 333, 336-337

INDEX

Hadley's device, 278, 279, 284, *291*
Haenel and Haenel Aydt rifles, *316*, *317*, 320, *321*, *322*, *323*, 326-328
Harpers Ferry muskets, 277
Hatcher, Colonel, 250
Hayes, William, 81 n.
Heel bullets, 217
Henry (Alexander) actions, 233, 263, 332
Hepburn, Lewis Lobell, 136, 139
Hepburn action, 139-144, 163. See also Remington Hepburn rifles.
Hopkins and Allen single-shot rifles, 304-307, 309; Take Down models, 305, *306*, 307; Junior, 305-306; series for rim-fire cartridges, 306; Schuetzen, 306-307; .32/20, 307
Howe, James V., 344

Ideal Manufacturing Company, 227

Jenkins, Dr. Paul, 274, 275
Johnson, Charles C., 1, 254, 330, 336, 342, 344, 346, 352, 353, 357, 359, 365

Kahrs, Frank J., 137, 163
Kennedy repeating rifles, 274
Kessler action, 320, 322-324, 336
Kolbe action, 320

Laidley, Col. T. S. S., 268
Laidley and Emery, 268
Lawrence pellet primer mechanism, 166, 168
Leopold's Banana Lubricant, 227
Leopold Olio Wads, 228
Levers, Ballard, 10, *11*, 67
Lovell, Hervey, 329, 330, 331
Lower, J. P., 171, 364
Lubrication, ammunition, 217, 226-228
Lyman Gun Sight Corporation, 189, 224, 226

Malcolm telescopic sight, 54
Mann, Dr., 227
Mann-Niedner firing pin, 344
Marble-Goss, 368
Marlin, John M., 14
Marlin, J. M., Company, 2, 4, 6, 14

Marlin Firearms Company, 2, 14; catalogues quoted, 20-25, 28-33
Martini-Henry rifle, 331-332
Martini system, 250; Rook rifles, 262, 336-337; German, 262, 315, 320, 324, 325, 326, 327; Martini BSA, *341*, 368
Mayer, Frank, 184
Maynard rifles, 277-297; cartridges, 278-279, 280, *281*, *282*, *283*, *291*; action, 279; sights, 279; Hadley's devices, 279, *284*, *285*, *291*; tools and reloading accessories, 279, 284, *285*, 289; Creedmoor targets, 293, 295; ammunition, 292-296
Listing—
Gallery No. 1, 283
Gallery or Small Game Hunting No. 2, 283-284
Hunter's No. 5, 285
Hunter's No. 7, 285-286
Hunter's No. 8, 286
Hunter's No. 11, 288
Hunting or Target No. 3, 284
Hunting or Target No. 4, 284
Hunting or Target No. 9, 286
Long Range Creedmoor No. 14, 289, 296
Mid Range Target and Hunting No 10, 286, 288
Mid Range No. 12, 288
Mid Range Target No. 13, 288
Percussion Sporting, 277, 287
Shot Gun No. 1, 290
Shot Gun No. 2, 291
Shot Gun No. 3, 291
Sporting No. 6, 285
Sporting No. 11, 287
Target No. 15, 290
Target No. 16, 282, 287, 290, 296

Niedner Rifle Corporation, 330, 333, 344, 367

Patch guide, 289
Peabody, Henry O., 249
Peabody-Martini rifles, 250-267; engraved model, *251*; "What Cheer" and other cartridges, 252, 254-260; action, 258, 260, *261*; altered by

382 INDEX

Francotte, 262; description, 262-267; tools, 265; assembling and dismounting, 266-267; foreign adoption of, 311.
Listing—
Creedmoor Long Range, 251, 252, 253, 254, 259
Creedmoor Mid Range, 251, 252, 253, 259
Kill Deer, 251, 252, 253, 259, 266
Match, 261, 266
Mid Range, 252, 254-255
Military, 260, 264
Rough and Ready, 251
Peabody rifles, 249-250; military rifle, 249-250; action, 258. See also Peabody-Martini rifles.
Peterson, A. W., 175, 346, 367
Phoenix rifles, 269-276; system, 273-274; calibers, 274-275; cartridges, 275.
Listing—
Gallery, 275
Military carbine, 276
Military rifle, 276
Schuetzen target, 276
Sporting and target, 272, 273, 275
Pistols: Stevens, 76, 77; Remington, 133, 138-139, 145, 160, 161; Wesson, 234, 236-237; Wurfflein, 244; Büchel and Tell, 321
Pope, H. M., 77, 78, 79-80, 81, 81 n., 175
Providence Tool Company, 249, 250, 251, 258, 262, 264

Rabbeth, F. J., 227
Remington, E., 114
Remington Arms Company, 114; barrel, 189, 194, 198
Remington Hepburn rifles, 119, 120-123, 125-131, 139-144, 155, 217, 340; remodeling, 354-357.
Listing—
Creedmoor Improved, 120-121
Creedmoor Long Range, 121
Creedmoor Long Range Military, 123, 140
Creedmoor Mid Range, 143, 160
Hunter's. See Sporting No. 3.

Remington Hepburn rifles (Cont.)
Listing (Cont.)—
Improved No. 3, 120
Match, 122
Match No. 3, 130
Match Grade B, 143, 160
Schuetzen Match (New Special), 129-130, 134, 137
Schuetzen "Special," 134, 142, 155, 162
Short and Mid Range, 122
Sporting No. 3 (Basic), 120, 121, 125-126, 128-129, 141, 143, 159, 160
Remington-Rider rolling-block action, 113, 114, 115, 116-119, 122, 123-129, 131, 134-140
Remington Rolling-block rifles, 114 ff., 147, 216, 268, 272.
Listing—
Adirondack, 115
Black Hills, 116
Buffalo (Sporting No. 1), 116, 145, 160
Civil Guard, 117
Creedmoor Long Range, 117, 135-137, 145, 160
Creedmoor Mid Range No. 3, 131
Deer, 115
Egyptian, 116
High Power No. 3, 129
Match, 122
Match Grade A (early Schuetzen No. 3), 130, 143, 160
Match Grade B No. 3, 130-131, 156
Match "Special" Grade B No. 3, 131
Mid Range No. 1, 118-119
Military, 116-117, 123, 131-132, 145, 160
Schuetzen .38/55, 147, 161
Short and Mid Range, 122
Short Range No. 1, 118
Spanish, 116
"Special" No. 5, 125, 161
Sporting No. 1, 114-115, 116, 117, 132, 143, 160
Sporting No. 2, 119, 124, 132
Sporting No. 4, 123-124
Sporting and Target No. 7, 125, 135, 137-138

INDEX 383

Sporting and Target No. 7 (Cont.)
  Springfield, .58, 117
  Take Down No. 4, *145*, 160
  Take Down No. 6, 124, *161*
  United States, 117
Remington single-shot pistols, 133, 138-139, *145*, 160, *161*; cartridges used in, 127, 128, 146-159
Remington single-shot rifles, 114-164; cartridges used in, 127, 128, 134, 136; auxiliary rifle barrel, tools, and implements, 133-134; loading tools, molds, and accessories, 150, 151, 152, 153. See also other Remington headings.
Remington-Walker action, 163
Remodeling, 338-369; Winchester, 342-346; Stevens 44½, 346-354; Remington Hepburn, 354-357; Farquharson, 357; BSA Martini, 357; Sharps Borchardt, 357-361; Ballard, 362-368
Roberts, N. H., 146, 147, 215-216, 310
Rook rifle, 262, 336-337
Ross, F. C., 77
Rowland, Charles W., 227
Rupertus (J.) Rifle, *195*

Satterlee, L. D., 2, 12 n., 115, 116, 165, 269, 275
Sawyer, C. W., 274
Schalke, George, 81 n.
Schilling, V. Chr., rifles, *312*, *313*
Schoverling and Daly, 14
Schoyen, George, 224, 227
Schoyen and Peterson, 224
Schuetzen rifles, Swiss and German, 311 ff.
Sharpe, Philip B., 250
Sharps Borchardt rifles, 165, *169*, *171*, 172-200, *189*, *193*; set triggers, 172, *173*, *175*, 194; paneled models, 176, *177*, *178*; vernier sights, 179-183; remodeling, 357-361.
  Listing—
  Business, 176
  Creedmoor Long Range, 176
  Express .45, *174*, 176, 194, 292
  Hunter's, 176
  Long Range, *171*, 176, *197*, 199

Sharps Borchardt rifles (Cont.)
  Listing (Cont.)—
  Mid Range, 176, *197*, 199, 359
  Military, 172, *174-175*, 176, 188, *196*, *197*, 198, 357-359
  Officer's .45-70, *174*
  Short Range, 176, *197*, 199
  Sporting, *174*, 176, 358
  Target Mid Range, 178-179
Sharps cartridges, 136, 167, *178*, *179*, *180*, *181*, *182*, 183-184, *185*, *186*, *187*, 188-193; patching bullets, 193
Sharps rifles, 165-200; hammerless actions, 165-172.
  Listing—
  Creedmoor side-hammer, 168-171
  Military carbine, *197*, 198
  Slanting Breech, *167*, *196*, 198
  Sporting (early), *166*, *167*, 168
  Sporting (heavier), **170**, *171*-172, *196*, 198
  Target, **170**
  See also Sharps Borchardt rifles.
Sheldon, Colonel H. P., 199-200
Shellhamer, Thomas, 330, 333
Shotguns: Ballard, 26, 27; Stevens, 52, 58, 59, 76; Remington, 122-123, 133, *159*; Winchester, 204, 210, *211*, *212*; Wurfflein, 243; Maynard, 290, 291; Sharps, 297; British, 331
Single-shot rifles, foreign, 311-337; remodeling, see Remodeling.
Smith, Winston O., 165, 166
Snider rifle, 274
Springfield military rifle, 358
Springfield Officers Model (1873), *195*
Stahl-Martini rifles, 315, 320, 324, 325, 336
Stevens (J.) Arms and Tool Company, 50, 296
Stevens bicycle rifles. See Stevens pocket rifles.
Stevens Conlin Rifle No. 38, 101
Stevens Everlasting center-fire shells, 59
Stevens Gould Rifle No. 37, 101
Stevens Ideal English Model 044½, 78, 92-93, 94, 96, 98, 112, 340; Ladies Model No. 56, 101-102
Stevens Ideal No. 44 models, 51, 64-92, 112-113; trigger levers, 67; engraved models, 68; extras, 74-78, 102.

Stevens Ideal No. 44 models (Cont.)
  Listing—
    Armory Model No. 414, 102
    Basic No. 44, 66-67, 97
    Ladies Model No. 55, 73-74, 102
    Modern Range No. 47, 69
    Modern Range No. 48, 69
    Range Model No. 45, 67-69
    Range Model No. 46, 69
    Walnut Hill No. 49, 69-71
    Walnut Hill No. 50, 71
    Schuetzen No. 51, 71-72, 73, 81
    Schuetzen Junior No. 52, 72-73
    Schuetzen Special No. 54, 73
Stevens Ideal No. 44½ series, 50, 51, 78, 92-103, 112-113; extras, 101; remodeling, 340, 341, 346-354.
  Listing—
    Armory Model No. 414, 102
    Basic No. 44½, 98
    Ladies Model No. 55, 101
    Ladies Model No. 56, 80, 112
    Modern Range No. 47, 79, 99, 112
    Range No. 45, 79, 98-99, 112
    Schuetzen No. 51, 80, 81, 99-100, 112
    Schuetzen Junior No. 52, 51, 70, 80, 100, 112
    Schuetzen Special No. 54, 51, 71, 80, 100-101, 112
    Semi-military model No. 404, 102
    Walnut Hill No. 49, 51, 80, 99, 112
Stevens Maynard Junior Rifle, 297
Stevens Pocket Pistols: Vernier New Model Pistol No. 40½, 76; Diamond Model Pistol No. 43, 77; Target pistols, 77
Stevens Pocket (Bicycle) Rifles and Shotguns, 50-51, 58-59, 75-77, 101.
  Listing—
    New Model Rifle No. 40, 76
    New Model Shotgun No. 39, 76
    Reliable Pocket Rifle No. 42, 76
Stevens-Pope rifles, 62, 63; barrels and accessories, 77-92; Ideal models, 88-89; Special Pope Model, 89-92
Stevens Repeating Rifle model 425, 50
Stevens single-shot rifles, 50-113, 216-217; tip-up series, 51-61; cartridges used in, 55, 56, 57, 61, 104-111;
early action and models, 60, 75-77; Ideal No. 44 models, 64-92; Favorite models, 65, 75, 97; trigger levers, 67, 91; engraved models, 68, 70, 71, 72, 74, 75; butt plates, 91; Ideal No. 44½ models, 92-103; reboring services, 103-104; illustrations described, 112-113. See also other Stevens headings.
Stevens Tip-up rifles, 51-61, 52, 54, 58.
  Listing—
    Expert Rifle No. 5, 53
    Expert Rifle No. 6, 53
    Gallery Rifle No. 2, 51
    Gallery Rifle No. 4, 53
    Hunter's Pet rifles, 54, 58-59
    Ladies rifles, 52, 53, 56-58
    New Model Range Rifle, 55-56
    Pistol model No. 41, 76
    Pocket (Bicycle) rifles, 54, 58-59
    Premier Rifle No. 7, 53, 55
    Premier Rifle No. 8, 53, 55, 78, 112
    Range Rifle No. 10, 56, 74, 75, 78, 112
    Shotguns, 52, 53, 58, 59
    Sporting Rifle No. 1, 52, 53
    Target rifle, 52, 53
    Tip-up Rifle No. 1, 51
    Tip-up Rifle No. 3, 51, 53
Swinburn action, 332
Swiss and German single-shot rifles, 311-330; Swiss Martinis, 313, 326, 334. See also German single-shot rifles.

Tabatière rifle, 274
Tables—
  I. Rifling Twists, 370-371
  II. Sight Slots, 371
  III. Case Lengths and Factory Load Cartridge Data, 372-375
  IV. Case Lengths and Loads of Rim Fire Cartridges, 375
Targets, Creedmoor, 293, 295
Tedman, Allyn, 347
Tell target pistols, 321
Toggenburger, Frederich, 195
Toggenburger Martini Rifle, 195
Triggers, Ballard, 16, 17, 18; set, 172, 173, 175, 194
Tryon, George K., 251

INDEX

Union Metallic Cartridge Company, 47, 104 n., 111, 154, 183, 189, 190, 214, 254, 255, 296

Vickers rifles, 336
Vickery, W. F., 344, 358, 366

Wagar, J. V. K., 165, 184, 202, 260, 346
Wainwright, Fred, 234
Walker, L. N., 163
Walker Special Schuetzen barrels, 162, 163
Wesson (F.) rifles, 216-217, 233-240; tip-up models, 233, 235; falling-block models, 233-234, 235, 240; breech-loading models, 234, 236, 237-238, 239; cartridges, 236-237.
Listing—
Creedmoor models, **234**
Falling-block model, **233**
Long Range Creedmoor, 234
Long Range No. 1, 235
Long Range No. 2, 235
Long Range Champion, 237, 238
Mid Range .42 Russian Berdan, 234, 235
Mid Range Sporting and Gallery, 238, 240
Pocket (pistol), 234, 236-237, 239
Tip-up models, 233, 235
Tip-up target, 235
Westley Richards action, 332, 334
"What Cheer" rifles and cartridges. *See* Peabody rifles *and* Peabody-Martini rifles.
What Cheer Target Range, 252, 254
Whitney, Eli, 268
Whitney, Eli, III, 274
Whitney Arms Company, 274
Whitney rollingblock rifles, 268-269, 270, 271, 272.
Listing—
Creedmoor Long Range, 269
Creedmoor Mid Range, 269
Gallery, 269

Whitney rollingblock rifles (Cont.)
Listing (Cont.)—
Light carbine, 269
Military, 269
Military carbine, 269
Sporting and target, 269, 273
Winchester single-shot falling-block rifles, 201-232; high-wall action types, 202; Express action, 202, 206; Browning model, 202, 203, 231, 232; low-wall action, 202-203, 309; take-down versions, 203-204, 210, 213; repeating shotguns, 204; cartridges, 204-206, 208, 214-229; sights, 206; target models, 207-208; extras, 208; calibers, 208; price list, 209; system, 214; loading tools, etc., 222-228; lubricants, 227; remodeling, 342-346.
Listing—
Express, 202, 206, 229, 230
First model, 201, 202, 203
High side-wall, 229, 231
Schuetzen, 207, 231, 232
Sporting (Plain), 207, 209, 229, 230
Sporting (Special), 207, 209, 229, 231, 232
Take down, 204, 212-214
Take down Schuetzen, 211
Target (Special), 207
Winchester-Winder muskets, 202, 204, 209
Winder, Colonel C. B., 204
Winder musket. *See* Winchester-Winder musket.
Witsil, W. E., 146
Wotkyns, Captain, 250
Wurfflein rifles, 216-217, 241-248, 345; action design, 242; shotgun, 243; sporting and gallery, 243, 244, 246; target pistol, 244; loading and reloading shells, 245-246; mid-range target, 246; cartridges, 246-247; sights, 247; loading tools, 248

Zischang, A. O., 175